# REDEMPTION

# HYMNAL

---

*" Be filled with the spirit ; speaking to yourselves
in psalms and hymns and spiritual songs, singing
and making melody in your heart to the Lord."*
—Ephesians 5. 18, 19.

---

**KINGSWAY PUBLICATIONS**
EASTBOURNE

*First published* 1951

*Made and printed in Great Britain for*
KINGSWAY PUBLICATIONS LTD
*Lottbridge Drove, Eastbourne, E. Sussex BN23 6NT by*
*Richard Clay (The Chaucer Press) Ltd, Bungay, Suffolk*

# PREFACE

*Abridged from the Music Edition.*

This collection of hymns has been compiled to meet the need of companies of believers all over the British Isles who are rejoicing in a scriptural experience of the grace and power of the Holy Spirit similar, they humbly affirm, to that received by the early Christians on the Day of Pentecost, and enjoyed throughout the primitive apostolic churches. The inconvenience of not possessing an adequate compilation of hymns in one book suited to their distinctive testimony eventually led to a decision to prepare and publish such a collection. The widely representative Committee that was appointed now present the result of their labours of several years.

These hymns emphasize the Deity of the Lord Jesus Christ, and the glory of His cross as central in the redemption, by His blood, of sinful men. They provide for the worship of the Father in spirit and in truth, and express the aspirations of those who long to be holy as He is holy. Their basis of doctrine is belief that the Bible is the Word of God that liveth and abideth for ever, by which men are born again and through which they grow in grace and in the knowledge of our Lord and Saviour. All these truths have glowed with new and deeper power and beauty through the baptism in the Holy Spirit received as a definite experience with scriptural evidence. Because existing hymn books contain an inadequate selection of hymns that embody this vital testimony, one special aim in compiling this collection has been to supply that which is lacking. A hymnal is now proffered that combines rich devotional hymns in abundance with stirring revival hymns that present the Gospel in all its depth, winsomeness and simplicity. It is equally suitable for the regular life and work of the local churches, for great conventions and evangelistic campaigns.

The hymns of the Methodist Revival, many of the best of which will be found in this collection, served to impress its great doctrinal and experimental truths upon the multitudes who sang them. In publishing this grand collection in the middle of the Twentieth Century the Committee believe that these hymns also will indelibly impress the burning truths of the Pentecostal Revival upon the many thousands who will sing them with the spirit and with the understanding also.

THE HYMNAL COMMITTEE.

# CONTENTS

# Section I

## WORSHIP

### (1) ADORATION AND PRAISE

**1** Lord of all being, throned afar,
   Thy glory flames from sun and
      star;
Centre and soul of every sphere,
Yet to each loving heart how near.

2 Sun of our life, Thy quickening ray
Sheds on our path the glow of day;
Star of our hope, Thy softened light
Cheers the long watches of the
      night.

3 Our midnight is Thy smile with-
      drawn;
Our noontide is Thy gracious dawn;
Our rainbow arch, Thy mercy's
      sign;
All, save the clouds of sin, are
      Thine.

4 Lord of all life, below, above,
Whose light is truth, whose warmth
      is love,
Before Thy ever-blazing throne
We ask no lustre of our own.

5 Grant us Thy truth to make us free,
And kindling hearts that burn for
      Thee,
Till all Thy living altars claim
One holy light, one heavenly flame.
                      *O. W. Holmes.*


**2** All hail the power of Jesu's
      name!
   Let angels prostrate fall;
Bring forth the royal diadem,
   And crown Him Lord of all.

2 Crown Him, ye martyrs of our God,
   Who from His altar call;
Extol the stem of Jesse's rod,
   And crown Him Lord of all.

3 Ye chosen seed of Israel's race,
   A remnant weak and small,
Hail Him who saves you by His
      grace,
   And crown Him Lord of all.

4 Ye Gentile sinners, ne'er forget
   The wormwood and the gall;
Go, spread your trophies at His feet,
   And crown Him Lord of all.

5 Let every kindred, every tribe,
   On this terrestrial ball,
To Him all majesty ascribe,
   And crown Him Lord of all.

6 O that with yonder sacred throng
   We at His feet may fall,
Join in the everlasting song,
   And crown Him Lord of all.
                      *Edward Perronet.*


**3** Praise Him, praise Him, Jesus our
      blessed Redeemer,
   Sing, O earth, His wonderful
      love proclaim.
Hail Him! hail Him! highest arch-
      angels in glory,
   Strength and honour give to His
      holy name.
Like a shepherd, Jesus will guard
      His children,
   In His arms He carries them all
      day long.
O ye saints that dwell on the moun-
      tain of Zion,
   Praise Him! praise Him! ever in
      joyful song.

2 Praise Him, praise Him, Jesus our
      blessed Redeemer,
   For our sins He suffered and bled
      and died;
He, our rock, our hope of eternal
      salvation,
   Hail Him! hail Him! Jesus the
      Crucified.
Loving Saviour, meekly enduring
      sorrow,
   Crowned with thorns that cruelly
      pierced His brow;
Once for us rejected, despised and
      forsaken,
   Prince of Glory, ever triumphant
      now.

3 Praise Him, praise Him, Jesus our
    blessed Redeemer,
  Heavenly portals loud with ho-
    sannas ring;
Jesus, Saviour, reigneth for ever
  and ever,
  Crown Him, crown Him, Prophet
    and Priest and King!
Death is vanquished! Tell it with
  joy, ye faithful,
  Where is now thy victory, boast-
    ing grave?
Jesus lives! no longer thy portals
  are cheerless,
  Jesus lives, the mighty and strong
    to save.
                    *Fanny J. Crosby.*

**4** WE worship and adore Thee
    Before the mercy seat,
  We give Thee praise and glory,
    Dear Lord, it is so sweet.

2 We worship and adore Thee
    Who once for us was slain,
  Thou liv'st and reign'st in Glory,
    Thou soon wilt come again.

3 We worship and adore Thee,
    For Thy redeeming Grace,
  Thou set Thy love upon us,
    To Thee be all the praise.

4 We worship and adore Thee,
    A tribute, Lord, we bring,
  Of praise and glad thanksgiving,
    And crown Thee King of kings.

**5** PRAISE, my soul, the King of
    heaven;
  To His feet thy tribute bring;
Ransomed, healed, restored, for-
  given,
  Who like thee His praise should
    sing?
    Praise Him! praise Him!
  Praise the everlasting King.

2 Praise Him for His grace and
    favour
  To our fathers in distress;
Praise Him, still the same for ever,
  Slow to chide and swift to bless:
    Praise Him! praise Him!
  Glorious in His faithfulness.

3 Father-like He tends and spares us;
  Well our feeble frame He knows;
In His hands He gently bears us,
  Rescues us from all our foes:
    Praise Him! praise Him!
  Widely as His mercy flows.

4 Angels, help us to adore Him!
  Ye behold Him face to face;
Sun and moon, bow down before
  Him;
  Dwellers all in time and space.
    Praise Him! praise Him!
  Praise with us the God of grace.
                    *H. F. Lyte.*

**6** THE God of Abraham praise,
    Who reigns enthroned above,
Ancient of everlasting days,
    And God of love!
Jehovah! great I AM!
  By earth and heav'n confest,
I bow, and bless the sacred Name,
    For ever blest.

2   The God of Abraham praise,
    At whose supreme command
From earth I rise, and seek the joys
    At His right hand.
  I all on earth forsake,
    Its wisdom, fame, and power;
  And Him my only portion make,
    My shield and tower.

3   He by Himself hath sworn;
    I on His oath depend:
I shall, on eagles' wings upborne,
    To heaven ascend.
  I shall behold His face,
    I shall His power adore.
And sing the wonders of His grace
    For evermore.

4   The whole triumphant host
    Give thanks to God on high;
" Hail, Father, Son, and Holy
    They ever cry.     [Ghost!"
Hail, Abraham's God and mine!
  I join the heavenly lays;
All might and majesty are Thine,
    And endless praise.
                  *Thomas Olivers.*

**7** WITH harps and with vials there
    stand a great throng
  In the presence of Jesus, and sing
    this new song.
Unto Him Who hath loved us and washed us
  from sin,
Unto Him be the glory for ever !  Amen

2 All these once were sinners, defiled in His sight,
  Now arrayed in pure garments in praise they unite.

3 He maketh the rebel a priest and a king,
  He hath bought us and taught us this new song to sing.

4 How helpless and hopeless we sinners had been,
  If He never had loved us till cleansed from our sin.

5 Aloud in His praises our voices shall ring,
  So that others, believing, this new song shall sing.

  *A. T. Pierson.*

**8** OH, for a thousand tongues to sing
  My great Redeemer's praise,
  The glories of my God and King,
  The triumphs of His grace!

2 My gracious Master and my God,
  Assist me to proclaim,
  To spread through all the earth abroad
  The honours of Thy name.

3 Jesus! the name that charms our fears,
  That bids our sorrows cease;
  'Tis music in the sinner's ears,
  'Tis life, and health, and peace.

4 He breaks the power of cancelled sin,
  He sets the pris'ner free; [sin,
  His blood can make the foulest clean,
  His blood availed for me. [clean,

5 Hear Him, ye deaf; His praise, ye dumb,
  Your loosened tongues employ;
  Ye blind, behold your Saviour come;
  And leap, ye lame, for joy!
  *Charles Wesley.*

**9** YE servants of God,
  Your Master proclaim,
  And publish abroad
  His wonderful name;
  The name all victorious
  Of Jesus extol;
  His kingdom is glorious,
  And rules over all.

2 God ruleth on high,
  Almighty to save;
  And still He is nigh,
  His presence we have!
  The great congregation
  His triumph shall sing,
  Ascribing salvation
  To Jesus our King.

3 Salvation to God,
  Who sits on the throne;
  Let all cry aloud,
  And honour the Son:
  The praises of Jesus
  All angels proclaim,
  Fall down on their faces,
  And worship the Lamb.

4 Then let us adore
  And give Him His right;
  All glory and power,
  All wisdom and might;
  All honour and blessing,
  With angels above;
  And thanks never-ceasing,
  And infinite love.

  *Charles Wesley.*

**10** O WORSHIP the King,
  All glorious above,
  O gratefully sing
  His power and His love;
  Our Shield and Defender,
  The Ancient of Days,
  Pavilioned in splendour,
  And girded with praise.

2 O tell of His might,
  O sing of His grace,
  Whose robe is the light,
  Whose canopy space.
  His chariots of wrath
  The deep thunder-clouds form,
  And dark is His path
  On the wings of the storm.

3 Thy bountiful care,
  What tongue can recite?
  It breathes in the air,
  It shines in the light,
  It streams from the hills,
  It descends to the plain,
  And sweetly distils
  In the dew and the rain.

4 Frail children of dust,
   And feeble as frail;
In Thee do we trust,
   Nor find Thee to fail;
Thy mercies, how tender,
   How firm to the end,
Our Maker, Defender,
   Redeemer, and Friend!

5 O measureless Might!
   Ineffable Love!
While angels delight
   To hymn Thee above,
The humbler creation,
   Though feeble their lays,
With true adoration
   Shall lisp to Thy praise.
*R. Grant.*

**11** O GOD, of good the unfathomed
     sea!
Who would not give his heart to
   Thee?
   Who would not love Thee with
   his might?
O Jesu, lover of mankind,
Who would not his whole soul and
   mind,
   With all his strength, to Thee
   unite.

2 Thou shin'st with everlasting rays;
Before th'insufferable blaze
   Angels with both wings veil their
   eyes:
Yet free as air Thy bounty streams
On all Thy works; Thy mercy's
   beams
   Diffusive as Thy sun's arise.

3 Fountain of good! All blessing
   flows
   From Thee; no want Thy fulness
   knows;
   What but Thyself canst Thou de-
   sire?
Yet, self-sufficient as Thou art,
Thou dost desire my worthless
   heart;
   This, only this, dost Thou require.

4 High throned on heav'n's eternal
   hill,
   In number, weight, and measure
   still
Thou sweetly orderest all that is:

And yet Thou deign'st to come to
   me,
And guide my steps, that I, with
   Thee
   Enthroned, may reign in endless
   bliss.
*Johann Scheffler ; tr. John Wesley.*

**12** O WORSHIP the Lord in the
     beauty of holiness!
   Bow down before Him, His
   glory proclaim;
With gold of obedience and incense
   of lowliness,
   Kneel and adore Him, the Lord
   is His name.

2 Low at His feet lay thy burden of
   carefulness,
   High on His heart He will bear it
   for thee,
Comfort thy sorrows, and answer
   thy prayerfulness,
   Guiding thy steps as may best
   for thee be.

3 Fear not to enter His courts in the
   slenderness
   Of the poor wealth thou wouldst
   reckon as thine:
Truth in its beauty and love in its
   tenderness:
   These are the offerings to lay on
   His shrine.

4 These, though we bring them in
   trembling and fearfulness,
   He will accept for the name that
   is dear;
Mornings of joy give for evenings
   of tearfulness,
   Trust for our trembling, and
   hope for our fear.

5 O worship the Lord in the beauty
   of holiness!
   Bow down before Him, His glory
   proclaim;
With gold of obedience and incense
   of lowliness,
   Kneel, and adore Him, the Lord
   is His name.
*J. S. B. Monsell.*

**13** COME, let us join our cheerful songs
With angels round the throne;
Ten thousand thousand are their tongues,
But all their joys are one.

2 " Worthy the Lamb that died," they
" To be exalted thus:"    [cry,
"Worthy the Lamb," our lips reply,
" For He was slain for us."

3 Jesus is worthy to receive
Honour and power divine:
And blessings more than we can
Be, Lord, for ever Thine.    [give

4 Let all that dwell above the sky,
And air, and earth, and seas,
Conspire to lift Thy glories high,
And speak Thine endless praise.

5 The whole creation join in one,
To bless the sacred name
Of Him that sits upon the throne,
And to adore the Lamb.
*Isaac Watts.*

**14** HARK! the song of jubilee,
Loud as mighty thunders roar,
Or the fulness of the sea
When it breaks upon the shore:
" Hallelujah! for the Lord
God omnipotent shall reign:
Hallelujah!" let the word
Echo round the earth and main.

2 " Hallelujah!" hark! the sound
From the depths unto the skies,
Wakes above, beneath, around,
All creation's harmonies;
See Jehovah's banner furled,
Sheathed His sword; He speaks—
'tis done,
And the kingdoms of this world
Are the kingdom of His Son.

3 He shall reign from pole to pole
With illimitable sway;
He shall reign when like a scroll
Yonder heavens have passed
away·
Then the end; beneath His rod
Man's last enemy shall fall;
" Hallelujah!" Christ in God,
God in Christ is All in all!
*J. Montgomery.*

**15** O THE deep, deep love of Jesus,
Vast, unmeasured, boundless,
Rolling as a mighty ocean    [free!
In its fulness over me.
Underneath me, all around me,
Is the current of Thy love;
Leading onward, leading homeward,
To my glorious rest above.

2 O the deep, deep love of Jesus,
Spread His praise from shore to
How He loveth, ever loveth, [shore;
Changeth never, nevermore;
How He watches o'er His loved
ones,
Died to call them all His own;
How for them He intercedeth,
Watcheth o'er them from the
throne.

3 O the deep, deep love of Jesus,
Love of every love the best:
'Tis an ocean vast of blessing,
'Tis a haven sweet of rest.
O the deep, deep love of Jesus,
'Tis a heaven of heavens to me;
And it lifts me up to glory,
For it lifts me up to Thee.
*S. Trevor Francis.*

**16** WITH gladness we worship, rejoice as we sing,
Free hearts and free voices how
blessed to bring,
The old, thankful story shall scale
Thine abode,
Thou King of all glory, most bountiful God.

2 Thy right would we give Thee—
true homage Thy due,
And honour eternal, the universe
through,
With all Thy creation, earth, heaven
and sea,
In one acclamation we celebrate
Thee.

3 Renewed by Thy Spirit, redeemed
by Thy Son,
Thy children revere Thee for all
Thou hast done.
O Father! returning to love and to
light,
Thy children are yearning to praise
Thee aright.

4 We join with the angels, and so
    there is given
  From earth Hallelujah, in answer
    to heaven.
  Amen! Be Thou glorious below
    and above,
  Redeeming, victorious, and infinite
    Love!

  *G. Rawson.*

**17** SALVATION! O the joyful sound!
    What music to our ears!
  A sov'reign balm for every wound,
    A cordial for our fears.

  Glory, honour, praise, and power,
    Be unto the Lamb for ever !
  Jesus Christ is our Redeemer :
    Hallelujah ! Hallelujah !
    Hallelujah ! Praise the Lord.

2 Salvation! O Thee bleeding Lamb,
    To Thee the praise belongs;
  Salvation shall inspire our hearts,
    And dwell upon our tongues.

3 Salvation! Let the echo fly
    The spacious earth around;
  While all the armies of the sky
    Conspire to raise the sound.

  *Isaac Watts and W. W. Shirley.*

**18** THOU great Redeemer, dying
    Lamb,
    We love to hear of Thee;
  No music's like Thy charming
    Nor half so sweet can be. [name

2 O may we ever hear Thy voice
    In mercy to us speak !
  And in our Priest we will rejoice,
    Thou great Melchizedek !

3 Our Jesus shall be still our theme
    While in this world we stay:
  We'll sing our Jesu's lovely name
    When all things else decay.

4 When we appear in yonder cloud,
    With all that favoured throng,
  Then will we sing more sweet, more
    loud,
    And Christ shall be our song.

  *John Cennick.*

**19** PRAISE ye the Lord! 'Tis good
    to raise [praise :
  Your hearts and voices in His
  His nature and His works invite
  To make this duty our delight.

2 He formed the stars, those heavenly
    flames, [names;
  He counts their numbers, calls their
  His wisdom's vast, and knows no
    bound,
  A deep where all our thoughts are
    drowned.

3 Sing to the Lord! Exalt Him high,
  Who spreads His clouds along the
    sky;
  There He prepares the fruitful rain,
  Nor lets the drops descend in vain.

4 He makes the grass the hills adorn,
  And clothes the smiling fields with
    corn;
  The beasts with food His hands
    supply,
  And the young ravens when they
    cry.

5 What is the creature's skill or force?
  The sprightly man, or warlike
    horse?
  The piercing wit, the active limb?
  All are too mean delights for Him.

6 But saints are lovely in His sight,
  He views His children with delight;
  He sees their hope, He knows their
    fear,
  And looks, and loves His image
    there.

  *Isaac Watts.*

**20** Now in a song of grateful praise,
    To Thee, O Lord, my voice I'll
    raise:
  With all Thy saints I'll join to tell,
  My Jesus hath done all things well.

2 How sov'reign, wonderful, and free
  Has been Thy love to sinful me!
  Thou sav'dst me from the jaws of
    hell;
  My Jesus hath done all things well.

3 Since e'er my soul has known His
    love,
  What mercies He has made me
    prove!
  Mercies which do all praise excel!
  My Jesus hath done all things well.

4 And when to that bright world I
    rise,
And join the anthems of the skies,
Above the rest this note shall swell,
My Jesus hath done all things well.
                        *Samuel Medley.*

**21** BEGIN, my soul, some heav'nly
        theme;
    Awake, my voice, and sing
The mighty works, or mightier
    Of our eternal King.    [name,

2 Tell of His wondrous faithfulness,
    And sound His power abroad;
Sing the sweet promise of His
    And the performing God. [grace,

3 Proclaim salvation from the Lord,
    For wretched, dying men:
His hand hath writ the sacred word
    With an immortal pen.

4 Engraved as in eternal brass,
    The mighty promise shines;
Nor can the powers of darkness rase
    Those everlasting lines.

5 His every word of grace is strong
    As that which built the skies;
The voice that rolls the stars along
    Speaks all the promises.

6 Now shall my fainting heart rejoice
    To know Thy favour sure:
I trust the all-creating voice,
    And faith desires no more.
                        *Isaac Watts.*

**22** WHEN morning gilds the skies,
    My heart awaking cries,
    " May Jesus Christ be praised!"
Alike at work and prayer
To Jesus I repair:
    " May Jesus Christ be praised!"

2 When sleep her balm denies,
    My silent spirit sighs,
    " May Jesus Christ be praised!"
When evil thoughts molest,
With this I shield my breast—
    " May Jesus Christ be praised!"

3 Does sadness fill my mind,
    A solace here I find,
    " May Jesus Christ be praised!"
Or fades my earthly bliss,
My comfort still is this,
    " May Jesus Christ be praised!"

4 To God, the Word, on high,
    The hosts of angels cry,
    " May Jesus Christ be praised!"
Let mortals, too, upraise
Their voice in hymns of praise:
    " May Jesus Christ be praised!"

5 Let earth's wide circle round,
    In joyful notes resound,
    " May Jesus Christ be praised!"
Let air, and sea, and sky,
From depth to height, reply,
    " May Jesus Christ be praised!"

6 Be this, while life is mine,
    My canticle divine,
    " May Jesus Christ be praised!"
Be this th'eternal song
Through all the ages on,
    " May Jesus Christ be praised!"
                        *tr. E. Caswall.*

**23** My heart and voice I raise,
    To spread Messiah's praise;
    Messiah's praise let all repeat;
The universal Lord,
By whose almighty word
    Creation rose in form complete.

2 A servant's form He wore,
    And in His body bore
    Our dreadful curse on Calvary:
He like a victim stood,
And poured His sacred blood,
    To set the guilty captives free.

3 But soon the Victor rose
    Triumphant o'er His foes,
    And led the vanquished host in
        chains:
He threw their empire down,
His foes compelled to own,
    O'er all the great Messiah reigns.

4 With mercy's mildest grace,
    He governs all our race
    In wisdom, righteousness, and
Who to Messiah fly        [love:
Shall find redemption nigh,
    And all His great salvation prove.

5 Hail, Saviour, Prince of Peace!
    Thy kingdom shall increase,
    Till all the world Thy glory see,
And righteousness abound,
As the great deep profound,
    And fill the earth with purity!
                        *B. Rhodes.*

**24** COME, sound His praise abroad,
And hymns of glory sing!
Jehovah is the sovereign God,
The universal King!

Praise ye the Lord, Hallelujah,
Praise ye the Lord, Hallelujah,
Hallelujah, Hallelujah,
Hallelujah, Praise ye the Lord !

2　He formed the deeps unknown;
He gave the seas their bound:
The wat'ry worlds are all His own,
And all the solid ground.

3　Come, worship at His throne,
Come, bow before the Lord:
We are His work, and not our own,
He formed us by His word.

4　To-day attend His voice,
Nor dare provoke His rod;
Come, like the people of His choice,
And own your gracious God.
　　　　　　　*Isaac Watts.*

**25** LORD, enthroned in heav'nly
splendour,
First begotten from the dead,
Thou alone, our strong Defender,
Liftest up Thy people's head.
Alleluia.
Jesu, True and Living Bread!

2 Here our humblest homage pay we;
Here in loving reverence bow;
Here, for faith's discernment pray
we,
Lest we fail to know Thee now.
Alleluia.
Thou art here, we ask not how.

3 Though the lowliest form doth veil
As of old in Bethlehem, [Thee
Here as there Thine angels hail
Thee,
Branch and Flower of Jesse's
Alleluia. [stem.
We in worship join with them.

4 Paschal Lamb, Thine Offering, fin-
ished
Once for all when Thou wast
In its fulness undiminished [slain,
Shall for evermore remain,
Alleluia.
Cleansing souls from every stain.

5 Life-imparting Heavenly Manna,
Stricken Rock with streaming
Side,
Heav'n and earth with loud Ho-
sanna,
Worship Thee, the Lamb who
Alleluia. [died.
Risen, ascended, glorified!

**26** ALLELUIA! sing to Jesus!
His the sceptre, His the
Alleluia! His the triumph, [throne:
His the victory alone;
Hark! the songs of peaceful Sion
Thunder like a mighty flood;
Jesus out of every nation
Hath redeemed us by His blood.

2 Alleluia! not as orphans
Are we left in sorrow now;
Alleluia, He is near us,
Faith believes, nor questions how;
Though the cloud from sight re-
ceived Him,
When the forty days were o'er,
Shall our hearts forget His promise,
"I am with you evermore"?

3 Alleluia! bread of angels,
Thou on earth our food, our
Alleluia! here the sinful [stay:
Flee to Thee from day to day;
Intercessor, Friend of sinners,
Earth's Redeemer, plead for me,
Where the songs of all the sinless
Sweep across the crystal sea.

4 Alleluia! King eternal,
Thee the Lord of lords we own;
Alleluia! born of Mary,
Earth Thy footstool, heaven Thy
throne.
Thou within the veil hast entered,
Robed in flesh, our great High
Priest;
Thou on earth both Priest and
Victim:
In the Eucharistic Feast.
　　　　　　*W. Chatterton Dix.*

**27** GOD is love; that anthem olden,
Sing the glorious orbs of light,
In their language glad and golden,
Telling to us day and night
Their great story,
God is love and God is light.

2 Through that precious love He sought us,
  Wand'ring from His holy ways,
With that precious Life He bought [us;
  Then let all our future days
  Tell this story:
  Love is life—our lives be praise.

3 Gladsome is the theme and glorious,
  Praise to Christ our gracious Head,
Christ, the risen Christ, victorious,
  Death and hell hath captive led.
  Glory, glory!
  Love is life—and Death is dead.

4 Up to Him let each affection
  Daily rise and round Him move;
Our whole lives one resurrection
  To the Life of life above;
  Their glad story,
  God is life, and God is love.
               *J. S. B. Monsell.*

**28** PRAISE to the Holiest in the height,
  And in the depth be praise:
In all His words most wonderful,
  Most sure in all His ways.

2 O loving wisdom of our God!
  When all was sin and shame,
A second Adam to the fight,
  And to the rescue came.

3 O wisest love! that flesh and blood
  Which did in Adam fail,
Should strive afresh against the foe,
  Should strive and should prevail.

4 And that a higher gift than grace
  Should flesh and blood refine,
God's presence, and His very self
  And essence all-divine.

5 O generous love! that He, who
  In man for man the foe, [smote
The double agony in man
  For man should undergo.

6 And in the garden secretly,
  And on the Cross on high,
Should teach his brethren, and in-
  To suffer and to die.    [spire

7 Praise to the Holiest in the height,
  And in the depth be praise:
In all His words most wonderful,
  Most sure in all His ways.
               *J. H. Newman.*

**29** HAIL, Thou once despisèd Jesus!
  Hail, Thou Galilean King!
Thou didst suffer to release us,
  Thou didst free salvation bring:
Hail, Thou agonizing Saviour,
  Bearer of our sin and shame;
By Thy merits we find favour;
  Life is given through Thy name!

2 Paschal Lamb, by God appointed,
  All our sins were on Thee laid;
By almighty love anointed,
  Thou hast full atonement made:
All Thy people are forgiven
  Through the virtue of Thy blood;
Opened is the gate of heaven:
  Peace is made 'twixt man and God.

3 Jesus, hail! enthroned in glory,
  There for ever to abide;
All the heavenly host adore Thee,
  Seated at Thy Father's side.
There for sinners Thou art plead-ing,
  There Thou dost our place pre-pare,
Ever for us interceding,
  Till in glory we appear.

4 Worship, honour, power and bless-ing,
  Thou art worthy to receive;
Loudest praises, without ceasing,
  Meet it is for us to give.
Help, ye bright angelic spirits,
  Bring your sweetest, noblest lays;
Help to sing our Saviour's merits,
  Help to chant Immanuel's praise!
               *J. Bakewell.*

**30** COME, my brethren, praise your Saviour,
  Let your songs with rapture swell,
Through His grace have ye found favour,
  Who His boundless love can tell?
  Sing His praises,
  For He hath done all things well.

2 Louder yet, yea grander, greater,
  As your gladsome hearts rejoice
In your Saviour, Lord, Creator,
  Swell, O swell the trembling [chords;
  Wake the echoes!
  Louder than the ocean's roar.

3 What! ye tire? shame upon you!
  Dare ye cease to sing His praise?
Shall the very stones provoke you?
  Louder sing your wondrous lays,
    Till creation
  Owns His mighty power to save.

4 Blessèd Lord, we will adore Thee,
  Praise Thee, bless Thee, shout
      and sing,
  Till that day when we shall see
      Thee,
  Crowning Thee, all glorious King;
      Hallelujah!
  How the courts of glory ring.
                    *E. T. Mellor.*

**31** I'LL praise my Maker while I've
      breath,
  And when my voice is lost in death,
    Praise shall employ my nobler
        powers;
  My days of praise shall ne'er be
      past,
  While life and thought and being
      last,
    Or immortality endures.

2 Happy the man whose hopes rely
  On Israel's God; He made the sky
    And earth and seas, with all their
        train;
  His truth for ever stands secure;
  He saves the oppressed, He feeds
      the poor,
    And none shall find His promise
        vain.

3 The Lord gives eyesight to the
      blind;
  The Lord supports the fainting
      mind;
    He sends the lab'ring conscience
        peace;
  He helps the stranger in distress,
  The widow and the fatherless,
    And grants the pris'ner sweet re-
        lease.

4 I'll praise Him while He lends me
      breath;
  And when my voice is lost in death,
    Praise shall employ my nobler
        powers;

My days of praise shall ne'er be
    past,
While life and thought and being
    last,
  Or immortality endures.
                    *Isaac Watts.*

**32** MY God, how wonderful Thou
      art,
  Thy majesty how bright!
How beautiful Thy mercy-seat,
  In depths of burning light!

2 How dread are Thine eternal years,
    O everlasting Lord,
  By prostrate spirits day and night
    Incessantly adored!

3 How beautiful, how beautiful,
    The sight of Thee must be,
  Thine endless wisdom, boundless
    And awful purity!        [power

4 O how I fear Thee, living God,
    With deepest, tenderest fears,
  And worship Thee with trembling
    And penitential tears!      [hope,

5 Yet I may love Thee too, O Lord,
    Almighty as Thou art,
  For Thou hast stooped to ask of me
    The love of my poor heart.

6 No earthly father loves like Thee;
    No mother, e'er so mild,
  Bears and forbears as Thou hast
      done
    With me, Thy sinful child.

7 Father of Jesus, love's reward,
    What rapture will it be
  Prostrate before Thy throne to lie,
    And gaze, and gaze on Thee!
                    *F. W. Faber.*

**33** O LORD of heav'n and earth and
      sea,
  To Thee all praise and glory be;
  How shall we show our love to
      Who givest all?        [Thee,

2 Thou didst not spare Thine only
      Son,
  But gav'st Him for a world undone;
  And freely with the blessèd One
      Thou givest all.

3 We lose what on ourselves we
    spend,
We have as treasure without end
Whatever, Lord, to Thee we lend,
    Who givest all.

4 To Thee, from whom we all derive
Our life, our gifts, our power to
    give!
O may we ever with Thee live,
    Who givest all.

5 Thou giv'st the Spirit's blessèd
    dower,
Spirit of life, and love, and power,
And dost His sevenfold graces
    shower,
    Upon us all.

6 For souls redeemed, for sins for-
    given,
For means of grace and hopes of
    heaven,
Father, all praise to Thee be given,
    Who givest all.

*C. Wordsworth.*

**34** SING, O thou happy habitant
    Of Christ the everlasting
    Rock;
Secure in Love's imprisonment
    From sin's assault and Satan's
    shock.

2 This mighty Rock is ever sure,
    'Twas riv'n for thy sake long ago,
All those shall evermore endure
    Who this enduring Hiding know.

3 Sing, happy dove, within the cleft
    Of this Rock-Fortress high and
    strong,
With joy, of every care bereft,
    Out-sing the happy angels song.

4 Speak to this Rock alone, apart.
    And sparkling waters will out-
    burst,
Waters to bless thy barren heart
    And quench thy constant, killing
    thirst.

5 Here honey heav'nly sweet is found,
    Here golden oil of gladness
    springs,
    Here fire, while angels stand
    around,
    Consumes thy daily offerings.

6 On this Rock built, the gates of hell
    Shall not prevail against thee;
    though
    Great tempests beat and torrents
    swell,
      Their hate shall not thee over-
      throw.

7 When overwhelmed I am with fear,
    To It my soul shall strongly cry,
The Rock shall hide and hold me
    near,
The Rock is higher far than I!

8 Rejoice, inhabitant of heaven,
    Until Emmanuel for thee come;
Thy praise unto the Rock be given,
    The Rock, thine everlasting
    Home.

*Harold Horton.*

**35** O SAVIOUR, precious Saviour,
    Whom yet unseen we love,
O name of might and favour,
    All other names above!
We worship Thee, we bless Thee,
    To Thee alone we sing:
We praise Thee, and confess Thee
    Our holy Lord and King.

2 O Bringer of salvation,
    Who wondrously hast wrought,
Thyself the revelation
    Of love beyond our thought;
We worship Thee, we bless Thee,
    To Thee alone we sing;
We praise Thee, and confess Thee
    Our gracious Lord and King.

3 In Thee all fulness dwelleth,
    All grace and power divine;
The glory that excelleth,
    O Son of God, is Thine;
We worship Thee, we bless Thee,
    To Thee alone we sing;
We praise Thee, and confess Thee
    Our glorious Lord and King.

4 Oh, grant the consummation
    Of this our song above
In endless adoration,
    And everlasting love!
Then shall we praise and bless
    Thee
    Where perfect praises ring,
And evermore confess Thee
    Our Saviour and our King.

*Frances R. Havergal.*

**36** IMMORTAL, invisible, God only
    wise,
In light inaccessible hid from our
    eyes,
Most blessèd, most glorious, the
    Ancient of Days,
Almighty, victorious, Thy great
    name we praise.

2 Unresting, unhasting, and silent as
    light,
Nor wanting, nor wasting, Thou
    rulest in might!
Thy justice like mountains high
    soaring above,
Thy clouds which are fountains of
    goodness and love.

3 To all life Thou givest—to both
    great and small;
In all life Thou livest, the true life
    of all;
We blossom and flourish as leaves
    on the tree,
And wither and perish—but nought
    changeth Thee.

4 Great Father of Glory, pure Father
    of Light,
Thine angels adore Thee, all veil-
    ing their sight;
All laud we would render; O help
    us to see:
'Tis only the splendour of light
    hideth Thee.

5 Immortal, invisible, God only wise,
In light inaccessible hid from our
    eyes,
Most blessèd, most glorious, the
    Ancient of Days,
Almighty, victorious, Thy great
    name we praise.
        *Walter Chalmers Smith.*

**37** ANGEL voices, ever singing
    Round Thy throne of light,
Angel harps, for ever ringing,
    Rest not day nor night;
Thousands only live to bless Thee,
    And confess Thee
        Lord of Might.

2 Thou who art beyond the farthest
    Mortal eye can scan,
Can it be that Thou regardest
    Songs of sinful man?

Can we know that Thou art near us
    And wilt hear us?
        Yea, we can.

3 In Thy house, great God, we offer
    Of Thine own to Thee,
And for Thine acceptance proffer,
    All unworthily,     [voices
Hearts, and minds, and hands, and
    In our choicest
        Psalmody.

4 Honour, glory, might, and merit
    Thine shall ever be,
Father, Son, and Holy Spirit,
    Blessèd Trinity.
Of the best that Thou hast given
    Earth and heaven
        Render Thee.
        *Mary F. Pott.*

**38** PRAISE the Lord! ye heav'ns,
    adore Him;
Praise Him, angels in the height;
Sun and moon, rejoice before Him;
    Praise Him, all ye stars and light.

2 Praise the Lord, for He hath
    spoken;
Worlds His mighty voice obeyed;
Laws, that never shall be broken,
    For their guidance He hath made.

3 Praise the Lord, for He is glorious;
    Never shall His promise fail:
God hath made His saints vic-
    torious;
    Sin and death shall not prevail.

4 Praise the God of our salvation;
    Hosts on high His power pro-
    claim;
Heaven and earth, and all creation,
    Laud and magnify His name.

**39** PRAISE to the Lord, the Al-
    mighty, the King of creation;
O my soul, praise Him, for He is
    thy health and salvation;
    All ye who hear,
    Brothers and sisters draw near,
Praise Him in glad adoration.

2 Praise to the Lord, who doth pros-
per thy work and defend thee;
Surely His goodness and mercy
here daily attend thee;
Ponder anew
What the Almighty can do,
If with His love He befriend thee.

3 Praise to the Lord, who, when tem-
pests their warfare are waging,
Who, when the elements madly
around thee are raging,
Biddeth them cease,
Turneth their fury to peace,
Whirlwinds and waters assuaging.

4 Praise to the Lord, who when dark-
ness and sin is abounding,
Who, when the godless do triumph,
all virtue confounding,
Sheddeth His light,
Chaseth the horrors of night,
Saints with His mercy surrounding.

5 Praise to the Lord!  O let all that
is in me adore Him!
All that hath life and breath, come
now with praises before Him!
Let the Amen
Sound from His people again:
Gladly for aye we adore Him.
*Joachim Neander.*

**40** ETERNAL God! we raise to Thee,
Our songs of praise this solemn
hour;
Now let Thy Spirit make us free,
To magnify Thy grace and
power;
We worship, and Thy name adore,
And Thou art blest for evermore.

2 To Thee all holy angels sing,
The seraph and the cherub
throng,
Worship the everlasting King,
In notes of unexpiring song;
Before Thy throne their anthem
raise,
And fill the heavens with their
praise.

3 The God of patriarchs who face
Thy throne while round the seers
stand,
Oh, how they magnify Thy grace,
Delight to go at Thy command:
The prophets and the saintly throng
Extol Thy name with heavenly
song.

4 The God of all the martyred host,
The slain upon the rock of
shame,
Of Thee they make their glorious
boast,
And fall in wonder at Thy name.
The Church throughout remotest
bounds
Now sings Thy praise till heav'n re-
sounds!
*D. P. Williams.*

**41** O CHRIST, whose glory fills our
days,
Whose beauty shines from shore
to shore;
Our gladdest songs on high we
raise
To Thee whom earth and heav'n
adore.

2 Thy glory Thou to us hast shown,
Thy name proclaimèd by Thy
word;
Thy majesty is surely known,
Thy praise among all people
heard.

3 The drooping spirit lives again,
The fainting heart regains its
power,
The sick and lame, Thy promise
claim
In this Thy great appointed
hour.

4 With what a wealth of faith and
hope
Thy word is grasped, the weak
made strong;
We stretch our hands to touch Thy
robe
And healed and blessed, Thy
praise prolong.
*W. G. Hathaway.*

**42** O MAGNIFY the Lord with me,
　Ye people of His choice!
Let all to whom He lendeth breath
Now in His name rejoice;
For love's blest revelation,
For rest from condemnation,
For uttermost salvation,
　To Him give thanks.

　Let all . . . the people praise Thee,
　Let all . . . the people praise Thee !
　Let all . . . the people praise Thy name
　For ever and for evermore.
　　For evermore, O Lord !
　Let all . . . the people praise Thee,
　Let all . . . the people praise Thee,
　Let all . . . the people praise Thy name
　　For ever and for evermore.

2 O praise Him for His holiness,
　His wisdom and His grace;
Sing praises for the precious blood
　Which ransomed all our race;
In tenderness He sought us,
From depths of sin He brought us,
The way of life then taught us,
　To Him give thanks.

3 Had I a thousand tongues to sing,
　The half could ne'er be told
Of love so rich, so full and free,
　Of blessings manifold;
Of grace that faileth never,
Peace flowing as a river
From God the glorious Giver,
　To Him give thanks.
　　　　　　　　　　*Mrs. C. H. Morris.*

**43** SHALL hymns of grateful love
　　Through heav'n's high arches
And all the hosts above　　[ring,
　Their songs of triumph sing;
And shall not we take up the
　strain,
And send the echo back again?

2 Shall every ransomed tribe
　Of Adam's scattered race
To Christ all power ascribe,
　Who saved them by His grace;
And shall not we take up the strain,
And send the echo back again?

3 Shall they adore the Lord,
　Who bought them with His
　　blood,
And all the love record
　That led them home to God;
And shall not we take up the
　strain,
And send the echo back again?

4 Oh! spread the joyful sound,
　The Saviour's love proclaim,
And publish all around
　Salvation through His name;
Till all the world take up the
　strain,
And send the echo back again!
　　　　　　　　　　*J. J. Cummins.*

## (2) THANKSGIVING AND
## REJOICING

**44** LET me sing—for the glory of
　　heaven
Like a sunbeam has swept o'er
　　my heart;
I would praise Thee for sins all
　　forgiven,
For Thy love, which shall never
　　depart.

2 If Thy works praise Thee, Giver
　　of Good,
　If the sun shines his praise unto
　　　Thee,
If the wind, as it sighs through the
　　wood,
　Makes a murmur of song from
　　　each tree—

3 Then these lips, sure, a tribute shall
　　bring,
　Though unworthy the praises
　　　must be;
Shall all nature be vocal and sing,
　And no psalm of rejoicing from
　　　me?

4 O wonderful, glorious Redeemer!
　I would worship Thee, Saviour
　　　Divine;
And rejoice, though surrounded
　　with praises,
　Thou wilt still hear a song such
　　　as mine:

5 A song of a sinner forgiven,
　And a song that is music to Thee;
A song of a pilgrim to heaven,
　Yes, a song from a sinner like
　　　me!
　　　　　　　　　　*S. Trevor Francis.*

**45** Be glad in the Lord, and rejoice,
All ye that are upright in
heart;
And ye that have made Him your
choice,
Bid sadness and sorrow depart.

Rejoice ! . . . rejoice ! . . .
Be glad in the Lord and rejoice !
Rejoice ! . . . rejoice ! . . .
Be glad in the Lord and rejoice !

2 Be joyful, for He is the Lord,
On earth and in heaven supreme;
He fashions and rules by His word;
The " Mighty " and " Strong " to
redeem.

3 What though in the conflict for
right
Your enemies almost prevail !
God's armies, just hid from your
sight,
Are more than the foes which
assail.

4 Though darkness surround you by
day,
Your sky by the night be o'er-
cast,
Let nothing your spirit dismay,
But trust till the danger is past.

5 Be glad in the Lord, and rejoice,
His praises proclaiming in song;
With harp, and with organ, and
voice,
The loud hallelujahs prolong !
*M.E. Servoss.*

**46** My God, I thank Thee, who
hast made
The earth so bright,
So full of splendour and of joy,
Beauty and light;
So many glorious things are here,
Noble and right.

2 I thank Thee, too, that Thou hast
Joy to abound; [made
So many gentle thoughts and deeds,
Circling us round;
That in the darkest spot of earth
Some love is found.

3 I thank Thee more that all my joy
Is touched with pain;
That shadows fall on brightest
That thorns remain; [hours,
So that earth's bliss may be my
And not my chain. [guide,

4 For Thou who knowest, Lord, how
Our weak heart clings, [soon
Hast given us joys, tender and true,
Yet all with wings,
So that we see, gleaming on high,
Diviner things.

5 I thank thee, Lord, that Thou hast
The best in store; [kept
I have enough, yet not too much,
To long for more;
A yearning for a deeper peace
Not known before.

6 I thank Thee, Lord, that here our
Though amply blest, [souls,
Can never find, although they seek
A perfect rest—
Nor ever shall, until they lean
On Jesus' breast.
*Adelaide Anne Proctor.*

**47** To God be the glory, great
things He hath done,
So loved He the world that He gave
us His Son,
Who yielded His life an atonement
for sin,
And opened the Life Gate that all
may go in.

Praise the Lord, praise the Lord,
Let the earth hear His voice,
Praise the Lord, praise the Lord,
Let the people rejoice !
O come to the Father through Jesus the Son,
And give Him the glory, great things He
hath done.

2 O perfect redemption, the purchase
of blood,
To every believer the promise of
God;
The vilest offender who truly be-
lieves,
That moment from Jesus a pardon
receives.

3 Great things He hath taught us,
great things He hath done,
And great our rejoicing through
Jesus the Son;
But purer, and higher, and greater
will be
Our wonder, our transport when
Jesus we see.
*Fanny J. Crosby.*

**48** My Saviour suffered on the tree,
  Glory to the bleeding Lamb;
O come and praise the Lord with me!
  Glory to the bleeding Lamb.

The Lamb, the Lamb, the bleeding Lamb,
I love the sound of Jesu's name ;
It sets my spirit all in a flame,
Glory to the bleeding Lamb !

2 He bore my sins and curse and shame,
  Glory to the bleeding Lamb;
And I am saved through Jesu's name,
  Glory to the bleeding Lamb.

3 I know my sins are all forgiven,
  Glory to the bleeding Lamb;
And I am on my way to heaven,
  Glory to the bleeding Lamb.

4 And when the storms of life are o'er,
  Glory to the bleeding Lamb;
I'll sing upon a happier shore,
  Glory to the bleeding Lamb.

5 And this my ceaseless song shall be,
  Glory to the bleeding Lamb;
That Jesus tasted death for me,
  Glory to the bleeding Lamb.


**49** THIS is the day the Lord hath made,
  He calls the hours His own;
Let heav'n rejoice, let earth be glad,
  And praise surround the throne.

2 To-day He rose and left the dead,
  And Satan's empire fell;
To-day the saints His triumph spread,
  And all His wonders tell.

3 Hosanna to the anointed King,
  To David's holy Son!
Help us, O Lord! descend and bring
  Salvation from Thy throne.

4 Blest be the Lord, who comes to men
  With messages of grace;
Who comes in God His Father's name,
  To save our sinful race.

5 Hosanna, in the highest strains
  The church on earth can raise;
The highest heavens in which He reigns
  Shall give Him nobler praise.
                                        *Isaac Watts.*


**50** Now thank we all our God,
  With hearts, and hands, and voices;
Who wondrous things hath done,
  In whom His world rejoices;
Who, from our mothers' arms,
  Hath blessed us on our way
With countless gifts of love,
  And still is ours to-day.

2 O may this bounteous God
  Through all our life be near **us**,
With ever-joyful hearts
  And blessèd peace to cheer **us**,
And keep us in His grace,
  And guide us when perplexed,
And free us from all ills
  In this world and the next.

3 All praise and thanks to God
  The Father now be given,
The Son, and Him who reigns
  With Them in highest heaven—
The one, eternal God,
  Whom earth and heaven adore;
For thus it was, is now,
  And shall be evermore.
    *Martin Rinkart ; tr. Catherine Winkworth.*


**51** MY soul shouts glory to the Son of God,
  For the work free grace hath done;
My faith looks upward with a steadfast eye
  That is clear as the noonday sun.

Hallelujah ! Hallelujah !
  Hallelujah to the Saviour I adore ;
I will praise Him, I will praise Him,
  Hallelujah ! I will praise Him evermore.

2 My soul shouts glory to the Son of God,
  Not a cloud nor a care I see;
My hope is clinging with a perfect trust
  To the cross He has borne for me.

3 My soul shouts glory to the Son of
    God,
  In His secret place I dwell;
His constant presence overshades
    me there,
  And my joy there is none can tell.

4 My soul shouts glory to the Son of
    God,
  And I know it will not be long;
Till o'er the river, where the saints
    have gone,
  I shall join their eternal song.
               *Fanny J. Crosby.*

**52** PRAISE the Saviour, ye who
    know Him;
Who can tell how much we owe
Gladly let us render to Him [Him?
  All we have and are.

2 "Jesus" is the name that charms
    us;
  He for conflicts fits and arms us;
Nothing moves and nothing harms
    us,
    When we trust in Him.

3 Trust in Him, ye saints for ever;
  He is faithful, changing never;
Neither force nor guile can sever
    Those He loves from Him.

4 Keep us, Lord, oh, keep us cleaving
  To Thyself and still believing,
Till the hour of our receiving
    Promised joys in heaven.

5 Then we shall be where we would
    be;
Then we shall be what we should
    be;
Things which are not now, nor
    could be,
    Then shall be our own.
               *T. Kelly.*

**53** PRAISE, praise ye the name of
    Jehovah, our God;
Declare, oh, declare ye His glories
    abroad;
Proclaim ye His mercy from nation
    to nation.
Till the uttermost islands have
    heard His salvation.

For His love floweth on, free and full as
  a river ;
And His mercy endureth for ever and ever.

2 Praise, praise ye the Lamb, who for
    sinners was slain;
Who went down to the grave and
    ascended again;
And who soon shall return when
    these dark days are o'er,
To set up His Kingdom in glory
    and power.

3 Then the heavens and the earth and
    the sea shall rejoice;
The fields and the forest shall lift
    their glad voice:
The sands of the desert shall flour-
    ish in green,
And Lebanon's glory be shed o'er
    the scene.

4 Her bridal attire, and her festal
    array,
All nature shall wear on that glori-
    ous day;
For her King cometh down, with
    His people to reign,
And His presence shall bless her
    with Eden again.
             *Horatius Bonar.*

**54** JOY to the world; the Lord is
    come!
  Let earth receive her King;
Let ev'ry heart prepare Him room,
  And heav'n and nature sing.

2 Joy to the world; the Saviour
    reigns!
  Let men their songs employ;
While fields and floods, rocks, hills
    and plains,
  Repeat the sounding joy.

3 He rules the world with truth and
    grace;
  And makes the nations prove
The glories of His righteousness,
  And wonders of His love.
             *Isaac Watts.*

**55** PRAISE the King of Glory, He
    is God alone;
Praise Him for the wonders He to
    us hath shown;
For His promised presence all the
    pilgrim way,
For the flaming pillar, and the
    cloud by day.

Praise . . . Him, shining angels, strike . . . your harps of gold ;
All . . . His hosts adore Him, who . . . His face behold . . .
Through . . . His great dominion, while . . . the ages roll,
All His works shall praise Him ; bless the Lord, my soul !

2 Praise Him for redemption, free to every soul;
Praise Him for the Fountain that can make us whole;
For His gifts of kindness and His loving care,
For the blest assurance that He answers prayer.

3 Praise Him for the trials sent as cords of love,
Binding us more closely to the things above;
For the faith that conquers, hope that naught can dim,
For the land where loved ones gather unto Him.

*E. E. Hewitt.*

**56** AWAKE, awake, O heart of mine !
Sing praise to God above;
Take up the song of endless years,
And sing redeeming love !
Redeemed by Him who bore my sins,
When on the cross He died;
Redeemed and purchased with His blood,
Redeemed and sanctified.

Awake, awake . . . O heart of mine ! . . .
Sing praise, sing praise . . . to God above . . .
Take up the song . . . of endless years . . .
And sing . . . redeeming love ! . . .

2 Redeemed by Him, my Lord and King,
Who saves me day by day;
My life and all its ransomed powers
Could ne'er His love repay.
And yet His mercy condescends
My humble gift to own;
And through the riches of His grace
He brings me near His throne.

3 Oh, love unchanging, love sublime !
Not all the hosts above
Can reach the height or sound the depth
Of God's eternal love.
This wondrous love enfolds the world,
It fills the realms above;
'Tis boundless as eternity;
Oh, praise the God of love.

*Fanny J. Crosby.*

**57** O JESUS, King most wonderful,
Thou Conqueror renowned;
Thou Sweetness most ineffable,
In whom all joys are found.

2 When once Thou visitest the heart,
Then truth begins to shine;
Then earthly vanities depart,
Then kindles love divine.

3 Jesus! Thy mercies are untold,
Through each returning day;
Thy love exceeds a thousand-fold
Whatever we can say.

4 May every heart confess Thy name,
And ever Thee adore;
And, seeking Thee, itself inflame
To seek Thee more and more.

5 Thee may our tongues for ever bless;
Thee may we love alone;
And ever in our lives express
The image of Thine own.

6 Grant us, while here on earth we stay,
Thy love to feel and know;
And when from hence we pass away
To us Thy glory show.

*Bernard of Clairvaux ; tr. E. Caswall.*

**58** WHEN the morning stars were singing,
And the world was newly born,
And all life was filled with music,
Music of the morn,
There was One above the splen-
Who commanded it to be; [dour,
And in all the heavenly radiance,
None so fair as He!

2 When man's heart was growing
    weary
  And his feet had gone astray,
And his God seemed high in
    heaven,
  Very far away;    [Saviour,
Then there came from heaven, the
  To whom shepherds bowed the
    knee,
And the wise men made their offer-
  None so wise as He!    [ings,

3 When my early hope was darkened
  By the sin that won the day,
  And I stumbled in the shadows,
    Groping for the way;
Then His grace and promise beck-
    oned,
  And He welcomed even me;
And in all the human story,
  None so kind as He!

4 Ever clear, and ever clearer,
  Shall His glory yet increase,
And the praises of His people
  Never, never cease:
They shall grow into His likeness,
  For His beauty they shall see,
And in all the ransomed future,
  None so great as He!
             *W. Y. Fullerton.*

**59** FATHER, what can to Thee be
    giv'n
  For all Thy mercies blest;
For riches of Thy glorious grace,
  And for the bliss of rest?

2 My weary soul doth pant for Thee,
  In dry and thorny land;
And in the howling wilderness
  I find Thy guiding Hand.

3 Thou lovest me with love unknown,
  When no one can console,
And, like the apple of Thine eye,
  Preservest Thou my soul.

4 Thou leadest me, and Thou alone,
  In paths Thou knowest best;
I trust Thee when I cannot trace
  The way to future rest.

5 Within Thy hand I place my own,
  And thus my path pursue,
  Content to walk with Thee alone,
  Till glory fills my view.
             *D. P. Williams.*

## (3) ASPIRATION

**60** ETERNAL Light! Eternal Light!
  How pure the soul must be,
When, placed within Thy searching
    sight,
  It shrinks not, but, with calm de-
    light,
  Can live, and look on Thee!

2 The spirits that surround Thy
    throne
  May bear the burning bliss;
But that is surely theirs alone,
Since they have never, never known
  A fallen world like this.

3 Oh, how shall I, whose native
    sphere
  Is dark, whose mind is dim,
Before the Ineffable appear,
And on my naked spirit bear
  The uncreated beam?

4 There is a way for man to rise
  To that sublime abode:
  An offering and a sacrifice,
  A Holy Spirit's energies,
  An advocate with God,—

5 These, these prepare us for the
    sight
  Of Holiness above:
The sons of ignorance and night
May dwell in the Eternal Light,
  Through the Eternal Love!
             *T. Binney.*

**61** I NEED Thee, precious Saviour,
  Oh, Thou art all to me;
Before the Throne for ever
  I stand complete in Thee.
Though Satan loud accuses,
  Yet I can ever see,
The blood of Christ most precious,
  The sinner's perfect plea.

2 I need Thee, precious Saviour,
  I need a friend like Thee:
A friend to soothe and comfort,
  A friend to care for me;
I need Thy heart, Lord Jesus,
  To feel each anxious care;
To bear my every burden,
  And all my sorrow share.

3 I need Thee, precious Saviour,
   I need Thee day by day,
To fill me with Thy fulness,
   To lead me on my way:
I need Thy Holy Spirit
   To teach me what I am—
To show me more of Jesus,
   To point me to the Lamb.

4 I need Thee, precious Saviour,
   And hope to see Thee soon,
Encircled with the rainbow,
   And seated on Thy throne;
There, with Thy blood-bought
   My joy shall ever be,     [people,
To sing Thy praise, Lord Jesus,
   And ever gaze on Thee.
                          *F. Whitfield.*

**62** JESUS, Thy boundless love to me
      No thought can reach, no
         tongue declare;
O knit my thankful heart to Thee,
   And reign without a rival there;
Thine wholly, Thine alone, I am;
   Lord, with Thy love my heart
      inflame.

2 O grant that nothing in my soul
   May dwell but Thy pure love
      alone;
O may Thy love possess me whole,
   My joy, my treasure, and my
      crown;
All coldness from my heart remove;
   May every act, word, thought, be
      love.

3 O Love, how cheering is Thy ray!
   All pain before Thy presence
      flies;
Care, anguish, sorrow, melt away,
   Where'er Thy healing beams
      arise;
O Jesus, nothing may I see—
   Nothing desire, or seek, but Thee.

4 In suffering be Thy love my peace,
   In weakness be Thy love my
      power;
And when the storms of life shall
      cease,
   Jesus, in that important hour,
In death, as life, be Thou my
      Guide,
   And save me, who for me hast
      died.
                 *P. Gerhardt ; tr. J. Wesley.*

**63** JESUS, my eyes are unto Thee,
      For Thou art all I long to see,
Since Thou hast suffered on the
      That I might live.     [tree,

2 Jesus, my heart is fixed on Thee,
   Waiting for all Thou hast for me,
Seeking a closer walk with Thee,
      Thy paths to see.

3 Jesus, my soul still pants for Thee,
   For Thou art all in all to me,
And when Thy blessèd face I see,
      At rest I'll be.

4 Jesus, for Thy great love I yearn,
   Even for those God's ways who
      spurn,
That through Thy love from death
      they'll turn,
      To Thee and live.

5 Oh, that my steps may quickened
      be
   To follow Him who still loves me,
And bids me through eternity,
      With Him to dwell.

6 Jesus, of Him shall be my song,
   Who loved me patiently and long,
My life, my all, henceforth belong
      To Him alone.
                          *M. Bairstow.*

**64** JESUS, stand among us
      In Thy risen power;
Let this time of worship
   Be a hallowed hour.

2 Breathe Thy Holy Spirit
   Into every heart;
Bid the fears and sorrows
   From each soul depart.

3 Thus with quickened footsteps
   We'll pursue our way,
Watching for the dawning
   Of eternal day.
                          *W. Pennefather.*

**65** FILL Thou my life, O Lord my
      God,
   In every part with praise,
That my whole being may proclaim
   Thy being and Thy ways.

2 Not for the lip of praise alone,
   Not e'en the praising heart,
I ask, but for a life made up
   Of praise in every part:

3 Praise in the common things of life.
    Its goings out and in:
  Praise in each duty and each deed,
    However small and mean.

4 Fill every part of me with praise;
    Let all my being speak
  Of Thee and of Thy love, O Lord.
    Poor though I be and weak.

5 So shalt Thou, Lord, from me, e'en
    Receive the glory due;   [me,
  And so shall I begin on earth
    The song for ever new.

6 So shall no part of day or night
    From sacredness be free;
  But all my life, in every step,
    Be fellowship with Thee.
            *Horatius Bonar.*

**66** LET me come closer to Thee,
    Lord Jesus,
  Oh, closer day by day;
  Let me lean harder on Thee, Lord
  Yes, harder all the way.   [Jesus.

2 Let me show forth Thy beauty,
    Lord Jesus,
  Like sunshine on the hills;
  Oh, let my lips pour forth Thy
    sweetness
  In joyous sparkling rills!

3 Yes, like a fountain, precious Lord
    Jesus,
  Make me and let me be;
  Keep me and use me daily, Lord
  For Thee, for only Thee. [Jesus,

4 In all my heart and will, Lord
  Be altogether King;   [Jesus,
  Make me a loyal subject, Lord
  To Thee in everything.  [Jesus,

5 Thirsting and hung'ring for Thee,
    Lord Jesus,
  With blessèd hunger here,
  Longing for home on Zion's moun-
    tain—
  No thirst, no hunger there.
             *J. L. Lyne.*

**67** LORD Jesus Christ, we seek Thy
    face;
  Within the veil we bow the knee;
  Oh, let Thy glory fill the place,
    And bless us while we wait on
    Thee.

2 We thank Thee for the precious
    blood
    That purged our sins and brought
    us nigh;
  All cleansed and sanctified to God,
    Thy holy Name to magnify.

3 Shut in with Thee, far, far above
    The restless world that wars
    below;
  We seek to learn and prove Thy
    love,
    Thy wisdom and Thy grace to
    know.

4 The brow that once with thorns
    was bound,
    Thy hands, Thy side, we fain
    would see;
  Draw near, Lord Jesus, glory
    crowned,
    And bless us while we wait on
    Thee.
            *Alex Stewart.*

**68** O FOR a closer walk with God,
    A calm and heavenly frame,
  A light to shine upon the road
  That leads me to the Lamb.

2 Where is the blessedness I knew
    When first I saw the Lord?
  Where is that soul-refreshing view
  Of Jesus and His word?

3 What peaceful hours I once en-
    joyed!
  How sweet their memory still!
  But they have left an aching void
  The world can never fill.

4 Return, O holy Dove! return,
    Sweet messenger of rest!
  I hate the sins that made Thee
    mourn,
  And drove Thee from my breast.

5 The dearest idol I have known,
    Whate'er that idol be,
  Help me to tear it from Thy throne,
  And worship only Thee.

6 So shall my walk be close with
    God,
  Calm and serene my frame;
  So purer light shall mark the road
  That leads me to the Lamb.
            *W. Cowper.*

**69** O Love Divine, how sweet Thou
art!
When shall I find my willing heart
All taken up by Thee?
I thirst, I faint, I die to prove
The greatness of redeeming love,
The love of Christ to me.

2 Stronger His love than death or
hell!
Its riches are unsearchable;
The first-born sons of light
Desire in vain its depths to see;
They cannot reach the mystery,
The length, and breadth, and
height.

3 God only knows the love of God:
Oh, that it now were shed abroad
In this poor stony heart!
For love I sigh, for love I pine:
This only portion, Lord, be mine—
Be mine this better part!
*Charles Wesley.*

**70** My goal is God Himself, not
joy, nor peace,
Nor even blessing, but Himself,
my God:
'Tis His to lead me there, not mine,
but His—
" At any cost, dear Lord, by any
road!"

2 So faith bounds forward to its goal
in God,
And love can trust her Lord to
lead her there;
Upheld by Him, my soul is following hard,
Till God hath full fulfilled my
deepest prayer.

3 No matter if the way be sometimes
dark,
No matter though the cost be ofttimes great,
He knoweth how I best shall reach
the mark,
The way that leads to Him must
needs be strait.

4 One thing I know, I cannot say
Him nay;
One thing I do, I press toward
my Lord;

My God, my glory here, from day
to day,
And in the glory there my Great
Reward.
*F. Brook.*

**71** Love divine, all loves excelling,
Joy of heav'n, to earth come
down!
Fix in us Thy humble dwelling,
All Thy faithful mercies crown.
Jesus, Thou art all compassion,
Pure, unbounded love Thou art;
Visit us with Thy salvation,
Enter every trembling heart.

2 Breathe, oh, breathe Thy loving
Spirit
Into every troubled breast!
Let us all in Thee inherit,
Let us find the promised rest;
Take away the love of sinning;
Alpha and Omega be;
End of faith, as its beginning,
Set our hearts at liberty.

3 Come, almighty to deliver,
Let us all Thy grace receive!
Suddenly return, and never,
Never more Thy temples leave;
Thee we would be always blessing,
Serve Thee as Thy hosts above,
Pray, and praise Thee without ceas-
Glory in Thy perfect love. [ing,

4 Finish then Thy new creation,
Pure and spotless may we be;
Let us see our whole salvation
Perfectly secured by Thee!
Changed from glory into glory,
Till in heaven we take our place;
Till we cast our crowns before
Thee,
Lost in wonder, love, and praise.
*Charles Wesley.*

**72** My God, the spring of all my
joys,
The life of my delights,
The glory of my brightest days,
And comfort of my nights!

2 In darkest shades, if Thou appear,
My dawning is begun:
Thou art my soul's bright morning
star,
And Thou my rising sun.

3 The opening heavens around me
  shine,
  With beams of sacred bliss,
If Jesus shows His mercy mine,
And whispers I am His.

4 My soul would leave this heavy
  clay,
  At that transporting word;
Run up with joy the shining way,
To meet my dearest Lord.
  *Isaac Watts.*

**73** HERE from the world we turn,
  Jesus to seek;
Here may His loving voice
  Graciously speak!
Jesus, our dearest Friend,
While at Thy feet we bend,
Oh, let Thy smile descend!
  'Tis Thee we seek.

2 Come, Holy Comforter,
  Presence divine,
Now in our longing hearts
  Graciously shine!
Oh, for Thy mighty power!
Oh, for a blessèd shower,
Filling this hallowed hour
  With joy divine.

3 Saviour, Thy work revive!
  Here may we see
Those who are dead in sin
  Quickened by Thee!
Come to our hearts tonight,
Make every burden light,
Cheer Thou our waiting sight;
  We long for Thee.
  *Fanny J. Crosby.*

**74** LORD of the worlds above,
  How pleasant and how fair
The dwellings of Thy love,
  Thine earthy temples, are!
    To thine abode
    My heart aspires,
    With warm desires
    To see my God.

2 O happy souls that pray
  Where God delights to hear!
O happy men that pay
  Their constant service there!
    They praise Thee still,
    And happy they
    Who love the way
    To Zion's hill!

3 They go from strength to strength,
  Through this dark vale of tears,
Till each o'ercomes at length,
  Till each in heaven appears:
    O glorious seat!
    Thou God, our King,
    Shalt thither bring
    Our willing feet.

4 God is our sun and shield,
  Our light and our defence;
With gifts His hands are filled,
  We draw our blessings thence:
    He shall bestow
    Upon our race
    His saving grace,
    And glory too.

5 The Lord His people loves;
  His hand no good withholds
From those His heart approves,
  From holy, humble souls
    Thrice happy he,
    O Lord of Hosts,
    Whose spirit trusts
    Alone in Thee!
  *Isaac Watts.*

**75** THOU Shepherd of Israel, and
  mine,
  The joy and desire of my heart,
For closer communion I pine,
  I long to reside where Thou art.

2 The pasture I languish to find,
  Where all who their Shepherd
  obey,
Are fed on His bosom reclined,
  And screened from the heat of
  the day.

3 Ah, show me that happiest place,
  That place of Thy people's
  abode,
Where saints in an ecstasy gaze,
  And hang on a crucified God.

4 Thy love for a sinner declare,
  Thy passion and death on the
My spirit to Calvary bear,   [tree,
  To suffer and triumph with Thee.

5 'Tis there, with the lambs of Thy
  flock,
  There only I covet to rest;
To lie at the foot of the Rock,
  Or rise to be hid in Thy breast.

6 'Tis there I would always abide,
  And never a moment depart,
Concealed in the cleft of Thy side,
  Eternally hid in Thy heart.

7 How good is the God we adore,
    Our faithful, unchangeable
      Friend:
  Whose love is as great as His
      power,
    And knows neither measure nor
      end.

8 'Tis Jesus, the First and the Last,
  Whose Spirit shall guide us safe
      home;
  We'll praise Him for all that is
      past,
    And trust Him for all that's to
      come.
        *Charles Wesley (first 6 vv.).*

**76** NEARER, still nearer, close to
      Thy heart,
  Draw me, my Saviour, so precious
      Thou art;
  Fold me, O fold me close to Thy
      breast,
  Shelter me safe in that " Haven of
      Rest."

2 Nearer, still nearer, nothing I
      bring,
  Naught as an offering to Jesus my
      King;
  Only my sinful, now contrite heart,
  Grant me the cleansing Thy blood
      doth impart.

3 Nearer, still nearer, Lord, to be
      Thine,
  Sin, with its follies, I gladly resign;
  All of its pleasures, pomp and its
      pride,
  Give me but Jesus my Lord cruci-
      fied.

4 Nearer, still nearer, while life shall
      last,
  Till all its struggles and trials are
      past;
  Then through eternity, ever I'll be
  Nearer, my Saviour, still nearer to
      Thee.
        *Mrs. C. H. Morris.*

**77** IT passeth knowledge, that dear
      love of Thine,
  My Jesus, Saviour; yet this soul of
      mine
  Would of Thy love, in all its
      breadth and length,
  Its height and depth, its everlasting
      strength,
    Know more and more.

2 It passeth telling, that dear love of
      Thine,
  My Jesus, Saviour; yet these lips of
      mine
  Would fain proclaim to sinners far
      and near,
  A love which can remove all guilty
      fear,
    And love beget.

3 It passeth praises, that dear love of
      Thine,
  My Jesus, Saviour; yet this heart of
      mine
  Would sing that love, so rich, so
      full, so free,
  Which brings a rebel sinner, such
      as me,
    Nigh unto God.

4 But though I cannot sing, or tell,
      or know
  The fulness of Thy love, while here
      below,
  My empty vessel I may freely
      bring:
  O Thou, who art of love the living
      spring,
    My vessel fill.

5 I am an empty vessel—not one
      thought
  Or look of love, I ever to Thee
      brought;
  Yet I may come, and come again to
      Thee,
  With this, the empty sinner's only
      plea—
    Thou lovest me.

6 Oh, fill me, Jesus Saviour, with Thy
      love!
  Lead, lead me to the living fount
      above;
  Thither may I, in simple faith, draw
      nigh,
  And never to another fountain fly,
    But unto Thee.

7 And when my Jesus, face to face, I
 see,
 When at His lofty throne I bow the
  knee,
 Then of His love, in all its breadth
  and length,
 Its height and depth, its everlasting
  strength,
   My soul shall sing.
       *Mary Shekleton.*

**78** IF I but knew Thee as Thou art,
   O Loveliness unknown,
 With what desire, O Lord, my
  heart,
 Would claim Thee for its own.

2 Thy glory would my shame conceal,
 Thy purity my dross;
 I should rejoice with Thee to feel
 The sorrow of the cross.

3 But I am dull and blind, O Lord,
 Unapt of Thee to learn;
 Thee I but dimly in Thy word,
 As in a glass, discern.

4 With faith's warm finger, through
  the veil,
 I seek to touch Thy hand;
 I feel the imprint of the nail
 And partly understand.

5 But, ah, my lonely spirit tires
 Of knowing Thee in part.
 O Jesus, how my soul desires
 To see Thee as Thou art!
      *I. MacPherson.*

### (4) COMMUNION

**79** TALK with us, Lord, Thyself re-
   veal,
 While here o'er earth we rove;
 Speak to our hearts, and let us feel
 The kindling of Thy love.

2 With Thee conversing, we forget
 All time, and toil, and care;
 Labour is rest, and pain is sweet,
 If Thou, my God art here.

3 Here then, my God, vouchsafe to
  stay,
 And bid my heart rejoice;
 My bounding heart shall own Thy
  sway,
 And echo to Thy voice.

4 Thou callest me to seek Thy face;
 'Tis all I wish to seek;
 To attend the whispers of Thy
  grace,
 And hear Thee inly speak.

5 Let this my every hour employ,
 Till I Thy glory see;
 Enter into my Master's joy,
 And find my heaven in Thee.
      *Charles Wesley.*

**80** I CANNOT breathe enough of
   Thee,
 O gentle breeze of love,
 More fragrant than the myrtle tree
 The Rose of Sharon is to me,
 The balm of heaven above.

2 I cannot gaze enough on Thee,
 Thou Fairest of the fair;
 My heart is filled with ecstasy,
 As in Thy face of radiancy
 I see such beauty there.

3 I cannot work enough for Thee,
 My Saviour, Master, Friend;
 I do not wish to go out free,
 But ever, always, willingly,
 To serve Thee to the end.

4 I cannot sing enough of Thee,
 The sweetest name on earth,
 A note so full of melody
 Comes from my heart so joyously,
 And fills my soul with mirth.

5 I cannot speak enough of Thee,
 I have so much to tell:
 Thy heart it beats so tenderly
 As thou dost draw me close to
  Thee,
 And whisper " All is well."
     *W. Spencer Walton.*

**81** No more veil! God bids me
   enter
 By the new and living way—
 Not in trembling hope I venture,
 Boldly I His call obey:
 There, with Him, my God I meet,
 God upon the mercy seat!

2 In the robes of spotless whiteness,
 With the blood of priceless
  worth,
 He has gone into that brightness,
 Christ rejected from the earth—
 Christ accepted there on high,
 And in Him do I draw nigh.

3 Oh, the welcome I have found
    there,
   God in all His love made
    known!
Oh, the glories that surround there,
   Those accepted in His Son!
Who can tell the depths of bliss
Spoken by the Father's kiss?

4 One with Him, O Lord, before
    Thee,
   There I live, and yet not I;
Christ it is who there adores Thee;
   Who more dear, or who more
    nigh?
All the Father's heart mine own—
Mine—and yet His Son's alone.

5 All the worth I have before Him
   Is the value of the Blood;
I present when I adore Him,
   Christ the first-fruits unto God;
Him with joy doth God behold,
Thus is my acceptance told.
*Frances Bevan.*

82 "WITHIN the Veil:" Be this,
    belov'd, thy portion,
   Within the secret of thy Lord to
    dwell;
Beholding Him, until thy face His
    glory,
   Thy life His love, thy lips His
    praise shall tell.

2 "Within the Veil," for only as thou
    gazest
   Upon the matchless beauty of His
    face,
Canst thou become a living revela-
    tion
   Of His great heart of love, His
    untold grace.

3 "Within the Veil," His fragrance
    poured upon thee,
   Without the Veil, that fragrance
    shed abroad;
"Within the Veil," His hand shall
    tune the music
   Which sounds on earth the
    praises of thy Lord.

4 "Within the Veil," thy spirit deeply
    anchored,
   Thou walkest calm above a
    world of strife;

"Within the Veil" thy soul with
    Him united,
   Shall live on earth His resur-
    rection life.
*Freda Hanbury Allen.*

83 COME ye yourselves apart, and
    rest awhile,
   Weary, I know it, of the press
    and throng;
Wipe from your brow the sweat
    and dust of toil,
   And in My quiet strength again
    be strong.

2 Come ye aside from all the world
    holds dear,
   For converse which the world
    has never known;
Alone with Me, and with My
    Father here,
   With Me, and with My Father
    not alone.

3 Come, tell Me all that ye have said
    and done,
   Your victories and failures, hopes
    and fears;
I know how hardly souls are wooed
    and won;
   My choicest wreaths are always
    wet with tears.

4 Come ye, and rest, the journey is
    too great,
   And ye will faint beside the way
    and sink;
The bread of life is here for you
    to eat,
   And here for you the wine of
    love to drink.

5 Then, fresh from converse with
    your Lord, return
   And work till daylight softens in-
    to even,
The brief hours are not lost in
    which ye learn
   More of your Master and His
    rest in heaven.
*E. H. Bickersteth.*

84 DEAR Lord and Father of man-
    kind,
   Forgive our foolish ways!
Re-clothe us in our rightful mind,
In purer lives Thy service find,
   In deeper reverence, praise.

2 In simple trust like theirs who
 Beside the Syrian sea,  [heard,
The gracious calling of the Lord,
Let us, like them, without a word
Rise up and follow Thee.

3 O Sabbath rest by Galilee!
 O calm of hills above,
Where Jesus knelt to share with
The silence of eternity,  [Thee
Interpreted by love.

4 With that deep hush subduing all
 Our words and works that drown
The tender whisper of Thy call,
As noiseless let Thy blessing fall
As fell Thy manna down.

5 Drop Thy still dews of quietness,
 Till all our strivings cease; [stress,
Take from our souls the strain and
And let our ordered lives confess
The beauty of Thy peace.

6 Breathe through the heats of our
  desire
 Thy coolness and Thy balm;
Let sense be dumb, let flesh retire;
Speak  through  the  earthquake,
  wind, and fire,
O still, small voice of calm!
      *J. G. Whittier.*

**85**  HERE is love, vast as the ocean,
 Loving-kindness as the flood;
When the Prince of Life my ransom,
Shed for me His precious blood.
Who His love will not remember?
Who can cease to sing His praise?
He shall never be forgotten,
 Through  heav'n's  everlasting
  days.

2 On the mount of crucifixion,
 Fountains opened deep and wide,
Through the flood-gates of God's
  mercy,
 Flowed the vast and gracious tide;
Grace and love like mighty rivers
 Poured incessant from above,
And heav'n's peace and perfect jus-
  tice
 Kissed a guilty world in love.

3 Let me all Thy love accepting,
 Love Thee, ever all my days;
Let me seek Thy kingdom only
 And my life be to Thy praise;

Thou alone shalt be my glory,
 Nothing in the world I see;
Thou hast cleansed and sanctified
  me,
Thou Thyself hast set me free.

4 In Thy truth Thou dost direct me
 By Thy Spirit through Thy Word;
And Thy grace my need is meeting,
 As I trust in Thee, my Lord.
All Thy fulness Thou art pouring
 In Thy love and power in me,
Without measure, full and bound-
 As I yield myself to Thee. [less,

**86**  NOTHING between, Lord, nothing
  between;
 Let me Thy glory see,
 Draw my soul close to Thee,
 Then speak in love to me—
  Nothing between.

2 Nothing between, Lord, nothing be-
  tween;
 Let not earth's din and noise
 Stifle Thy still small voice;
 In it let me rejoice—
  Nothing between.

3 Nothing between, Lord, nothing
  between;
 Nothing of earthly care,
 Nothing of tear or prayer,
 No robe that self may wear—
  Nothing between.

4 Nothing between, Lord, nothing
  between;
 Unbelief disappear,
 Vanish each doubt and fear,
 Fading when Thou art near—
  Nothing between.

5 Nothing between, Lord, nothing
  between;
 Till Thine eternal light,
 Rising on earth's dark night,
 Bursts on my open sight—
  Nothing between.
      *E. H. H.*

**87**  THE sands of time are sinking,
 The dawn of heaven breaks;
The summer morn I've sighed for,
 The fair sweet morn awakes;
Dark, dark hath been the midnight,
 But dayspring is at hand,
And glory, glory dwelleth
 In Immanuel's land.

2 O Christ, He is the fountain,
  The deep, sweet well of love;
The streams on earth I've tasted,
  More deep I'll drink above;
There to an ocean fulness
  His mercy doth expand,
And glory, glory dwelleth
  In Immanuel's land.

3 With mercy and with judgment,
  My web of time He wove,
And aye the dews of sorrow
  Were lustred by His love:
I'll bless the hand that guided,
  I'll bless the heart that planned,
When throned where glory dwelleth
  In Immanuel's land.

4 Oh, I am my Belovèd's,
  And my Belov'd is mine!
He brings a poor vile sinner
  Into His " House of wine;"
I stand upon His merit,
  I know no other stand,
Not e'en where glory dwelleth
  In Immanuel's land.

5 The bride eyes not her garment,
  But her dear bridegroom's face;
I will not gaze at glory,
  But on my King of grace;
Not at the crown He gifteth,
  But on His piercèd hand;
The Lamb is all the glory
  Of Immanuel's land.

6 I've wrestled on towards heaven,
  'Gainst storm, and wind, and tide;
Now like a weary trav'ller
  That leaneth on His guide;
Amid the shades of evening,
  While sinks life's lingering sand.
I hail the glory dawning
  In Immanuel's land.
                    *A. R. Cousin.*

**88** SPEAK, Lord, in Thy stillness,
    While I wait on Thee;
Hushed my heart to listen
  In expectancy.

2 Speak, O blessèd Master,
  In this quiet hour;
Let me see Thy face, Lord,
  Feel Thy touch of power.

3 For the words Thou speakest,
  " They are life indeed;"
Living bread from heaven,
  Now my spirit feed!

4 Satiate my being,
  With Thy fulness fill;
As the dew descending,
  Let Thy speech distil.

5 All to Thee is yielded,
  I am not mine own;
Blissful, glad surrender,
  I am Thine alone.

6 Speak, Thy servant heareth;
  Be not silent, Lord!
Waits my soul upon Thee
  For the quickening word.

7 Fill me with the knowledge
  Of Thy glorious will;
All Thine own good pleasure
  In Thy child fulfil.

8 Like a watered garden,
  Full of fragrance rare,
Lingering in Thy presence,
  Let my life appear.
                    *E. May Grimes.*

**89** JESUS, the very thought of Thee
    With sweetness fills my breast;
But sweeter far Thy face to see,
  And in Thy presence rest.

2 Nor voice can sing, nor heart can
    frame,
  Nor can the memory find
A sweeter sound than Thy blest
  O Saviour of mankind.   [name,

3 O Hope of every contrite heart,
  O Joy of all the meek,
To those who fall, how kind Thou
    art!
  How good to those who seek!

4 But what to those who find? Ah,
    this
  Nor tongue nor pen can show;
The love of Jesus, what it is,
  None but His loved ones know.

5 Jesus, our only joy be Thou,
  As Thou our prize wilt be;
Jesus, be Thou our glory now,
  And through eternity.
                  *Bernard of Clairvaux.*

**90** JESUS, Jesus, Jesus,
    Sweetest name on earth:
How can I, a sinner,
  Come to know its worth?

2 Oh! the sinful sorrow,
  Oh! the strangest shame,
That I saw no beauty
  In that sacred Name.

3 Never felt the sweetness,
  Never knew the grace,
Never saw the love-pain
  In that wounded face!

4 Never found the mystery
  In that simple word
Jesus, Jesus, Jesus,
  Saviour, Lover—Lord.

5 Now 'tis past and over,
  Gone my sin and shame,
Jesus, Jesus did it,
  Glory to His Name!

6 I have seen the glory
  Of His tender face,
I have felt with wonder
  Thrills of holy grace.

7 Wonderful compassion
  Reaching even me,
Bows my humbled spirit
  In captivity.

8 Jesus! Jesus! Jesus!
  Loved me in my shame,
Oh! the joy and rapture
  Of that sacred Name.
                    *A. Paget Wilkes.*

**91** My heart is resting, O my God,
  I will give thanks and sing;
My heart is at the secret source
  Of every precious thing.

2 Now the frail vessel Thou hast
    made
  No hand but Thine shall fill;
For the waters of this world have
    failed
  And I am thirsty still.        [failed

3 I thirst for springs of heavenly life,
  And here all day they rise;
I seek the treasure of Thy love,
  And close at hand it lies.

4 And a new song is in my mouth,
  To long-loved music set—
Glory to Thee for all Thy grace
  I have not tasted yet.

5 "Thou art my Portion," saith my
    soul,
  Ten thousand voices say,
And the music of their glad Amen
  Will never die away.
                    *Anna L. Waring.*

**92** I LIFT my heart to Thee,
  Saviour divine;
For Thou art all to me,
  And I am Thine.
Is there on earth a closer bond than
    this
That my Belovèd's mine, and I am
    His?

2    Thine am I by all ties;
      But chiefly Thine,
    That through Thy sacrifice
      Thou, Lord, art mine.
By Thine own cords of love, so
    sweetly wound
Around me, I to Thee am closely
    bound.

3    To Thee, Thou dying Lamb,
      I all things owe;
    All that I have, and am,
      And all I know.
All that I have is now no longer
    mine,
And I am not my own; Lord, I am
    Thine.

4    How can I, Lord, withhold
      Life's brightest hour
    From Thee; or gathered gold,
      Or any power?
Why should I keep one precious
    thing from Thee,
When Thou hast given Thine own
    dear self to me?

5    I pray Thee, Saviour, keep
      Me in Thy love,
    Until death's holy sleep
      Shall me remove
To that fair realm where, sin and
    sorrow o'er,
Thou and Thine own are one for
    evermore.
                    *C. E. Mudie.*

**93** ALONE upon the mount of God
  I stand,
    With silenced heart His voice to
    hear;
  'Tis love itself hath led this hungry
    soul
    Unto the place of vision clear.

2 How wonderful amid this hush
    divine,
    Entranced, God's beauty to be-
    hold;

To wait whilst deep with deep
    doth meet and merge,
And love its secrets doth unfold.

3 Within the shadow of almighty love,
    This soul at last hath found its
      home,
Embosomed in the faithfulness of
    Him
    From whom it nevermore shall
      roam.

4 O blessèd heights of fellowship
    with God,
    Where love creative reigns
      supreme,
And springs of never-failing healing
    rise,
    To gladden, strengthen and re-
      deem.

5 O heart of God, Thy grace and
    tenderness
    Now wraps this ravished soul
      around;
No human mind could e'er conceive
    the joy
    In fellowship with Thee here
      found.
          *E. C. W. Boulton.*

**94** JESUS, I am resting, resting,
    In the joy of what Thou art;
I am finding out the greatness
Of Thy loving heart.
Thou hast bid me gaze upon Thee,
And Thy beauty fills my soul,
For, by Thy transforming power,
    Thou hast made me whole.

    Jesus, I am resting, resting,
      In the joy of what Thou art ;
    I am finding out the greatness
      Of Thy loving heart.

2 Oh, how great Thy loving kindness,
    Vaster, broader than the sea!
Oh, how marvellous Thy goodness,
    Lavished all on me!
Yes, I rest in Thee, Beloved,
    Know what wealth of grace is
      Thine,
Know Thy certainty of promise,
    And have made it mine.

3 Simply trusting Thee, Lord Jesus,
    I behold Thee as Thou art;
And Thy love so pure, so change-
      less,
    Satisfies my heart.

Satisfies its deepest longings,
    Meets, supplies its every need,
Compasseth me round with bless-
      ings;
    Thine is love indeed!

4 Ever lift Thy face upon me,
    As I work and wait for Thee;
Resting 'neath Thy smile, **Lord**
    Jesus,
    Earth's dark shadows flee.
Brightness of my Father's glory,
    Sunshine of my Father's face,
Keep me ever trusting, resting,
    Fill me with Thy grace.
          *Jean Sophia Pigott.*

**95** DWELLING in the secret place,
    Overshadowed by His grace,
Looking up into His face,
    Seeing only Jesus.

2 Hidden there from all alarm,
Safe from danger, fear and harm;
Holden up by His strong arm,
    Seeing only Jesus.

3 Dwelling there, how truly blest!
Leaving all, how sweet to rest,
Head upon my Saviour's breast,
    Seeing only Jesus.

4 Resting there, no more to roam,
Drawing near to heaven and home,
Waiting there until He come,
    Seeing only Jesus.
          *Grace Clement.*

**96** THOU the Rose of Sharon,
    Let Thy praises roll;
Lily of the valley,
    Flower of my soul;
Chiefest of ten thousand,
    Round my heart entwine;
I am my Beloved's,
    My Belov'd is mine.

    Thou the Rose of Sharon,
      Let Thy praises roll !
    Lily of the valley,
      Flower of my soul.

2 Lead me by still waters,
    Hold me by the hand;
And upon the mountains
    Give me grace to stand;
Wind and storm and fire
    Raging, but my choice
Ever is to listen
    For Thy still, small voice.

3 Jesus, Lord and Master,
  Glorious Nazarene:
Close behind Thy reapers
  I would humbly glean:
But Thy grace hath brought me
  To Thy house above,
And Thy banner o'er me,
  Evermore is Love.

4 Water cannot quench it,
  Floods can never drown;
Substance cannot buy it,
  Love's a priceless crown:
Oh, the wondrous story,
  Mystery divine;
I am my Belovèd's,
  My Belov'd is mine.
                    *R. Kelso Carter.*

**97** THERE is a place of quiet rest,
  Near to the heart of God;
A place where sin cannot molest,
  Near to the heart of God.

  O Jesus, blest Redeemer,
    Sent from the heart of God;
  Hold us, who wait before Thee,
    Near to the heart of God.

2 There is a place of comfort sweet,
  Near to the heart of God;
A place where we our Saviour meet,
  Near to the heart of God.

3 There is a place of full release,
  Near to the heart of God;
A place where all is joy and peace,
  Near to the heart of God.

**98** JESUS, let Thy splendour
  Like a mantle fall,
On this waiting spirit,
  Whilst I yield Thee all;
Clothe me with Thy beauty,
  Bathe me in Thy will,
And with life triumphant
  All my nature fill.

  Fellowship with Jesus,
    This is victory;
  They who own His Lordship
    Know true liberty.

2 Give to me a vision
  Reaching to the throne.
Let me see earth's problems
  In that light alone;
'Tis Thy Word assures me
  All shall work for good,
Things that long have baffled
  Soon be understood.

3 Blessèd cross of Jesus,
  I Thy power would prove,
'Neath Thy shadow living,
  Naught this soul shall move.
Sanctify me wholly,
  Purge from every stain,
All that makes for bondage,
  Let it now be slain.

4 Fired with holy passion,
  Moved by urge divine,
What shall henceforth hinder
  Vict'ry being mine?
Men may raise their war-cry,
  Lift their standards high,
But before love's challenge
  Each vain thought shall fly.
                    *E. C. W. Boulton.*

### (5) PSALMS

**99** THE Lord's my Shepherd, I'll
    not want;
  He makes me down to lie
In pastures green; He leadeth me
  The quiet waters by.

2 My soul He doth restore again;
  And me to walk doth make
Within the paths of righteousness,
  E'en for His own name's sake.

3 Yea, though I walk in death's dark
    vale,
  Yet will I fear none ill;
For Thou art with me: and Thy rod
  And staff me comfort still.

4 My table Thou hast furnishèd
  In presence of my foes;
My head Thou dost with oil anoint
  And my cup overflows.

5 Goodness and mercy all my life
  Shall surely follow me,
And in God's house for evermore
  My dwelling place shall be.
                    *Whittingham and Rous.*

**100** PLEASANT are Thy courts above,
    In the land of light and love;
Pleasant are Thy courts below,
  In this land of sin and woe.
Oh, my spirit longs and faints
For the converse of Thy saints,
For the brightness of Thy face,
For Thy fulness, God of grace!

2 Happy birds that sing and fly
Round Thy altars, O Most High!
Happier souls that find a rest
In a heavenly Father's breast!
Like the wandering dove that found
No repose on earth around,
They can to their ark repair,
And enjoy it ever there.

3 Happy souls! their praises flow
Even in this vale of woe;
Waters in the desert rise,
Manna feeds them from the skies.
On they go from strength to
strength,
Till they reach Thy throne at
length;
At Thy feet adoring fall,
Who hast led them safe through all.

4 Lord, be mine this prize to win:
Guide me through a world of sin;
Keep me by Thy saving grace;
Give me at Thy side a place.
Sun and shield alike Thou art;
Guide and guard my erring heart:
Grace and glory flow from Thee;
Shower, oh shower them, Lord, on
me!                    *H. F. Lyte.*

### PART I.

**101** How lovely is Thy dwelling
place,
O Lord of hosts, to me!
The tabernacles of Thy grace
How pleasant, Lord, they be!

2 My thirsty soul longs vehemently,
Yea faints, Thy courts to see:
My very heart and flesh cry out,
O living God for Thee.

3 Behold, the sparrow findeth out
An house wherein to rest;
The swallow also for herself
Hath purchasèd a nest,

4 E'en Thine own altars, where she
safe
Her young ones forth may
bring,
O Thou almighty Lord of hosts,
Who art my God and King.

5 Blest are they in Thy house that
dwell;
They ever give Thee praise.
Blest is the man whose strength
Thou art,
In whose heart are Thy ways,

### PART II.

6 Who, passing through dark Baca's
vale,
Therein do dig up wells;
Also the rain that falleth down
The pools with water fills.

7 So they from strength unwearied
go
Still forward unto strength,
Until in Zion they appear
Before the Lord at length.

8 Lord God of hosts, my prayer
hear;
O Jacob's God give ear.
See God our shield, look on the
face
Of Thine anointed dear.

9 For in Thy courts one day excels
A thousand; rather in
My God's house will I keep a
door
Than dwell in tents of sin.

10 For God the Lord's a sun and
shield:
He'll grace and glory give,
And will withhold no good from
them
That uprightly do live.

11 O Thou that art the Lord of hosts,
That man is truly blessed
Who by assurèd confidence
On Thee alone doth rest.

**102** FROM all that dwell below the
skies
Let the Creator's praise arise:
Hallelujah!
Let the Redeemer's Name be sung
Through every land in every tongue.
Hallelujah!

2 Eternal are Thy mercies, Lord:
Eternal truth attends Thy word:
Hallelujah!
Thy praise shall sound from shore
to shore
Till suns shall rise and set no more.
Hallelujah!
                    *Isaac Watts.*

**103** THE King of love my Shepherd
is,
Whose goodness faileth never;
I nothing lack if I am His,
And He is mine for ever.

2 Where streams of living water flow
   My ransomed soul He leadeth,
And where the verdant pastures grow,
   With food celestial feedeth.

3 Perverse and foolish oft I strayed,
   But yet in love He sought me,
And on His shoulder gently laid,
   And home rejoicing brought me.

4 In death's dark vale I fear no ill
   With Thee, dear Lord, beside me;
Thy rod and staff my comfort still,
   Thy cross before to guide me.

5 And so through all the length of days
   Thy goodness faileth never;
Good Shepherd, may I sing Thy praise
   Within Thy house for ever.
                    *Henry W. Baker.*

**104** O GOD, our help in ages past,
   Our hope for years to come,
Our shelter from the stormy blast,
   And our eternal home.

2 Under the shadow of Thy throne
   Thy saints have dwelt secure:
Sufficient is Thine arm alone,
   And our defence is sure.

3 Before the hills in order stood,
   Or earth received her frame,
From everlasting Thou art God,
   To endless years the same.

4 A thousand ages in Thy sight
   Are like an evening gone,
Short as the watch that ends the night
   Before the rising sun.

5 Time like an ever-rolling stream,
   Bears all its sons away;
They fly forgotten, as a dream
   Dies at the opening day.

6 O God, our help in ages past,
   Our hope for years to come,
Be Thou our guard while troubles last,
   And our eternal home.
                    *Isaac Watts.*

**105** SWEET is the work, my God, my King
   To praise Thy name, give thanks and sing;
To show Thy love by morning light,
And talk of all Thy truth at night.

2 Sweet is the day of sacred rest,
No mortal cares disturb my breast,
O may my heart in tune be found,
Like David's harp of solemn sound!

3 My heart shall triumph in the Lord,
And bless His works and bless His word:
Thy works of grace, how bright they shine!
How deep Thy counsels, how divine!

4 And I shall share a glorious part,
When grace has well refined my heart,
And fresh supplies of joy are shed,
Like holy oil, to cheer my head.

5 Then shall I see, and hear, and know,
All I desired or wished below;
And every power find sweet employ
In that eternal world of joy.
                    *Isaac Watts.*

**106** ALL people that on earth do dwell,
   Sing to the Lord with cheerful voice;
Him serve with mirth, His praise forthtell;
   Come ye before Him and rejoice.

2 Know that the Lord is God indeed;
   Without our aid He did us make;
We are His flock, He doth us feed,
   And for His sheep He doth us take.

3 Oh enter then His gates with praise,
   Approach with joy His courts unto;
Praise, laud, and bless His name always,
   For it is seemly so to do.

4 For why? the Lord our God is good;
   His mercy is for ever sure;
His truth at all times firmly stood,
   And shall from age to age endure.
                    *William Kethe.*

**107** O THOU, my soul, bless God the Lord;
   And all that in me is
Be stirrèd up His holy name
   To magnify and bless.

2 Bless, O my soul, the Lord thy God,
   And not forgetful be
Of all His gracious benefits
   He hath bestowed on thee:

3 All thine iniquities who doth
   Most graciously forgive:
Who thy diseases all and pains
   Doth heal, and thee relieve:

4 Who doth redeem thy life, that thou
   To death may'st not go down:
Who thee with loving-kindness doth
   And tender mercies crown.

**108**   I to the hills will lift mine
   eyes,
   From whence doth come mine
   aid;
My safety cometh from the Lord,
   Who heaven and earth hath
   made.

2 Thy foot He'll not let slide, nor
   will
   He slumber that thee keeps:
Behold, He that keeps Israel,
   He slumbers not, nor sleeps.

3 The Lord thee keeps, the Lord thy
   shade
   On thy right hand doth stay:
The moon by night thee shall not
   smite,
   Nor yet the sun by day.

4 The Lord shall keep thy soul; He
   shall
   Preserve thee from all ill:
Henceforth thy going out and in
   God keep for ever will.
                    *Scottish Psalter.*

**109**   Let us with a gladsome mind
   Praise the Lord for He is kind;

For His mercies shall endure,
Ever faithful, ever sure.

2 Let us sound His name abroad,
   For of gods He is the God;

3 He, with all-commanding might,
   Filled the new-made world with
   light;

4 All things living He doth feed,
   His full hand supplies their need;

5 He His chosen race did bless
   In the wasteful wilderness;

6 He hath with a piteous eye
   Looked upon our misery;

7 Let us then with gladsome mind
   Praise the Lord, for He is kind.
                       *John Milton.*

**110**   Praise the Lord, His glories
   show,
   Hallelujah!
Saints within His courts below,
   Hallelujah!
Angels round His throne above,
   Hallelujah!
All that see and share His love.
   Hallelujah!

2 Earth to heaven, and heaven to
   Hallelujah!          [earth,
Tell His wonders, sing His worth;
   Hallelujah!
Age to age and shore to shore,
   Hallelujah!
Praise Him, praise Him evermore!
   Hallelujah!

3 Praise the Lord, His mercies trace,
   Hallelujah!
Praise His providence and grace,
   Hallelujah!
All that He for man hath done,
   Hallelujah!
All He sends us through His Son.
   Hallelujah!

4 Strings and voices, hands and hearts,
   Hallelujah!
In the concert bear your parts;
   Hallelujah!
All that breathe, your Lord adore,
   Hallelujah!
Praise Him, praise Him evermore!
   Hallelujah!
                       *H. F. Lyte.*

**111**   I waited for the Lord my
   God,
   And patiently did bear:
At length to me He did incline
   My voice and cry to hear.

2 He took me from a fearful pit,
   And from the miry clay,
And on a rock He set my feet,
   Establishing my way.

3 He put a new song in my mouth,
   Our God to magnify:
Many shall see it, and shall fear,
   And on the Lord rely.

4 O blessèd is the man whose trust
   Upon the Lord relies;
   Respecting not the proud, nor such
   As turn aside to lies.

5 In Thee let all be glad, and joy,
   Who seeking Thee abide;
   Who Thy salvation love, say still,
   The Lord be magnified.

*John Hopkins.*

# Section II

## THE GODHEAD

### (1) THE TRINITY

**112** THE Lord Jehovah reigns;
   His throne is built on high,
The garments He assumes
   Are light and majesty:
His glories shine with beams so
   bright,
No mortal eye can bear the sight.

2 The thunders of His hand
   Keep the wide world in awe;
His wrath and justice stand
   To guard His holy law;
And where His love resolves to
   bless,
His truth confirms and seals the
   grace.

3 Through all His mighty works
   Amazing wisdom shines,
Confounds the powers of hell,
   And breaks their dark designs;
Strong is His arm, and shall fulfil,
His great decrees and sovereign
   will.

4 And will this sovereign King
   Of Glory condescend?
And will He write His name
   My Father and my Friend?
I love His name, I love His word,
Join all my powers to praise the
   Lord.        *Isaac Watts.*

**113** HOLY, holy, holy, Lord God
   Almighty!
Early in the morning our song shall
   rise to Thee;
Holy, holy, holy, merciful and
   mighty,
God in Three Persons, blessèd
   Trinity!

2 Holy, holy, holy! all the saints
   adore Thee,
Casting down their golden crowns
   around the glassy sea;
Cherubim and seraphim falling
   down before Thee,
Which wert and art, and evermore
   shalt be.

3 Holy, holy, holy! though the darkness hide Thee,
Though the eye of sinful man Thy
   glory may not see,
Only Thou art holy; there is none
   beside Thee,
Perfect in power, in love, and
   purity.

4 Holy, holy, holy, Lord God
   Almighty!
All Thy works shall praise Thy
   name in earth and sky and sea;
Holy, holy, holy, merciful and
   mighty,
God in Three Persons, blessèd
   Trinity!

*Reginald Heber.*

**114** COME, Thou almighty King,
   Help us Thy name to sing,
   Help us to praise;
Father, all-glorious,
O'er all victorious,
Come, and reign over us,
   Ancient of Days!

2 Come, Thou incarnate Word,
Gird on Thy mighty sword:
   Our prayer attend;
Come, and Thy people bless,
And give Thy Word success:
Spirit of holiness,
   On us descend.

3 Come, Holy Comforter,
Thy sacred witness bear,
In this glad hour;
Thou, who almighty art,
Now rule in every heart,
And ne'er from us depart,
Spirit of power!

4 To the great One in Three,
The highest praises be,
Hence evermore!
His sovereign majesty
May we in glory see,
And to eternity
Love and adore.    *Charles Wesley.*

**115** THOU whose almighty word
Chaos and darkness heard,
And took their flight,
Hear us, we humbly pray,
And where the gospel day
Sheds not its glorious ray,
Let there be light!

2 Thou who didst come to bring
On Thy redeeming wing
Healing and sight,
Health to the sick in mind,
Sight to the inly blind,
Oh now to all mankind
Let there be light!

3 Spirit of truth and love,
Life-giving, holy Dove,
Speed forth Thy flight:
Move on the water's face,
Spreading the beams of grace,
And in earth's darkest place
Let there be light!

4 Blessèd and holy Three,
Glorious Trinity,
Wisdom, love, might;
Boundless as ocean's tide
Rolling in fullest pride,
Through the earth far and wide,
Let there be light!    *J. Marriott.*

**116** O GOD, Thou bottomless
abyss!
Thee to perfection who can
know?
O height immense!  What words
suffice
Thy countless attributes to show?

2 Unfathomable depths Thou art;
Oh plunge me in Thy mercy's
sea!

Void of true wisdom is my heart;
With love embrace and cover me.

3 Eternity Thy fountain was,
Which, like Thee, no beginning
knew;
Thou wast ere time began his race,
Ere glowed with stars th'ethereal
blue.

4 Greatness unspeakable is Thine,
Greatness, whose undiminished
ray,
When short-lived worlds are lost,
shall shine,
When earth and heaven are fled
away.

5 Unchangeable, all-perfect Lord,
Essential life's unbounded sea,
What lives and moves, lives by Thy
word;
It lives, and moves, and is from
Thee.

6 High is Thy power above all
height,
Whate'er Thy will decrees is
done;
Thy wisdom, equal to Thy might,
Only to Thee, O God, is known.
*E. Lange, tr. by J. Wesley.*

## (2) CREATION AND PROVIDENCE

**117** GOD moves in a mysterious
way
His wonders to perform;
He plants His footsteps in the sea,
And rides upon the storm.

2 Deep in unfathomable mines
Of never-failing skill,
He treasures up His bright designs,
And works His sovereign will.

3 Ye fearful saints, fresh courage
take!
The clouds ye so much dread
Are big with mercy; and shall
break
In blessings on your head.

4 Judge not the Lord by feeble sense,
But trust Him for His grace;
Behind a frowning providence
He hides a smiling face.

5 His purposes will ripen fast,
   Unfolding every hour;
The bud may have a bitter taste,
   But sweet will be the flower.
6 Blind unbelief is sure to err,
   And scan His work in vain;
God is His own interpreter,
   And He will make it plain.
*W. Cowper.*

**118** NONE is like Jeshurun's God,
   So great, so strong, so high;
Lo! He spreads His wings abroad,
   He rides upon the sky:
Israel is His first-born son;
   God, th'almighty God, is thine;
See Him to Thy help come down,
   The excellence divine.
2 Thee the great Jehovah deigns
   To succour and defend;
Thee the eternal God sustains,
   Thy Maker and thy Friend:
Israel, what hast thou to dread?
   Safe from all impending harms,
Round thee and beneath are spread
   The everlasting arms.
3 In a land of corn and wine
   His lot shall be below;
Comforts there, and blessings join,
   And milk and honey flow;
Jacob's well is in his soul:
   Gracious dew his heavens distil,
Fill his soul, already full,
   And shall for ever fill.
4 Blest, O Israel art Thou!
   What people is like thee?
Saved from sin by Jesus, now
   Thou art and still shalt be;
Jesus is thy sevenfold shield,
   Jesus is thy flaming sword;
Earth, and hell, and sin shall yield
   To God's almighty Word.
*Charles Wesley.*

**119** WE plough the fields and scatter
   The good seed on the land,
But it is fed and watered
   By God's almighty hand;
He sends the snow in winter,
   The warmth to swell the grain,
The breezes and the sunshine,
   And soft refreshing rain.
All good gifts around us
Are sent from heaven above,

Then thank the Lord, oh, thank the Lord,
   For all His love.
2 He only is the Maker
   Of all things near and far,
He paints the wayside flower,
   He lights the evening star;
The winds and waves obey Him,
   By Him the birds are fed;
Much more to us His children
   He gives our daily bread.
3 We thank Thee then, O Father,
   For all things bright and good,
The seed-time and the harvest,
   Our life, our health, our food;
Accept the gifts we offer
   For all Thy love imparts,
And, what Thou most desirest,
   Our humble, thankful hearts.
*Matthias Claudius; tr. Miss Jane M. Campbell.*

**120** WHEN all Thy mercies, O my God,
   My rising soul surveys,
Transported with the view, I'm lost
   In wonder, love and praise.
2 Unnumbered comforts on my soul
   Thy tender care bestowed,
Before my infant heart conceived
   From whom these comforts flowed.
3 Through hidden dangers, toils, and deaths,
   It gently cleared my way;
And through the pleasing snares of vice,
   More to be feared than they.
4 When worn with sickness oft hast Thou
   With health renewed my face;
And when in sins and sorrows sunk,
   Revived my soul with grace.
5 Ten thousand thousand precious gifts
   My daily thanks employ; [gifts
Nor is the least a cheerful heart
   That tastes those gifts with joy.
6 Through every period of my life
   Thy goodness I'll pursue;
And after death, in distant worlds,
   The glorious theme renew.
7 Through all eternity to Thee
   A joyful song I'll raise;
But oh, eternity's too short
   To utter all Thy praise.
*Joseph Addison.*

**121** SUMMER suns are glowing
  Over land and sea;
Happy light is flowing,
  Bountiful and free.
Everything rejoices
  In the mellow rays;
All earth's thousand voices
  Swell the psalm of praise.

2 God's free mercy streameth
  Over all the world,
And His banner gleameth,
  Everywhere unfurled.
Broad, and deep, and glorious,
  As the heav'n above,
Shines in might victorious,
  His eternal love.

3 Lord, upon our blindness
  Thy pure radiance pour;
For Thy loving-kindness
  Make us love Thee more.
And when clouds are drifting
  Dark across our sky,
Then, the veil uplifting,
  Father, be Thou nigh.

4 We will never doubt Thee,
  Though Thou veil Thy light;
Life is dark without Thee,
  Death with Thee is bright.
Light of Light, shine o'er us
  On our pilgrim way;
Go Thou still before us
  To the endless day.
                                *W. W. How.*

**122** THE spacious firmament on high,
With all the blue ethereal sky,
And spangled heavens, a shining frame,
Their great Original proclaim.

2 Th'unwearied sun, from day to day,
Doth his Creator's power display;
And publishes to every land
The work of an almighty hand.

3 Soon as the evening shades prevail,
The moon takes up the wondrous tale,
And nightly to the listening earth
Repeats the story of her birth:

4 While all the stars that round her burn,
And all the planets in their turn,

Confirm the tidings as they roll,
And spread the truth from pole to pole.

5 What though in solemn silence all
Move round this dark terrestrial ball;
What though no real voice nor sound
Amidst their radiant orbs be found:

6 In reason's ear they all rejoice,
And utter forth a glorious voice,
For ever singing as they shine:
The hand that made us is divine!
                            *Joseph Addison.*

**123** THOUGH troubles assail,
  And dangers affright;
Though friends should all fail,
  And foes all unite—
Yet one thing secures us,
  Whatever betide:
The Scripture assures us,
  "The Lord will provide."

2 The birds, without barn
  Or storehouse, are fed;
From them let us learn
  To trust for our bread:
His saints what is fitting
  Shall ne'er be denied,
So long as 'tis written,
  "The Lord will provide."

3 His call we obey
  Like Abram of old,
Not knowing our way;
  But faith makes us bold:
For though we are strangers,
  We have a good Guide;
And trust in all dangers:
  "The Lord will provide."

4 No strength of our own
  Or goodness we claim;
Yet since we have known
  The Saviour's great name,
In this our strong tower
  For safety we hide—
Almighty His power:
  "The Lord will provide."
                              *John Newton.*

**124** I SING th'almighty power of God,
  That made the mountains rise,
That spread the flowing seas abroad,
  And built the lofty skies.

2 I sing the wisdom that ordained
  The sun to rule the day;
The moon shines full at His com-
    mand,
  And all the stars obey.

3 I sing the goodness of the Lord,
  That filled the earth with food;
He formed the creatures with His
    word,
  And then pronounced them good.

4 Lord, how Thy wonders are dis-
    played
  Where'er I turn mine eye,
If I survey the ground I tread,
  Or gaze upon the sky;

5 There's not a plant or flower below
  But makes Thy glories known,
And clouds arise and tempests blow
  By order from Thy throne.

6 God's hand is my perpetual guard,
  He guides me with His eye;
Why should I then forget the Lord,
  Whose love is ever nigh?
                    *Isaac Watts.*

**125** STANDING at the portal
  Of the op'ning year,
Words of comfort meet us,
  Hushing ev'ry fear,
Spoken through the silence
  By our Father's voice,
Tender, strong, and faithful,
  Making us rejoice.

    Onward, then, and fear not,
      Children of the day !
    For His Word shall never,
      Never pass away !

2 I, the Lord, am with thee,
    Be thou not afraid!
I will help and strengthen,
    Be thou not dismayed!
Yea, I will uphold thee
    With My own right hand;
Thou art called and chosen
    In My sight to stand.

3 For the year before us,
    O what rich supplies!
For the poor and needy
    Living streams shall rise;
For the sad and sinful
    Shall His grace abound,
For the faint and feeble
    Perfect strength be found.

4 He will never fail us,
    He will not forsake;
His eternal covenant
    He will never break!
Resting on His promise,
    What have we to fear?
God is all-sufficient
    For the coming year.
                    *Frances R. Havergal.*

**126** HIGH in the heav'ns, eternal
    God,
  Thy goodness in full glory
      shines;          [cloud
Thy truth shall break through ev'ry
  That veils and darkens Thy
      designs.

2 For ever firm Thy justice stands,
    As mountains their foundations
      keep;
  Wise are the wonders of Thy hands;
    Thy judgments are a mighty deep.

3 Thy providence is kind and large,
    Both man and beast Thy bounty
      share;
  The whole creation is Thy charge,
    But saints are Thy peculiar care.

4 My God, how excellent Thy grace,
    Whence all our hope and com-
      fort springs!
  The sons of Adam in distress
    Fly to the shadow of Thy wings.

5 From the provisions of Thy house
    We shall be fed with sweet
      repast;
  When mercy like a river flows,
    And brings salvation to our taste.

6 Life, like a fountain rich and free,
    Springs from the presence of the
      Lord;
  And in Thy light our souls shall
      see
  The glories promised in Thy
      Word.
                    *Isaac Watts.*

**127** O LOVE of God, how strong
    and true;
  Eternal, and yet ever new;
Uncomprehended and unbought,
  Beyond all knowledge and all
      thought!

2 O heavenly Love, how precious
    still,
In days of weariness and ill,
In nights of pain and helplessness,
To heal, to comfort, and to bless.

3 O wide embracing, wondrous Love;
We read Thee in the sky above,
We read Thee in the earth below,
In seas that swell and streams that
    flow.

4 We read Thee best in Him who
    came
To bear for us the Cross of shame,
Sent by the Father from on high,
Our life to live, our death to die.

5 We read Thy power to bless and
    save
E'en in the darkness of the grave;
Still more in resurrection light
We read the fulness of Thy might.

6 O Love of God, our shield and stay
Through all the perils of our way;
Eternal Love, in Thee we rest,
For ever safe, for ever blest.
*Horatius Bonar.*

**128** COME, ye thankful people,
    come,
Raise the song of harvest home:
All is safely gathered in,
Ere the winter storms begin;
God our Maker doth provide
For our wants to be supplied;
Come to God's own temple, come,
Raise the song of harvest-home!

2 All the world is God's own field,
Fruit unto His praise to yield;
Wheat and tares together sown,
Unto joy or sorrow grown;
First the blade, and then the ear,
Then the full corn shall appear;
Lord of harvest, grant that we
Wholesome grain and pure may be.

3 For the Lord our God shall come,
And shall take His harvest home;
From His field shall in that day
All offences purge away;

Give His angels charge at last
In the fire the tares to cast;
But the fruitful ears to store
In His garner evermore.

4 Even so, Lord, quickly come
To Thy final Harvest-home,
Gather Thou Thy people in,
Free from sorrow, free from sin;
There for ever purified,
In Thy presence to abide:
Come, with all Thine angels, come;
Raise the glorious Harvest-home.
*H. Alford.*

**129** FOR the beauty of the earth,
    For the beauty of the skies,
For the love which from our birth
    Over and around us lies;
Christ, our God, to Thee we raise
This our sacrifice of praise.

2 For the beauty of each hour
    Of the day and of the night,
Hill and vale, and tree and flower,
    Sun and moon and stars of light;
Christ, our God, to Thee we raise
This our sacrifice of praise.

3 For the joy of ear and eye,
    For the heart and mind's delight,
For the mystic harmony
    Linking sense to sound and
      sight;
Christ, our God, to Thee we raise
This our sacrifice of praise.

4 For the joy of human love,
    Brother, sister, parent, child,
Friends on earth and friends above,
    For all gentle thoughts and mild;
Christ, our God, to Thee we raise
This our sacrifice of praise.

5 For each perfect gift of Thine
    To our race so freely given,
Graces human and divine,
    Flowers of earth and buds of
      heaven;
Christ, our God, to Thee we raise
This our sacrifice of praise.
*F. S. Pierpoint.*

# Section III

## THE LORD JESUS CHRIST

### (1) HIS INCARNATION

**130** OH come, all ye faithful,
Joyful and triumphant,
To Bethlehem hasten now with
Lo! in a manger   [glad accord;
Lies the King of angels;

Oh, come, let us adore Him,
Oh, come, let us adore Him,
Oh, come, let us adore Him, Christ the Lord!

2  Raise, raise, choirs of angels,
Songs of loudest triumph;
Through heaven's high arches be
your praises poured;
Now to our God be
Glory in the highest;

3  Amen! Lord, we bless Thee,
Born for our salvation,
O Jesus! for ever be Thy name
Word of the Father,   [adored;
Now in flesh appearing;

*18th Century.*

**131** WHILE shepherds watched
their flocks by night,
All seated on the ground,
The angel of the Lord came down,
And glory shone around.

2 Fear not! said he; for mighty
dread
Had seized their troubled mind:
Glad tidings of great joy I bring
To you and all mankind.

3 To you, in David's town, this day
Is born, of David's line,
A Saviour, who is Christ the Lord;
And this shall be the sign:

4 The heavenly Babe you there shall
find
To human view displayed,
All meanly wrapped in swaddling
And in a manger laid.   [bands

5 Thus spake the seraph; and forth-
with
Appeared a shining throng
Of angels praising God, who thus
Addressed their joyful song:

6 All glory be to God on high,
And to the earth be peace;
Goodwill henceforth from heaven
to men
Begin and never cease!

*Nahum Tate.*

**132** CHRISTIANS, awake, salute the
happy morn,
Whereon the Saviour of mankind
was born:
Rise to adore the mystery of love,
Which hosts of angels chanted from
above;
With them the joyful tidings first
begun   [Son.
Of God incarnate and the Virgin's

2 Then to the watchful shepherds it
was told,   [voice: Behold,
Who heard the angelic herald's
I bring good tidings of a Saviour's
birth   [earth:
To you and all the nations upon
This day hath God fulfilled His
promised word,
This day is born a Saviour, Christ
the Lord.

3 He spake; and straightway the
celestial choir   [conspire,
In hymns of joy, unknown before,
The praises of redeeming love they
sang,   [lujahs rang;
And heaven's whole orb with halle-
God's highest glory was their an-
them still,
Peace upon earth, and unto men
goodwill.

4 To Bethlehem straight the enlight-
ened shepherds ran,
To see the wonder God had
wrought for man:  [God, return,
Then to their flocks, still praising
And their glad hearts with holy
rapture burn;   [proclaim,
Amazed, the wondrous tidings they
The first apostles of His infant
fame.

5 Oh may we keep and ponder in our
    mind                    [mankind;
God's wondrous love in saving lost
Trace we the Babe, who hath re-
    trieved our loss,
From the poor manger to the bitter
    Cross;                   [grace,
Tread in His steps, assisted by His
Till man's first heavenly state again
    takes place.

6 Then may we hope, the angelic
    hosts among,             [song;
To sing, redeemed, a glad triumphal
He that was born upon this joyful
    day                      [play;
Around us all His glory shall dis-
Saved by His love, incessant we
    shall sing               [King.
Eternal praise to heaven's almighty
                        *John Byrom.*

**133**  As with gladness men of old
    Did the guiding star behold,
As with joy they hailed its light,
Leading onward, beaming bright;
So, most gracious Lord, may we
Evermore be led to Thee.

2 As with joyful steps they sped,
Saviour, to Thy lowly bed,
There to bend the knee before
Thee, whom heaven and earth
So may we with willing feet [adore;
Ever seek the mercy-seat.

3 As they offered gifts most rare
At Thy cradle rude and bare;
So may we with holy joy,
Pure, and free from sin's alloy,
All our costliest treasures bring,
Christ, to Thee, our heavenly King.

4 Holy Jesus, every day
Keep us in the narrow way;
And, when earthly things are past,
Bring our ransomed souls at last
Where they need no star to guide,
Where no clouds Thy glory hide.

5 In the heavenly country bright
Need they no created light:
Thou its light, its joy, its crown,
Thou its sun which goes not down;
There for ever may we sing
Hallelujahs to our King.
                    *W. Chatterton Dix.*

**134**  BRIGHTEST and best of the sons
    of the morning,
Dawn on our darkness, and lend
    us thine aid;             [ing,
Star of the East, the horizon adorn-
Guide where our infant Re-
    deemer is laid.

2 Cold on His cradle the dew-drops
    are shining;       [of the stall;
Low lies His head with the beasts
Angels adore Him in slumber re-
    clining,            [of all.
Maker, and Monarch, and Saviour

3 Say, shall we yield Him, in costly
    devotion,            [divine,
Odours of Edom, and offerings
Gems of the mountain and pearls
    of the ocean,
Myrrh from the forest or gold
    from the mine?

4 Vainly we offer each ample obla-
    tion;           [favour secure;
Vainly with gifts would His
Richer by far is the heart's adora-
    tion;               [the poor.
Dearer to God are the prayers of

5 Brightest and best of the sons of
    the morning,        [us thine aid;
Dawn on our darkness, and lend
Star of the East, the horizon adorn-
    ing,            [deemer is laid.
Guide where our infant Re-
                        *R. Heber.*

**135**  HARK! the herald-angels sing
    Glory to the new-born King,
Peace on earth, and mercy mild,
God and sinners reconciled.
Joyful, all ye nations rise,
Join the triumph of the skies;
With the angelic host proclaim,
Christ is born in Bethlehem.

Hark! the herald-angels sing
Glory to the new-born King.

2 Christ, by highest heaven adored,
Christ, the everlasting Lord,
Late in time behold Him come,
Offspring of a virgin's womb!
Veiled in flesh the Godhead see;
Hail the incarnate Deity!
Pleased as man with men to dwell,
Jesus, our Immanuel.

3 Mild He lays His glory by,
  Born that man no more may die,
  Born to raise the sons of earth,
  Born to give them second birth.
  Hail the heaven-born Prince of
    Peace!
  Hail the Sun of Righteousness!
  Light and life to all He brings,
  Risen with healing in His wings.
            *Charles Wesley.*

**136** THOU art the Everlasting Word,
  The Father's only Son;
God, manifestly seen and heard,
  And Heaven's belovèd One.
Worthy, O Lamb of God, art Thou,
That every knee to Thee should bow.

2 In Thee, most perfectly expressed,
  The Father's glories shine;
Of the full Deity possessed;
  Eternally divine.

3 But the high myst'ries of Thy name
  An angel's grasp transcend:
The Father only—glorious claim—
  The Son can comprehend.

4 Yet, loving Thee, on whom His
  Ineffable doth rest,    [love
Thy glorious worshippers above,
  As one with Thee, are blest.
            *J. Conder.*

### (2) HIS LIFE AND WORK

**137** OH, how sweet the glorious
    message,
  Simple faith may claim;
Yesterday, today, forever,
  Jesus is the same.
Still He loves to save the sinful,
  Heal the sick and lame:
Cheer the mourner, still the tem-
  Glory to His name!    [pest,
Yesterday, to-day, for ever,
  Jesus is the same,
All may change, but Jesus never!
  Glory to His name,
Glory to His name,
  Glory to His name,
All may change, but Jesus never!
  Glory to His name.

2 Him who pardoned erring Peter,
  Never need'st thou fear;
He that came to faithless Thomas,
  All thy doubt will clear.
He who let the loved disciple
  On His bosom rest,
Bids thee still, with love as tender,
  Lean upon His breast.

3 He who 'mid the raging billows,
  Walked upon the sea;
Still can hush our wildest tempest,
  As on Galilee.
He who wept and prayed in
  In Gethsemane,    [anguish,
Drinks with us each cup of tremb-
  In our agony.    [ling,

4 As of old He walked to Emmaus,
  With them to abide;
So through all life's way He walk-
  Ever near our side.    [eth,
Soon again shall we behold Him,
  Hasten, Lord, the day!
But 'twill still be "this same Jesus,"
  As He went away.
            *A. B. Simpson.*

**138** OH, where is He that trod the
    sea?
  Oh, where is He that spake?—
And demons from their victims flee,
  The dead their slumbers break;
The palsied rise in freedom strong,
  The dumb men talk and sing,
And from blind eyes, benighted
    long,
  Bright beams of morning spring.

2 Oh, where is He that trod the sea?
  Oh, where is He that spake?—
And piercing words of liberty
  The deaf ears open shake;
And mildest words arrest the haste
  Of fever's deadly fire,
And strong ones heal the weak
    who waste
  Their life in sad desire.

3 Oh, where is He that trod the sea?
  My soul, the Lord is here:
Let all thy fears be hushed in thee;
  To leap, to look, to hear
Be thine; thy needs He'll satisfy:
  Art thou diseased or dumb?
Or dost thou in thy hunger cry?
  "I come," saith Christ, "I come."
            *T. T. Lynch.*

**139** O THOU who art love's primal
    flame,
To whom all beauty owes its name,
  We worship at Thy Cross;
So vast Thine everlasting love,
  Thou didst forsake Thy throne
  To take the place of loss. [above,

2 To reach this cold and cheerless
  clime,  [time,
Thou didst descend the steeps of
Thy light and truth to bring;
So dark man's lost and sinful state,
  Thou didst anew the race create,
And take from death its sting.

3 Thyself as Lord Thou hast revealed,
Jesus through whom the sick are
  The mighty Nazarene;  [healed,
The Way, the Truth, the Living
  Bread,  [the dead,
Whose touch of power doth raise
And makes the vilest clean.

4 O Christ Thou hast the vail now
  rent,
And to Thy Church the Spirit sent,
  A pentecostal dower;  [wind,
With tongues of fire and rushing
Thou hast upon Thy loved ones
  In resurrection power.  [shined

5 Those stripes of Thine the ransom
  are  [far,
For those who wandered from Thee
And found no place of rest;
How deep, how full, love's crimson
  tide,  [hide,
Within those wounds a world may
At home upon Thy breast.
> *E. C. W. Boulton.*

**140** Come, ev'ry joyful heart,
  That loves the Saviour's name,
Your noblest powers exert
  To celebrate His fame;
Tell all above and all below,
The debt of love to Him you owe.

2 He left His starry crown,
  And laid His robes aside;
On wings of love came down,
  And wept, and bled, and died:
What He endured no tongue can
  tell,  [hell.
To save our souls from death and

3 From the dark grave He rose—
  The mansion of the dead;
And thence His mighty foes
  In glorious triumph led:
Up through the sky the Conqueror
  rode,  [God.
And reigns on high, the Saviour

4 From thence He'll quickly come—
  His chariot will not stay—
And bear us safely home
  To realms of endless day:
There shall we see His lovely face,
And ever be in His embrace.
> *S. Stennett.*

**141** One there is above all others,
  Well deserves the name of
    Friend;
His is love beyond a brother's,
  Costly, free, and knows no end:
They who once His kindness prove,
Find it everlasting love.

2 Which of all our friends, to save us,
  Could or would have shed his
    blood?
But our Jesus died to have us
  Reconciled in Him to God:
This was boundless love indeed;
Jesus is a Friend in need.

3 When He lived on earth abasèd
  "Friend of sinners" was His
    name;
Now above all glories raisèd,
  He rejoices in the same;
Still He calls them brethren, friends,
And to all their wants attends.

4 Oh, for grace our hearts to soften!
  Teach us, Lord, at length to love;
We, alas! forget too often
  What a Friend we have above;
But when home our souls are
  brought
We shall love Thee as we ought.
> *John Newton.*

**142** One day when heaven was
  filled with His praises,
One day when sin was as black
  as could be,  [virgin,
Jesus came forth to be born of a
Dwelt amongst men, my example is
  He!

Living, He loved me; dying, He saved me;
Buried, He carried my sins far away,
Rising, He justified freely for ever:
One day He's coming—oh, glorious day.

2 One day they led Him up Calvary's
  mountain,  [on the tree;
One day they nailed Him to die
Suffering anguish, despised and re-
  jected;  [is He!
Bearing our sins, my Redeemer

3 One day they left Him alone in the
 garden,   [ing free;
One day He rested, from suffer-
Angels came down o'er His tomb
 to keep vigil;  [is He!
Hope of the hopeless, my Saviour

4 One day the grave could conceal
 Him no longer, [from the door;
One day the stone rolled away
Then He arose, over death He had
 conquered;   [more!
Now is ascended, my Lord ever-

5 One day the trumpet will sound
 for His coming, [will shine;
One day the skies with His glory
Wonderful day my belovèd ones
 bringing;    [mine!
Glorious Saviour, this Jesus is
     *J. Wilbur Chapman.*

**143** WHEN the Saviour dwelt below,
  Pity in His bosom reigned;
Sympathy He loved to show,
 Nor the meanest suit disdained.

2 Round Him thronged the blind, the
 lame,    [sessed;
Deaf and dumb, diseased, pos-
None in vain for healing came,
 All the Saviour freely blessed.

3 He could make the leper whole;
 Thousands at a meal He fed;
Winds and waves could He control;
 By a word He raised the dead.

4 List'ning sinners round Him pressed
 Whilst He taught the way to bliss;
Even enemies confessed,
 "No man ever spake like this."

5 Be Thy love to me revealed;
 Be Thy grace by me possessed;
Touch me, and I shall be healed;
 Bless me, and I shall be blessed.

**144** MY song is love unknown;
  My Saviour's love to me;
Love to the loveless shown,
 That they might lovely be.
  O who am I,
   That for my sake,
  My Lord should take
  Frail flesh, and die?

2 He came from His blest Throne,
 Salvation to bestow:
But men made strange, and none

The longed-for Christ would
 But O my Friend! [know.
 My Friend indeed,
 Who at my need
 His life did spend.

3 Sometimes they strew His way,
 And His sweet praises sing;
Resounding all the day,
 Hosannas to their King.
  Then: Crucify!
   Is all their breath,
  And for His death
  They thirst and cry.

4 Why, what hath my Lord done?
 What makes this rage and spite?
He made the lame to run,
 He gave the blind their sight.
  Sweet injuries!
   Yet they at these
  Themselves displease,
  And 'gainst Him rise.

5 They rise and needs will have
 My dear Lord made away;
A murderer they save;
 The Prince of life they slay.
  Yet cheerful He
   To suffering goes,
  That He His foes
  From thence might free.

6 In life, no house, no home
 My Lord on earth might have;
In death, no friendly tomb
 But what a stranger gave.
  What may I say?
   Heav'n was His home;
  But mine the tomb
  Wherein He lay.

7 Here might I stay and sing,
 No story so divine;
Never was love, dear King,
 Never was grief like Thine.
  This is my Friend,
   In whose sweet praise
  I all my days
  Could gladly spend.
     *S. Crossman.*

**145** HARK! the glad sound, the
  Saviour comes,
The Saviour promised long;
Let every heart prepare a throne,
 And every voice a song.

2 He comes, the prisoner to release
　　In Satan's bondage held;
　The gates of brass before Him
　　The iron fetters yield. 　[burst.

3 He comes the broken heart to bind,
　　The bleeding soul to cure;
　And with the treasures of His grace
　　To enrich the humble poor.

4 Our glad hosannas, Prince of Peace.
　　Thy welcome shall proclaim;
　And heaven's eternal arches ring
　　With Thy belovèd name.
　　　　　　　　　　　　*P. Doddridge.*

**146** Jesus my Saviour to Bethle-
　　　hem came, 　　　　[shame;
　Born in a manger to sorrow and
　Oh, it was wonderful—blest be His
　Seeking for me, for me! [name!
　　Seeking for me ! . . . for me ! . . .
　　Oh, it was wonderful—blest be His name !
　　Seeking for me, for me !

2 Jesus my Saviour, on Calvary's tree,
　Paid the great debt, and my soul
　　He set free;
　Oh, it was wonderful—how could it
　Dying for me, for me! [be?—
　　Dying for me ! . . . for me ! . . .
　　Oh, it was wonderful—how could it be ?
　　Dying for me, for me !

3 Jesus my Saviour, the same as of
　　old, 　　　　　　　[the fold,
　While I was wandering afar from
　Gently and long did He plead with
　Calling for me, for me! [my soul,
　　Calling for me ! . . . for me ! . . .
　　Gently and long did He plead with my soul,
　　Calling for me, for me !

4 Jesus my Saviour shall come from
　　on high— 　　　　　　[fly;
　Sweet is the promise as weary years
　Oh, I shall see Him descending the
　Coming for me, for me! [sky,
　　Coming for me ! . . . for me ! . . .
　　Oh, I shall see Him descending the sky,
　　Coming for me, for me !
　　　　　　　　　　　　　　　*A. N.*

**147** Thou didst leave Thy throne
　　　And Thy kingly crown,
　When Thou camest to earth for me;
　　But in Bethlehem's home
　　Was there found no room
　For Thy holy nativity:
　　O come to my heart, Lord Jesus;
　There is room in my heart for Thee.

2 　　Heaven's arches rang
　　　When the angels sang,
　Proclaiming Thy royal degree;
　　But of lowly birth
　　Cam'st Thou, Lord, on earth,
　And in great humility:
　　O come to my heart, Lord Jesus;
　There is room in my heart for Thee.

3 　　The foxes found rest,
　　　And the birds their nest,
　In the shade of the cedar tree;
　　But Thy couch was the sod,
　　O Thou Son of God,
　In the deserts of Galilee:
　　O come to my heart, Lord Jesus;
　There is room in my heart for Thee.

4 　　Thou camest, O Lord,
　　　With the living word
　That should set Thy people free;
　　But, with mocking scorn,
　　And with crown of thorn,
　They bore Thee to Calvary:
　　O come to my heart, Lord Jesus;
　Thy cross is my only plea.

5 　　When heav'n's arches ring,
　　　And her choirs shall sing,
　At Thy coming to victory,
　　Let Thy voice call me home,
　　Saying, " Yet there is room,
　There is room at My side for thee!"
　And my heart shall rejoice, Lord
　　Jesus, 　　　　　　　[me.
　When Thou comest and callest for
　　　　　　　　　　　*E. E. S. Elliott.*

**148** Wonderful birth, to a manger
　　　He came, 　　　　[proclaim
　Made in the likeness of man, to
　God's boundless love for a world
　　sick with sin, 　　　[come in.
　Pleading with sinners to let Him
　　　Wonderful name He bears,
　　　Wonderful crown He wears,
　　Wonderful blessings His triumphs afford';
　　　Wonderful Calvary,
　　　Wonderful grace for me,
　　Wonderful love of my wonderful Lord !

2 Wonderful life, full of service so
　　free, 　　　　　　　[was He;
　Friend to the poor and the needy
　Unfailing goodness on all He bes-
　　　　　　　　　　　　[towed,
　Undying faith in the vilest He
　　showed.

3 Wonderful death, for it meant not
  defeat,                    [complete,
Calvary made His great mission
Wrought our redemption, and when
  He arose,                     [foes.
Banished for ever the last of our

4 Wonderful hope, He is coming
  again,                      [reign;
Coming as King o'er the nations to
Glorious promise, His word cannot
  fail,                    [prevail!
His righteous kingdom at last must

*A. H. Ackley.*

**149** I CANNOT tell why He, whom
  angels worship,           [of men,
Should set His love upon the sons
Or why, as Shepherd, He should
  seek the wanderers,
  To bring them back they know
  not how or when.
But this I know, that He was born
  of Mary,            [His only home,
When Bethlehem's manger was
And that He lived at Nazareth and
  laboured,          [world, is come.
And so the Saviour, Saviour of the

2 I cannot tell how silently He suf-
  fered,              [place of tears,
As with His peace He graced this
Or how His heart upon the Cross
  was broken,        [thirty years.
The crown of pain to three and
But this I know, He heals the bro-
  ken-hearted,        [lurking fear,
And stays our sin, and calms our
And lifts the burden from the heavy
  laden,           [the world, is here.
For yet the Saviour, Saviour of

3 I cannot tell how He will win the
  nations,               [heritage,
How He will claim His earthly
How satisfy the needs and aspira-
  tions                     [sage.
Of east and west, of sinner and of
But this I know, all flesh shall see
  His glory,            [has sown,
And He shall reap the harvest He
And some glad day His sun shall
  shine in splendour
  When He the Saviour, Saviour of
  the world, is known.

4 I cannot tell how all the lands
  shall worship,   [storm is stilled,
When, at His bidding, every
Or who can say how great the jubi-
  lation             [love are filled.
When all the hearts of men with
But this I know, the skies will thrill
  with rapture,        [voices sing,
And myriad, myriad human
And earth to heaven, and heaven to
  earth, will answer:
  At last the Saviour, Saviour of
  the world, is King.

*W. Y. Fullerton.*

**150** TELL me the story of Jesus.
  Write on my heart every
  word!
Tell me the story most precious,
  Sweetest that ever was heard.
Tell how the angels in chorus
  Sang, as they welcomed His birth.
" Glory to God in the highest,
  Peace and good tidings to earth."
    Tell me the story of Jesus,
    Write on my heart every word,
    Tell me the story most precious,
    Sweetest that ever was heard.

2 Fasting alone in the desert,
  Tell of the days that He passed;
How He was tried and was tempted,
  Yet was triumphant at last.
Tell of the years of His labours,
  Tell of the sorrows He bore;
He was despised and afflicted,
  Homeless, rejected, and poor.

3 Tell of the cross where they nailed
  Dying in anguish and pain; [Him,
Tell of the grave where they laid
  Tell how He liveth again. [Him;
Love, in that story so tender,
  Clearer than ever I see;     [per,
Stay, let me weep while you whis-
  Love paid the ransom for me.

*Fanny J. Crosby.*

**151** THOU who didst leave Thy
  Father's Throne
On Calvary to die alone
That from our sins we might be free
Saviour Divine! we worship Thee.

2 Thou who didst tread this earth
  below                      [know,
That all Thy healing power might
The lame to walk, the blind to see,
Healer Divine! we worship Thee.

3 Thou who didst send the Holy Ghost
  To fill our hearts, and be the Host
  Empowered for service thus to be
  Baptizing Lord! we worship Thee

4 Thou who hast gone a place to prepare,
  Where we shall all Thy glories share
  Until Thy blessed face we see,
  Our coming King! we worship Thee.          *Mrs. G. Turner.*

## (3) HIS CHARACTER AND TITLES

**152** Join all the glorious names
        Of wisdom, love and power,
  That mortals ever knew,
      That angels ever bore:          [worth.
  All are too mean to speak His
  Too mean to set my Saviour forth.

2 Great Prophet of my God,
    My tongue would bless Thy
  By Thee the joyful news          [name;
    Of our salvation came:
  The joyful news of sins forgiv'n,
  Of hell subdued, and peace with heav'n.

3 Jesus, my great High Priest,
    Offered His blood and died;
  My guilty conscience seeks
    No sacrifice beside;
  His powerful blood did once atone—          throne.
  And now it pleads before the

4 My dear Almighty Lord
    My Conqueror and my King!
  Thy matchless power and love,
    Thy saving grace, I sing:
  Thine is the power—oh, may I sit
  In willing bonds beneath Thy feet.

5 Then let my soul arise,
    And tread the tempter down;
  My Captain leads me forth
    To conquest and a crown.
  The feeblest saint shall win the day,
  Though death and hell obstruct the way.          *Isaac Watts.*

**153** Name of Jesus! highest Name!
        Name that earth and heaven adore!
  From the heart of God it came,
  Leads me to God's heart once more.

2 Name of Jesus! living tide!
    Days of drought for me are past;
  How much more than satisfied
    Are the thirsty lips at last!

3 Name of Jesus! dearest Name!
    Bread of heaven, and balm of
  Oil of gladness, surest claim [love:
    To the treasures stored above.

4 Jesus gives forgiveness free,
    Jesus cleanses all my stains;
  Jesus gives His life to me,
    Jesus always He remains.

5 Only Jesus! fairest Name!
    Life, and rest, and peace, and
  Jesus, evermore the same,          [bliss,
    He is mine, and I am His.
            *Tersteegen ; tr. Mrs. Bevan.*

**154** Let earth and heaven agree,
        Angels and men be joined,
  To celebrate with me
    The Saviour of mankind;
  To adore the all-atoning Lamb,
  And bless the sound of Jesu's name.

2 Jesus, transporting sound!
    The joy of earth and heaven;
  No other help is found,
    No other name is given,
  By which we can salvation have;
  But Jesus came the world to save.

3 Jesus, harmonious name!
    It charms the hosts above;
  They evermore proclaim
    And wonder at His love;
  'Tis all their happiness to gaze
  'Tis heaven to see our Jesu's face.

4 His name the sinner hears,
    And is from sin set free;
  'Tis music in his ears,
    'Tis life and victory;
  New songs do now his lips employ,
  And dances his glad heart for joy.

5 Stung by the scorpion sin,
    My poor expiring soul
  The balmy sound drinks in,
    And is at once made whole:
  See there my Lord upon the tree!
  I hear, I feel, He died for me.

6 O unexampled love!
    O all-redeeming grace!
  How swiftly didst Thou move

To save a fallen race!
What shall I do to make it known
What Thou for all mankind hast
done?

7 O for a trumpet voice,
  On all the world to call;
To bid their hearts rejoice
  In Him who died for all;
For all my Lord was crucified,
For all, for all my Saviour died!

*Charles Wesley.*

**155** How sweet the name of Jesus
  sounds
  In a believer's ear;  [wounds
It soothes his sorrows, heals his
And drives away his fear.

2 It makes the wounded spirit whole,
  And calms the troubled breast;
'Tis manna to the hungry soul,
  And to the weary rest.

3 Dear name, the Rock on which I
  My shield and hiding-place,  [build
My never-failing treasury, filled
  With boundless stores of grace.

4 Jesus, my Shepherd, Saviour
  Friend,
  My Prophet, Priest and King,
My Lord, my Life, my Way, my
  Accept the praise I bring.  [End,

5 Weak is the effort of my heart,
  And cold my warmest thought;
But when I see Thee as Thou art
  I'll praise Thee as I ought.

6 I would Thy boundless love pro-
  With every fleeting breath;  [claim
So shall the music of Thy name
  Refresh my soul in death.

*John Newton.*

**156** THERE is a name I love to hear,
  I love to sing its worth,
It sounds like music in mine ear,
  The sweetest name on earth.

2 It tells me of a Saviour's love,
  Who died to set me free,
It tells me of His precious blood,
  The sinner's perfect plea.

3 It bids my trembling soul rejoice,
  And dries each rising tear;
It tells me in a " still small voice,"
  To trust and never fear.

4 Jesus, the name I love so well,
  The name I love to hear,
No saint on earth its worth can tell,
  No heart conceive how dear.

5 This name shall shed its fragrance
  Along this thorny road,  [still
Shall sweetly smooth the rugged hill
  That leads me up to God.

6 And there, with all the blood-
  bought throng,
  From sin and sorrow free,
I'll sing the new eternal song
  Of Jesus' love to me.

*Frederick Whitfield.*

**157** CROWN Him with many
  crowns,
  The Lamb upon His Throne;
Hark! how the heav'nly anthem
  All music but its own:  [drowns
Awake, my soul, and sing
  Of Him who died for thee,
And hail Him as thy matchless
  Through all eternity.  [King

2  Crown Him the Virgin's Son,
  The God incarnate born,  [won
Whose arm those crimson trophies
  Which now His brow adorn;
Fruit of the mystic Rose,
  As of that Rose the Stem;
The Root whence mercy ever flows,
  The Babe of Bethlehem.

3  Crown Him the Lord of love:
  Behold His hands and side,
Those wounds yet visible above
  In beauty glorified:
No angel in the sky
  Can fully bear that sight,
But downward bends his burning
  At mysteries so bright.  [eye

4  Crown Him the Lord of life,
  Who triumphed o'er the grave,
And rose victorious in the strife
  For those He came to save;
His glories now we sing,
  Who died, and rose on high,
Who died, eternal life to bring,
  And lives, that death may die.

5  Crown Him the Lord of peace,
  Whose power a sceptre sways
From pole to pole, that wars may
  cease,
  And all be prayer and praise:

His reign shall know no end,
And round His piercèd feet
Fair flowers of Paradise extend
Their fragrance ever sweet.

6    Crown Him the Lord of years,
The Potentate of time,
Creator of the rolling spheres,
Ineffably sublime:
All hail, Redeemer, hail!
For Thou hast died for me;
Thy praise shall never, never fail
Throughout eternity.
*Matthew Bridges and Godfrey Thring.*

**158**    TAKE the name of Jesus with
you,
Child of sorrow and of woe;
It will joy and comfort give you—
Take it then where'er you go.

Precious name, . . . oh, how sweet ! . . .
Hope of earth and joy of heaven ;
Precious name, . . . oh, how sweet ! . . .
Hope of earth and joy of heaven.

2 Take the name of Jesus ever,
As a shield from every snare;
If temptations round you gather,
Breathe that holy name in prayer.

3 Oh, the precious name of Jesus!
How it thrills our souls with joy,
When His loving arms receive us,
And His songs our tongues employ!

4 At the name of Jesus bowing,
Falling prostrate at His feet;
King of kings in heaven we'll
crown Him,
When our journey is complete.
*Mrs. L. Baxter.*

**159**    I'VE found the " Pearl of great-
est price,"
My heart doth sing for joy,
And sing I must, for Christ I have—
Oh, what a Christ have I!

2 My Christ, He is " the Lord of
lords,"
The Sovereign " King of kings,"
The risen " Sun of Righteousness,
With healing in His wings."

3 My Christ, He is " the Tree of
That in God's Eden grows; [Life,"
The living "clear as crystal" stream
Whence life for ever flows.

4 Christ is my Meat, Christ is my
Drink,
My Medicine, and my Health;
My Portion, mine Inheritance,
Yea, all my boundless Wealth.
*J. Mason.*

**160**    THE name of Jesus is so sweet,
I love its music to repeat;
It makes my joys full and complete,
The precious name of Jesus.

" Jesus ! " oh, how sweet the name !
" Jesus ! " every day the same !
" Jesus ! " let all saints proclaim
Its worthy praise for ever.

2 I love the name of Him whose
heart
Knows all my griefs and bears a
part;
Who bids all anxious fears depart,
I love the name of Jesus.

3 That name I fondly love to hear,
It never fails my heart to cheer;
Its music dries the falling tear;
Exalt the name of Jesus.

4 No word of man can ever tell
How sweet the name I love so well;
Oh, let its praises ever swell!
Oh, praise the name of Jesus.
*W. C. Martin.*

### (4) HIS SUFFERINGS AND DEATH

**161**    WHEN I survey the wondrous
cross                      [died,
On which the Prince of glory
My richest gain I count but loss,
And pour contempt on all my
pride.

2 Forbid it, Lord, that I should boast,
Save in the death of Christ, my
God :                       [most,
All the vain things that charm me
I sacrifice them to His blood.

3 See, from His head, His hands, His
feet,                        [down,
Sorrow and love flow mingled
Did e'er such love and sorrow meet,
Or thorns compose so rich a
crown?

4 Were the whole realm of nature
mine,                      [small;
That were an offering far too
Love so amazing, so divine, [all.
Demands my soul, my life, my
*Isaac Watts.*

**162** O SACRED head once wounded,
　　With grief and pain weighed
How scornfully surrounded　[down,
With thorns, Thine only crown!
How pale art Thou with anguish,
With sore abuse and scorn!
How does that visage languish
Which once was bright as morn!

2 O Lord of Life and Glory,
What bliss till now was Thine!
I read the wondrous story,
　I joy to call Thee mine.
Thy grief and Thy compassion
Were all for sinners' gain;
Mine, mine was the transgression,
But Thine the deadly pain.

3 What language shall I borrow
To praise Thee, heavenly Friend,
For this Thy dying sorrow,
Thy pity without end?
Lord, make me Thine for ever,
Nor let me faithless prove;
O let me never, never
Abuse such dying love!

4 Be near me, Lord, when dying;
O show Thyself to me;
And, for my succour flying,
Come, Lord, to set me free:
These eyes, new faith receiving,
From Jesus shall not move;
For he who dies believing
Dies safely through Thy love.
　　*Bernard of Clairvaux and Gerhardt ;*
　　　　*tr. Dr. Alexander.*

**163** O HEAD once filled with
　　bruises,
Oppressed with pain and scorn:
O'erwhelmed with sore abuses,
Mocked with a crown of thorn!
O head to death once wounded,
In shame upon the tree,
In glory now surrounded,
With brightest Majesty!

2 Thou, Lord, of all transcendent;
Thou life-creating Sun
To worlds on Thee dependent—
Yet bruised and spit upon!
O Lord! what Thee tormented
Was our sin's heavy load;
We had the debt augmented
Which Thou didst pay in blood.

3 We give Thee thanks unfeignèd,
Lord Jesus, Friend in need,
For what Thy soul sustainèd,
When Thou for us didst bleed;
Grant us to lean unshaken
Upon Thy faithfulness,
Until to glory taken,
We see Thee face to face.
　　　　　　　*Gerhardt.*

**164** WHAT a wonderful, wonderful
　　Saviour,　　[me!
Who would die on the cross for
Freely shedding His precious life-
　　blood,　　　　[free.
That the sinner might be made

He was nailed to the cross for me,
He was nailed to the cross for me,
　On the cross crucified,
　For me He died ;
He was nailed to the cross for me.

2 Thus He left His heavenly glory
To accomplish His Father's plan:
He was born of the Virgin Mary,
Took upon Him the form of man.

3 He was wounded for our transgres-
　　sions,
And He carried our sorrows too;
He's the Healer of every sickness,
This He came to the world to do.

4 So He gave His life for others
In redeeming this world from sin,
And He's gone to prepare a man-
　　sion,
That at last we may enter in.
　　　　　　*F. A. Graves.*

**165** KING of my life, I crown Thee
　　now,
Thine shall the glory be;
Lest I forget Thy thorn-crowned
Lead me to Calvary.　　[brow,

　Lest I forget Gethsemane,
　Lest I forget Thine agony,
　Lest I forget Thy love for me,
　Lead me to Calvary.

2 Show me the tomb where Thou
　　wast laid,
Tenderly mourned and wept:
Angels in robes of light arrayed,
Guarded Thee whilst Thou slept.

3 Let me, like Mary, through the
　　gloom,
Come with a gift to Thee:
Show to me now the empty tomb,
Lead me to Calvary.

4 May I be willing, Lord, to bear
   Daily my cross for Thee;
Even Thy cup of grief to share,
   Thou hast borne all for me.

5 Fill me, O Lord, with Thy desire
   For all who know not Thee;
Then touch my lips with holy fire,
   To speak of Calvary.
      *Jenny Evelyn Mussey.*

**166**   EXTENDED on a cursèd tree,
     Besmeared with dust, and
       sweat, and blood,
See there, the King of Glory see!
Sinks and expires the Son of God.

2 Who, who, my Saviour, this hath
   done?        [wound?
Who could Thy sacred body
No guilt Thy spotless heart hath
   known,       [found.
No guile hath in Thy lips been

3 I, I alone, have done the deed!
   'Tis I Thy sacred flesh have torn:
My sins have caused Thee, Lord, to
   bleed,       [thorn
Pointed the nail, and fixed the

4 The burden, for me to sustain
   Too great, on Thee, my Lord
     was laid;     [pain:
To heal me, Thou hast borne my
To bless me, Thou a curse wast
   made.

5 My Saviour, how shall I proclaim?
   How pay the mighty debt I owe?
Let all I have and all I am,
   Ceaseless to all Thy glory show.

6 Too much to Thee I cannot give;
   Too much I cannot do for Thee;
Let all Thy love, and all Thy grief
   Graven on my heart for ever be!
      *Gerhardt.*

**167**   'TIS finished! the Messiah dies:
     Cut off for sins, but not His
Accomplished is the sacrifice, [own:
   The great redeeming work is
   done.

2 'Tis finished! all the debt is paid;
   Justice divine is satisfied; [made;
The grand and full atonement
God for a guilty world hath died.

3 The veil is rent in Christ alone;
   The living way to heaven is seen;
The middle wall is broken down,
   And all mankind may enter in.

4 The types and figures are fulfilled,
   Exacted is the legal pain;
The precious promises are sealed;
   The spotless Lamb of God is
   slain.

5 The reign of sin and death is o'er
   And all may live from sin set
     free;
Satan hath lost his mortal power;
   'Tis swallowed up in victory.

6 Saved from the legal curse I am,
   My Saviour hangs on yonder
     tree:
See there the meek, expiring Lamb!
   'Tis finished! He expires for me.

7 Accepted in the Well-beloved,
   And clothed in righteousness
     divine,
I see the bar to heaven removed;
   And all Thy merits, Lord, are
   mine.

8 Death, hell, and sin are now sub-
     dued;
All grace is now to sinners given;
   And lo, I plead th'atoning blood,
And in Thy right I claim Thy
   heaven.     *Charles Wesley.*

**168**   THERE is a green hill far away,
     Without a city wall,
Where the dear Lord was cruci
Who died to save us all.   [fied,

2 We may not know, we cannot tell
   What pains He had to bear;
But we believe it was for us
   He hung and suffered there.

3 He died that we might be forgiven,
   He died to make us good,
That we might go at last to heaven,
   Saved by His precious blood.

4 There was no other good enough
   To pay the price of sin;
He only could unlock the gate
   Of heaven, and let us in.

5 O dearly, dearly has He loved,
   And we must love Him too,
And trust in His redeeming blood,
   And try His works to do.
      *Mrs. C. F. Alexander.*

**169**  NOT all the blood of beasts,
  On Jewish altars slain,
Could give the guilty conscience
Or wash away the stain. [peace,

2  But Christ the heavenly Lamb,
  Takes all our sins away;
A sacrifice of nobler name
And richer blood than they.

3  My faith would lay her hand
  On that dear head of Thine,
While like a penitent I stand,
And there confess my sin.

4  My soul looks back to see
  The burdens Thou didst bear,
When hanging on the cursèd tree,
And knows her guilt was there.

5  Believing, we rejoice
  To see the curse remove: [voice
We bless the Lamb with cheerful
And sing His bleeding love!
*Isaac Watts.*

**170**  "MAN of sorrows," what a
  name
  For the Son of God who came
Ruined sinners to reclaim!
  Hallelujah! what a Saviour!

2  Bearing shame and scoffing rude,
In my place condemned He stood;
Sealed my pardon with His blood:
  Hallelujah! what a Saviour!

3  Guilty, vile, and helpless we,
Spotless Lamb of God was He;
"Full atonement," can it be?
  Hallelujah! what a Saviour!

4  Lifted up was He to die,
"It is finished," was His cry;
Now in heaven exalted high;
  Hallelujah! what a Saviour!

5  When He comes, our glorious King,
All His ransomed home to bring;
Then anew this song we'll sing:
  Hallelujah! what a Saviour!
*P. P. Bliss.*

**171**  WE sing the praise of Him who
  died,
  Of Him who died upon the cross;
The sinner's hope let men deride,
  For this we count the world but
  loss.

2  Inscribed upon the cross we see
  In shining letters, "God is love;"
He bears our sins upon the tree,
  He brings us mercy from above.

3  The Cross! it takes our guilt away;
  It holds the fainting spirit up;
It cheers with hope the gloomy day,
  And sweetens every bitter cup.

4  It makes the coward spirit brave,
  And nerves the feeble arm for
  fight;
It takes its terror from the grave,
  And gilds the bed of death with
  light.

5  The balm of life, the cure of woe,
  The measure and the pledge of
  love,
The sinner's refuge here below,
  The angels' theme in heaven
  above.
*T. Kelly.*

**172**  GIVE me a sight, O Saviour,
  Of Thy wondrous love to me;
Of the love that brought Thee down
  To die on Calvary.        [to earth,
  Oh, make me understand it,
  Help me to take it in ;
  What it meant to Thee, the Holy One,
  To bear away my sin.

2  Was it the nails, O Saviour,
  That bound Thee to the tree?
Nay, 'twas Thine everlasting love,
  Thy love for me, for me.

3  Oh, wonder of all wonders,
  That through Thy death for me,
My open sins, my secret sins,
  Can all forgiven be.

4  Then melt my heart, O Saviour,
  Bend me, yea, break me down,
Until I own Thee Conqueror,
  And Lord and Sovereign crown.
*Katherine A. M. Kelly.*

**173**  O LOVE divine! what hast
  Thou done?        [me!
  The immortal God hath died for
The Father's co-eternal Son
  Bore all my sins upon the tree;
The immortal God for me hath
  died;
My Lord, my Love, is crucified.

2 Behold Him, all ye that pass by,
    The bleeding Prince of life and peace!
Come, sinners, see your Maker die,
    And say, was ever grief like His?
Come. feel with me His blood applied:
My Lord, my Love, is crucified:

3 Is crucified for me and you,
    To bring us rebels back to God:
Believe, believe the record true,
    Ye all are bought with Jesu's blood,
Pardon for all flows from His side:
My Lord, my Love, is crucified.

4 Then let us sit beneath His Cross,
    And gladly catch the healing stream,
All things for Him account but loss,
    And give up all our hearts to Him;
Of nothing think or speak beside:
My Lord, my Love, is crucified.
                  *Charles Wesley.*

**174**   BENEATH the cross of Jesus
       I fain would take my stand—
The shadow of a mighty Rock,
    Within a weary land;
A home within the wilderness,
    A rest upon the way,
From the burning of the noontide
    And the burden of the day. [heat,

2 O safe and happy shelter,
    O refuge tried and sweet,
O trysting-place where heaven's love
    And heaven's justice meet!
As to the holy patriarch
    That wondrous dream was given.
So seems my Saviour's cross to me,
    A ladder up to heaven.

3 There lies, beneath its shadow,
    But on the farther side,
The darkness of an awful grave
    That gapes both deep and wide;
And there between us stands the cross,
    Two arms outstretched to save;
Like a watchman set to guard the
    From that eternal grave. [way

4 Upon that cross of Jesus,
    Mine eyes at times can see

The very dying form of One
    Who suffered there for me;
And from my smitten heart, with
    Two wonders I confess— [tears,
The wonders of His glorious love,
    And my own worthlessness.

5 I take, O cross, thy shadow
    For my abiding place;
I ask no other sunshine than
    The sunshine of His face:
Content to let the world go by,
    To know no gain nor loss—
My sinful self my only shame,
    My glory all the cross.
             *Miss E. C. Clephane.*

**175**   By the Cross of Jesus standing
      Love our straitened souls expanding,
                    [grace!
Taste we now the peace and
Health from yonder Tree is flowing,
Heav'nly light is on it glowing.
    From the blessèd Suff'rer's face.

2 Here is pardon's pledge and token,
    Guilt's strong chain for ever broken,
           Righteous peace securely made;
Brightens now the brow once shaded,
Freshens now the face once faded,
    Peace with God now makes us glad.

3 All the love of God is yonder,
    Love above all thought and wonder,
           Perfect love that casts out fear!
Strength, like dew, is here distilling,
Glorious life our souls is filling—
    Life eternal, only here!

4 Here the living water welleth;
Here the Rock, now smitten, telleth
    Of salvation freely given;
This the fount of love and pity,
This the pathway to the city,
    This the very gate of heaven.
             *Horatius Bonar.*

**176**   I STAND amazed in the presence
      Of Jesus the Nazarene,
And wonder how He could love me,
    A sinner, condemned. unclean.

How marvellous ! how wonderful !
    And my song shall ever be ;
How marvellous ! how wonderful !
    Is my Saviour's love for me !

2 For me it was in the garden
    He prayed—" Not My will, but Thine: "
He had no tears for His own griefs.
    But sweat drops of blood for mine.

3 In pity angels beheld Him,
    And came from the world of light
To comfort Him in the sorrows
    He bore for my soul that night.

4 He took my sins and my sorrows,
    He made them His very own;
He bore the burden to Calvary,
    And suffered, and died alone.

5 When with the ransomed in glory
    His face I at last shall see,
'Twill be my joy through the ages
    To sing of His love for me.
              *C. H. Gabriel.*

**177** JESUS was slain for me,
    At Calvary.
Crownèd with thorns was He,
    At Calvary.
There He in anguish died,
There from His opened side,
Poured forth the crimson tide,
    At Calvary.

2 Pardoned is all my sin,
    At Calvary.
Cleansed is my heart within,
    At Calvary.
Now robes of praise I wear,
Gone are my grief and care,
Christ bore my burdens there,
    At Calvary.

3 Wondrous His love for me,
    At Calvary.
Glorious His victory,
    At Calvary.
Vanquished are death and hell,
Oh, let His praises swell,
Ever my tongue shall tell
    Of Calvary.    *Geo. Perfect.*

**178** ALAS! and did my Saviour bleed?
    And did my Sovereign die?
Would He devote that sacred head
    For such a worm as I?

2 Was it for crimes that I had done
    He groaned upon the tree?
Amazing pity! grace unknown!
    And love beyond degree!

3 Well might the sun in darkness hide
    And shut his glories in.
When Christ, the mighty Maker, died
    For man, the creature's sin.

4 Thus might I hide my blushing face,
    Whilst His dear cross appears,
Dissolve my heart in thankfulness,
    And melt mine eyes to tears.

5 But drops of grief can ne'er repay
    The debt of love I owe;
Here, Lord, I give myself away;
    'Tis all that I can do.
              *Isaac Watts.*

**179** To Calvary, Lord, in spirit now
    Our weary souls repair,
To dwell upon Thy dying love,
    And taste its sweetness there.

2 Sweet resting-place of every heart
    That feels the plague of sin.
Yet knows that deep mysterious joy,
    The peace of God within.

3 There through Thine hour of deepest woe,
    Thy suffering spirit passed;
Grace there its wondrous victory gained,
    And love endured its last.

4 Dear suffering Lamb, Thy bleeding wounds
    With cords of love divine,
Have drawn our willing hearts to Thee.
    And linked our life with Thine.

5 Our longing eyes would fain behold
    That bright and blessed brow,
Once wrung with bitterest anguish,
    Its crown of glory now.    [wear
              *E. Denny.*

### (5) HIS RESURRECTION

**180** JESUS lives! no longer now
    Can thy terrors, Death, appal me;
Jesus lives! by this I know
From the grave He will recall me;
    Brighter scenes at death commence;
    This shall be my confidence.

2 Jesus lives! to Him the Throne
High o'er heaven and earth is given;
    I may go where He is gone,
Live and reign with Him in heaven:

God through Christ forgives offence;
This shall be my confidence.

3 Jesus lives! for me He died;
Hence will I, to Jesus living,
    Pure in heart and act abide,
Praise to Him and glory giving;
    Freely God doth aid dispense;
    This shall be my confidence.

4 Jesus lives! my heart knows well
Nought from me His love shall sever;
    Life, nor death, nor powers of hell,
Part me now from Christ for ever:
    God will be a sure defence;
    This shall be my confidence.

5 Jesus lives! henceforth is death
Entrance-gate of life immortal;
    This shall calm my trembling breath,
When I pass its gloomy portal:
    Faith shall cry, as fails each sense,
    Lord, Thou art my Confidence.
        *C. F. Gellert ; tr. F. E. Cox.*

**181** THINE be the glory, risen, conquering Son,
Endless is the victory Thou o'er death hast won;    [stone away,
Angels in bright raiment rolled the
Kept the folded grave-clothes where Thy body lay.

    Thine be the glory, risen, conqu'ring Son,
    Endless is the victory Thou o'er death hast won.

2 Lo! Jesus meets us, risen from the tomb;    and gloom;
Lovingly He greets us, scatters fear
Let the Church with gladness, hymns of triumph sing,
For her Lord now liveth, death hath lost its sting.

3 No more we doubt Thee, glorious Prince of life;
Life is nought without Thee; aid us in our strife:
Make us more than conquerors through Thy deathless love:
Bring us safe through Jordan to Thy home above.
        *E. L. Budry.*

**182** CHRIST is risen! Hallelujah!
    Risen our victorious Head.
Sing His praises! Hallelujah!
    Christ is risen from the dead.
Gratefully our hearts adore Him,
    As His light once more appears;
Bowing down in joy before Him,
    Rising up from grief and tears.

    Christ is risen ! Hallelujah !
    Risen our victorious Head.
    Sing His praises ! Hallelujah !
    Christ is risen from the dead.

2 Christ is risen! All the sadness
    Of His earthly life is o'er,
Through the open gates of gladness
    He returns to life once more;
Death and hell before Him bending,
    He doth rise, the Victor now,
Angels on His steps attending,
    Glory round His wounded brow.

3 Christ is risen! Henceforth never
    Death or hell shall us enthral,
We are Christ's, in Him for ever
    We have triumphed over all;
All the doubting and dejection
    Of our trembling hearts have ceased:
'Tis His day of resurrection,
    Let us rise and keep the feast.
        *J. S. B. Monsell.*

**183** HE dies! He dies! the lowly Man of Sorrows,
On whom were laid our many griefs and woes;    [awful billows,
Our sins He bore, beneath God's
And He hath triumphed over all our foes.

    " I am He that liveth, that liveth, and was dead ;
    I am He that liveth, that liveth, and was dead ;
        And  behold . . . I  am  alive . . . for evermore . . .
        Behold . . . I  am  alive . . . for evermore . . .
    I am He that liveth, that liveth, and was dead ;
        And  behold, . . . I  am  alive . . . for e . . . vermore."

2 He lives! He lives! what glorious consolation!    [hand;
    Exalted at His Father's own right
He pleads for us, and by His intercession    [to stand.
Enables all His saints by grace

3 He comes! He comes! Oh, blest
   anticipation!   [faithful word;
In keeping with His true and
To call us to our heavenly con-
   summation—   [the Lord."
Caught up, to be " for ever with
             *C. Russell Hurditch.*

**184**  CHRIST the Lord is risen today!
              Hallelujah!
Sons of men and angels say,
              Hallelujah!
Raise your songs and triumphs high:
              Hallelujah!
Sing, ye heavens; thou earth reply:
              Hallelujah!

2 Love's redeeming work is done,
Fought the fight, the battle won:
Lo! our sun's eclipse is o'er;
Lo! he sets in blood no more:

3 Vain the stone, the watch, the seal,
Christ hath burst the gates of hell;
Death in vain forbids Him rise;
Christ hath opened Paradise.

4 Lives again our glorious King:
Where, O death, is now thy sting?
Once He died our souls to save:
Where's thy victory, O grave?

5 Soar we now where Christ hath led,
Following our exalted Head;
Made like Him, like Him we rise;
Ours the cross, the grave, the skies.

6 Hail! the Lord of earth and heaven;
Praise to Thee by both be given,
Thee we greet triumphant now:
Hail! the Resurrection, Thou!
             *Charles Wesley.*

**185**  JESUS Christ is risen today,
    Our triumphant holy day,
Who did once upon the cross,
Suffer to redeem our loss.

2 Hymns of praise then let us sing,
Unto Christ, our heavenly King,
Who endured the cross and grave,
Sinners to redeem and save.

3 But the pain which He endured,
Our salvation hath procured;
Now above the sky He's King,
Where the angels ever sing.

4 Sing we to our God above
Praise eternal as His love;

Praise Him, all ye heavenly host,
Father, Son, and Holy Ghost.
             *Lyra Davidica.*

**186**  Low in the grave He lay—
    Jesus, My Saviour!
Waiting the coming day—
    Jesus, My Lord!

Up from the grave He arose, . . .
With a mighty triumph o'er His foes ; . . .
He arose, a Victor from the dark domain,
And He lives for ever with His saints to
   reign ;
   He arose ! . . . He arose ! . . .
   Hallelujah ! Christ arose !

2 Vainly they watch His bed—
    Jesus, my Saviour!
Vainly they seal the dead—
    Jesus, my Lord!

3 Death cannot keep His prey—
    Jesus, my Saviour!
He tore the bars away—
    Jesus, my Lord!    *Robert Lowry.*

## (6) HIS ASCENSION AND EXALTATION

**187**  LOOK, ye saints! the sight is
    glorious;
See the Man of Sorrows now
From the fight return victorious,
Every knee to Him shall bow:
   Crown Him! crown Him!
Crowns become the Victor's brow.

2 Crown the Saviour! angels crown
   Him,
Rich the trophies Jesus brings;
In the seat of power enthrone Him,
While the vault of heaven rings;
   Crown Him! crown Him!
Crown the Saviour King of kings.

3 Sinners in derision crowned Him,
   Mocking thus the Saviour's claim;
Saints and angels crowd around
   Him,
Own His title, praise His Name:
   Crown Him! crown Him!
Spread abroad the Victor's fame.

4 Hark, those bursts of acclamation!
   Hark, those loud triumphant
   chords!
Jesus takes the highest station:
   O what joy the sight affords!
   Crown Him! crown Him!
King of kings, and Lord of lords!
            *Thomas Kelly.*

## The Lord Jesus Christ

**188** HAIL the day that sees Him rise,
        Alleluia!
To His throne above the skies;
        Alleluia!
Christ, the Lamb for sinners given,
        Alleluia!
Enters now the highest heaven.
        Alleluia!

2 There the glorious triumph waits
Lift your heads, eternal gates;
He hath conquered death and sin;
Take the King of glory in.

3 Lo! the heaven its Lord receives,
Yet He loves the earth He leaves;
Though returning to His throne,
Still He calls mankind His own.

4 See! He lifts His hands above;
See! He shows the prints of love;
Hark! His gracious lips bestow
Blessings on His Church below.

5 Still for us He intercedes
His prevailing death He pleads,
Near Himself prepares our place,
He the first-fruits of our race.

6 Lord, though parted from our sight
Far above the starry height,
Grant our hearts may thither rise,
Seeking Thee above the skies.
*Charles Wesley.*

**189** IN the Name of Jesus
    Every knee shall bow,
Every tongue confess Him
    King of glory now:
'Tis the Father's pleasure
    We should call Him Lord,
Who from the beginning
    Was the Mighty Word.

2 At His voice, creation
    Sprang at once to sight,
All the angel faces,
    All the hosts of light,
Thrones and Dominations,
    Stars upon their way,
All the heavenly Orders,
    In their great array.

3 Humbled for a season,
    To receive a Name
From the lips of sinners
    Unto whom He came;
Faithfully He bore it,
    Spotless to the last,
Brought it back victorious,
    When from death He passed.

4 Bore it up triumphant,
    With its human light,
Through all ranks of creatures,
    To the central height;
To the Throne of Godhead,
    To the Father's breast,
Filled it with the glory
    Of that perfect rest.

5 In your hearts enthrone Him;
    There let Him subdue
All that is not holy,
    All that is not true;
Crown Him as your Captain
    In temptation's hour;
Let His Will enfold you
    In its light and power.

6 Brothers, this Lord Jesus
    Shall return again
With His Father's glory,
    With His angel train;
For all wreaths of empire
    Meet upon His brow.
And our hearts confess Him
    King of glory now.
*Caroline M. Noel.*

**190** JESUS shall reign where'er the sun
Doth his successive journeys run;
His kingdom stretch from shore to shore,
Till suns shall rise and set no more.

2 For Him shall endless prayer be made,   [head;
And praises throng to crown His
His Name like sweet perfume shall
With every morning sacrifice. [rise

3 People and realms of every tongue
Dwell on His love with sweetest song;
And infant voices shall proclaim
Their young hosannas to His Name.

4 Blessings abound where'er He reigns;   [chains;
The prisoner leaps to lose his
The weary find eternal rest;
And all the sons of want are blest.

5 Where He displays His healing power;   [more;
Death and the curse are known no
In Him the tribes of Adam boast
More blessings than their father lost.

6 Let every creature rise and bring,
  Its grateful honours to our King;
  Angels descend with songs again,
  And earth prolong the joyful strain.
  *Isaac Watts.*

**191** MAJESTIC sweetness sits en-
    throned
  Upon the Saviour's brow;
  His head with radiant glories
    crowned,
  His lips with grace o'erflow.

2 No mortal can with Him compare,
  Among the sons of men;
  Fairer is He than all the fair
  That fill the heavenly train.

3 He saw me plunged in deep distress,
  He flew to my relief;
  For me He bore the shameful cross,
  And carried all my grief.

4 To Him I owe my life and breath,
  And all the joys I have;
  He makes me triumph over death,
  He saves me from the grave.

5 To heaven, the place of His abode,
  He brings my weary feet,
  Shows me the glories of my God,
  And makes my joy complete.

6 Since from His bounty I receive
  Such proofs of love divine;
  Had I a thousand hearts to give,
  Lord, they should all be Thine!
  *Samuel Stennett.*

**192** THE head that once was crowned
    with thorns,
  Is crowned with glory now;
  A royal diadem adorns
  The mighty Victor's brow.

  He lives . . . He lives . . .
  I know that my Redeemer lives.

2 The highest place that heaven
  Is His by sov'reign right; [affords,
  The King of kings, the Lord of lords,
  And heaven's eternal Light.

3 The joy of all who dwell above,
  The joy of all below,
  To whom He manifests His love,
  And grants His name to know.

4 To them the cross, with all its
    shame,
  With all its grace is given;
  Their name, an everlasting name,
  Their joy, the joy of heaven.

5 The cross He bore is life and
    health,
  Though shame and death to Him;
  His people's hope, His people's
  Their everlasting theme. [wealth,
  *T. Kelly.*

**193** CLAP your hands, ye people all,
  Praise the God on whom ye
    call;
  Lift your voice, and shout His
    praise;
  Triumph in His sovereign grace!

2 Glorious is the Lord most High,
  Terrible in majesty;
  He His sovereign sway maintains,
  King o'er all the earth He reigns.

3 Jesus is gone up on high,
  Takes His seat above the sky:
  Shout the angel-choirs aloud,
  Echoing to the trump of God.

4 Sons of earth, the triumph join,
  Praise Him with the host divine;
  Emulate the heavenly powers,
  Their victorious Lord is ours.

5 Shout the God enthroned above,
  Trumpet forth His conquering love;
  Praises to our Jesus sing,
  Praises to our glorious King!

6 Power is all to Jesus given,
  Power o'er hell, and earth, and
    heaven!
  Power He now to us imparts;
  Praise Him with believing hearts.

7 Wonderful in saving power,
  Him let all our hearts adore;
  Earth and heaven repeat the cry,—
  " Glory be to God most High!"
  *Charles Wesley.*

**194** JESUS, when made in the like-
    ness of men, [the Cross;
  Humbled Himself to the death of
  No reputation belonged to Him
    then; [it no loss.
  Emptying Himself, He esteemed

  Far above all ! . . . Far above all ! . . .
  God hath exalted Him far above all ! . . .
  Crown Him as Lord, at His feet humbly fall,
  Jesus, Christ Jesus, is far above all !

2 Name that through ages to come
  shall out-ring: [was slain!
  Jesus, the Lamb, who for sinners
  Soon to this earth He is coming as
    King, [reign.
  Coming in power and in glory to

## The Lord Jesus Christ

3 Kingdoms of earth shall be yielded
  to God;  [on the throne!
Glorious the reign, with our Lord
Chained the usurper, and broken
  his rod:  [own.
Jesus as King every nation shall

4 Jesus, my Saviour, I yield unto
  Thee;  [and Lord,
Reign in my heart as Redeemer
Make me what Thou wouldest have
  me to be,  [with Thy word.
Filled with Thy Spirit, and filled

**195** REJOICE, the Lord is King!
  Your Lord and King adore;
Mortals, give thanks and sing,
  And triumph evermore;
Lift up your heart, lift up your
Rejoice, again I say, rejoice! [voice,

2 Jesus the Saviour reigns,
  The God of truth and love;
When He had purged our stains,
  He took His seat above;
Lift up your heart, lift up your
Rejoice, again I say, rejoice! [voice,

3 His kingdom cannot fail;
  He rules o'er earth and heaven;
The keys of death and hell
  Are to our Saviour given;
Lift up your heart, lift up your
Rejoice, again I say, rejoice! [voice,

4 Rejoice in glorious hope;
  Jesus the Judge shall come,
And take His servants up
  To their eternal home:
We soon shall hear th'archangel's
  voice;  [rejoice!
The trump of God shall sound,
     *Charles Wesley.*

**196** THE golden gates are lifted up,
  The doors are opened wide,
The King of Glory is gone in
Unto His Father's side.

2 Thou art gone up before us, Lord,
  To make for us a place,
That we may be where now Thou
And look upon God's face. [art,

3 And ever on our earthly path
  A gleam of glory lies,
A light still breaks behind the cloud
That veiled Thee from our eyes.

4 Lift up our hearts, lift up our
  minds;
Let Thy dear grace be given,
That while we wander here below,
Our treasure be in heaven;

5 That where Thou art, at God's right
  hand,
Our hope, our love, may be:
Dwell Thou in us, that we may
For evermore in Thee. [dwell
    *Mrs. C. F. Alexander.*

**197** GOLDEN harps are sounding,
  Angel voices ring,
Pearly gates are opened—
  Opened for the King;
Jesus, King of glory,
  Jesus, King of love,
Is gone up in triumph
  To His throne above.

 All His work is ended,
  Joyfully we sing,
 Jesus hath ascended ;
  Glory to our King !

2 He who came to save us,
  He who bled and died
Now is crowned with glory
  At His Father's side.
Nevermore to suffer,
  Nevermore to die;
Jesus, King of glory,
  Is gone up on high.

3 Praying for His children
  In that blessèd place,
Calling them to glory,
  Sending them His grace;
His bright home preparing,
  Faithful ones for you;
Jesus ever liveth,
  Ever loveth too.
    *Frances R. Havergal.*

**198** SEE the Conqueror mounts in
  triumph,
See the King in royal state
Riding on the clouds His chariot
  To His heavenly palace gate;
Hark! the choirs of angel voices
  Joyful hallelujahs sing,
And the portals high are lifted
  To receive their heavenly King.

2 Who is this that comes in glory,
  With the trump of jubilee?
Lord of battles, God of armies,
  He has gained the victory;

He who on the Cross did suffer,
He who from the grave arose,
He has vanquished sin and Satan,
He by death has spoiled His foes.

3 He has raised our human nature
In the clouds to God's right hand;
There we sit in heavenly places,
There with Him in glory stand:
Jesus reigns adored by angels;
Man with God is on the throne;
Mighty Lord, in Thine ascension
We by faith behold our own.

4 Glory be to God the Father;
Glory be to God the Son,
Dying, risen, ascending for us,
Who the heavenly realm has won;
Glory to the Holy Spirit;
To One God in Persons Three
Glory both in earth and heaven,
Glory, endless glory be!
*Christopher Wordsworth.*

199 God is gone up on high,
With a triumphant noise;
The clarions of the sky
Proclaim the angelic joys!
Join all on earth, rejoice and sing;
Glory ascribe to glory's King.

2 God in the flesh below,
For us He reigns above:
Let all the nations know
Our Jesu's conquering love!
Join all on earth, rejoice and sing;
Glory ascribe to glory's King.

3 All power to our great Lord
Is by the Father given;
By angel hosts adored,
He reigns supreme in heaven:
Join all on earth, rejoice and sing;
Glory ascribe to glory's King.

4 High on His holy seat
He bears the righteous sway;
His foes beneath His feet
Shall sink and die away:
Join all on earth, rejoice and sing;
Glory ascribe to glory's King.

5 His foes and ours are one,
Satan, the world, and sin;
But He shall tread them down,
And bring His kingdom in:
Join all on earth, rejoice and sing;
Glory ascribe to glory's King.

6 Till all the earth, renewed
In righteousness divine,
With all the hosts of God
In one great chorus join:
Join all on earth, rejoice and sing,
Glory ascribe to glory's King.
*Charles Wesley.*

(7) HIS HEAVENLY MINISTRY

200 Arise, my soul, arise,
Shake off thy guilty fears;
The bleeding sacrifice
In my behalf appears;
Before the throne my surety stands,
My name is written on His hands.

2 He ever lives above,
For me to intercede;
His all redeeming love,
His precious blood to plead;
His blood atoned for all our race,
And sprinkles now the throne of
grace.

3 Five bleeding wounds He bears,
Received on Calvary;
They pour effectual prayers,
They strongly plead for me;
"Forgive him, oh, forgive," they cry,
"Nor let that ransomed sinner die."

4 The Father hears Him pray,
His dear Anointed One:
He cannot turn away
The presence of His Son:
His Spirit answers to the blood,
And tells me I am born of God.

5 My God is reconciled,
His pard'ning voice I hear;
He owns me for His child,
I can no longer fear;
With confidence I now draw nigh,
And "Father, Abba, Father," cry.
*Charles Wesley.*

201 Where high the heavenly tem-
ple stands,                [hands,
The house of God not made with
A great High Priest our nature
wears,
The Patron of mankind appears.

2 He who for men their Surety stood,
   And poured on earth His precious blood,
Pursues in heaven His mighty plan,
The Saviour and the Friend of man.

3 Though now ascended up on high,
   He bends on earth a Brother's eye;
Partaker of the human name,
He knows the frailty of our frame.

4 Our Fellow-sufferer yet retains
   A fellow-feeling of our pains;
And still remembers, in the skies,
His tears, and agonies, and cries.

5 In every pang that rends the heart
   The Man of Sorrows had a part;
He sympathises with our grief,
And to the sufferer sends relief.

6 With boldness, therefore, at the throne,
   Let us make all our sorrows known;
And ask the aid of heavenly power
To help us in the evil hour.
                    *Scottish Paraphrase, 1781.*

**202** A GOOD High Priest is come,
        Supplying Aaron's place,
     And taking up his room,
        Dispensing life and grace.
The law of Aaron's priesthood came,
But grace and truth by Jesus' name.

2 He once temptations knew,
     And woes of every kind,
  That He might succour show
     To every tempted mind;
In every point the Lamb was tried
Like us, and then for us He died.

3 He died, but lives again,
     And by the altar stands;
  There shows how He was slain,
     Opening His piercèd hands;
Our Priest abides, and pleads our cause,
Transgressors of His righteous laws.

4 I other priests disclaim,
     Their laws and offerings too;
  None but the bleeding Lamb
     The mighty work can do;
He shall have all the praise, for He
Hath loved and lived and died for me.
                    *John Cennick.*

**203** AND didst Thou love the race
        that loved not Thee?
     And didst Thou take to heaven a
        human brow? [marvellous sea?
Dost plead with man's voice by the
Art Thou his kinsman now?

2 O God, O kinsman, loved, but not
     enough!                [death!
  O Man, with eyes majestic after
Whose feet have toiled along our
     pathways rough,
Whose lips drawn human breath!

3 By that one likeness which is ours
     and Thine,        [hold us kin,
  By that one nature which doth
  By that high heaven where, sinless,
     Thou dost shine,
To draw us sinners in:

4 By Thy last silence in the judgment
     hall,              [deadly tree,
  By long foreknowledge of the
  By darkness, by the wormwood and
     the gall,
I pray Thee visit me.

5 Come, lest this heart should, cold
     and cast away,      [entertain—
  Die e'er the Guest adored she
  Lest eyes that never saw Thine
     earthly day
Should miss Thy heavenly reign.
                    *Jean Ingelow.*

**204** I KNOW that my Redeemer
        lives,
What joy the blest assurance gives!
He lives, He lives, who once was
     dead;
He lives, my everlasting Head.

2 He lives, to bless me with His love;
  He lives, to plead for me above;
  He lives, my hungry soul to feed;
  He lives, to help in time of need.

3 He lives, and grants me daily breath;
  He lives, and I shall conquer death;
  He lives, my mansion to prepare;
  He lives, to lead me safely there.

4 He lives, all glory to His name;
  He lives, my Saviour, still the same;
  What joy the blest assurance gives,
  I know that my Redeemer lives!
                    *Samuel Medley.*

# Section IV

## THE HOLY SPIRIT

### (1) HIS PERSON AND WORK

**205** SPIRIT of faith, come down,
Reveal the things of God;
And make to us the Godhead known,
And witness with the blood.

2 Tis thine the blood to apply,
And give us eyes to see
Who did for every sinner die
Hath surely died for me.

3 No man can truly say
That Jesus is the Lord,
Unless Thou take the veil away,
And breathe the living word.

4 Then, only then, we feel,
Our interest in His blood,
And cry, with joy unspeakable:
Thou art my Lord, my God.

5 O that the world might know
The all-atoning Lamb!
Spirit of faith, descend, and show
The virtue of His name.

6 The grace which all may find
The saving power impart;
And testify to all mankind,
And speak in every heart.

7 Inspire the living faith,
Which whosoe'er receives,
The witness in himself he hath,
And consciously believes.

8 The faith that conquers all,
And doth the mountain move,
And saves whoe'er on Jesus call,
And perfects them in love.
*Charles Wesley.*

**206** OUR blest Redeemer, ere He breathed
His tender, last farewell,
A Guide, a Comforter, bequeathed
With us to dwell.

2 He came in tongues of living flame,
To teach, convince, subdue;

All-powerful as the wind He came,
As viewless too.

3 He came sweet influence to impart,
A gracious, willing Guest;
Where He can find one humble heart
Wherein to rest.

4 And His that gentle voice we hear,
Soft as the breath of even,
That checks each thought, and calms each fear,
And speaks of heaven.

5 And every virtue we possess,
And every conquest won,
And every thought of holiness
Are His alone.

6 Spirit of purity and grace,
Our weakness pitying see:
O make our heart Thy dwelling-place,
And worthier Thee.

7 O praise the Father, praise the Son;
Blest Spirit, praise to Thee;
All praise to God, the Three in One,
The One in Three.
*Harriet Auber.*

**207** OPEN my eyes, that I may see
Glimpses of truth Thou hast for me;
Place in my hands the wonderful key
That shall unclasp and set me free.
Silently now I wait for Thee,
Ready, my God, Thy will to see;
Open my eyes, illumine me,
Spirit Divine!

2 Open my ears, that I may hear
Voices of truth Thou sendest clear;
And while the wave-notes fall on my ear,
Everything false will disappear.
Silently now I wait for Thee,
Ready, my God, Thy will to see;
Open my ears, illumine me,
Spirit Divine!

3 Open my mouth, and let me bear
   Gladly the warm truth everywhere.
   Open my heart and let me prepare
   Love with Thy children thus to
     share.
    Silently now I wait for Thee,
    Ready, my God, Thy will to see;
    Open my heart, illumine me,
      Spirit Divine!

4 Open my mind, that I may read
   More of Thy love in word and deed;
   What shall I fear while yet Thou
    dost lead?
   Only for light from Thee I plead.
    Silently now I wait for Thee,
    Ready, my God, Thy will to see;
    Open my mind, illumine me,
      Spirit Divine!

5 Open my way, that I may bring
   Trophies of grace to Thee, my King;
   Echoed in love Thy word shall out-
    ring,
   Sweet as the note that angels sing.
    Silently now I wait for Thee,
    Ready, my God, Thy will to see;
    Open my way, illumine me,
      Spirit Divine!
       *Clara H. Scott and Fred P. Morris.*

**208** O BREATH of God, breathe on
    us now,       [pray;
   And move within us while we
  The spring of our new life art Thou,
  The very light of our new day.

2 O strangely art Thou with us, Lord,
   Neither in height nor depth to
    seek :       [heard;
  In nearness shall Thy voice be
  Spirit to spirit Thou dost speak.

3 Christ is our Advocate on high;
   Thou art our Advocate within:
  O plead the truth and make reply
  To every argument of sin.

4 But ah, this faithless heart of mine!
   The way I know; I know my
    guide:
  Forgive me, O my Friend divine,
  That I so often turn aside.

5 Be with me when no other friend
   The mystery of my heart can
    share;

And be Thou known, when fears
    transcend,
  By Thy best name of Comforter.
        *Alfred H. Vine.*

**209** GRACIOUS Spirit, dwell with me!
    I myself would gracious be,
  And with words that help and heal
  Would Thy life in mine reveal,
  And with actions bold and meek
  Would for Christ my Saviour speak.

2 Truthful Spirit, dwell with me!
   I myself would truthful be,
  And with wisdom kind and clear
  Let Thy life in mine appear,
  And with actions brotherly
  Speak my Lord's sincerity.

3 Tender Spirit, dwell with me!
   I myself would tender be:
  Shut my heart up like a flower
  At temptation's darksome hour;
  Open it when shines the sun,
  And His love by fragrance own.

4 Mighty Spirit, dwell with me!
   I myself would mighty be,
  Mighty so as to prevail
  Where unaided man must fail,
  Ever by a mighty hope
  Pressing on and bearing up.

5 Holy Spirit, dwell with me!
   I myself would holy be;
  Separate from sin, I would
  Choose and cherish all things good,
  And, whatever I can be,
  Give to Him who gave me Thee.
        *T. T. Lynch.*

**210** SPIRIT Divine, attend our pray-
    ers,
   And make our hearts Thy home;
  Descend with all Thy gracious
    powers,
   O come, great Spirit, come.

2 Come as the light—to us reveal
   Our need of Thee below;
  And lead us in those paths of life
  Where all the righteous go.

3 Come as the fire—and purge our
   With sacrificial flame;   [hearts
  Let our whole self an offering be
  To our Redeemer's name.

4 Come as the dew—and sweetly
   This consecrated hour;   [bless
  May barrenness rejoice to own
  Thy fertilising power.

5 Come as the Dove—and spread Thy
    wings,
    The wings of peaceful love;
And let Thy Church on earth be-
    come
    Blest as the Church above.

6 Come as the wind—with rushing
    And pentecostal grace;   [sound
That all of woman born may see
    The glory of Thy face.

                   *A. Reed.*

**211** COME, Holy Spirit, like a dove
    descending,    [to pray;
    Rest Thou upon us while we meet
Show us the Saviour, His great love
    revealing;   [Truth, the Way.
Lead us to Him, the Life, the

2 Come, Holy Spirit, every cloud dis-
    pelling;    [Master's name:
Fill us with gladness, through the
Bring to our mem'ry words that He
    hath spoken.
    Then shall our tongues His won-
    drous grace proclaim.

3 Come, Holy Spirit, sent from God
    the Father—
    Thou Friend and Teacher, Com-
    forter and Guide—
Our thoughts directing, keep us
    close to Jesus,    [abide.
And in our hearts for evermore

                *Robert Bruce.*

**212** O HOLY Spirit, come,
    Anoint us one and all,
And let some mighty deed be done,
    While at Thy feet we fall.

2 Thy Presence now we feel,
    To Thee our all we give,
Oh, let Thy love our spirits seal
    Henceforth for Thee to live.

3 The glow of love divine
    Refines us, at Thy feet;
For this our souls will always pine
    And yearn to be complete.

4 O Unction from on high,
    Come, permeate within;
Then I shall bear Thy searching
    Without a trace of sin.    [eye

               *D. P. Williams.*

**213** COME, Thou everlasting Spirit,
    Bring to every thankful mind
All the Saviour's dying merit,
    All His sufferings for mankind:
True Recorder of His passion,
    Now the living faith impart;
Now reveal His great salvation
    Unto every faithful heart.

2 Come, Thou witness of His dying;
    Come, Remembrancer divine;
Let us feel Thy power applying
    Christ to every soul, and mine.
Yes, in me, in me He dwelleth;
    I in Him, and He in me!
And my empty soul He filleth,
    Here and through eternity.

               *Charles Wesley.*

## (2) THE PENTECOSTAL FULNESS

**214** ARE you looking for the ful-
    ness of the blessing of the Lord
In your heart and life to-day?
Claim the promise of your Father,
    come according to His word,
    In the blessed old-time way.

   He will fill your heart to-day to over-
    flow . . . ing,
   As the Lord commandeth you, " Bring your
    vessels, not a few ";
   He will fill your heart to-day to over-
    flow . . . ing
   With the Holy Ghost and power.

2 Bring your empty earthen vessels,
    clean through Jesus' precious
    blood,
    Come, ye needy, one and all;
And in human consecration wait be-
    fore the throne of God,
    Till the Holy Ghost shall fall.

3 Like the cruse of oil, unfailing is
    His grace for evermore,
And His love unchanging still;
And according to His promise with
    the Holy Ghost and power,
    He will every vessel fill.

               *Mrs. C. H. Morris.*

**215** O LORD, " with one accord,"
    We gather round Thy Throne,
To hear Thy holy Word,
    To worship Thee alone.
Now send from heaven the Holy
Be this another Pentecost!    [Ghost,

2    We have no strength to meet
        The storms that round us lower,
    Keep Thou our trembling feet
        In every trying hour;
    More than victorious shall we be
    If girded with Thy panoply.

3    Where is the mighty wind
        That shook the holy place,
    That gladdened every mind,
        And brightened every face?
    And where the cloven tongues of
        flame        [Lamb?
    That marked each follower of the

4    There is no change in Thee,
        Lord God the Holy Ghost,
    Thy glorious majesty
        Is as at Pentecost!
    O may our loosened tongues pro-
        claim,        [same.
    That Thou, our God, art still the

5    And may that living wave,
        That issues from on high,
    Whose golden waters lave
        Thy throne eternally:
    Flow down in power on us to-day,
    And none shall go unblessed away!

6    Anoint us with Thy grace,
        To yield ourselves to Thee;
    To run our daily race,
        With joy and energy,
    Until we hear the Bridegroom say,
    "Rise up my love, and come away."
                *W. Pennefather.*

**216**    Now I feel the sacred fire,
        Kindling, flaming, glowing,
Higher still, and rising higher,
    All my soul o'erflowing;
Life immortal I receive;
    Oh, the wondrous story;
I was dead, but now I live,
    Glory! glory! glory!

2    Now I am from bondage freed,
        Every bond is riven,
Jesus makes me free indeed,
    Just as free as heaven;
'Tis a glorious liberty;
    Oh, the wondrous story!
I was bound, but now I'm free,
    Glory! glory! glory!

3    Let the testimony roll,
        Roll through every nation
Witnessing from soul to soul,
    This immense salvation;

Now I know it's full and free
    Oh, the wondrous story!
For I feel it saving me,
    Glory! glory! glory!

4    Glory be to God on high,
        Glory be to Jesus!
He hath brought salvation nigh
    From all sin He frees us;
Let the golden harps of God,
    Ring the wondrous story;
Let the pilgrims shout aloud
    Glory! glory! glory!

5    Let the trump of jubilee
        The glad tidings thunder,
Jesus sets the captives free,
    Bursts their bonds asunder;
Fetters break and dungeons fall,
    Oh, the wondrous story,
This salvation's free to all,
    Glory! glory! glory!

**217**    I'M rejoicing night and day,
        As I walk the pilgrim way,
For the hand of God in all my life
    I see,
    And the reason of my bliss,
    Yes, the secret all is this:
That the Comforter abides with me.

    He abides, . . . He abides, . . .
    Hallelujah, He abides with me !
    I'm rejoicing night and day,
    As I walk the narrow way,
    For the Comforter abides with me.

2    Once my heart was full of sin,
    Once I had no peace within,
Till I heard how Jesus died upon
    the tree;
    Then I fell down at His feet,
    And there came a peace so sweet,
Now the Comforter abides with me.

3    He is with me everywhere,
    And He knows my every care,
I'm as happy as a bird and just as
    For the Spirit has control, [free;
    Jesus satisfies my soul,
Since the Comforter abides with me.

4    There's no thirsting for the things
    Of the world—they've taken
        wings;
Long ago I gave them up, and in-
    stantly
    All my night was turned to day,
    All my burdens rolled away,
Now the Comforter abides with me.
               *Herbert Buffum.*

**218** HALLELUJAH sing exulting
 For the Holy Ghost has come,
To prepare a chosen people
 For their Lord and heavenly
  home.
Soon in clouds of Light appearing,
 Faithful to His promised word,
We shall see Him, therefore, breth-
 ren,     [Lord.
Watch and pray and serve the
Come, believing, cleanse your gar-
 ments
 In the blood on Calv'ry shed,
From the old, set free for ever,
 Formed anew in Christ our Head.

**2** Fall upon us, mighty Spirit
 In Thy fulness from above;
New creating, all conforming
 In us, to the Lord we love.
To Thy service consecrated
 And with hearts from self set
  free,
Burning with Love's pure devotion
 We will live and die for Thee.
Gifts and graces for His members
 Thou art come, abroad to shed,
Thus through signs and wonders
 bringing
 Glory to our risen Head.

**3** Hark, the ransomed choir is singing
 Hallelujah to the Lamb.
Glory, honour, praise and worship,
 Hail Him as the great I AM.
See the Bride in dazzling raiment
 Hastes her glorious Lord to meet;
Come, Lord Jesus, we await Thee,
 While we worship at Thy feet.
Hallelujah! Everlasting
 Glory dawns upon us now,
As we hear with joy and rapture
 His clear summons: "Enter
 thou!"   *Martin Gensichen.*

**219** THE power that fell at Pente-
  cost,
 When in the upper room,
Upon the watching, waiting ones,
 The Holy Ghost had come,
Remaineth evermore the same;
 Unchanging still, O praise His
  name.

 The power, . . . the power, . . . the Pente-
  costal power
 Is just the same to-day, . . .
 Is just the same to-day, . . .

 The power, . . . the power, . . . the Pentecostal power,
 Is just . . . the same to-day.

**2** " Ye shall have power (said Jesus)
  when
 The Holy Ghost is come;"
Your loosened tongues shall speak
 His praise,
 Your lips no more be dumb;
The timid, shrinking ones be brave,
 To reach a hand the lost to save.

**3** The wavering shall steadfast be-
  come,
 The weak in faith be strong,
With holy boldness going forth,
 Denouncing sin and wrong;
With burning zeal each heart
 aflame,
 A whole salvation to proclaim.

**4** Breathe on us now the Holy Ghost,
 The young and old inspire;
Let each receive his Pentecost,
 Set hearts and tongues afire!
Thou wonderful transforming power,
 Come now in this accepted hour.
    *Mrs. C. H. Morris.*

**220** " THE Holy Spirit's power
 Ye need," the Master said;
" So wait till comes the hour
 When on you He is shed."
So praise did all their souls employ
As tarried they with fervent joy.

**2** And when ten days were passed
 With one accord were they,
Heaven's windows long closed fast,
 Were opened on that day;
With rushing mighty wind and
 flame,
The promised Holy Spirit came.

**3** Their loosened tongues were filled
 With strange and wondrous
  words;
Heaven's life their hearts had
 thrilled,
 God's goodness they declared;
" And unto all," th'Apostle said,
" Is the like gift, since Christ has
 bled."

**4** Come now, ye sons of men,
 This message now receive,
The Holy Spirit's given
 To all who will believe;

Ye, too, may know His mighty power,
And speak with tongues this very hour.
5 Then charity divine,
Your yearning hearts shall fill
T'wards those who now repine,
Held in sin's bondage still;
For these your zeal shall never tire
To snatch them from th'e'erlasting fire.
*E. T. Mellor.*

**221** "I WILL not leave you comfortless,"
But if I go away,
Will send the Holy Comforter,
Your royal Guest for evermore,
Abiding day by day.

Has He come to you, to you, to you?
Has the Comforter come to you? . . .
The Lord will reprove the world of sin,
When the Comforter comes to you. . .

2 Church of the Living God, arise
The fulness to receive;
Until the lost in every place,
Shall feel the need of saving grace,
And shall on Christ believe.

3 God's skies are full of Pentecosts,
For you, for me, for all;
Then let us humbly, boldly press,
Our heritage in Christ possess,
That power from heaven may fall.

4 Then quickly "back to Pentecost,"
That blessed upper room;
And pray the mighty Lord of Hosts
To send on us the Holy Ghost,
And tarry till He come.
*Mrs. C. H. Morris.*

**222** HOLY Ghost, we bid Thee welcome, [art;
Source of life and power Thou
Promise of our heavenly Father
Now thrice welcome to my heart.

Welcome, welcome, welcome,
Holy Ghost, we welcome Thee:
Come in power and fill the temple,
Holy Ghost, we welcome Thee.

2 Here like empty earthen vessels,
Lying at the Master's feet,
Small but clean through Jesus' merit, [plete.
Wait till Thou Thy work com-

3 Come like dew from heaven falling,
Come like spring's refreshing shower;

Holy Ghost, for Thee we're calling,
Come in all Thy quickening power.

4 Hearts are open to receive Thee,
Though we've grieved Thee o'er and o'er,
Holy Ghost, we greatly need Thee,
Come, abide for evermore.
*Mrs. C. H. Morris.*

**223** COME to me, O blessèd Spirit,
Enter Thou my heart to-day;
I am longing to receive Thee,
Come, and ever with me stay.

I am waiting, I am willing,
Thine and only Thine to be;
Make my heart Thy living temple,
Come to-day and dwell in me.

2 Come to me in all Thy fulness,
Take possession of my soul;
Take the will I scarce can yield Thee,
Sanctify and cleanse the whole.

3 Loving Spirit, make me loving,
Melt my heart and cleanse from [sin,
Satisfy my restless longings,
Make me fair and pure within.

4 Holy Ghost, I now receive Thee!
I accept Thy mighty power;
And, by faith, I claim Thy presence
In this solemn, sacred hour.

I believe Thee! I believe Thee!
And the blessing now I claim
Of Thy fulness, gracious Spirit;
Glory to Thy holy name!
*Annie M. Potter.*

**224** BREATHE upon us, Lord, from heaven,
Fill us with the Holy Ghost;
Promise of the Father given,
Send us now a Pentecost.

Breathe upon us, breathe upon us,
With Thy love our hearts inspire;
Breathe upon us, breathe upon us,
Lord baptize us now with fire.

2 While the Spirit hovers o'er us,
Open all our hearts, we pray;
To Thine image, Lord, restore us,
Witness in our souls to-day.

3 From all sin grant us exemption,
Wash us in the cleansing flood;
Let us know the full redemption
Purchased for us by the blood.

4 Lift us, Lord, O lift us higher,
  From the carnal mind set free;
Fill us with refining fire,
  Give us perfect liberty.
        *R. Kelso Carter.*

**225** O GLADSOME day of praise,
  O day of joy divine!
The Christ who died is risen again,
  In glory now to shine.
He hath gone up on high,
  Ten thousand hosts attend;
He takes the throne in majesty,
  All powers before Him bend.

2 The heavens resound with praise,
  Earth owns His regal state:
A glorious company of saints
  His promised gift await.
For ere the Saviour went
  In triumph through the cloud,
Said He, " The Holy Ghost shall
    come."
  Then at His feet they bowed.

3 In ecstacy and joy,
  With songs of love and grace,
As one they tarry for their God,
  As one they seek His face.
Nor can they be denied—
  They ask in Jesu's name:
Behold! He comes! the Spirit
    comes
In wind and fiery flame.

4 The old prophetic word
  Becomes His Church's dower:
" Upon all flesh " is now outpoured
  This plenitude of power.
Who own Him Christ the Lord
  May all His fulness prove;
Yea, boldly now this gift we claim,
  Through His redeeming love.

5 All-powerful Lord on high,
  Dazzling in splendour bright,
Enlarge our souls, our hearts in-
  With Pentecostal might!   [spire
We dare not let Thee go—
  Thou art our one desire:   [down!
Oh, rend the heavens, in power come
  Baptize us, Lord, with fire!
        *L. F. W. Woodford.*

**226** Joys are flowing like a river,
  Since the Comforter has come;
He abides with us for ever,
  Makes the trusting heart His
    home.

Blessed quietness, holy quietness,
  What assurance in my soul !
On the stormy sea, He speaks peace to me,
  How the billows cease to roll.

2 Bringing life, and health, and glad-
    ness,
  All around this heavenly Guest;
Banished unbelief and sadness,
  Changed our weariness to rest.

3 Like the rain that falls from heaven,
  Like the sunlight from the sky,
So the Holy Ghost is given,
  Coming on us from on high.

4 What a wonderful salvation,
  Where we always see His face;
What a perfect habitation,
  What a quiet resting-place.
        *Mamie Payne Ferguson.*

**227** OH, spread the tidings round,
    wherever man is found,
Wherever human hearts and human
  woes abound; [the joyful sound:
Let every Christian tongue proclaim
  The Comforter has come!

The Comforter has come, the Comforter
  has come !
The Holy Ghost from heaven, the Father's
  promise given ;
Oh, spread the tidings round, wherever man
  is found—
  The Comforter has come !

2 Lo, the great King of kings, with
  healing in His wings,
To every captive soul a full deliv-
  'rance brings;
And through the vacant cells the
  song of triumph rings;
  The Comforter has come!

3 O boundless Love divine! how shall
  this tongue of mine
To wond'ring mortals tell the
  matchless grace divine—
That I a child of hell, should in
  His image shine!
  The Comforter has come!

4 Sing, till the echoes fly above the
  vaulted sky,   [low reply,
And all the saints above to all be-
  In strains of endless love, the song
  that ne'er will die:
  The Comforter has come!
        *F. Bottome.*

**228** THE Holy Ghost to me is given,
An earnest of my home in
heaven;
Since He has taken full control,
I've Pentecost in my soul.

I've Pentecost in my soul, . . .
I've Pentecost in my soul ; . . .
The Spirit has come for ever to abide ;
I've Pentecost in my soul.

2 He deigns to dwell my heart within,
And quells the power of pardoned
sin; [may roll,
Though o'er my head dark clouds
I've Pentecost in my soul.

3 I shout aloud with sacred joy,
His praises shall my powers em-
ploy;
His blessèd name my tongue extol,
For Pentecost in my soul.

4 And when I reach yon world of
bliss,
A land more glorious far than this,
I'll sing while countless ages roll,
I've Pentecost in my soul.

5 Then seek this gift without delay,
Receive the royal Guest to-day;
Yield all to His benign control,
Let Pentecost fill your soul.
*Thoro Harris.*

**229** Do you seek a land where
there comes no night,
Blessed Beulah land, where the sun
shines bright, [by sight,
Where we walk by faith and not
Baptized with the Holy Ghost?

Will you be baptized in this faith ? . . .
Baptized with the Holy Ghost ?
To be free, indeed, 'tis the power you need,
Baptized with the Holy Ghost.

2 Will you take Him now as your all
in all, [may fall?
Let the self be slain, that the power
Will you now in faith for the bless-
ing call,
Baptized with the Holy Ghost?

3 'Tis the Canaan land for our weary
feet, [rest complete;
With our wand'rings o'er, and our
Where we dwell with Christ in com-
munion sweet,
Baptized with the Holy Ghost.
*Mrs. C. H. Morris.*

**230** Ho, every one that is thirsty in
spirit, [sad;
Ho, every one that is weary and
Come to the fountain, there's ful-
ness in Jesus, [and be glad.
All that you're longing for, come

" I will pour water on him that is thirsty,
I will pour floods upon the dry ground;
Open your heart for the gift I am bringing ;
While you are seeking Me, I will be
found."

2 Child of the world, are you tired of
your bondage? [untrue?
Weary of earth-joys, so false, so
Thirsting for God and His fulness
of blessing? [you!
List to the promise, a message for

3 Child of the Kingdom, be filled with
the Spirit! [can meet:
Nothing but fulness thy longing
'Tis the enduement for life and for
service; [so sweet.
Thine is the promise, so certain,
*Lucy J. Rider.*

### (3) HIS MANIFESTATION AND
POWER

**231** LORD God, the Holy Ghost,
In this accepted hour,
As on the day of Pentecost,
Descend in all Thy power!

2 We meet with one accord
In our appointed place,
And wait the promise of our Lord,
The Spirit of all grace.

3 Like mighty rushing wind
Upon the waves beneath,
Move with one impulse every mind,
One soul, one feeling breathe.

4 The young, the old inspire
With wisdom from above, [fire
And give us hearts and tongues of
To pray, and praise, and love.

5 Spirit of Light, explore
And chase our gloom away,
With lustre shining more and more
Unto the perfect day!

6 Spirit of Truth, be Thou
In life and death our Guide!
O Spirit of Adoption, now
May we be sanctified.
*J. Montgomery.*

**232** OF gifts and powers miracu-
lous,
Endowments rare we sing,
Equipment of anointed hearts
Shed forth by Christ the King,
Designed from heaven God's light
and power
To helpless earth to bring.

2 O blest diversity of Gifts,
The Spirit's Super-Sense,
Strong currents of Infinity,
Gleams of Omnisciènce,
Outpourings of Almightiness,
That Risen Hands dispense!

O blessèd proofs of living Love
In Apostolic days,
Rejected long by formal minds—
Now, to God's endless praise,
Re-risen in this later age
Like dawn's returning blaze!

4 Shine forth in richer radiance,
Break out in rarer might,
In miracles and mighty signs,
In this earth's darkling night,
That once again Thy Church may
Victorious in the fight.        [be

5 O  may  Thy  members,  Mighty
Most earnestly desire,     [Christ,
Most covetously thirst once more,
Most fervently aspire,
Till each arises furnished new
With ministries of fire!

6 Shall  we  neglect  God's  glorious
His gospel grace to speed? [plan
Shall we despise rare instruments
Of evangelic deed?
Lord, once again give gifts to men
In this late hour of need.
                        *Harold Horton.*

**233** LORD, Thy ransomed Church is
waking
Out of slumber far and near,
Knowing that the morn is breaking
When   the   Bridegroom   shall
appear:
Waking up to claim the treasure
With  Thy  precious  life-blood
bought,
And to trust in fuller measure
All  Thy  wondrous  death  hath
wrought.

2 Praise to Thee for this glad shower,
Precious drops of latter rain;
Praise, that by Thy Spirit's power
Thou hast quickened us again;
That Thy Gospel's priceless trea-
sure
Now is borne from land to land,
And that all the Father's pleasure
Prospers in Thy piercèd hand.

3 Praise to Thee for saved ones yearn-
ing          [throng;
O'er  the  lost  and  wandering
Praise for voices daily learning
To upraise the glad new song:
Praise to Thee for sick ones hast-
ing          [hem!
Now  to  touch  Thy  garment's
Praise for souls believing—tasting
All Thy love has won for them.

4 Set on fire our heart's devotion
With the love of Thy dear name;
Till o'er every land and ocean
Lips and lives Thy Cross pro-
claim,
Fix our eyes on Thy returning,
Keeping  watch  till  Thou  shalt
come;          [ing;
Loins well girt, lamps brightly burn-
Then, Lord, take Thy servants
home.          *Sarah G. Stock.*

**234** COME, Holy Spirit, raise our
songs
To reach the wonders of that day,
When,  with  Thy  fiery  cloven
tongues,          [display.
Thou didst such glorious scenes

2 Lord, we believe to us and ours,
The Apostolic promise given;
We wait the Pentecostal showers,
The Holy Ghost sent down from
heaven.

3 Assembled here with one accord,
Calmly  we  wait  the  promised
grace,
The purchase of our dying Lord;
Come, Holy Ghost and fill the
place.

4 If every one that asks may find,
If still Thou dost on sinners fall,
Come as a mighty rushing wind;
Great grace be now upon us all.
                        *Charles Wesley.*

**235** TARRY for the Spirit,
　　He shall come in showers,
Energising wholly
　　All your ransomed powers;
Signs shall follow service
　　In the Holy Ghost,
Then the Church of Jesus
　　Prove a mighty host.

　　On, then, Church of Jesus,
　　　Claim your Pentecost;
　　God shall now baptize thee
　　　In the Holy Ghost.

2 " Rivers " is Thy promise,
　　This shall be our plea,
Less than this can never
　　Meet our cry for Thee;
Tired of lukewarm service,
　　And the loss it brings,
We would live entirely
　　For eternal things.

3 When the Spirit cometh,
　　Loosened lips shall tell,
Of the wondrous blessing
　　Which upon them fell;
Life of Jesus springing,
　　Like a well within,
Hearts with loud hosannas,
　　Constantly shall ring.

4 When with joy we follow
　　In Christ's triumph train,
And our lives are flooded
　　With the Latter Rain;
Then the world around us
　　Shall the impact feel,
Of a Church with vision,
　　Fired with holy zeal.

5 Then the Lord of glory
　　Shall be magnified,
He who trod the winepress,
　　Fully satisfied;
Walking in the Spirit,
　　Condemnation o'er,
Blessèd life of worship,
　　Now and evermore.
　　　　　　　　*E. C. W. Boulton.*

**236** O SPIRIT of the living God,
　　In all Thy plenitude of grace,
Where'er the foot of man hath trod,
　　Descend on our apostate race.

2 Give tongues of fire and hearts of
　　　love,
　　To preach the reconciling word;

Give power and unction from above
　　Whene'er the joyful sound is
　　　heard.

3 Be darkness, at Thy coming, light;
　　Confusion order in Thy path:
Souls without strength inspire with
　　　might;
　　Bid mercy triumph over wrath.

4 O Spirit of the Lord, prepare
　　All the round earth her God to
　　　meet;　　　　　　　　[air,
Breathe Thou abroad, like morning
　　Till hearts of stone begin to beat.

5 Baptize the nations; far and nigh
　　The triumphs of the cross record;
The name of Jesus glorify,
　　Till every kindred call Him Lord.

6 God, from eternity, hath willed
　　All flesh shall His salvation see:
So be the Father's love fulfilled,
　　The Saviour's sufferings crowned
　　　through Thee.
　　　　　　　　*James Montgomery.*

**237** WHEN first the risen Lord of
　　　power
　　His chosen ones sent forth,
A charge He gave, that solemn hour,
　　To preach His saving worth.
" Go ye," said He, " to all man-
　　　kind;　　　　　　　　[find:
Declare My Word, and ye shall
These signs shall surely follow them
　　Who on My Name believe."

2 " No demons shall before them
　　　　　　　　　　　　[stand,
　　No poison do them harm:
Nor subtle serpent in their hand
　　Cause pain or dread alarm."
For Satan's kingdom He o'ercame.
To give His people right to claim:
These signs shall surely follow them
　　Who on My Name believe.

3 " They shall with other tongues de-
　　　　　　　　　　　　[clare
　　The wonders of their God;
The sick beneath their hands, by
　　　prayer,
　　Shall rise, to prove My Word."
So let it be! Firm as His Throne
Stands this clear promise to His
　　　own:
These signs shall surely follow them
　　Who on My Name believe.

4 Crowned with the flame of Pente-
   A faithful, fearless band  [cost,
  Proclaimed His Name: a ransomed
   Arose from every land.  [host
The Lord worked with them from
   on High,
His proven Word could none deny:
These signs shall surely follow them
  Who on My Name believe.

5 No word of Thine is void of power;
   No promise, Lord, is vain.
  Be this a Pentecostal hour—
   Confirm Thy Word again!
Nor canst Thou fail! Thou art the
   same
As when of old Thou didst pro-
   claim:  [them
These signs shall surely follow
  Who on My Name believe.
*L. F. W. Woodford.*

**238** LORD, in Thy presence we are
   met,
   A full salvation to proclaim;
To testify of grace received,
   Or offered now in Jesus' Name;
Dear Lord, to Thee our spirits cry,
Our every longing satisfy.

2 We ask Thee, Lord—for Thou art
   here—
   Make this a Pentecostal hour,
When hungering souls from Thee
   receive
   Pardon, or purity, or power;
Unstop deaf ears, let blind eyes
Bring souls into Thy liberty.  [see,

3 Thou knowest sin-sick souls are
   Sick with depravity within,  [here,
Restless, discouraged, wearied ones,
   And Thou art here to cleanse
    from sin;  [whole ";
Oh! speak the word " I will, be
And save and sanctify each soul.

4 Grant to Thy servants boldness now,
   That faithfully they speak Thy
    Word,  [heal."
  " By stretching forth Thy hand to
  Let signs and wonders from the
   Lord,
Here in our midst to-day be done,
So, Father, glorify Thy Son.

5 We wait—according to Thy Word,
  Lord, let it to Thy servants be;

May nothing—self, pride, prejudice,
  Or unbelief—still hinder Thee;
Bless'd Spirit, have unhindered way
In yielded hearts and lives to-day.
*Mary E. Maxwell.*

**239** GOD sent His mighty power
    To this poor, sinful heart,
To keep me every hour,
  And needful grace impart:
And since His Spirit came
  To take supreme control,
The love enkindled flame
  Is burning in my soul.

   'Tis burning in my soul,
   'Tis burning in my soul;
 The fire of heavenly love is **burning in my**
   soul;
    The Holy Spirit came,
    All glory to His name !
 The fire of heavenly love is burning in **my**
   soul.

2 Before the Cross I bow,
  Upon the altar lay
A willing off'ring now,
  My all from day to day.
My Saviour paid the price,
  My name He sweetly calls;
Upon the sacrifice
  The fire from heaven falls.

3 No good that I have done,
  His promise I embrace;
Accepted in the Son,
  He saves me by His grace;
All glory be to God!
  Let hallelujahs roll;
His love is shed abroad,
  The fire is in my soul.
*Delia T. White.*

**240** THY sons and daughters, Lord,
    behold,
More precious than the finest gold,
  O guide them with Thine eye!
Thy Holy Spirit richly pour,
And fill their hearts this gracious
  That they may prophesy.  [hour,

2 May signs and wonders still be
   wrought,  [brought
And numbers, by their preaching
  To know the truth divine:
May all the powers of hell give
   way,  [pray,
And thousands, taught to sing and
In holy worship join.

3 Endue them, Lord, with power and
    grace,
  To preach Thy word in every place,
    To sinners born to die:
  Enlarge their power of doing good,
  That millions, sprinkled with Thy
    blood,
    May meet Thee in the sky.

4 Bring them at last to see Thy face,
  And triumph in redeeming grace,
    With all Thy saints in light;
  And, seated round Thy throne
    divine,
  With angels and archangels join
    To worship in Thy sight.

**241**  O MEN of God, arise! the
    Lord                      [Word
  Has given thee in His wondrous
  Great promises of mighty signs
  To ratify the sacred lines
  Of His Salvation's perfect plan
  As thou dost preach to fallen man.

2 If He, the Lord of Glory, need
  Arresting sign and glowing deed—
  Credentials of Messiahship—
  Thy helpless hand and faltering lip
  Must surely share an equal flame
  To blazon forth Messiah's Name!

3 These signs shall follow them, He
    saith,                    [faith:
  Who speak His Word in simple
  They shall with heaven's authority
  Bid foul tormenting spirits flee;
  They shall in other tongues speak
    things
  Beyond the range of finite wings—

4 (So spake they after Pentecost
  High myst'ries of the Holy Ghost);
  They shall the fearsome serpent
    tame,
  And bind its venom in His Name;
  If any deadly thing they take
  It shall not hurt them, for His
    sake;

5 Upon the sick they shall lay hands,
  Who shall arise from Satan's bands,
  Leaving their fev'rous beds of pain
  To leap like youngling harts again.
  O men of God! These signs *must*
  As Christ's authority to thee! [be

6 There is no other way! The Word
  Not heav'n-confirmed must fall un-
    heard,
  For wondrous act and mighty sign
  Are still the Saviour's own design
  To wing His message to each heart,
  And bid the pow'rs of hell depart.
                        *Harold Horton.*

**242**  LORD Jesus, Thou Thy Church
    hast graced
    With gifts supernal and divine;
  Gifts of Thy Spirit, pure and chaste
    With heavenly lustre here to
    shine.
  Ascending to Thy Father's throne,
  Thou hast bestowed them on Thine
    own.

2 In Thee, our living Head, are stored
    Treasures of wisdom, light and
    love;                   [poured
  On us, Thy members, Thou hast
    This wealth of blessing from
    above.
  Oh, may we prove, this very hour,
  The nine-fold splendour of Thy
    power!

3 Speak, Lord! By Word of Wisdom
    pure,
    Thy will reveal, Thy mind impart;
  By Word of Knowledge, swift and
    sure,                    [heart.
    Illume, instruct, and guide each
  So shall we trace Thy way divine,
  Line upon line, in clear design.

4 Thy mighty faith on us bestow,
    Beyond our measure or our
    thought;
  Let gifts of healing from Thee flow,
  And wonders in Thy name be
    wrought.
  Make bare Thine arm, confirm Thy
    word,                    [Lord!
  That all may own Thee Christ and

5 Touch Thou our lips! We would
    aspire
    To speak the praises of Thy love,
  Gifted with pure prophetic fire
    And holy unction from above;
  Whilst, through Thy searching Spirit,
    taught                 [thought.
  The secret springs of life and

6 With tongues of men or seraph
strain,                [in prayer;
Speak forth Thy words, in praise.
Then make each heaven-sent mes-
sage plain,
That we Thy glories may declare.
Grace every gift with love's high
theme:
Yea, reign o'er all, O Love supreme!
*L. F. W. Woodford.*

## (4) PENTECOSTAL REVIVAL

**243** IN Thy name, O blessed Savi-
our,
Gathered in this sacred place;
Here we seek a Father's blessing,
Plead and pray for needed grace;
From the ocean of Thy fulness,
Boundless, fathomless and free;
Let a tidal wave come sweeping,
Setting hearts at liberty.
Lift the floodgates, lift the floodgates,
Let the tide come sweeping in ;
Blessed tide of full salvation,
Washing, cleansing, from all sin.

2 Lift the floodgates, let salvation
In tremendous currents flow,
To the uttermost fulfilling
Thy blest mission here below;
Until myriads of sinners,
Borne on love's resistless tide,
Shall be swept into the kingdom,
And believers sanctified.

3 It is coming, we believe it,
Thou dost hear and answer
prayer;
It is coming, we shall see it,
Thine almighty arm made bare;
Tides of power, tides of glory,
Holy tides of perfect love,
Satisfying, overflowing,
Coming on us from above.
*Mrs. C. H. Morris.*

**244** LORD, as of old at Pentecost
Thou didst Thy power dis-
play,
With cleansing, purifying flame
Descend on us to-day.
Lord, send the old-time power, the Pente-
costal power !
Thy floodgates of blessing on us throw
open wide !
Lord, send the old-time power, the Pente-
costal power,
That sinners be converted and Thy name
glorified !

2 For mighty works for Thee prepare,
And strengthen every heart;
Come, take possession of Thine
And nevermore depart.    [own,

3 All self consume, all sin destroy!
With earnest zeal endue
Each waiting heart to work for
Oh Lord, our faith renew! [Thee;

4 Speak, Lord, before Thy throne we
Thy promise we believe,    [wait,
And will not let Thee go until
The blessing we receive!
*Charlotte G. Homer.*

**245** "THERE shall be showers of
blessing ":
This is the promise of love;
There shall be seasons refreshing,
Sent from the Saviour above.
Show . . . ers of blessing,
Showers of blessing we need ;
Mercy drops round us are falling,
But for the showers we plead.

2 "There shall be showers of bless-
Precious reviving again; [ing"—
Over the hills and the valleys,
Sound of abundance of rain.

3 "There shall be showers of bless-
ing:"
Send them upon us, O Lord!
Grant to us now a refreshing;
Come, and now honour Thy
Word.

4 "There shall be showers of bless-
ing,"
Oh, that to-day they might fall,
Now, as to God, we're confessing,
Now as on Jesus we call!

5 "There shall be showers of bless-
If we but trust and obey; [ing,"
There shall be seasons refreshing,
If we let God have His way.
*El Nathan.*

**246** REVIVE Thy work, O Lord!
Thy mighty arm make bare;
Speak with the voice that wakes the
dead,
And make Thy people hear!
Revive Thy work, O Lord, . . .
While here to Thee we bow ; . . .
Descend, O gracious Lord, descend,
Oh, come and bless us now !

2     Revive Thy work, O Lord!
        Disturb this sleep of death;
  Quicken the smouldering embers
    By Thine Almighty breath. [now

3     Revive Thy work, O Lord!
        Create soul-thirst for Thee;
  And hungering for the bread of life,
    Oh, may our spirits be!

4     Revive Thy work, O Lord!
        Exalt Thy precious name:
  And by the Holy Ghost, our love
  For Thee and Thine inflame.

*Albert Midlane (arr. F. J. Crosby.)*

**247**   THERE'S a sound upon the
        waters,
  There's a murmur in the air,
  For a wave of coming glory moves
    my soul;
  There's the sign of a revival—
  All ye saints, prepare for war;
  For the hosts of God are marching
    to the goal.

    Hallelujah ! Hallelujah ! Hallelujah to the
      Lord ;
    We shall triumph, we shall triumph
    Through the everlasting Word ;
    There's a sound upon the waters,
    There's a murmur in the air ;
    For a sound of coming glory moves my soul.

2  Sing, the Lord has come to battle,
  He's a mighty Man of war,
  He is girding on the sword to smite
    the foe;
  He will lead His people onward
  In the fulness of His power—
  Hark! the hosts of God are singing
    as they go.

3  We are coming, we are coming
  To the help of Judah's King,
  Every heart and hand is ready for
    the fray;
  Lift the Banner of Salvation,
  Jesus leads us—march away!
  Glory, glory, we shall win the well-
    fought day!

*J. Flanagan.*

**248**   FOR a world-wide revival,
        Blessèd Master, we pray,
  Let the power of the highest
    Be upon us to-day;
  For this world dearly purchased
    By the blood of God's Son,
  Back from Satan's dominion
    And from sin must be won.

    Send the power, O Lord,
    Send the power, O Lord,
    Send the Holy Ghost power, let it now be
      outpoured,
    Send it surging and sweeping like the waves
      of the sea,
    Send a world-wide revival, and begin it in me.

2 Send the showers of blessing,
    As declared in Thy Word,
  Let the Spirit of promise
    On all flesh be outpoured;
  Send the latter rain on us,
    Till the land overflows,
  Till the desert rejoicing
    Blossoms forth as the rose.

3 There's a sound of a going
    In the mulberry trees,
  News of nations awaking,
    Borne upon every breeze;
  For the prayers of His children,
    God in mercy doth own,
  The revival's beginning,
    And the power's coming down.

*Mrs. C. H. Morris.*

**249**   THEY were gathered in an up-
        per chamber,
  As commanded by the risen Lord,
  And the promise of the Father
  There they sought with one
    accord,       [descended
  When the Holy Ghost from heav'n
    Like a rushing wind and tongues
    of fire:
  So, dear Lord, we seek Thy blessing,
    Come with glory now our hearts
    inspire.

    Let the fire fall, let the fire fall,
      Let the fire from heaven fall ; . . .
    We are waiting and expecting,
      Now in faith, dear Lord, we call ; . . .
    Let the fire fall, let the fire fall,
      On Thy promise we depend ;
    From the glory of Thy presence
    Let the Pentecostal fire descend.

2 As Elijah we would raise the altar
    For our testimony clear and true,
  Christ the Saviour, loving Healer,
    Coming Lord, Baptizer too,
  Ever-flowing grace and full salva-
    tion       [planned;
    For a ruined race Thy love has
  For this blessèd revelation,
    For Thy written word we dare
    to stand.

3 'Tis the covenanted promise given,
    To as many as the Lord shall call,
  To the fathers and their children,

To Thy people, one and all;
So rejoicing in Thy word unfailing
We draw nigh in faith Thy powe
  to know—
Come, O come, Thou burning Spirit
Set our hearts with heav'nly fire
  aglow.

4 With a living coal from off Thy altar
  Touch our lips to swell Thy won-
    drous praise,
To extol Thee, bless, adore Thee,
  And our songs of worship raise;
Let the cloud of glory now descend-
  ing
Fill our hearts with holy ecstacy,
Come in all Thy glorious fulness,
  Blessèd Holy Spirit, have Thy
    way.

*H. Tee.*

**250** THERE'LL be showers of blessing from our Father's hand,
On His word of promise we may
  firmly stand;
There'll be rains refreshing on the
  thirsty land
    When the tithes are gathered in.

Tithes of love and willing service,
Tithes of silver and of gold ;
When the tithes . . . are gathered in . . .
When the tithes . . . are gathered in . . .
There'll be blessings more than we can
  contain,
When the tithes . . . are gathered in . . .

2 There'll be shouts of triumph from
  the conquering host,
There'll be perfect freedom in the
  Holy Ghost;   [cost,
Every one empowered as at Pente-
    When the tithes are gathered in.

3 Then will come the dawning of the
  reign of peace,
When the wars and conflicts shall
  forever cease,
And for struggling saints shall come
  a sweet release,
    When the tithes are gathered in.

4 We will rob no longer, then, our
  Lord and King, [gladly bring.
What to Him belongeth we will
And we'll shout hosanna, while the
  glad harps ring,
    When the tithes are gathered in.
*Mrs. C. H. Morris.*

**251** BLOW, pentecostal breeze,
  Breathe, apostolic blast,
Stir pentecostal hearts at ease,
  And sinners slumb'ring fast!

2  Breathe, Holy Ghost to-day,
  Dispel the ancient sloth;
The guilty deadness sweep away
  In resurrection growth.

3  Make sweeter graces bloom,
  And lovelier virtues shine,
And mightier influences perfume
  A world by purchase thine.

4  Revive the ancient glow,
  The fierce prophetic fire,
The ancient miracle bestow,
  The former power inspire.

5  Breathe on this soul of ours,
  On branch and stem and root,
Till Christ shall smell His fragrant
    flowers
  And taste His ripened fruit.

6  Breathe on us, Mighty Breath,
  On leaf and naked clod,
Breathe o'er the church's creeping
  The pulsing life of God. [death

7  Breathe till the perfume flows
  O'er wastes where sins abound,
Till Calv'ry's gospel-incense blows
  The stricken world around!
*Harold Horton.*

**252** THOU Christ of burning,
    cleansing flame,
  Send the fire!
Thy blood-bought gift to-day we
  Send the fire!   [claim,
Look down and see this waiting
  host,
Give us the promised Holy Ghost,
We want another Pentecost,
  Send the fire!

2 God of Elijah, hear our cry!
  Send the fire!
Oh, make us fit to live or die!
  Send the fire!
To burn up every trace of sin,
To bring the light and glory in,
The revolution now begin,
  Send the fire!

3 'Tis fire we want, for fire we plead,
  Send the fire!
The fire will meet our every need,
  Send the fire!

For strength to ever do the right,
For grace to conquer in the fight,
For power to walk the world in
    Send the fire!    [white,

4 To make our weak heart strong and
    Send the fire!    [brave,
To live a dying world to save,
    Send the fire!
Oh, see us on Thy altar lay
Our lives, our all, this very day;
To crown the offering now, we
    Send the fire!    [pray,

*William Booth.*

**253** FLOODS of revival,
    Lord, let them fall;
Streams of salvation
    Reaching to all.
Pour out Thy Spirit,
    Great is our need;
Sweep o'er our beings
    Now whilst we plead.

*Spirit divine, O quicken us now,*
  *Whilst in Thy presence, humbly we bow,*
*Set all our hearts ablaze with Thy love,*
*Teach us the secret of life from above.*

2 Utterly yielded,
    Longing to know
All the blest fulness
    Love can bestow.
Ready and willing,
    Eager to give
Perfect obedience,
    Bravely to live.

3 Raise up a people
    Holy and free;
Hearts with a vision
    Like unto Thee;
Souls that would rather
    Die than give in;
Lives with a passion
    Victory to win.

4 O for a deluge—
    Holy Ghost power;
Lord, we are waiting,
    Send it this hour.
Open the windows
    Of heav'n we pray;
All on the altar
    Gladly we lay.

*E. C. W. Boulton.*

**254** O BREATH of Life, come sweep-
    ing through us,    [power;
Revive Thy Church with life and
O Breath of Life, come cleanse, re-
    new us,    [hour.
And fit Thy Church to meet this

2 O Wind of God, come bend us,
    break us,
Till humbly we confess our need;
Then in Thy tenderness remake us,
    Revive, restore, for this we plead.

3 O Breath of Love, come breathe
    within us,    [heart:
Renewing thought and will and
Come, Love of Christ, afresh to
    win us,
Revive Thy Church in every part.

4 O Heart of Christ, once broken for
    us,    [and rest;
'Tis there we find our strength
Our broken contrite hearts now
    solace,    [blest.
And let Thy waiting Church be

5 Revive us, Lord! Is zeal abating
While harvest fields are vast and
    white?    [ing,
Revive us, Lord, the world is wait-
Equip Thy Church to spread the
    light.    *Mrs. B. P. Head.*

**255** GOD is here, and that to bless
    us    [power;
With the Spirit's quickening
See the cloud already bending,
    Waits to drop the grateful shower.

*Let it come, O Lord, we pray Thee,*
  *Let the shower of blessing fall ;*
*We are waiting, we are waiting,*
  *Oh, revive the hearts of all.*

2 God is here! we feel His presence
    In this consecrated place;
But we need the soul refreshing
    Of His free unbounded grace.

3 God is here! oh, then, believing,
    Bring to Him our one desire;
That His love may now be kindled,
    Till its flame each heart inspire.

4 Saviour, grant the prayer we offer,
    While in simple faith we bow,
From the windows of Thy mercy
    Pour us out a blessing now.

*James L. Black.*

**256** " WITH one accord " within an
upper room      [met;
The faithful followers of Jesus
One was the hope of every waiting
soul,      [heart was set.
And on one object great each

2 " With one accord "—until the
mighty gift      [poured;
Of Pentecostal power was out-
Then forth as witnesses possessed
of God—      [Lord!
To preach the resurrection of the

3 " With one accord " within the
House of God,
A Hallelujah song is daily raised,
As with the voice of one, from
vocal hearts      [praised.
Jehovah's name is glorified and

4 Pour down Thy Spirit once again,
dear Lord;      [ter rain ";
Our cry goes up to Thee for "lat-
Unite Thy people as the "heart of
one,"      [again!
And Pentecostal days shall come
      *E. May Grimes.*

**257** SEARCH me, O God, and know
my heart to-day;
Try me, O Lord, and know my
thoughts I pray:      [me.
See if there be some wicked way in
Cleanse me from every sin and set
me free.

2 I praise Thee, Lord, for cleansing
me from sin;      [within;
Fulfil Thy Word, and make me pure
Fill me with fire, where once I
burned with shame      [name.
Grant my desire to magnify Thy

3 Lord, take my life, and make it
wholly Thine;      [love divine;
Fill my poor heart with Thy great
Take all my will, my passion, self
and pride;      [abide.
I now surrender—Lord, in me

4 O Holy Ghost, revival comes from
Thee;      [me:
Send a revival—start the work in
Thy Word declares Thou wilt sup-
ply our need;      [bly plead.
For blessing now, O Lord, I hum-
      *Edwin Orr.*

**258** THERE'S a shout in the camp,
" Keep the fires brightly
burning
All the night long,"
That the lost may return to the fold
of the shepherd
From paths of wrong.

There's a shout in the camp,
   Hallelujah ! Glory to God !
There's an echo in heaven,
   Hallelujah ! Glory to God !

2 There's a shout in the camp for the
vict'ry is coming
O'er Satan's power;
Through the word of the Lord we
the battle are gaining
This very hour.

3 There's a shout in the camp over
sinners returning
Home to the fold,
From the byways of sin with its
burden of sorrow
To joy untold.

4 There's a shout in the camp, 'tis a
glad " Hallelujah!
Praise ye the Lord!"
All who trust in His name shall re-
ceive His Salvation,
'Tis God's own word.
      *C. Austin Miles.*

**259** HERE in Thy name we are
gathered,
Come and revive us, O Lord;
" There shall be showers of bless-
ing,"
Thou hast declared in Thy word.

Oh, graciously hear us,
   Graciously hear us we pray ;
Pour from Thy windows upon us
   Showers of blessing to-day.

2 Oh! that the showers of blessing
Now on our souls may descend,
While at the footstool of mercy
Pleading Thy promise, we bend!

3 " There shall be showers of bless-
Promise that never can fail; [ing,"
Thou wilt regard our petition;
Surely our faith will prevail.

4 Showers of blessing, we need them,
Showers of blessing from Thee;
Showers of blessing, oh, grant them,
Thine all the glory shall be.
      *Jennie Garnett.*

# Section V

## THE HOLY SCRIPTURES

**260** BREAK Thou the bread of life,
Dear Lord, to me,
As Thou didst break the loaves
Beside the sea;
Beyond the sacred page
I seek Thee, Lord;
My spirit pants for Thee,
O Living Word!

2 Break Thou the bread of life,
O Lord, to me,
That hid within my heart
Thy Word may be:
Mould Thou each inward thought,
From self set free,
And let my steps be all
Controlled by Thee.

3 Open Thy Word of Truth,
That I may see
Thy message written clear
And plain for me;
Then in sweet fellowship
Walking with Thee,
Thine image on my life
Engraved will be.

4 O send Thy Spirit, Lord
Now unto me,
That He may touch my eyes,
And make me see:
Show me the truth concealed
Within Thy Word,
And in Thy Book revealed
I see the Lord.

5 Bless Thou the truth, dear Lord,
To me, to me,
As Thou didst bless the bread
By Galilee:
Then shall all bondage cease,
All fetters fall;
And I shall find my peace,
My All in All!

*Mary A. Lathbury,*
*v. 4, Alexander Groves.*

**261** STANDING on the promises of
Christ our King,       [ring:
Through eternal ages let His praises
Glory in the highest, I will shout
and sing,
Standing on the promises of God.

Stand . . . ing, stand . . . ing,
Standing on the promises of God my
Saviour,
Stand . . . ing, stand . . . ing,
I'm standing on the promises of God.

2 Standing on the promises that can-
not fail,       [and fear assail
When the howling storms of doubt
By the living word of God I shall
prevail,
Standing on the promises of God.

3 Standing on the promises I now can
see       [blood for me;
Perfect, present cleansing in the
Standing in the liberty where Christ
makes free,
Standing on the promises of God.

4 Standing on the promises of Christ
the Lord,       [strong cord,
Bound to Him eternally by love's
Overcoming daily with the Spirit's
sword,
Standing on the promises of God.

*R. Kelso Carter.*

**262** LORD, Thy Word abideth,
And our footsteps guideth,
Who its truth believeth,
Light and joy receiveth.

2 When our foes are near us,
Then Thy Word doth cheer us,
Word of consolation,
Message of salvation.

3 When the storms are o'er us,
And dark clouds before us,
Then its light directeth,
And our way protecteth.

4 Who can tell the pleasure,
Who recount the treasure,
By Thy Word imparted
To the simple-hearted?

5 Word of mercy, giving
Succour to the living;
Word of life, supplying
Comfort to the dying!

6 O that we, discerning
Its most holy learning,
Lord, may love and fear Thee,
Evermore be near Thee!

*H. W. Baker.*

**263** THY Word is like a garden, Lord,
With flowers bright and fair,
And every one that seeks may find
A lovely garland there.

2 Thy Word is like a deep, deep mine,
And jewels rich and rare
Are hidden in its mighty depths
For every searcher there.

3 Thy Word is like the starry host;
A thousand rays of light
Are seen to guide the traveller,
And make his pathway bright.

4 Thy Word is like a glorious choir,
And loud its anthems ring;
Though many tongues and parts
It is one song they sing. [unite,

5 Thy Word is like an armoury,
  Where soldiers may repair,
And find for life's long battle-day
All needful weapons there.

6 Oh! may I love Thy precious Word,
May I explore its mine!
May I its fragrant flowers glean,
May light upon me shine!

7 Oh! may I find my armour there,—
Thy Word my trusty sword;
I'll learn to fight with every foe
The battle of the Lord.

*Edwin Hodder.*

**264** How firm a foundation, ye saints of the Lord,
Is laid for your faith in His excellent Word! [He hath said,
What more can He say than to you
You who unto Jesus for refuge have fled?

2 Fear not, I am with Thee, O be not dismayed! [Thee aid:
I, I am thy God and will still give
I'll strengthen thee, help thee, and cause thee to stand,
Upheld by My righteous, omnipotent hand.

3 When through the deep waters I call thee to go, [overflow:
The rivers of grief shall not thee
For I will be with thee in trouble to bless: [distress.
And sanctify to thee thy deepest

4 The soul that on Jesus hath leaned for repose, [foes!
I will not, I will not, desert to its
That soul, though all hell should endeavour to shake, [sake!
I'll never, no, never, no, never for-

*George Keith.*

**265** THY Word, O Lord, Thy precious Word alone,
Can lead me on;
By this, until the darksome night
Lead Thou me on; [be gone,
Thy Word is light, Thy Word is life and power, [hour!
By it, O guide me in each trying

2 This all I have; around no light
O lead me on! [appears,
With eyes on Thee, though gazing through my tears,
Lead Thou me on!
The good and best might lead me far astray, [I pray!
Omniscient Saviour, lead Thou me,

3 Whate'er my path, led by Thy
O lead me on! [Word, 'tis good;
Be my poor heart Thy blessèd Word's abode,
Lead Thou me on!
Thy Holy Spirit gives the light to see, [following Thee!
And leads me, by Thy Word, close

4 Led by aught else, I tread a devious
O lead me on! [way:
Speak, Lord, and help me ever to
Lead Thou me on! [obey,
My every step shall then be well defined, [mind!
And all I do according to Thy

*A. Midlane.*

**266** INSPIRER of the ancient seers,
Who wrote from Thee the sacred page, [years;
The same through all succeeding
To us, in our degenerate age,
The spirit of Thy Word impart,
And breathe the life into our heart.

2 While now Thine oracles we read
    With earnest prayer and strong
       desire,        [ceed.
Oh, let Thy Spirit from Thee pro-
Our souls to awaken and inspire,
Our weakness help, our darkness
    chase,
And guide us by the light of grace.

3 Whene'er in error's paths we rove,
    The living God through sin for-
       sake,        [prove,
Our conscience by Thy Word re-
Convince and bring the wanderers
    back.        [sword,
Deep wounded by Thy Spirit's
And then by Gilead's balm re-
    stored.

4 The sacred lessons of Thy grace,
    Transmitted through Thy Word,
       repeat,
And train us up in all Thy ways,
    To make us in Thy will com-
       plete;
Fulfil Thy love's redeeming plan,
And bring us to a perfect man.

5 Furnish'd out of Thy treasury,
    Oh, may we always ready stand
To help the souls redeemed by Thee.
    In what their various states de-
       mand        [prove,
To teach, convince, correct, re-
And build them up in holiest love!
*Charles Wesley.*

**267**  THE Spirit breathes upon the
       Word,
    And brings the truth to sight;
Precepts and promises afford,
    A sanctifying light.

2 A glory gilds the sacred page,
    Majestic, like the sun:
It gives a light to every age,
    It gives, but borrows none.

3 The Hand that gave it still supplies
    The gracious light and heat;
Its truths upon the nations rise—
    They rise, but never set.

4 Let everlasting thanks be Thine
    For such a bright display,
As makes a world of darkness shine
    With beams of heavenly day.

5 My soul rejoices to pursue
    The steps of Him I love,
Till glory breaks upon my view
    In brighter worlds above.
*William Cowper.*

**268**  O WORD of God incarnate,
       O wisdom from on high,
O truth unchanged, unchanging,
    O Light of our dark sky,
We praise Thee for the radiance
    That from the hallowed page,
A lantern to our footsteps,
    Shines on from age to age.

2 The Church from her dear Master
    Received the gift divine,
And still that light she lifteth,
    O'er all the earth to shine;
It is the golden casket
    Where gems of truth are stored;
It is the heaven-drawn picture
    Of Christ, the living Word;

3 It floateth like a banner
    Before God's host unfurled;
It shineth like a beacon
    Above the darkling world;
It is the chart and compass
    That, o'er life's surging sea,
'Mid mists, and rocks, and quick-
       sands,
    Still guides, O Christ, to Thee.

4 O make Thy Church, dear Saviour,
    A lamp of burnished gold,
To bear before the nations
    Thy true light, as of old;
O teach Thy wandering pilgrims
    By this their path to trace,
Till, clouds and darkness ended,
    They see Thee face to face.
*W. W. How.*

**269**  COME, O Thou Prophet of the
       Lord,
    Thou great interpreter divine,
Explain Thine own transmitted
    word,
    To teach and to inspire is Thine,
Thou only canst Thyself reveal,
Open the book and loose the seal.

2 Whate'er the ancient prophets spoke
    Concerning Thee, O Christ, make
       known;
Chief subject of the sacred book,
    Thou fillest all, and Thou alone;
Yet there our Lord we cannot see,
Unless Thy Spirit lend the key.

3 Now, Jesus, now the veil remove,
　The folly of our darkened heart;
Unfold the wonders of Thy love,
　The knowledge of Thyself im-
　　part:
Our ear, our inmost soul, we bow,
　Speak, Lord, Thy servants hearken
　now.　　　　　*Charles Wesley.*

**270**　HUNGRY, Lord, for Thy word
　　　　of truth,
　Sitting at my Saviour's feet;
Rising, gleaning, just like Ruth,
　Feed me on the finest of the
　wheat.

Bread of life it is now to me,
　Honey, wine and meat ;
In Thy love I will ever be
　Fed upon the finest of the wheat.

2 Work for the Master I will do,
　Trusting in His strength so great;
Living in His pastures new,
　Feed me on the finest of the
　wheat.

3 Then to the harvest let us go,
　Reaping in His fields so sweet;
Workers for Jesus, He wants you
　Fed upon the finest of the wheat.
　　　　　　　　*F. A. Graves.*

**271**　THY words unto my taste are
　　　　sweet,　　　　　[love;
　O Lord of hosts, Thy truth I
The light it sheds before my feet
　Streams from Thy dazzling place
　above.

2 O joy, within the page to find
　Such wondrous treasures all my
　own;
To trace the mysteries of Thy mind,
　And reach the splendours of Thy
　throne!

3 No human wisdom touched that
　height,　　　　　　[strain;
　No creature tongue sang that high
Thy breath breathed forth the holy
　light,　　,　　　　　[plain.
　Thy finger scrolled the message

4 Yet, Mighty Word, Thou stoopedst
　low
　To faltering lip and feeble hand,
For humble men spake long ago
　Such wisdom as Thy Spirit
　planned,

5 To profit him that hungereth
　With rich delight and doctrine
　pure,　　　　　　　[faith
To quicken love and strengthen
　And make his heavenly calling
　sure.

6 O Truth, who grandly traced the
　Way,
　O Love, who trod it with delight,
Grant all Thy children grace, we
　pray,　　　　　　　[sight.
　To walk well-pleasing in Thy
　　　　　　　　*Harold Horton.*

**272**　OH, wonderful, wonderful
　　　　Word of the Lord!
　True wisdom its pages unfold:
And though we may read them a
　thousand times o'er.
They never, no, never grow old.
Each line hath a treasure, each pro-
　mise a pearl,
　That all if they will may secure;
And we know that when time and
　the world pass away,
　God's Word shall for ever endure.

2 Oh, wonderful, wonderful Word of
　the Lord!
　The Lamp that our Father above
So kindly has lighted to teach us
　the way　　　　　　[love!
　That leads to the arms of His
Its warnings, its counsels, are faith-
　ful and just;　　　　[pure;
　Its judgments are perfect and
And we know that when time and
　the world pass away,
　God's Word shall for ever endure.

3 Oh, wonderful, wonderful Word of
　the Lord!
　Our only salvation is there;
It carries conviction down deep in
　the heart,
　And shows us ourselves as we are.
It tells of a Saviour, and points to
　the cross,　　　　　[secure;
　Where pardon we now may
For we know that when time and
　the world pass away,
　God's Word shall for ever endure.

4 Oh, wonderful, wonderful Word of
  the Lord!                [past!
  The hope of our friends in the
  Its truth where so firmly they an-
      chored their trust,
  Through ages eternal shall last.
Oh, wonderful, wonderful Word of
  the Lord!
  Unchanging, abiding, and sure;
For we know that when time and
  the world pass away,
Gods Word shall for ever endure.
                        *Julia Sterling.*

**273** FATHER of mercies, in Thy
        Word
What endless glory shines!
For ever be Thy name adored
For these celestial lines.

2 Here may the wretched sons of
  Exhaustless riches find;    [want
Riches, above what earth can grant,
  And lasting as the mind.

3 Here the fair tree of knowledge
  And yields a free repast;  [grows,
Sublimer sweets than nature knows
  Invite the longing taste.

4 Here the Redeemer's welcome voice
  Spreads heavenly peace around;
And life and everlasting joys
  Attend the blissful sound.

5 Divine instructor, gracious Lord,
  Be Thou for ever near;
Teach me to love Thy sacred Word,
  And view my Saviour there.
                        *Anne Steele.*

# Section VI

# THE GOSPEL

## (1) PROCLAMATION AND INVITATION

**274** "WHOSOEVER heareth!" shout,
        shout the sound!
Send the blessèd tidings all the
  world around!  [man is found:
Spread the joyful news wherever
  "Whosoever will may come."

"Whosoever will!" "whosoever will!"
Send the proclamation over vale and hill:
'Tis the loving Father calls the wanderer
  home;
"Whosoever will may come."

2 Whosoever cometh need not delay;
Now the door is open, enter while
  you may;            [Way,
Jesus is the true and only Living
  "Whosoever will may come."

3 "Whosoever will!" the promise is
  secure;            [endure;
"Whosoever will," for ever shall
"Whosoever will"—'tis life for
  evermore;
  "Whosoever will may come."
                        *P. P. Bliss.*

**275** ALL ye that pass by,
        To Jesus draw nigh:

To you is it nothing that Jesus
  should die?
  Your ransom and peace,
  Your surety He is:    [like His.
Come, see if there ever was sorrow

2   For what you have done
    His blood must atone:
The Father hath stricken for you
    His dear Son.
    The Lord, in the day
    Of His anger, did lay
Your sins on the Lamb, and He
    bore them away.

3   He answered for all:
    O come at His call,  [ment fall!
And low at His cross with astonish-
    But lift up your eyes
    At Jesus' cries:        [dies.
Impassive, He suffers; immortal, He

4   He dies to atone
    For sins not His own;
Your debt He hath paid, and your
    work He hath done.
    Ye all may receive
    The peace He did leave,
Who made intercession — "My
    Father, forgive!"

5  For you and for me
    He prayed on the tree:
The prayer is accepted, the sinner
    That sinner am I,     [is free.
    Who on Jesus rely,  [not deny.
And come for the pardon God will

6  My pardon I claim;
    For a sinner I am,
A sinner believing in Jesus' name.
    He purchased the grace
    Which now I embrace:
O Father, Thou know'st He hath
    died in my place.

7  His death is my plea;
    My Advocate see,
And hear the blood speak that hath
    answered for me.
    My ransom He was
    When He bled on the cross;
And by losing His life He hath
    carried my cause.

*Charles Wesley.*

**276**  WONDERFUL story of love; tell
    it to me again;
Wonderful story of love; wake the
    immortal strain!
Angels with rapture announce it,
    shepherds with wonder receive it;
Sinner, O won't you believe it?
    wonderful story of love.

    Won . . .der . . .ful ! Won . . .der . . .ful !
    Won . . .der . . .ful !
    Wonderful story of love !

2 Wonderful story of love; though
    you are far away;
Wonderful story of love; still He
    doth call to-day;
Calling from Calvary's mountain,
    down from the crystal bright
    fountain,
E'en from the dawn of creation,
    wonderful story of love.

3 Wonderful story of love; Jesus
    provides a rest;
Wonderful story of love; for all the
    pure and blest;
Rest in those mansions above us,
    with those who've gone on be-
    fore us,
Singing the rapturous chorus, won-
    derful story of love.

*J. M. Driver.*

**277**  HARK! the gospel news is
    sounding,
    Christ has suffered on the tree;
Streams of mercy are abounding,
    Grace for all is rich and free.
      Now, poor sinner,
    Come to Him who died for thee.

2 Oh! escape to yonder mountain,
    Refuge find in Him to-day;
Christ invites you to the fountain,
    Come and wash your sins away;
      Do not tarry,
    Come to Jesus while you may.

3 Grace is flowing like a river,
    Millions there have been sup-
Still it flows as fresh as ever [plied;
    From the Saviour's wounded side;
      None need perish,    [died.
    All may live, for Christ hath

4 Christ alone shall be our portion;
    Soon we hope to meet above;
Then we'll bathe in the full ocean
    Of the great Redeemer's love;
      All His fulness
    We shall then forever prove.

*H. Bourne and W. Sanders.*

**278**  THE cross it standeth fast:
      Hallelujah! hallelujah!
Defying ev'ry blast:
      Hallelujah! hallelujah!
The winds of hell have blown,
The world its hate hath shown,
Yet it is not overthrown:
      Hallelujah for the cross!

    Hallelujah, hallelujah, hallelujah for the
      cross !
    Hallelujah, hallelujah, it shall never suffer
      loss !

2 It is the old cross still:
      Hallelujah! hallelujah!
Its triumph let us tell:
      Hallelujah! hallelujah!
The grace of God here shone
Through Christ the blessèd Son,
Who did for sin atone:
      Hallelujah for the cross!

3 'Twas here the debt was paid:
      Hallelujah! hallelujah!
Our sins on Jesus laid:
      Hallelujah! hallelujah!
So round the cross we sing
Of Christ our offering,
Of Christ our living King:
      Hallelujah for the cross!

*Horatius Bonar, arr.*

**279** SINNERS Jesus will receive!
　　　Sound this word of grace to
　　　　　all
Who the heavenly pathway leave,
　All who linger, all who fall!

Sing it o'er . . . and o'er again, . . .
Christ receiv . . . eth sinful men ; . . .
Make the mes . . . sage clear and plain : . . .
Christ receiveth sinful men.

2 Come: and He will give you rest;
　Trust Him; for His word is plain;
He will take the sinfulest;
　Christ receiveth sinful men.

3 Now my heart condemns me not,
　Pure before the law I stand;
He who cleansed me from all spot
　Satisfied its last demand.

4 Christ receiveth sinful men,
　Even me with all my sin;
Purged from every spot and stain,
　Heaven with Him I enter in.
*Neumeister ; arr. D. W. W.*

**280** "COME unto Me, ye weary,
　　　And I will give you rest:"
Oh, blessèd voice of Jesus,
　Which comes to hearts oppressed!
It tells of benediction,
　Of pardon, grace, and peace,
Of joy that hath no ending,
　Of love which cannot cease.

2 "Come unto Me, ye wanderers,
　And I will give you light:"
Oh, loving voice of Jesus,
　Which comes to cheer the night!
Our hearts were filled with sadness,
　And we had lost our way;
But morning brings us gladness,
　And songs the break of day.

3 "And whosoever cometh,
　I will not cast him out:"
Oh, welcome voice of Jesus,
　Which drives away our doubt,
Which calls us very sinners,
　Unworthy though we be
Of love so free and boundless,
　To come, dear Lord, to Thee!
*W. C. Dix.*

**281** COME, let us sing of a wonder-
　　　ful love,
　　Tender and true;　　　[above,
Out of the heart of the Father

Streaming to me and to you.
　Wonderful love,
Dwells in the heart of the Father
　above.

2 Jesus the Saviour this Gospel to
　　Joyfully came—　　　　[tell
　Came with the helpless and hope-
　　less to dwell,
　Sharing their sorrow and shame:
　　Seeking the lost,
Saving, redeeming at measureless
　cost.

3 Jesus is seeking the wanderers yet—
　　Why do they roam?　　　[get:
　Love only waits to forgive and for-
　　Home! weary wanderers, home!
　　Wonderful love,
Dwells in the heart of the Father
　above.

4 Come to my heart, O Thou won-
　　derful love!
　　Come and abide;
Lifting my life till it rises above
　Envy and falsehood and pride:
　　Seeking to be,
Lowly and humble, a learner of
　Thee.
*Robert Walmsley.*

**282** LOOK to Jesus, and be saved,
　　　See Him hanging on the tree;
Guilty art thou and enslaved,
　But He bears thy guilt for thee.

2 Look, till thou canst see thy sin
　In His body crucified;
All the lusts that lurked within,
　All thy wilfulness and pride.

3 Look, and see the judgment fall
　On that guiltless, guilt-bowed
　　head;
He is made our sin: for all
　One hath died, and all are dead.

4 Look to Jesus, look and live,
　He has died thy death for thee;
Look, and trust, and love, and give
　All thou art His prize to be.

5 Look with awe, till wondering love
　Melts thy heart and dims thine
　　eyes,
And, with prostrate saints above,
　Rapt in praise thy spirit lies.
*W. Hay Aitken.*

**283** COME, ye sinners, lost and
hopeless,
Jesus' blood can make you free;
For He saved the worst among you,
When He saved a wretch like me.

And I know, . . . yes, I know, . . .
Jesus' blood can make the vilest sinner
clean. . . .

2 To the faint He giveth power,
Through the mountain makes a
way;
Findeth water in the desert,
Turns the night to golden day.

3 In temptation He is near thee,
Holds the powers of hell at bay;
Guides you to the path of safety,
Gives you grace for every day.

4 He will keep thee while the ages
Roll throughout eternity;
Though earth hinders and hell
rages,
All must work for good to thee.

*Mrs. A. W. Waterman.*

**284** JESUS only is our Message,
Jesus all our theme shall be,
We will lift up Jesus ever,
Jesus only will we see.

Jesus, only, Jesus ever,
Jesus all in all we sing ;
Saviour, Sanctifier, Healer,
Glorious Lord and coming King.

2 Jesus only is our Saviour,
All our guilt He bore away,
All our righteousness He gives us,
All our strength from day to day.

3 Jesus is our Sanctifier,
Cleansing us from self and sin,
And with all His Spirit's fulness,
Filling all our hearts within.

4 Jesus only is our Healer,
All our sicknesses He bare,
And His risen life and fulness,
All His members still may share.

5 Jesus only is our Power,
His the gift of Pentecost;
Jesus, breathe Thy power upon us,
Fill us with the Holy Ghost.

6 And for Jesus we are waiting,
Listening for the Advent call,
But 'twill still be Jesus only,
Jesus ever, all in all.

*A. B. Simpson.*

**285** COME, sinners, to the gospel
feast,
Let every soul be Jesus' guest;
Ye need not one be left behind,
For God hath bidden all mankind.

2 Sent by my Lord, on you I call;
The invitation is to all:
Come, all the world; come, sinner,
thou!
All things in Christ are ready now.

3 Come, all ye souls by sin oppressed,
Ye restless wanderers after rest,
Ye poor, and maimed, and halt, and
blind,
In Christ a hearty welcome find.

4 His love is mighty to compel;
His conquering love consent to feel,
Yield to His love's resistless power,
And fight against your God no
more.

5 This is the time; no more delay!
This is the Lord's accepted day;
Come in, this moment, at His call,
And live for Him who died for all.

*Charles Wesley.*

**286** THERE is a cleansing fountain,
It flows from Calvary,
'Twas opened by the Saviour,
From sin each soul to free:
And now His voice is calling
With accents, oh, so sweet—
" Come to the cleansing river,
Down at the Mercy-seat!"

Oh ! Calvary's stream is flowing,
Calvary's stream is flowing,
Flowing so free for you and for me,
Calvary's stream is flowing.

2 Though worn and heavy laden,
And burdened with your sin,
There's virtue in the river—
Oh, will you enter in?
There's healing in its waters,
There's cleansing in its stream;
Then look away to Calv'ry
Where mercy's light does beam.

3 This stream of life eternal
For you is flowing free;
Oh, bow yourself for cleansing,
And gain your liberty.
Then Christ shall be your Saviour,
And out of you shall flow
A life of peace and heaven,
God's Paradise below.

*J. C. Bateman.*

**287** I LOVE to tell the story
    Of unseen things above,
Of Jesus and His glory.
    Of Jesus and His love;
I love to tell the story
    Because I know it's true,
It satisfies my longing,
    As nothing else would do.

2 I love to tell the story,
    More wonderful it seems
Than all the golden fancies
    Of all the golden dreams;
I love to tell the story,
    It did so much for me,
And this is just the reason
    I tell it now to thee.

3 I love to tell the story,
    'Tis pleasant to repeat
What seems, each time I tell it,
    More wonderfully sweet:
I love to tell the story,
    For some have never heard
The message of salvation
    From God's own holy Word.

4 I love to tell the story,
    For those who know it best
Seem hungering and thirsting
    To hear it, like the rest;
And when, in scenes of glory,
    I sing the new, new song,
'Twill be—the old, old story
    That I have loved so long.
                        *Kate Hankey.*

**288** WOULD you be free from your
        burden of sin?
    There's power in the blood,
        power in the blood;
Would you o'er evil a victory win?
    There's wonderful power in the
        blood.

    There is power . . . power, wonder-working
        power
    In the blood . . . of the Lamb . . .
    There is power, . . . power, wonder-working
        power
    In the precious blood of the Lamb.

2 Would you be free from your pas-
        sion and pride?
    There's power in the blood, power
        in the blood;                [tide,
Come for a cleansing to Calvary's
    There's wonderful power in the
        blood.

3 Would you be whiter, much whiter
        than snow?
    There's power in the blood,
        power in the blood;    [flow,
Sin stains are lost in its life-giving
    There's wonderful power in the
        blood.

4 Would you do service for Jesus
        your King?
    There's power in the blood,
        power in the blood;    [to sing?
Would you live daily His praises
    There's wonderful power in the
        blood.            *L. E. Jones.*

**289** O WHAT a Saviour that He
        died for me!
From condemnation He hath made
        me free;            [saith He,
    " He that believeth on the Son,"
    " Hath everlasting life."

    " Verily, verily," I say unto you,
    " Verily, verily," message ever new ;
    " He that believeth on the Son " 'tis true,
    " Hath everlasting life."

2 All my iniquities on Him were laid,
    All my indebtedness by Him was
        paid;            [hath said,
    All who believe on Him, the Lord
    " Have everlasting life."

3 Though poor and needy I can trust
        my Lord,            [His word;
    Though weak and sinful I believe
    O glad message! ev'ry child of God
    " Hath everlasting life."

4 Though all unworthy, yet I will not
        doubt,            [cast out.
    For him that cometh, He will not
    " He that believeth," O the good
        news shout,
    " Hath everlasting life."
                    *Jas. McGranahan.*

**290** THERE is joy in the presence of
        the angels in heaven,
    When a sinner returns to his
        God;
    When in humble faith he welcomes
        the forgiveness freely given
    Through the shedding of the
        Saviour's precious Blood.

    And this joy is mine, . . .
    Boundless and Divine, . . .
Since I hearkened to the Gospel of His grace.

2 There is joy to the Father when He
    sees His erring son
  Coming back from his folly and
    shame;
  As he weeps in deep contrition o'er
    the sin that he has done,
  Pleading nothing but the worth of
    Jesus' name.

3 There is joy in the bosom of the
    Shepherd homeward bound,
  With the sheep on His shoulders
    strong;
  Though so weary, faint and bleat-
    ing, yet the wand'ring one is
    found,
  And the night is turned to noon-
    day with a song.

4 There is joy overflowing unto all
    who will believe,
  Who on Jesus will wholly rely;
  He will fully cleanse and pardon,
    He will comfort and relieve,
  Filling all the days with glory
    from on high.

5 Come, then, turn to the Saviour,
    seek Him now with heart and
    voice,        [love;
  And respond to the call of His
  Dare to take Him as your choice
    and He will cause you to rejoice,
  Till you hear His "Welcome
    home!" to realms above.

    And this joy Divine,
    Will be surely thine,
  If you hearken to the Gospel of His grace.
                *L. F. W. Woodford.*

**291**  COME thou with us, O soul
    oppressed, and we will do
    thee good;
  We are the people of the Lord re-
    deemed by Jesus' blood.
  He called us out of darkness, from
    the thraldom of our sin,
  And He gave us life and liberty,
    His peace and joy within.

    O come with us, we pray, this bright and
      heavenly way,
    The way of life, the way of joy and peace.
    If you come, for come you may, you will
      share with us to-day
    The pleasures of His love that never cease.

2 Come thou with us, there's room
    for all, and we will do thee good.
  Clear waters gush from out the
    Rock; we feast on heavenly food.
  He leads us by His Presence and
    His word of sure command,
  And He guides us o'er the desert
    to a broad celestial land.

3 Come thou with us, with firm re-
    solve, and we will do thee good;
  Now plant thy feet upon the road
    the saints of old have trod.
  Forsake the path of sin and choose
    the highway of the King,
  Where the ransomed of the Lord
    delight His saving grace to sing.

4 Come thou with us—for time is
    short—and we will do thee good;
  Nor linger till, alas, you find you
    cannot if you would.
  O haste to join us, even now, and
    swell the mighty throng
  Marching on with everlasting joy
    and singing Zion's song.
                *L. F. W. Woodford.*

**292**  THERE is no love like the love
    of Jesus—
  Never to fade or fall,
  Till into the fold of the peace of
  He has gathered us all.    [God

    Jesus' love, precious love,
      Boundless and pure and free ;
    Oh, turn to that love, weary wandering soul :
      Jesus pleadeth with thee !

2 There is no eye like the eye of
    Piercing so far away;    [Jesus,
  Ne'er out of the sight of its tender
  Can the wanderer stray.    [light

3 There is no voice like the voice of
    Jesus,
  Tender and sweet its chime,
  Like musical ring of a flowing
    spring
  In the bright summer time.

4 There is no heart like the heart of
    Jesus,
  Filled with a tender love;
  No throb nor throe that our hearts
    can know,
  But He feels it above.
                *W. E. Littlewood.*

**293** COME for the feast is spread;
    Hark to the call!
Come to the Living Bread,
    Broken for all;
Come to His " house of wine,"
Low on His breast recline,
All that He hath make thine;
    Come, sinner, come.

2 Come where the fountain flows—
    River of life—
Healing for all thy woes,
    Doubting and strife;
Millions have been supplied,
No one was e'er denied;
Come to the crimson tide,
    Come, sinner, come.

3 Come to the throne of grace,
    Boldly draw near;
He who would win the race
    Must tarry here;
Whate'er thy want may be
Here is the grace for thee,
Jesus thy only plea;
    Come, Christian, come.

4 Jesus, we come to Thee,
    Oh, take us in!
Set Thou our spirits free;
    Cleanse us from sin!
Then, in yon land of light,
All clothed in robes of white,
Resting not day nor night,
    Thee will we sing.   *H. Burton.*

**294** TELL me the old, old story
    Of unseen things above,
Of Jesus and His glory,
    Of Jesus and His love.
Tell me the story simply,
    As to a little child;
For I am weak and weary,
    And helpless and defiled.

2 Tell me the story slowly,
    That I may take it in,—
That wonderful redemption,
    God's remedy for sin.
Tell me the story often
    For I forget so soon!
The " early dew " of morning
    Has passed away at noon.

3 Tell me the story softly,
    With earnest tones, and grave;
Remember! I'm the sinner,
    Whom Jesus came to save.

Tell me the story always,
    If you would really be,
In any time of trouble
    A comforter to me.

4 Tell me the same old story,
    When you have cause to fear
That this world's empty glory
    Is costing me too dear.
Yes, and when that world's glory
    Is dawning on my soul,
Tell me the old, old story,
    " Christ Jesus makes thee whole."
                *Kate Hankey.*

**295** SOULS of men! why will ye
    scatter      [sheep?
Like a crowd of frightened
Foolish hearts, why will ye wander
    From a love so true and deep?

2 Was there ever kindest shepherd
    Half so gentle, half so sweet,
As the Saviour, who would have
    us
    Come and gather round His feet?

3 There's a wideness in God's mercy
    Like the wideness of the sea;
There's a kindness in His justice
    Which is more than liberty.

4 For the love of God is broader
    Than the measure of man's mind;
And the heart of the Eternal
    Is most wonderfully kind.

5 There is plentiful redemption
    In the blood that has been shed;
There is joy for all the members
    In the sorrows of the Head.

6 If our love were but more simple,
    We should take Him at His word,
And our lives would be all sun-
    shine
    In the sweetness of our Lord.
                *F. W. Faber.*

**296** 'TIS the grandest theme
    through the ages rung;
'Tis the grandest theme for a mor-
    tal tongue.  [world e'er sung,
'Tis the grandest theme that the
    " Our God is able to deliver
    thee."

    He is a . . . ble to deliver thee,
    He is a . . . ble to deliver thee :
Though by sin opprest, go to Him for rest ;
    Our God is able to deliver thee.

2 'Tis the grandest theme in the earth
    or main!       [tal strain,
'Tis the grandest theme for a mor-
'Tis the grandest theme, tell the
    world again,       [thee."
  " Our God is able to deliver

3 'Tis the grandest theme, let the tid-
    ings roll       [soul,
To the guilty heart, to the sinful
Look to God in faith, He will make
    thee whole,       [thee."
  " Our God is able to deliver
                *W. A. Ogden.*

**297** 'Twas Jesus, my Saviour, who
    died on the tree,
To open a fountain for sinners like
    me,       [don bestows,
His blood is the fountain that par-
And cleanses the foulest wherever
    it flows.

  For the conquering Saviour shall break
  every chain,
  And give us the vict'ry again and again.

2 And when I was willing with all
    things to part       [my heart,
He gave me my bounty, His love in
So now I am joined with the con-
    quering band,       [command.
Who are marching to glory at Jesus'

3 Though round me the storms of ad-
    versity roll, [compass my soul,
And the waves of destruction en-
In vain this frail vessel the tem-
    pest shall toss, [of the Cross.
My hopes rest secure on the blood

4 And when with the ransomed of
    Jesus, my Head, [shall be led,
From fountain to fountain I then
I'll fall at His feet and His mercy
    adore,       [evermore.
And sing of the blood of the Cross

5 Come, sinners, to Jesus! no longer
    delay!       [day,
A full free salvation He offers to-
Arouse your dark spirits, awake
    from your dream, [ing to Him.
And Christ will support you in com-
             *Henry Q. Wilson, arr.*

**298** Come, ye sinners, poor and
    needy,       [sore;
  Weak and wounded, sick and
Jesus ready stands to save you,

Full of pity, love and power:
  He is able,
He is willing, doubt no more.

2 Now, ye needy, come and welcome;
  God's free bounty glorify;
True belief and true repentance—
  Every grace that brings you
    Without money,       [nigh—
Come to Jesus Christ and buy.

3 Let not conscience make you linger,
  Nor of fitness fondly dream;
All the fitness He requireth
  Is to feel your need of Him:
    This He gives you—
  'Tis the Spirit's rising beam.

4 Come, ye weary, heavy-laden,
  Bruised and ruined by the Fall;
If you tarry till you're better,
  You will never come at all:
    Not the righteous—
  Sinners, Jesus came to call.

5 View Him, prostrate in the garden,
  On the ground your Maker lies!
On the awful tree behold Him,
  Hear Him cry before He dies,
    " It is finished!"
  Sinner, will not this suffice?

6 Lo, the incarnate God, ascended,
  Pleads the merit of His blood;
Venture on Him, venture wholly,
  Let no other trust intrude:
    None but Jesus
  Can do helpless sinners good.
              *J. Hart.*

**299** I've a message from the Lord,
    hallelujah !
The message unto you I'll give,
'Tis recorded in His word, hallelu-
    jah !       [live."
It is only that you " look and

  " Look and live," . . . my brother, live, . . .
  Look to Jesus now and live,
  'Tis recorded in His word, hallelujah !
  It is only that you " look and live."

2 I've a message full of love, halle-
    lujah !
  A message, O my friend, for you.
'Tis a message from above, halle-
    lujah !
  Jesus said it, and I know 'tis true.

3 Life is offered unto you, hallelujah!
  Eternal life your soul shall have,
  If you'll only look to Him, hallelujah!
  Look to Jesus who alone can save.
  
  *W. A. Ogden.*

**300** WEARY souls, that wander wide
  From the central point of bliss,
  Turn to Jesus crucified,
  Fly to those dear wounds of His;
  Sink into the cleansing flood;
  Rise into the life of God!

2 Find in Christ the way of peace,
  Peace unspeakable, unknown;
  By His pain He gives you ease,
  Life by His expiring groan;
  Rise, exalted by His fall,
  Find in Christ your all in all.

3 Oh believe the record true,
  God to you His Son hath given!
  Ye may now be happy too,
  Find on earth the life of heaven,
  Live the life of heaven above,
  All the life of glorious love.

4 This the universal bliss,
  Bliss for every soul designed;
  God's divinest promise this,
  God's great gift to all mankind:
  Blest in Christ this moment be!
  Blest to all eternity!
  
  *Charles Wesley.*

**301** BEAUTIFUL words of Jesus,
  Spoken so long ago,
  Yet, as we sing them over,
  Dearer to us they grow,
  Calling the heavy laden,
  Calling to hearts oppressed,
  "Come unto Me, ye weary,
  Come, I will give you rest."
    Hear the call of His voice so sweet ;
    Bring your load to the Saviour's feet ;
    Lean your heart on His loving breast,
    Come, O come and He will give you rest.

2 Beautiful words of Jesus,
  Cheering us, day by day;
  Throwing a gleam of sunshine
  Over a cloudy way:
  Casting on Him the burden
  We are too weak to bear,
  He will give grace sufficient,
  He will regard our prayer.

3 Beautiful words of Jesus,
  Tokens of endless rest,

When, by and by, we enter
  Into His presence blest;
  There shall we see His beauty,
  Meet with Him face to face;
  There shall we sing His glory,
  Praising His matchless grace.
  
  *E. E. Hewitt.*

**302** THE gospel bells are ringing,
  Over land, from sea to sea;
  Blessed news of free salvation
  Do they offer you and me.
  "For God so loved the world,
  That His only Son He gave!
  Whosoe'er believeth in Him
  Everlasting life shall have."
    Gospel bells ! . . . how they ring, . . .
    Over land from sea to sea ;
    Gospel bells . . . freely bring . . .
    Blessed news to you and me.

2 The gospel bells invite us
  To a feast prepared for all;
  Do not slight the invitation,
  Nor reject the gracious call.
  "I am the Bread of life;
  Eat of me, thou hungry soul;
  Though your sins be red as crimson,
  They shall be as white as wool."

3 The gospel bells give warning,
  As they sound from day to day,
  Of the fate which doth await them
  Who for ever will delay.
  "Escape thou for thy life!
  Tarry not in all the plain:
  Nor behind thee look, oh, never,
  Lest thou be consumed in pain."

4 The gospel bells are joyful
  As they echo far and wide,
  Bearing notes of perfect pardon,
  Through a Saviour crucified:
  "Good tidings of great joy
  To all people do I bring;
  Unto you is born a Saviour,
  Which is Christ, the Lord and King."  *S. Wesley Martin.*

**303** YE who the love of a mother
  have known, [may own,
  There is a love sweeter far you
  Love all-sufficient for sin to atone;
  Jesus is dearer than all.
    Dearer than all, yes, dearer than all,
    He is my King, before Him I fall ;
    No friend like Jesus my soul can enthral,
    Jesus is dearer, far dearer than all.

2 Jesus entreats you in Him to con-
    fide,        [ion and guide;
Make Him your constant compan-
He can do more than the whole
    world beside;
    Jesus is dearer than all.

3 Heaven, with all of its beauty so
    rare,        [pare;
With my Redeemer can never com-
He is the glory transcendent up
    there;
    Jesus is dearer than all.

                    *A. H. Ackley.*

**304** SOUND the gospel of grace
    abroad,
    There's life in the risen Lord.
Spread the news of the gift of God,
    There's life in the risen Lord.
    God above desires it!
    Sinful man requires it!

Tell it around, let it abound,
There's life in the risen Lord.

2 All by nature are doomed to die,
    So saith the Holy Word;
Welcome therefore the joyful cry,
    There's life in the risen Lord.
    Welcome news of gladness—
    Antidote of sadness.

3 Saints, apostles, and prophets, all
    Published with one accord,
This deliverance from the fall—
    This life in the risen Lord.
    Glory be to Jesus,
    Who from bondage frees us.

4 Pardon, power, and perfect peace
    The words of this life afford,
Never then let the tidings cease,
    Of life in the risen Lord.
    Open wide the portal,
    Unto every mortal.

                    *P. P. Bliss.*

**305** UNDER the burdens of guilt and
    care,
    Many a spirit is grieving,
Who in the joy of the Lord might
    Life everlasting receiving. [share,

    Life ! life ! eternal life !
    Jesus alone is the Giver !
    Life ! life ! abundant life !
    Glory to Jesus for ever !

2 Bearing our burden of guilt, there
    came
    One who is strong to deliver,
Bringing to men, through His won-
    drous name,
    Life " more abundant " for ever.

3 Burdened one, why will you longer
    bear
    Sorrows from which He releases?
Open your heart, and rejoicing
    share,
    Life " more abundant " in Jesus.

4 Leaving the mountain, the stream-
    let grows,
    Flooding the vale with a river;
So, from the hill of the Cross, there
    flows
    Life "more abundant" for ever.

5 Oh, for the floods on the thirsty
    land!
    Oh, for a mighty revival!
Oh, for a sanctified, fearless band,
    Ready to hail its arrival.

                    *W. Leslie.*

**306** THERE is life for a look at the
    Crucified One,     [thee.
    There is life at this moment for
Then look, sinner, look unto Him
    and be saved,     [tree.
    Unto Him who was nailed on the

    Look, look, look and live,
    There is life for a look at the Crucified One,
    There is life at this moment for thee.

2 Oh, why was He there as a Bearer
    of sin,     [laid?
    If on Jesus thy sins were not
Oh, why from His side flowed the
    sin-cleansing blood.     [paid?
    If His dying thy debt has not

3 It is not thy tears of repentance
    nor prayers,     [soul;
    But the blood that atones for the
On Him then believe, and a pardon
    receive,     [quite whole.
    For His blood can now make thee

4 We are healed by His stripes;
    wouldst thou add to the word?
    And He is our righteousness
    made;
The best robe of heaven He bids
    thee to wear,     [arrayed?
    Oh, couldst thou be better

5 Then doubt not thy welcome,
  since God has declared
There remaineth no more to be
  done;        [He appeared,
That once in the end of the world
And completed the work He begun.

6 But take, with rejoicing, from Jesus
  at once
The life everlasting He gives;
And know with assurance thou
  never canst die,        [lives.
Since Jesus thy righteousness
                      *Asa M. Hull.*

**307** FREE from the law, oh, happy
  condition,        [mission,
Jesus hath bled, and there is re-
Cursed by the law and bruised by
  the fall,        [all.
Grace hath redeemed us once for

  Once for all, oh, sinner receive it,
  Once for all, oh, brother believe it;
  Cling to the Cross, the burden will fall,
  Christ hath redeemed us once for all.

2 Now are we free—there's no con-
  demnation,
Jesus provides a perfect salvation;
" Come unto Me," oh, hear His
  sweet call,
Come, and He saves us once for all.

3 " Children of God," oh, glorious
  calling,        [falling;
Surely His grace will keep us from
Passing from death to life at His
  call,
Blessed salvation once for all.
                      *P. P. Bliss.*

**308** COME to the Saviour, make no
  delay;        [the way;
Here in His Word He has shown us
Here in our midst He's standing to-
Tenderly saying, " Come!" [day,

  Joyful, joyful will the meeting be,
  When from sin our hearts are pure and free,
  And we shall gather, Saviour, with Thee,
  In our eternal home.

2 "Suffer the children!" oh, hear His
  voice!        [joice!
Let every heart leap forth and re-
And let us freely make Him our
  Do not delay, but come. [choice,

3 Think once again, He's with us to-
  day;        [obey;
Heed now His blest command and

Hear now His accents tenderly say,
" Will you, My children, come?"
                      *George F. Root.*

**309** HAVE you been to Jesus for the
  cleansing power?
Are you washed in the blood of
  the Lamb?        [this hour?
Are you fully trusting in His grace
Are you washed in the blood of
  the Lamb?

  Are you washed . . . in the blood . . .
    In the soul-cleansing blood of the Lamb?
  Are your garments spotless? Are they
    white as snow?
  Are you washed in the blood of the Lamb?

2 Are you walking daily by the
  Saviour's side?        [the Lamb?
Are you washed in the blood of
Do you rest each moment in the
  Crucified?        [the Lamb?
Are you washed in the blood of

3 When the Bridegroom cometh will
  your robes be white?
Pure and white in the blood of
  the Lamb?        [mansions bright,
Will your soul be ready for the
And be washed in the blood of
  the Lamb?

4 Lay aside the garments that are
  stained by sin,        [the Lamb;
And be washed in the blood of
There's a fountain flowing for the
  soul unclean,        [Lamb.
Oh be washed in the blood of the
                      *Elisha A. Hoffman.*

## (2) WARNING AND
## REPENTANCE

**310** " ALMOST persuaded" now to
  believe;        [ceive;
" Almost persuaded" Christ to re-
Seems now some soul to say?—
" Go, Spirit, go Thy way:
  Some more convenient day
  On Thee I'll call."

2 " Almost persuaded:" come, come
  to-day!        [away!
" Almost persuaded:" turn not
  Jesus invites you here,
  Angels are lingering near,
  Prayers rise from hearts so dear,
  O wanderer, come!

3 " Almost persuaded : " harvest is
    past!     [at last!
" Almost persuaded : " doom comes
" Almost " cannot avail;
" Almost " is but to fail :
Sad, Sad, that bitter wail—
    " Almost "—*but lost*!

*P. P. Bliss.*

**311**  I HEAR Thy welcome voice,
    That calls me, Lord, to Thee
For cleansing in Thy precious blood
    That flowed on Calvary.

    I am coming, Lord,
      Coming now to Thee :
    Trusting only in the blood
      That flowed on Calvary.

2   Though coming weak and vile,
    Thou dost my strength assure :
Thou dost my vileness fully cleanse,
    Till spotless all and pure.

3   'Tis Jesus calls me on
    To perfect faith and love,
To perfect hope, and peace, and
    trust,
For earth and heaven above.

4   'Tis Jesus who confirms
    The blessed work within,
By adding grace to welcomed grace,
    Where reigned the power of sin.

5   And He the witness gives
    To loyal hearts and free,
That every promise is fulfilled,
    If faith but brings the plea.

6   All hail, atoning blood!
    All hail, redeeming grace!
All hail, the gift of Christ, our
    Lord,
    Our strength and righteousness!

*L. Hartsough.*

**312**  JESUS, lover of my soul,
    Let me to Thy bosom fly,
While the nearer waters roll.
    While the tempest still is high :
Hide me, O my Saviour, hide,
    Till the storm of life is past;
Safe into the haven guide;
    Oh, receive my soul at last.

2 Other refuge have I none;
    Hangs my helpless soul on Thee;
Leave, ah! leave me not alone,
    Still support and comfort me.

All my trust on Thee is stayed,
    All my help from Thee I bring;
Cover my defenceless head
    With the shadow of Thy wing.

3 Thou, O Christ! art all I want;
    More than all in Thee I find :
Raise the fallen, cheer the faint,
    Heal the sick, and lead the blind.
Just and holy is Thy name,
    I am all unrighteousness;
Vile and full of sin I am,
    Thou art full of truth and grace.

4 Plenteous grace with Thee is found,
    Grace to cover all my sin;
Let the healing streams abound,
    Make and keep me pure within :
Thou of life the fountain art,
    Freely let me take of Thee;
Spring Thou up within my heart,
    Rise to all eternity.

*Charles Wesley.*

**313**  TO-DAY Thy mercy calls me,
    To wash away my sin;
However great my trespass,
    Whate'er I may have been,
However long from mercy
    I may have turned away,
Thy blood, O Christ, can cleanse
    And make me white to-day. [me,

2 To-day Thy gate is open,
    And all who enter in,
Shall find a Father's welcome,
    And pardon for their sin;
The past shall be forgotten,
    A present joy be given,
A future grace be promised—
    A glorious crown in heaven.

3 O all-embracing mercy,
    Thou ever open door,
What should I do without Thee,
    When heart and eyes run o'er?
When all things seem against me,
    To drive me to despair,
I know one gate is open,
    One ear will hear my prayer.

*Oswald Allen.*

**314**  PASS me not, O gentle Saviour,
    Hear my humble cry;
While on others Thou art calling,
    Do not pass me by.

    Saviour, Saviour,
      Hear my humble cry ;
    While on others Thou art calling,
      Do not pass me by.

2 Let me, at Thy throne of mercy
Find a sweet relief;
Kneeling there in deep contrition,
Help my unbelief.

3 Trusting only in Thy merit
Would I seek Thy face;
Heal my wounded, broken spirit,
Save me by Thy grace.

4 Thou, the spring of all my comfort,
More than life to me—
Whom have I on earth beside Thee?
Whom in heaven but Thee?
*Fanny J. Crosby.*

**315** RING the bells of heaven! there
is joy to-day,
For a soul returning from the
wild; [on the way,
See! the Father meets him out up-
Welcoming His weary, wand'ring
child.

Glory ! glory ! how the angels sing !
Glory ! glory ! how the loud harps ring !
'Tis the ransomed army, like a mighty sea,
Pealing forth the anthem of the free !

2 Ring the bells of heaven! there is
joy to-day, [ciled;
For the wanderer now is recon-
Yes, a soul is rescued from his sin-
ful way, [child.
And is born anew a ransomed

3 Ring the bells of heaven! spread
the feast to-day! [strain!
Angels swell the glad triumphant
Tell the joyful tidings! bear it far
away!
For a precious soul is born again.
*W. O. Cushing.*

**316** How can a weary heart find
rest, [pressed;
By doubt dismayed, by sin op-
I strive to wash my sins away,
And weeping, pray both night and
day.

2 Hark, weary one, the work was
done
By God the Father's only Son,
Could all mankind unite to pray,
'Twould never wash one sin away.

3 For man is lost and dead in sin,
But Jesus died our souls to win,

He bore our guilt, endured our
shame,
Oh, blessèd be His holy name.

4 I now receive Him, and His power,
It fills my soul this very hour,
His changeless word I now believe,
And life eternal I receive.

**317** WHERE will you spend etern-
ity? [me!
This question comes to you and
Tell me, what shall your answer
be?
Where will you spend eternity?

2 Many are choosing Christ to-day,
Turning from all their sins away;
Heaven shall their happy portion
be:
Where will you spend eternity?

3 Leaving the strait and narrow way,
Going the downward road to-day,
Sad will the final ending be—
Lost through a long eternity!

4 Repent, believe this very hour,
Trust in the Saviour's grace and
power;
Then shall your joyous answer be,
Saved through a long eternity!
*E. A. Hoffman.*

**318** LORD, I hear of showers of
blessing,
Thou art scattering full and free.
Showers the thirsty land refreshing,
Let some drops now fall on me,
Even me.

2 Pass me not, O God, my Father,
Sinful though my heart may be,
Thou might'st leave me, but the
rather
Let Thy mercy light on me,
Even me.

3 Pass me not, O mighty Spirit,
Thou canst make the blind to see:
Witnesser of Jesus' merit,
Speak the word of power to me,
Even me.

4 Love of God, so pure and change-
less,
Blood of Christ, so rich and free;
Grace of God, so rich and bound- [less,
Magnify it all in me,
Even me.

5 Pass me not, Thy lost one bringing;
  Bind my heart, O Lord, to Thee,
Whilst the streams of life are
    springing,
  Blessing others, oh, bless me!
    Even me!   *Mrs. E. Codner.*

**319**  Depth of mercy: can there be
    Mercy still reserved for me?
Can my God his wrath forbear?
Me, the chief of sinners spare?

2 I have long withstood His grace,
  Long provoked Him to His face;
Would not hearken to His calls,
Grieved Him by a thousand falls.

3 Whence to me this waste of love?
  Ask my Advocate above!
See the cause in Jesus' face,
Now before the throne of grace.

4 There for me the Saviour stands,
  Shows His wounds, and spreads His
    hands:
God is love, I know, I feel;
Jesus lives and loves me still.

5 If I rightly read Thy heart,
  If Thou all compassion art,
Bow Thine ear, in mercy bow,
Pardon and accept me now!
            *Charles Wesley.*

**320**  When God of old the way of
    life
  Would teach to all His own,
He placed them safe beyond the
  Of death, by blood alone. [reach

    It is His word, . . . God's precious word, . . .
      It stands for ever true ;
    " When I the Lord . . . shall see the blood, . . .
      I will pass over you."

2 By Christ, the sinless Lamb of God,
  The precious blood was shed,
When He fulfilled God's holy word,
  And suffered in our stead.

3 O soul, for thee salvation thus
  By God is freely given;
The blood of Christ atones for sin,
  And makes us meet for heaven.

4 The wrath of God that was our due,
  Upon the Lamb was laid;
And by the shedding of His blood
  The debt for us was paid.

5 How calm the judgment hour shall
  To all who do obey    [pass

The word of God, and trust the
    blood,
And make that word their stay.
           *El Nathan.*

**321**  O Jesus, Thou art standing
    Outside the fast-closed door,
In lowly patience waiting
  To pass the threshold o'er.

2 Shame on us Christian brothers,
  His Name and sign who bear;
Oh, shame—thrice shame upon us
  To keep Him standing there.

3 O Jesus, Thou art knocking
  And lo! that hand is scarred,
And thorns Thy brow encircle,
  And tears Thy face have marred!

4 Oh, love that passeth knowledge,
  So patiently to wait!
Oh, sin that hath no equal,
  So fast to bar the gate!

5 O Jesus, Thou art pleading
  In accents meek and low,—
" I died for you, My children,
  And will ye treat me so?"

6 O Lord, with shame and sorrow
  We open now the door:
Dear Saviour enter, enter,
  And leave us never more!
           *W. W. How.*

**322**  Will your anchor hold in the
    storms of life?    [of strife;
When the clouds unfold their wings
When the strong tides lift and the
  cables strain,         [main?
Will your anchor drift, or firm re-

    We have an anchor that keeps the soul
    Steadfast and sure while the billows roll :
    Fastened to the Rock which cannot move,
    Grounded firm and deep in the Saviour's
      love !

2 It is safely moored, 'twill the storm
  withstand,      [our's hand;
For 'tis well secured by the Savi-
And the cables passed from His
  heart to mine,      [divine.
Can defy the blast, through strength

3 It will firmly hold in the straits of
  fear,         [reef is near,
When the breakers have told the
Though the tempest rave and the
  wild winds blow,    [o'erflow
Not an angry wave shall our bark

4 It will surely hold in the floods of
    death,          [latest breath,
When the waters cold, chill our
On the rising tide it can never fail,
While our hopes abide within the
    veil!

5 When our eyes behold, through the
    gathering night      [bright,
The city of gold, our harbour
We shall anchor fast by the heav-
    enly shore,       [more.
With the storms all past for ever-
*Priscilla J. Owens.*

## (3) GRACE AND FORGIVENESS

**323**   O WHAT a wonderful Saviour,
    In Jesus my Lord I have
    found,
Though I had sins without number,
    His grace unto me did abound.

His grace aboundeth more, . . .
His grace aboundeth more,
Though sin abounded in my heart,
His grace aboundeth more.

2 When a poor sinner He found me,
    No goodness to offer had I;
Often His law I had broken,
    And merited naught but to die.

3 Nothing of merit possessing,
    All helpless before Him I lay,
But in the precious blood flowing
    He washed all my sin-stains
    away.

4 In Him my gracious Redeemer,
    My Prophet, my Priest and my
    King;
Mercy I find and forgiveness,
    My all to His keeping I bring.

5 How can I keep from rejoicing?
    I'll sing of the joy in my soul;
Praising the love of my Saviour,
    While years of eternity roll.
*Kate Ulmer.*

**324**   AND can it be, that I should
    gain        [blood?
An interest in the Saviour's
Died He for me, who caused His
    pain?       [sued?
For me, who Him to death pur-
Amazing love! how can it be
That Thou, my God, shouldst die
    for me?

2 'Tis mystery all! The Immortal
    dies!       [design?
Who can explore His strange
In vain the first born seraph tries
    To sound the depth of love
    divine!
'Tis mercy all! let earth adore,
Let angel-minds inquire no more.

3 He left His Father's throne above
    (So free, so infinite His grace!)
Emptied Himself of all but love,
    And bled for Adam's helpless
    race:
'Tis mercy all, immense and free,
For, O my God, it found out me!

4 Long my imprisoned spirit lay
    Fast bound in sin and nature's
    night;
Thine eye diffused a quickening ray,
    I woke, the dungeon flamed with
    light:
My chains fell off, my heart was
    free,       [Thee.
I rose, went forth, and followed

5 No condemnation now I dread,
    Jesus, and all in Him, is mine;
Alive in Him, my living Head,
    And clothed in righteousness
    divine.
Bold I approach the eternal throne,
And claim the crown, through
    Christ, my own. *Charles Wesley.*

**325**   GRACE! 'tis a charming sound,
    Harmonious to the ear,
Heaven with the echo shall
    resound,
    And all the earth shall hear.

Saved by grace alone !
This is all my plea ;
Jesus died for all mankind,
And Jesus died for me.

2   'Twas grace that wrote my name
    In life's eternal book;   [Lamb,
'Twas grace that gave me to the
    Who all my sorrows took.

3   Grace taught my wand'ring feet
    To tread the heavenly road,
And new supplies each hour I meet,
    While pressing up to God.

4   Grace taught my soul to pray,
    And made mine eyes o'erflow;
'Tis grace has kept me to this day,
    And will not let me go.

5 Oh, let Thy grace inspire
My soul with strength divine!
May all my powers to Thee aspire,
And all my days be Thine.
*P. Doddridge.*

**326** JESUS, the name high over all,
In hell, or earth, or sky;
Angels and men before it fall
And devils fear and fly.

2 He breaks the power of cancelled
And sets the prisoner free; [sin,
His blood can make the foulest
His blood avails for me. [clean,

3 Jesus! the name to sinners dear,
The name to sinners given;
It scatters all their guilty fear;
It turns their hell to heaven.

4 Jesus the prisoner's fetters breaks,
And bruises Satan's head, [speaks,
Power into strengthless souls He
And life unto the dead.

5 Oh, that the world might taste and
The riches of His grace! [see
The arms of love that compass me
Would all mankind embrace.
*Charles Wesley.*

**327** O SWEET is the story of Jesus,
The wonderful Saviour of
men, [ner—
Who suffered and died for the sin-
I'll tell it again and again!

O won . . . derful, wonderful sto . . . ry,
The dear . . . est that ever was told, . . .
I'll repeat it in glo . . . ry, the wonderful
sto . . . ry,
Where I . . . shall His beauty behold. . . .

2 He came from the brightest of glory;
His blood as a ransom He gave,
To purchase eternal redemption,
And oh, He is mighty to save!

3 His mercy flows on like a river,
His love is unmeasured and free;
His grace is for ever sufficient,
It reaches and purifies me.
*C. H. Gabriel.*

**328** THE great Physician now is
near,
The sympathising Jesus;
He speaks the drooping heart to
cheer,
Oh, hear the voice of Jesus.

Sweetest note in seraph song,
Sweetest name on mortal tongue ;
Sweetest carol ever sung,
Jesus, blessed Jesus.

2 Your many sins are all forgiven,
Oh, hear the voice of Jesus:
Go on your way in peace to heaven,
And wear a crown with Jesus.

3 All glory to the dying Lamb!
I now believe in Jesus;
I love the blessed Saviour's name,
I love the name of Jesus.

4 His name dispels my guilt and fear,
No other name but Jesus,
Oh! how my soul delights to hear
The precious name of Jesus.
*Wm. Hunter.*

**329** IN the misty days of yore,
Jesus' precious blood had
power;
E'en the thief upon the Cross to
save; [home in Paradise,
Like a bird his spirit flies to its
Through the power of Calv'ry's
crimson wave.

And the blood . . . has never lost its
power, . . .
No, never ; . . . no, never ; . . .
Jesus' blood . . . avails for sin for ever, . . .
And will never lose its power.

2 I was lost and steeped in guilt, but
the blood for sinners spilt
Washed away my sins and set me
free;
Now and evermore the same,
praise, oh, praise His holy
name! [be.
Will the cleansing stream availing

3 God in mercy asks you why, brother sinner, will you die,
When such full redemption He
provides?
You have but to look and live, life
eternal He will give,
For the power of Calv'ry still
abides.

4 Bring your burdens, come to-day,
turn from all your sins away,
He can fully save and sanctify;
From the wrath to come now flee,
let your name recorded be
With the blood-washed, and re-
deem'd on high.
*Mrs. C. H. Morris.*

**330** In evil long I took delight,
    Unawed by shame or fear,
Till a new object met my sight
And stopped my wild career.

  Oh, the Lamb ! the bleeding Lamb !
    The Lamb of Calvary !
  The Lamb that was slain,
  That liveth again
    To intercede for me.

2 I saw One hanging on a tree
    In agonies and blood,
Who fixed His languid eyes on me,
    As near His cross I stood.

3 My conscience felt and owned my
      guilt,
    And plunged me in despair;
I saw my sins His blood had spilt,
    And helped to nail Him there.

4 A second look He gave which said,
    " I freely all forgive;
This blood is for thy ransom paid;
    I die that thou mayst live."

5 Thus while His death my sin dis-
    In all its blackest hue,   [plays
Such is the mystery of grace,
    It seals my pardon, too.
                *John Newton.*

**331** A ruler once came to Jesus
    by night,    [and light;
To ask Him the way of salvation
The Master made answer in words
    true and plain,
  " Ye must be born again !"

    " Ye must be born again ! . . .
    Ye must be born again ! . . .
    I verily, verily say unto you :
    Ye must be born again ! "

2 Ye children of men attend to the
    word    [Lord,
So solemnly uttered by Jesus, the
And let not this message to you be
    in vain,
  " Ye must be born again !"

3 O ye who would enter the glorious
    rest,    [song of the blest;
And sing with the ransomed the
The life everlasting if ye would
  " Ye must be born again."   [obtain,

4 A dear one in heaven thy heart
    yearns to see,    [ing for thee;
At the beautiful gates may be watch-
Then list to the note of this solemn
    refrain,
  " Ye must be born again."
                *W. T. Sleeper.*

**332** Years I spent in vanity and
    pride,
Caring not my Lord was crucified,
Knowing not it was for me He died
    On Calvary.

  Mercy there was great and grace was free,
  Pardon there was multiplied to me,
  There my burdened soul found liberty,
    At Calvary.

2 By God's Word at last my sin I
    learned,    [spurned,
Then I trembled at the law I'd
Till my guilty soul, imploring turned
    To Calvary.

3 Now I've given to Jesus everything,
Now I gladly own Him as my King,
Now my raptured soul can only
    Of Calvary.    [sing

4 Oh! the love that drew salvation's
    plan,    [to man,
Oh! the grace that brought it down
Oh! the mighty gulf that God did
    At Calvary.    [span
                *Wm. R. Newell.*

**333** What can wash away my
    stain?
Nothing but the blood of Jesus,
What can make me whole again?
Nothing but the blood of Jesus.

  Oh, precious is the flow
  That makes me white as snow ;
  No other fount I know,
  Nothing but the blood of Jesus.

2 For my cleansing this I see—
    Nothing but the blood of Jesus;
For my pardon this my plea,—
    Nothing but the blood of Jesus.

3 Nothing can for sin atone,
    Nothing but the blood of Jesus:
Nought of good that I have done,
    Nothing but the blood of Jesus.

4 This is all my hope and peace—
    Nothing but the blood of Jesus:
He is all my righteousness—
    Nothing but the blood of Jesus.

5 Now by this I overcome:
    Nothing but the blood of Jesus:
Now by this I'll reach my home:
    Nothing but the blood of Jesus!
                *R. Lowry.*

**334** GOD loved the world of sin-
ners lost
And ruined by the fall;
Salvation full, at highest cost,
He offers free to all.
Oh, 'twas love, 'twas wondrous love !
The love of God to me ;
It brought my Saviour from above,
To die on Calvary.

2 Eternal praises, Lord, to Thee,
Thou blessèd Son of God;
For Thy deep love in cleansing me,
In Thy most precious blood.

3 Love brings the glorious fulness in,
And to His saints makes known
The blessèd rest from inbred sin
Through faith in Christ alone.

4 Believing souls, rejoicing go;
There shall to you be given
A glorious foretaste, here below,
Of endless life in heaven.

5 Of victory now o'er Satan's power
Let all the ransomed sing,
And triumph in the dying hour
Through Christ, the Lord, our
King.        *Mrs. M. M. Stockton.*

**335** THERE is a fountain filled with
blood,
Drawn from Immanuel's veins,
And sinners plunged beneath that
flood
Lose all their guilty stains.

2 The dying thief rejoiced to see
That fountain in his day;
And there may I, though vile as he,
Wash all my sins away.

3 I do believe, I will believe,
That Jesus died for me!
That on the cross He shed His
blood,
From sin to set me free.

4 Dear dying Lamb! Thy precious
blood
Shall never lose its power,
Till all the ransomed church of God
Be saved to sin no more.

5 E'er since by faith I saw the stream
Thy flowing wounds supply,
Redeeming love has been my
theme,
And shall be till I die.
        *William Cowper.*

**336** BLESSED be the Fountain of
blood,
To a world of sinners revealed;
Blessèd be the dear Son of God;
Only by His stripes are we
healed.        [fold,
Though I've wandered far from His
Bringing to my heart pain and
woe,
Wash me in the blood of the Lamb,
And I shall be whiter than snow.
Whit . . . er than the snow, . . .
Whit . . . er than the snow, . . .
Wash me in the blood of the Lamb, . . .
And I shall be whiter than snow. . . .

2 Thorny was the crown that He
wore,
And the cross His body o'ercame;
Grievous were the sorrows He bore,
But He suffered thus not in vain.
May I to that Fountain be led,
Made to cleanse my sins here be-
low;
Wash me in the blood that He shed,
And I shall be whiter than snow.

3 Father, I have wandered from Thee,
Often has my heart gone astray;
Crimson do my sins seem to me :
Water cannot wash them away,
Jesus, to that Fountain of Thine,
Leaning on Thy promise I go,
Cleanse me by Thy washing divine,
And I shall be whiter than snow.
        *E. R. Latta.*

**337** WOULD Jesus have the sinner
die?        [tree?
Why hangs He then on yonder
What means that strange expiring
cry?
Sinners, He prays for you and me :
Forgive them, Father, oh forgive!
They know not that by Me they live.

2 Thou loving, all-atoning Lamb,
Thee—by Thy painful agony,
Thy blood-like sweat, Thy grief and
shame,
Thy cross and passion on the
tree,
Thy precious death and life—I
pray,
Take all, take all my sins away!

3 Oh let me kiss Thy piercèd feet,
And bathe and wash them with
my tears!

The story of Thy love repeat
  In every drooping sinner's ears,
That all may hear the quickening
    sound,
Since, I, e'en I, have mercy found.

4 Oh let Thy love my heart con-
    strain!
  Thy love for every sinner free,
That every fallen soul of man
  May taste the grace that found
    out me;      [prove
That all mankind with me may
  Thy sovereign everlasting love.
               *Charles Wesley.*

**338** GRACE of God the Father,
    Grace of God the Son,
Grace of God the Spirit,—blessèd
  Three in One,—
Came in all its beauty, light and
  life to bring.  [hearts to sing.
Chase away the shadows, make sad

  Grace, grace, wondrous gift of God to all
    the human race ;
  Grace, grace, bountiful and free, found in
    every place ;
  Grace, grace, beautiful and sweet, would all
    mankind embrace ;
  Grace, grace, every one may taste God's
    great gift of grace.

2 Where sin is abounding, Grace
    aboundeth more; [is the store;
Precious is the message, boundless
Never be discouraged, Grace is
    flowing free,    [than the sea.
Higher than the heavens, deeper

3 Now this grace is kindly offered
    every soul,
Come with all your burdens, Grace
  will make you whole:
" Him that cometh to Me I will not
    cast out,    [do not doubt."
But will love him freely,—come and
               *Tom Jones.*

**339** OH, this uttermost salvation!
    'Tis a fountain full and free,
Pure, exhaustless, ever flowing,
  Wondrous grace! it reaches me!

  It reaches me ! it reaches me !
  Wondrous grace ! it reaches me !
  Pure, exhaustless, ever flowing,
  Wondrous grace ! it reaches me !

2 How amazing God's compassion,
  That so vile a worm should prove
This stupendous bliss of heaven,
  This unmeasured wealth of love!

3 Jesus, Saviour, I adore Thee!
  Now Thy love I will proclaim;
I will tell the blessèd story,
  I will magnify Thy name!
              *Mary D. James.*

**340** I AM happy to-day and the sun
    shines bright,
  The clouds have been rolled
    away;    [will
For the Saviour said, whosoever
  May come with Him to stay.

  Whosoever, surely meaneth me,
  Surely meaneth me, O surely meaneth me ;
  Whosoever, surely meaneth me,
  Whosoever, meaneth me.

2 All my hopes have been raised, O
    His name be praised,
  His glory has filled my soul;
I've been lifted up, and from sin
  set free,
  His blood has made me whole.

3 O what wonderful love, O what
    grace divine,
  That Jesus should die for me;
I was lost in sin, for the world I
  pined,
  But now I am set free.
             *J. E. McConnell.*

**341** ROCK of Ages, cleft for me,
    Let me hide myself in Thee!
Let the water and the blood,
From Thy riven side which flowed,
Be of sin the double cure;
Cleanse me from its guilt and
  power.

2 Not the labours of my hands,
Can fulfil Thy law's demands;
Could my zeal no respite know,
Could my tears for ever flow,
All for sin could not atone;
Thou must save and Thou alone.

3 Nothing in my hand I bring,
Simply to Thy cross I cling;
Naked, come to Thee for dress;
Helpless, look to Thee for grace;
Foul, I to the fountain fly;
Wash me, Saviour, or I die.

4 While I draw this fleeting breath,
When my eyelids close in death,
When I soar to worlds unknown,
See Thee on Thy judgment throne,
Rock of Ages, cleft for me,
Let me hide myself in Thee.
             *A. M. Toplady.*

**342**  OH, now I see the cleansing
  wave!
The fountain deep and wide;
Jesus, my Lord, mighty to save,
  Points to His wounded side.

2 I see the new creation rise;
  I hear the speaking blood!
It speaks! polluted nature dies!
  Sinks 'neath the cleansing flood.

3 I rise to walk in heaven's own light,
  Above the world and sin, [white,
With heart made pure and garments
  And Christ enthroned within.

4 Amazing grace! 'tis heaven below
  To feel the blood applied;
And Jesus, only Jesus, know,
  My Jesus crucified.

*Phoebe Palmer.*

**343**  THERE is a story sweet to hear,
  I love to tell it too:
It fills my heart with hope and
  'Tis old, yet ever new.     [cheer,

'Tis old, . . . yet ever new,
'Tis old, . . . yet ever new,
I know, . . . I feel 'tis true,
'Tis old, yet ever new.

2 It tells me God the Son came down
  From glory's throne to die,
That I might live and wear a crown,
  And reign with Him on high.

3 It says He bore the cross for me,
  And suffered in my place,
That I from sin might ransomed be,
  And praise Him for His grace.

4 Oh wondrous love, so great, so vast,
  So boundless and so free!
Lord, at Thy feet myself I cast;
  My all I give to Thee!

*W. A. Williams.*

**344**  GREAT God of wonders! all
  Thy ways
Display the attributes divine;
But countless acts of pard'ning
  grace            [shine:
Beyond Thine other wonders
Who is a pard'ning God like Thee?
Or who has grace so rich and free?

2 In wonder lost, with trembling joy
  We take the pardon of our God;
Pardon for crimes of deepest dye,
  A pardon bought with Jesu's
  blood:

Who is a pard'ning God like Thee?
Or who has grace so rich and free?

3 Pardon—from an offended God!
  Pardon—for sins of deepest dye!
Pardon—bestowed through Jesu's
  blood!          nigh!
Pardon—that brings the rebel
Who is a pard'ning God like Thee?
Or who has grace so rich and free?

4 O may this strange, this matchless
  grace,
This God-like miracle of love,
Fill the wide earth with grateful
  praise,
As now it fills the choirs above!
Who is a pard'ning God like Thee?
Or who has grace so rich and free?

*Samuel Davies.*

### (4) THE APPEAL

**345**  WHO'LL be the next to follow
  Jesus?            [bear?
Who'll be the next His cross to
Someone is ready, someone is wait-
  ing,             [wear?
Who'll be the next a crown to

Who'll be the next, who'll be the next,
Who'll be the next to follow Jesus?
Who'll be the next to follow Jesus now?—
Follow Jesus now?

2 Who'll be the next to follow Jesus?
  Come and bow at His precious
  feet.            [den
Who'll be the next to lay every bur-
Down at the Father's Mercy-seat?

3 Who'll be the next to follow Jesus?
  Who'll be the next to praise His
  name?            [redemption,
Who'll swell the chorus of free
Sing, Hallelujah! Praise the
  Lamb?

*Mrs. Annie S. Hawks.*

**346**  JESUS is tenderly calling thee
  home—
Calling to-day, calling to-day!
Why from the sunshine of love wilt
  thou roam,
Farther and farther away?

Call . . . ing to-day! call . . . ing to-day! . . .
Je . . . sus is call . . . ing, is tenderly calling
to-day!

2 Jesus is calling the weary to rest—
 Calling to-day, calling to-day!
Bring Him thy burden and thou
  shalt be blest:
He will not turn thee away.

3 Jesus is waiting, oh, come to Him
  now—
 Waiting to-day, waiting to-day!
Come with thy sins, at His feet
  lowly bow;
Come, and no longer delay!

4 Jesus is pleading; oh, list to His
  voice—                    [day!
 Hear Him to-day, hear Him to-
They who believe on His name
  shall rejoice;
Quickly arise and away!
                        *Fanny J. Crosby.*

**347**  OH, what will you do with
    Jesus?
  The call comes low and sweet;
And tenderly He bids you
  Your burdens lay at His feet;
Oh soul so sad and weary,
  That sweet voice speaks to thee:
Then what will you do with Jesus?
  Oh, what shall the answer be?

> What shall the answer be?
> What shall the answer be?
> What will you do with Jesus?
> Oh, what shall the answer be?

2 Oh, what will you do with Jesus?
  The call comes loud and clear;
The solemn words are sounding
  In every listening ear;
Eternal life's in the question,
  And joy through eternity:
Then what will you do with Jesus?
  Oh, what shall the answer be?

3 Oh, think of the King of Glory—
  From heaven to earth come
His life so pure and holy;  [down;
  His death, His cross, His crown;
Of His Divine compassion,
  His sacrifice for thee:
Then what will you do with Jesus?
  Oh, what shall the answer be?
                        *Nath. Norton.*

**348**  ART thou weary, art thou lan-
    guid,
  Art thou sore distressed?
Come to Me, saith One, and, com-
  Be at rest!                [ing,

2 Hath He marks to lead me to Him,
  If He be my guide?
In His feet and hands are wound-
  And His side.          [prints,

3 Hath He diadem as Monarch
  That His brow adorns?
Yea, a crown in very surety,
  But of thorns!

4 If I find Him, if I follow,
  What His guerdon here?
Many a sorrow, many a labour,
  Many a tear.

5 If I still hold closely to Him,
  What hath He at last?
Sorrow vanquished, labour ended,
  Jordan past.

6 If I ask Him to receive me,
  Will He say me nay?
Not till earth and not till heaven
  Pass away.

7 Finding, following, cleaving, trust-
  Is He sure to bless?      [ing,
Saints, apostles, prophets, martyrs,
  Answer: Yes!
*Stephen the Sabaite (8th cent.) ; tr. J. M. Neale.*

**349**  I HAVE a Saviour, He's plead-
    ing in glory,
  A dear, loving Saviour though
    earth-friends be few;
And now He is watching in tender-
    ness o'er me:
  And oh, that my Saviour were
    your Saviour too!

> For you I am praying,
> For you I am praying,
> For you I am praying,
> I'm praying for you.

2 I have a Father: to me He has
    given                    [true;
  A hope for eternity, blessèd and
And soon He will call me to meet
    Him in heaven,
  But oh, may He lead you to go
    with me too!

3 I have a robe: 'tis resplendent in
    whiteness,                [view;
  Awaiting in glory my wondering
Oh, when I receive it all shining
    in brightness,
  Dear friend, could I see you re-
    ceiving one too!

4 I have a peace: it is calm as a
river,          [world never knew;
A peace that the friends of this
My Saviour alone is its Author and
Giver,          [given to you!
And oh, could I know it was

5 When Jesus has found you, tell
others the story,
That my loving Saviour is your
Saviour too;
Then pray that your Saviour may
bring them to glory,
And prayer will be answered,
'twas answered for you!

*Samuel O'M. Cluff.*

**350**  WILL you take Jesus to be your
Guide?
His love will brighten the way;
Safe in His keeping you may abide:
Will you take Jesus to-day?

Will you take Jesus to-day ?
Will you take Jesus to-day ?
He offers pardon and peace to all :
Will you take Jesus to-day ?

2 For you the Saviour was crucified,
Accept His love while you may;
The door of mercy stands open
wide:
Will you take Jesus to-day?

3 He longs to enter your heart of sin—
How can you turn Him away?
Throw wide the portal and let Him
Will you take Jesus to-day? [in:

4 I will take Jesus, my Lord and
His word I gladly obey;  [King,
My sins forgiven, His praise I'll
sing:
I will take Jesus to-day.

I will take Jesus to-day !
I will take Jesus to-day !
He offers pardon and peace to all :
I will take Jesus to-day !

*William W. Rock.*

**351**  IF you from sin are longing to
be free,
Look to the Lamb of God;
He, to redeem you, died on Cal-
Look to the Lamb of God. [vary,

Look to the Lamb of God,
Look to the Lamb of God,
For He alone is able to save you ;
Look to the Lamb of God.

2 When Satan tempts, and doubts and
fears assail,
Look to the Lamb of God;

You in His strength shall over all
prevail,
Look to the Lamb of God.

3 Are you aweary, does the way seem
long?
Look to the Lamb of God;
His love will cheer and fill your
heart with song,
Look to the Lamb of God.

4 Fear not when shadows on your
pathway fall,
Look to the Lamb of God;
In joy or sorrow Christ is all in all,
Look to the Lamb of God.

*H. G. Jackson.*

**352**  PRECIOUS, precious blood of
Jesus,
Shed on Calvary;
Shed for rebels, shed for sinners,
Shed for thee!

Precious, precious blood of Jesus,
Ever flowing free ;
Oh, believe it ; oh, receive it,
'Tis for thee.

2 Precious, precious blood of Jesus,
Let it make thee whole;
Let it flow in mighty cleansing
O'er thy soul.

3 Though thy sins are red like crim-
Deep in scarlet glow,     [son
Jesus' precious blood shall wash
White as snow.          [thee

4 Precious blood that hath redeemed
All the price is paid!     [us!
Perfect pardon now is offered,
Peace is made.

5 Now the holiest with boldness
We may enter in;
For the open fountain cleanseth
From all sin.

6 Precious blood! by this we conquer
In the fiercest fight,
Sin and Satan overcoming
By its might.

7 Precious blood whose full atone-
Makes us nigh to God!    [ment
Precious blood, our way of glory,
Praise and laud.

*Frances R. Havergal.*

**353** REDEMPTION! oh, wonderful story— [me:
Glad message for you and for
That Jesus has purchased our pardon,
And paid all the debt on the tree.

Believe it, O sinner, believe it ;
Receive the glad message—'tis true ;
Trust now in the crucified Saviour,
Salvation He offers to you.

2 From death unto life He hath brought us, [God;
And made us by grace sons of
A Fountain is opened for sinners:
Oh, wash and be cleansed in the blood!

3 No longer shall sin have dominion,
Though present to tempt and annoy; [tion,
For Christ in His blessèd redemp-
The power of sin shall destroy.

4 Accept now God's offer of mercy;
To Jesus, oh, hasten today;
For He will receive him that cometh,
And never will turn him away.
*S. M. Sayford.*

**354** JUST as I am, without one plea,
But that Thy blood was shed for me, [Thee,
And that Thou bidst me come to
O Lamb of God, I come.

2 Just as I am, and waiting not
To rid my soul of one dark blot,
To Thee, whose blood can cleanse each spot,
O Lamb of God, I come.

3 Just as I am—though tossed about
With many a conflict, many a doubt, [out,
Fightings and fears within, with-
O Lamb of God, I come.

4 Just as I am—poor, wretched, blind—
Sight, riches, healing of the mind,
Yea, all I need, in Thee to find,
O Lamb of God, I come.

5 Just as I am, Thou wilt receive,
Wilt welcome, pardon, cleanse, relieve;
Because Thy promise I believe,
O Lamb of God, I come.

6 Just as I am—Thy love unknown
Has broken every barrier down;
Now to be Thine, yea, Thine alone,
O Lamb of God, I come.

7 Just as I am, of that free love
The breadth, length, depth and height to prove,
Here for a season, then above,
O Lamb of God, I come.
*Charlotte Elliott.*

**355** JUST as I am, Thine own to be,
Friend of the young, who lovest me,
To consecrate myself to Thee,
O Jesus Christ, I come.

2 In the glad morning of my day,
My life to give, my vows to pay,
With no reserve, and no delay—
With all my heart, I come.

3 I would live ever in the light,
I would work ever for the right,
I would serve Thee with all my might—
Therefore to Thee I come.

4 Just as I am, young, strong, and free,
To be the best that I can be, [free,
For truth, and righteousness, and Thee,
Lord of my life—I come.

5 And for Thy sake to win renown,
And then to take the victor's crown,
And at Thy feet to lay it down,
O Master, Lord—I come.
*Marianne Farningham.*

**356** SOFTLY and tenderly Jesus is calling,—
Calling for you and for me;
See, on the portals He's waiting and watching,—
Watching for you and for me.

Come home, . . . come home, . . .
Ye who are weary, come home,
Earnestly, tenderly Jesus is calling,—
Calling, " O sinner, come home ! "

2 Why should we tarry when Jesus is pleading,—
Pleading for you and for me?
Why should we linger and heed not His mercies,—
Mercies for you and for me?

3 Time is now fleeting, the moments
 are passing,—
 Passing from you and from me?
Shadows are gathering, deathbeds
 are coming,—
 Coming for you and for me.

4 Oh for the wonderful love He has
 promised,—
 Promised for you and for me;
Though we have sinned He has
 mercy and pardon,—
 Pardon for you and for me.
 *Will L. Thompson.*

**357** SINNER, how thy heart is
 troubled,
 God is coming very near;
Do not hide thy deep emotion,
 Do not check that falling tear.

 Oh, be saved, His grace is free !
 Oh, be saved, He died for thee !

2 Jesus now is bending o'er thee,
 Jesus lowly, meek, and mild;
To the Friend who died to save
 thee,
 Wilt thou not be reconciled?

3 Art thou waiting till the morrow?
 Thou mayest never see its light;
Come at once! accept His mercy:
 He is waiting—come tonight!

4 With a lowly, contrite spirit,
 Kneeling at the Saviour's feet,
Thou canst feel, this very moment,
 Pardon — precious, pure, and
 sweet.

5 Let the angels bear the tidings
 Upward to the courts of heaven!
Let them sing with holy rapture,
 O'er another soul forgiven!
 *Fanny J. Crosby.*

**358** ONCE again the Gospel mess-
 age [heard,
 From the Saviour you have
Will you heed the invitation?
 Will you turn and seek the Lord?

 Come believing ! . . . come believing ! . . .
 Come to Jesus ! look and live ! . . .
 Come believing ! . . . come believing ! . . .
 Come to Jesus ! look and live !

2 Many summers you have wasted,
 Ripened harvests you have seen;
Winter snows by Spring have
 melted,
 Yet you linger in your sin.

3 Jesus for your choice is waiting;
 Tarry not: at once decide!
While the Spirit now is striving,
 Yield, and seek the Saviour's
 side.

4 Cease of fitness to be thinking;
 Do not longer try to feel;
It is *trusting*, and not *feeling*,
 That will give the Spirit's seal.

5 Let your will to God be given,
 Trust in Christ's atoning blood;
Look to Jesus now in heaven,
 Rest on His unchanging word.
 *D. W. Whittle.*

**359** SINNER, wheresoe'er thou art,
 At the Cross there's room;
Tell the burden of thy heart,
 At the Cross there's room.
Tell it in thy Saviour's ear,
Cast away thy every fear;
Only speak, and He will hear;
 At the Cross there's room.

2 Haste thee, wanderer, tarry not,
 At the Cross there's room;
Seek that consecrated spot;
 At the Cross there's room.
Heavy-laden, sore opprest,
Love can soothe thy troubled
In the Saviour find thy rest, [breast;
 At the Cross there's room.

3 Thoughtless sinner, come today,
 At the Cross there's room;
Hark! the Bride and Spirit say,
 At the Cross there's room.
Now a living Fountain see
Opened there for you and me,
Rich and poor, for bond and free:
 At the Cross there's room.

4 Blessèd thought! For every one
 At the Cross there's room;
Love's atoning work is done;
 At the Cross there's room.
Streams of boundless mercy flow,
Free to all who thither go:
Oh, that all the world might know,
 At the Cross there's room.
 *Fanny J. Crosby.*

**360** BEHOLD Me standing at the
 door,
And hear Me pleading evermore,
With gentle voice: Oh, heart of sin,
May I come in, may I come in?

Behold Me standing at the door,
And hear Me pleading evermore;
Say, weary heart, opprest with sin,
May I come in? may I come in?

2 I bore the cruel thorns for thee,
I waited long and patiently:
Say, weary heart, opprest with sin,
May I come in, may I come in?

3 I would not plead with thee in vain;
Remember all My grief and pain!
I died to ransom thee from sin,
May I come in, may I come in?

4 I bring thee joy from heaven above,
I bring thee pardon, peace and love:
Say, weary heart, opprest with sin,
May I come in, may I come in?
*Fanny J. Crosby.*

**361** Is there a heart that is waiting,
Longing for pardon today?
Hear the glad message proclaiming,
Jesus is passing this way.

Jesus is passing this way, . . .
This way, . . . to-day ; . . .
Jesus is passing this way, . . .
Is passing this way to-day.

2 Is there a heart that has wandered?
Come with thy burden today;
Mercy is tenderly pleading,
Jesus is passing this way.

3 Is there a heart that is broken?
Weary and sighing for rest?

Come to the arms of thy Saviour,
Pillow thy head on His breast.

4 Come to thy only Redeemer,
Come to His infinite love;
Come to the gate that is leading
Homeward to mansions above.
*Annie L. James.*

**362** HAVE you any room for Jesus,
He who bore your load of
sin?
As He knocks and asks admission,
Sinner, will you let Him in?

Room for Jesus, King of Glory,
Hasten now, His word obey,
Swing the heart's door widely open,
Bid Him enter while you may.

2 Room for pleasure, room for busi-
But for Christ the crucified, [ness,
Not a place that He can enter,
In your heart for which He died?

3 Have you any time for Jesus,
As in grace He calls again?
O to-day is time accepted,
To-morrow you may call in vain.

4 Room and time now give to Jesus,
Soon will pass God's day of
grace;
Soon thy heart left cold and silent,
And thy Saviour's pleading cease.
*D. W. Whittle.*

# Section VII

## THE CHRISTIAN LIFE

### (1) ASSURANCE AND
CONFIDENCE

**363** THOU hidden Source of calm
repose,
Thou all sufficient love divine;
My help and refuge from my foes,
Secure I am, if Thou art mine,
From sin and grief, from guilt and
shame:
I hide me, Jesus, in Thy name.

2 Thy mighty Name salvation is,
And keeps my happy soul above;
Comfort it brings, and power and
peace,

And joy and everlasting love;
To me, with Thy dear Name, are
given
Pardon and holiness and heaven.

3 Jesus, my all in all Thou art,
My rest in toil, mine ease in pain;
The med'cine of my broken heart;
In war, my peace; in loss, my
gain: [frown;
My smile beneath the tyrant's
In shame, my glory and my crown

4 In want, my plentiful supply;
In weakness, mine almighty
power;

In bonds, my perfect liberty;
  My light in Satan's darkest hour;
In grief, my joy unspeakable;  [all.
My life in death; my heaven, my

*Charles Wesley.*

**364** COME, sing my soul, and praise
  the Lord,     [blood;
Who hath redeemed thee by His
Delivered thee from chains that
  bound,     [ground.
And brought thee to redemption
Redemption ground, the ground of peace!
Redemption ground, O wondrous grace!
Here let our praise to God abound,
Who saves us on redemption ground!

2 Once from my God I wandered far,
And with His holy will made war;
But now my songs to God abound:
I'm standing on redemption ground.

3 O joyous hour when God to me
A vision gave of Calvary!
My bonds were loosed, my soul un-
  bound;
I sang upon redemption ground.

4 No works of merit now I plead,
But Jesus take for all my need;
No righteousness in me is found,
Except upon redemption ground.

5 Come, weary soul, and here find
  rest;
Accept redemption and be blest;
The Christ who died, by God is
  crowned
To pardon on redemption ground.

*El Nathan.*

**365** RESTING on the faithfulness of
  Christ our Lord,
Resting on the fulness of His own
  sure word;     [and power,
Resting on His wisdom, on His love
Resting on His covenant from hour
  to hour.

2 Resting 'neath His guiding hand for
  untracked days,  [noontide rays;
Resting 'neath His shadow from the
Resting at the eventide beneath His
  wing,     [King.
In the fair pavilion of our Saviour-

3 Resting in the fortress while the foe
  is nigh,  [waves roll high;
Resting in the lifeboat while the
Resting in His chariot for the swift,
  glad race,  [boundless grace.
Resting, always resting, in His

4 Resting in the pastures, and beneath the Rock,
Resting by the waters where He
  leads His flock;
Resting, while we listen at His
  glorious feet,  [rest complete!
Resting in His arms of love—oh,

5 Resting and believing, let us on-
  ward press,
Resting on Himself, "the Lord our
  Righteousness!"
Resting and rejoicing, let His saved
  ones sing—  our King!"
"Glory, glory, glory be to Christ

*Frances R. Havergal.*

**366** JESUS, Thy blood and right-
  eousness
My beauty are, my glorious dress;
'Midst flaming worlds, in these
  arrayed,
With joy shall I lift up my head.

2 Bold shall I stand in that great day,
For who aught to my charge shall
  lay?
Fully absolved through these I am,
From sin and fear, from guilt and
  shame.

3 When from the dust of death I rise,
To claim my mansion in the skies,
E'en then shall this be all my plea,
"Jesus hath lived, and died, for
  me."

4 This spotless robe the same appears,
When ruined nature sinks in years;
No age can change its glorious hue,
The robe of Christ is ever new.

5 Oh, let the dead now hear Thy
  voice,     [joice;
Bid, Lord, Thy banished ones re-
Their beauty this, their glorious
  dress,
Jesus, the Lord our Righteousness!

*Zinzendorf; tr. J. Wesley.*

**367** THOU hast snapped my fetters;
  Thou hast made me free:
Liberty and gladness,
  I have found in Thee;
Liberty from bondage,
  From my weary load,
Satan's slave no longer,
  Now a child of God!

I am Thine, Lord Jesus,
Ever Thine, Thine I am,
And my heart is singing,
" Glory to the Lamb."

2 Living in the sunshine,
Shining in Thy light,
Fighting as Thy soldier,
Mighty in Thy might;
Going on Thy mission,
Pointing men to Thee,
Telling of the Saviour
Who can set them free.

3 Such the life, Lord Jesus,
I would ever live,
Such the grateful tribute
I would ever give;
Witnessing for Thee, Lord,
Everywhere I go,
Of the Blood that cleanseth,
Washing white as snow.

4 And when life is ended,
When the vict'ry's won,
When I hear from Thee, Lord,
The glad words, " Well done,"
With what joy and rapture
Shall I sing of Thee,
Who from sin's dark chains didst
Set my spirit free!

**368** I CAME unto Jesus confessing
my sin,
Forsaking the wrongs of the past;
He promised me pardon and cleans-
ing within,
His promise I trusted at last.

His promises hold, hallelujah !
His promises hold, praise His name ;
His promises hold, hallelujah !
For He is for ever the same.

2 I sought for the Comforter pro-
mised to all
Who all on the altar would lay;
I trusted the promise and blessing
did fall
Upon me that glorious day.

3 He promised to keep me so safe in
His fold, [astray;
That no one should lead me
His arms everlasting will ever up-
hold,
And He will be with me alway.

4 My constant Companion, my Guide
and my Friend,
My Saviour, my Keeper is He;

His love and compassion shall
nevermore end,
In life or in death He keeps me.
*Haldor Lillenas.*

**369** REDEEMED, how I love to pro-
claim it, [Lamb;
Redeemed by the blood of the
Redeemed through His infinite
mercy,
His child and forever I am.

Redeemed, . . . Redeemed, . . .
Redeemed by the blood of the Lamb,
Redeemed, . . . Redeemed, . . .
His child and forever I am.

2 Redeemed and so happy in Jesus,
No language my rapture can tell;
I know that the light of His pre-
sence
With me doth continually dwell.

3 I think of my blessèd Redeemer,
I think of Him all the day long;
I sing, for I cannot be silent,
His love is the theme of my song.

4 I know I shall see in His beauty,
The King in whose law I delight;
Who lovingly guardeth my foot-
steps,
And giveth me songs in the night.

5 I know there's a crown that is wait-
ing
In yonder bright mansion for me;
And soon with the spirits made per-
fect,
At home with the Lord I shall be.
*Fanny J. Crosby.*

**370** BLESSED assurance, Jesus is
mine! [divine!
Oh, what a foretaste of glory
Heir of salvation, purchase of God,
Born of His Spirit, washed in His
blood.

This is my story, this is my song,
Praising my Saviour all the day long.

2 Perfect submission, perfect delight,
Visions of rapture now burst on
my sight, [above
Angels descending, bring from
Echoes of mercy, whispers of love.

3 Perfect submission, all is at rest,
I in my Saviour am happy and
blest,

Watching and waiting, looking
   above,
Filled with His goodness, lost in
   His love.

*Fanny J. Crosby.*

**371** I KNOW not why God's won-
   drous grace
   To me He hath made known,
Nor why, unworthy, Christ in love
   Redeemed me for His own.

But " I know whom I have believed,
  And am persuaded that He is able
To keep that which I've committed
  Unto Him against that day."

2 I know not how this saving faith
   To me He did impart,
Nor how believing in His Word
   Wrought peace within my heart.

3 I know not how the Spirit moves,
   Convincing men of sin,
Revealing Jesus through the Word,
   Creating faith in Him.

4 I know not what of good or ill
   May be reserved for me,
Of weary ways or golden days
   Before His face I see.

5 I know not when my Lord may
   come,
   At night or noonday fair,
Nor if I'll walk the vale with Him,
   Or " meet Him in the air."

*El Nathan.*

**372** THROUGH the love of God our
   Saviour,
   All will be well;
Free and changeless is His favour,
   All, all is well:
Precious is the blood that healed
   us,
Perfect is the grace that sealed us:
Strong the hand stretched forth to
   shield us,
   All must be well.

2 Though we pass through tribulation,
   All will be well;
Ours is such a full salvation,
   All, all is well:
Happy still in God confiding;
Fruitful if in Christ abiding;
Holy through the Spirit's guiding;
   All must be well.

3 We expect a bright to-morrow;
   All will be well;
Faith can sing through days of
   All, all is well:    [sorrow
On our Father's love relying,
Jesus every need supplying,
Or in living or in dying,
   All must be well.

*Mary Peters.*

**373** JESUS hath died and hath risen
   again,
   Pardon and peace to bestow;
Fully I trust Him; from sin's guilty
   Jesus saves me now.    [stain

Jesus saves me now !
Jesus saves me now !
Yes, Jesus saves me all the time,
  Jesus saves me now !

2 Sin's condemnation is over and
   gone,
   Jesus alone knoweth how;
Life and salvation my soul hath
   Jesus saves me now.    [put on;

3 Jesus is stronger than Satan and sin,
   Satan to Jesus must bow,
Therefore I triumph without and
   Jesus saves me now.    [within;

4 Sorrow and pain may beset me
   about,
   Nothing can darken my brow;
Battling in faith I can joyfully
   Jesus saves me now.    [shout:

**374** " THOU remainest," blest Re-
   deemer,
   Lord of peace and Lord of strife;
Jesus, Saviour, Lord for ever,
   " Thou remainest," Christ my life.

"Thou remainest," .. "Thou remainest," ..
  " Thou remainest," Christ my all ; . . .
Peace or conflict, joy or sorrow,
  " Thou remainest," Christ my all.

2 Satisfying every longing
   Of my sinful soul for grace;
From my weakness never turning,
   " Thou remainest," Christ my
   peace.

3 Earthly joys may soon be fading,
   Wintry frosts sweet flowers des-
   troy;
But above the cloud that's shading,
   " Thou remainest," Christ my joy.

4 One by one my loved may leave me,
  Voices sweet no more be heard;
But of God naught can bereave me,
  " Thou remainest," Christ my Lord.

5 When from earth Thou, Lord, shalt call me,
  Calm I'll lay my burden down;
For I know, what e'er befall me,
  " Thou remainest," Christ my crown.

*El Nathan.*

**375** 'Tis the promise of God full salvation to give
Unto him who on Jesus, His Son, will believe.

  Hallelujah ! 'tis done,
  I believe on the Son ;
I am saved by the blood of the Crucified One.

2 Though the pathway be lonely and dangerous too,
Surely Jesus is able to carry me through.

3 Many loved ones have I in yon heavenly throng,
They are safe now in glory, and this is their song.

4 There are prophets and kings in that throng I behold,
And they sing while they march through the streets of pure gold.

5 There's part in that chorus for you and for me,
And the theme of our praises for ever will be:

*P. P. Bliss.*

**376** I'm not ashamed to own my Lord,
  Or to defend His cause;
Maintain the honour of His Word,
  The glory of His cross.

  At the cross, at the cross, where I first saw the light,
  And the burden of my heart rolled away,
  It was there by faith I received my sight,
  And now I am happy all the day.

2 Jesus, my Lord! I know His name—
  His name is all my trust,
Nor will He put my soul to shame,
  Nor let my hope be lost.

3 Firm as His throne, His promise
  And He can well secure [stands,
What I've committed to His hands,
  Till the decisive hour.

4 Then will He own my worthless
  Before His Father's face; [name
And in the new Jerusalem,
  Appoint my soul a place.

*Isaac Watts.*

**377** My faith has found a resting-place,
  Not in device nor creed;
I trust the Ever-living One,
  His wounds for me shall plead.

  I need no other argument,
  I need no other plea,
  It is enough that Jesus died,
  And that He died for me.

2 Enough for me that Jesus saves,
  This ends my fear and doubt;
A sinful soul I come to Him,
  He'll never cast me out.

3 My heart is leaning on the word,
  The written word of God,
Salvation by my Saviour's Name,
  Salvation through His blood.

4 My great Physician heals the sick,
  The lost He came to save:
For me His precious blood He shed,
  For me His life He gave.

*L. H. Edmonds.*

**378** My hope is built on nothing
  less [ness;
Than Jesus' blood and righteous-
I dare not trust the sweetest frame,
But wholly lean on Jesus' name.

  On Christ, the solid rock, I stand ;
  All other ground is sinking sand.

2 When darkness seems to veil His face,
  I rest on His unchanging grace;
In every high and stormy gale,
  My anchor holds within the veil.

3 His oath, His covenant, and blood,
  Support me in the 'whelming flood;
When all around my soul gives way,
  He then is all my hope and stay.

4 When He shall come with trumpet sound,
  Oh, may I then in Him be found;
Dressed in His righteousness alone,
  Faultless to stand before the throne.

*Edward Mote.*

**379** Upon life's boundless ocean
    where mighty billows roll,
I've fixed my hope in Jesus, blest
    anchor of my soul;
When trials fierce assail me as
    storms are gathering o'er,
I rest upon His mercy and trust
    Him more.

    I've anchored in Jesus, the storms of life
      I'll brave,
    I've anchored in Jesus, I fear no wind or
      wave,
    I've anchored in Jesus for He hath power
      to save,
      I've anchored to the Rock of Ages.

2 He keeps my soul from evil and
    gives me blessèd peace,
His voice hath stilled the waters
    and bid their tumult cease;
My Pilot and Deliverer, to Him I
    all confide,     [at my side.
For always when I need Him, He's

3 He is my Friend and Saviour, in
    Him my anchor's cast,
He drives away my sorrows and
    shields me from the blast;
By faith I'm looking upward be-
    yond life's troubled sea,
There I behold a haven prepared
    for me.

*    L. E. Jones.*

**380** Loved with everlasting love,
    Led by grace that love to
    know,
Spirit breathing from above,
    Thou hast taught me it is so.
Oh, this full and perfect peace!
    Oh, this transport all divine!
In a love which cannot cease,
    I am His and He is mine.

2 Heaven above is softer blue,
    Earth around is sweeter green;
Something lives in every hue
    Christless eyes have never seen:
Birds with gladder songs o'erflow,
    Flowers with deeper beauties
    shine,
Since I know, as now I know,
    I am His and He is mine.

3 Things that once were wild alarms
    Cannot now disturb my rest;
Closed in everlasting arms,
    Pillowed on the loving breast:
Oh, to lie for ever here!
    Doubt and care and self resign,

While He whispers in my ear—
    I am His and He is mine.
4 His for ever, only His;
    Who the Lord and me shall part?
Ah, with what a rest of bliss,
    Christ can fill the loving heart!
Heaven and earth may fade and
    flee;
    Firstborn light in gloom decline;
But while God and I shall be,
    I am His and He is mine.

*    G. Wade Robinson.*

**381** What though clouds are hover-
    ing o'er me,
    And I seem to walk alone,
Longing, 'mid my cares and crosses,
    For the joys that now are flown!
If I've Jesus, "Jesus only,"
    Then my sky will have a gem;
He's the Sun of brightest splendour,
    And the star of Bethlehem.

2 What though all my earthly journey
    Bringeth naught but weary hours;
And, in grasping for life's roses,
    Thorns I find instead of flow'rs!
If I've Jesus, "Jesus only,"
    I possess a cluster rare;
He's the "Lily of the Valley,"
    And the "Rose of Sharon" fair.

3 What though all my heart is yearn-
    For the loved of long ago— [ing
Bitter lessons sadly learning
    From the shadowy page of woe!
If I've Jesus, "Jesus only,"
    He'll be with me to the end;
And, unseen by mortal vision,
    Angel bands will o'er me bend.

4 When I soar to realms of glory,
    And an entrance I await,
If I whisper, "Jesus only!"
    Wide will ope the pearly gate;
When I join the heavenly chorus,
    And the angel-hosts I see,
Precious Jesus, "Jesus only,"
    Will my theme of rapture be.

*    Hattie M. Conrey.*

**382** Come, let us all unite to sing—
    God is love!
While heaven and earth their praises
    God is love!     [bring
Let every soul from sin awake,
Each in his heart sweet music make,
And sweetly sing for Jesus' sake
    God is love!

God is love, . . .
God is love ! . . .
Come, let us all unite to sing :
God is love !

2 Oh, tell to earth's remotest bound,
God is love!
In Christ is full redemption found—
God is love!                    [away;
His blood can cleanse our sins
His Spirit turns our night to day,
And leads our souls with joy to
God is love!                      [say—

3 How happy is our portion here—
God is love!
His promises our spirits cheer—
God is love!
He is our Sun and Shield by day,
Our help, our hope, our strength,
our stay,
He will be with us all the way—
God is love!

4 What though my heart and flesh
God is love!            [shall fail—
Through Christ I shall o'er death
God is love!                   [prevail—
E'en Jordan's swell I will not fear,
For Jesus will be with me there,
My soul above the waves to bear—
God is love!

*Howard Kingsbury.*

**383** REJOICE in the Lord! oh, let
His mercy cheer;
He sunders the bands that en-
thrall;          [should we ever fear
Redeemed by His blood, why
Since Jesus is our " all in all "?

If God be for us, if God be for us,
If God be for us, who can be against us ?
Who ? who ? who ? who can be against
us, against us ?

2 Be strong in the Lord! rejoicing in
His might,
Be loyal and true day by day;
When evils assail, be valiant for the
right,                              [stay.
And He will be our strength and

3 Confide in His Word—His promises
so sure;          [amen ";
In Christ they are " yea and
Though earth pass away, they ever
shall endure,
'Tis written o'er and o'er again.

4 Abide in the Lord: secure in His
control,
'Tis life everlasting begun;
To pluck from His hand the weak-
est, trembling soul—
It never, never can be done!

*G. M. J.*

**384** DYING with Jesus, by death
reckoned mine;
Living with Jesus a new life divine;
Looking to Jesus till glory doth
shine;                           [Thine.
Moment by moment, O Lord, I am

Moment by moment I'm kept in His love,
Moment by moment I've life from above ;
Looking to Jesus till glory doth shine ;
Moment by moment, O Lord, I am Thine.

2 Never a battle with wrong for the
right,                             [fight;
Never a contest that He doth not
Lifting above us His banner so
white                         [His sight.
Moment by moment I'm kept in

3 Never a trial that He is not there,
Never a burden that He doth not
bear,                             [share
Never a sorrow that He doth not
Moment by moment I'm under His
care.

4 Never a heart-ache, and never a
groan,                          [moan,
Never a tear-drop, and never a
Never a danger but there on the
throne                        [His own.
Moment by moment He thinks of

5 Never a weakness that He doth not
feel,                             [heal;
Never a sickness that He cannot
Moment by moment, in woe or in
weal,                            [still.
Jesus my Saviour abides with me

*D. W. Whittle.*

**385** WHY should I fear the darkest
hour?
Or tremble at the tempter's power?
Jesus vouchsafes to be my Tower.

2 Though hot the fight, why quit the
field?
Why must I either flee or yield?
Since Jesus is my mighty Shield?

3 When creature comforts fade and
die,                            [should I?
Worldlings may weep, but why
Jesus still lives and still is nigh.

**4** Though all the flocks and herds
    were dead,
My soul a famine need not dread,
For Jesus is my living Bread.

**5** I know not what may soon betide,
Or how my wants shall be supplied;
But Jesus knows, and will provide.

**6** Though sin would fill me with dis-
    tress,
The throne of grace I dare address,
For Jesus is my Righteousness.

**7** Though faint my prayers and cold
    my love,
My steadfast hope shall not remove
While Jesus intercedes above.

**8** Against me earth and hell combine;
But on my side is power Divine;
Jesus is all, and He is mine.
                  *J. Newton.*

**386** A MIND at "perfect peace" with
    God;
  Oh, what a word is this!
A sinner reconciled through blood;
  This, this indeed is peace!

**2** By nature and by practice far,
  How very far from God!
Yet now by grace brought nigh to
    Him,
  Through faith in Jesus' blood.

**3** So nigh, so very nigh to God,
  I cannot nearer be;
For in the person of His Son
  I am as near as He.

**4** So dear, so very dear to God,
  More dear I cannot be;
The love wherewith He loves the
    Son—
  Such is His love to me!

**5** Why should I ever anxious be,
  Since such a God is mine?
He watches o'er me night and day,
  And tells me " Mine is thine."
             *Catesby Paget.*

**387** ON Thee my heart is resting!
    Ah, this is rest indeed!
What else, Almighty Saviour,
  Can a poor sinner need?
Thy light is all my wisdom,
  Thy love is all my stay;
Our Father's home in glory
  Draws nearer every day.

**2** My guilt is great, but greater
  The mercy Thou dost give;
Thyself, a spotless Offering,
  Hast died that I should live.
With Thee, my soul unfettered
  Has risen from the dust;
Thy blood is all my treasure,
  Thy word is all my trust.

**3** Through me, Thou gentle Master,
  Thy purposes fulfil,
I yield myself forever
  To Thy most holy will.
What though I be but weakness?
  My strength is not in me;
The poorest of Thy people
  Has all things, having Thee.

**4** When clouds are darkest round me
  Thou, Lord, art then most near,
My drooping faith to quicken,
  My weary soul to cheer.
Safe nestling in Thy bosom,
  I gaze upon Thy face;
In vain my foes would drive me
  From Thee, my hiding place,

**5** 'Tis Thou hast made me happy,
  'Tis Thou hast set me free,
To whom shall I give glory
  For ever, but to Thee?
Of earthly love and blessing
  Should every stream run dry,
Thy grace shall still be with me,
  Thy grace to live and die.
            *Thomas Monod.*

**388** DEAR Saviour, Thou art mine,
    How sweet the thought to
Let me repeat Thy name,    [me!
  And lift my heart to Thee.
  Mine ! mine ! mine ! I know Thou art
    mine ;
  Saviour, dear Saviour, I know Thou art
    mine.

**2** Thou art the sinner's friend,
  So I Thy friendship claim,
A sinner saved by grace,
  When Thy sweet message came.

**3** My hardened heart was touched;
  Thy pardoning voice I heard;
And joy and peace came in
  While listening to Thy word.

**4** So, let me sing Thy praise,
  So, let me call Thee mine.
I cannot doubt Thy word,
  I know that I am Thine.
            *Anna Hudson.*

**389** Now I have found the ground
  wherein    [main,
 Sure my soul's anchor may re-
The wounds of Jesus, for my sin
 Before the world's foundation
  slain;
Whose mercy shall unshaken stay,
When heaven and earth are fled
  away.

2 Father, Thine everlasting grace
 Our scanty thought surpasses far,
Thy heart still melts with tender-
  ness,
 Thy arms of love still open are,
Returning sinners to receive,
That mercy they may taste and live.

3 O love, thou bottomless abyss,
 My sins are swallowed up in
  Thee!
Covered is my unrighteousness,
 Nor spot of guilt remains on me,
While Jesu's blood through earth
 and skies
Mercy, free, boundless mercy, cries.

4 With faith I plunge me in this sea,
 Here is my hope, my joy, my rest;
Hither, when hell assails, I flee,
 I look into my Saviour's breast;
Away, sad doubt, and anxious fear!
Mercy is all that's written there.

5 Though waves and storms go o'er
 my head,   [friends be gone,
 Though strength, and health, and
Though joys be withered all and
 dead,     [drawn,
 Though every comfort be with-
On this my steadfast soul relies,
Father, Thy mercy never dies.

6 Fixed on this ground will I remain,
 Though my heart fail, and flesh
  decay;
This anchor shall my soul sustain,
 When earth's foundations melt
  away;     [prove,
Mercy's full power I then shall
Loved with an everlasting love.
       *tr. J. Wesley.*

**390** A DEBTOR to mercy alone,
 Of covenant mercy I sing;
Nor fear, with God's righteousness
 on,
My person and off'ring to bring.

The terrors of law and of God
 With me can have nothing to do;
My Saviour's obedience and blood
 Hide all my transgressions from
  view.

2 The work which His goodness be-
 gan,      [plete;
 The arm of His strength will com-
His promise is Yea and Amen,
 And never was forfeited yet.
Things future, nor things that are
 now,
 Nor all things below or above,
Can make Him His purpose forgo,
 Or sever my soul from His love.

3 My name from the palms of His
 hands
 Eternity will not erase;
Impressed on His heart it remains,
 In marks of indelible grace.
Yes, I to the end shall endure,
 As sure as the earnest is given;
More happy, but not more secure,
 The glorified spirits in heaven.
       *A. M. Toplady.*

**391** My soul is now united
  To Christ the Living Vine;
His grace I long have slighted,
 But now I know He's mine;
I was to God a stranger
 Till Jesus took me in;
He freed my soul from danger,
 And pardon'd all my sin.

2 Soon as my all I ventured
 On the atoning Blood,
The Holy Spirit entered,
 And I was born of God;
Still Christ is my Salvation—
 What can I covet more?
I fear no condemnation,
 My Father's wrath is o'er.

3 By floods and flames surrounded,
 I now my way pursue;
Nor shall I be confounded,
 With glory in my view;
I taste a heavenly pleasure,
 And need not fear a frown:
Christ is my joy and treasure,
 My glory and my crown.

4 Christians be not faint-hearted,
 Though least among the flock;
From Christ you'll ne'er be parted,
 While built upon the Rock;

Let's speed our pace to glory,
We soon shall meet above,
And tell the wondrous story
Of His redeeming love.

**392** I WOULD not ask for earthly
     store—
Thou wilt my need supply;
But I would covet, more and more,
The clear and single eye,
To see my duty face to face,
And trust Thee, Lord, for daily
     grace.

    Then shall my heart keep singing,
    While to the Cross I cling ;
  For rest is sweet at Jesus' feet,
    While homeward faith keeps winging,
    While homeward faith keeps winging.

2 I care not for the empty show
  That thoughtless worldlings see;
But gladly do the best I know,
  And leave the rest with Thee;
Well satisfied that sweet reward
Is sure to those who trust the Lord.

3 Whate'er the crosses mine shall be,
  I would not dare to shun;
But only ask to live for Thee,
  And that Thy will be done;
Thy will, O Lord, be mine each
    day,     [way.
While pressing on my homeward

4 And when at last, my labour o'er,
  I cross the narrow sea,
Grant, Lord, that on the other
    shore
  My soul may dwell with Thee;
And learn what here I cannot know,
Why Thou hast ever loved me so.
               *J. J. Maxfield.*

## (2) GROWTH IN GRACE

**393** I'M pressing on the upward
     way,
New heights I'm gaining every day;
Still praying as I onward bound,
" Lord, plant my feet on higher
    ground."

  Lord, lift me up and let me stand,
  By faith, on heaven's table-land ;
  Where love, and joy, and light abound,
  Lord, plant my feet on higher ground.

2 My heart has no desire to stay
Where doubts arise, and fears dis-
    may;     [these abound,
Though some may dwell where
My constant aim is higher ground.

3 Beyond the mist I fain would rise,
To rest beneath unclouded skies,
Above earth's turmoil peace is
    found     [ground.
By those who dwell on higher

4 I long to scale the utmost height,
Though rough the way, and hard
    the fight,     [sound,
My song, while climbing, shall re-
Lord, lead me on to higher ground.

5 Lord, lead me up the mountain
    side     [Guide;
I dare not climb without my
And, heaven gained, I'll gaze
    around,     [ground.
With grateful heart from higher
    *Johnson Oatman, Jr., and Ada R. Habershon.*

**394** MORE about Jesus would I
     know,
More of His grace to others show;
More of His saving fulness see,
More of His love who died for me.

  More, more about Jesus,
  More, more about Jesus ;
  More of His saving fulness see,
  More of His love who died for me.

2 More about Jesus let me learn,
More of His holy will discern;
Spirit of God, my teacher be,
Showing the things of Christ to me.

3 More about Jesus, in His Word,
Holding communion with my Lord;
Hearing His voice in every line,
Making each faithful saying mine.

4 More about Jesus, on His throne,
Riches in glory all His own;
More of His kingdom's sure in-
    crease;     [Peace.
More of His coming, Prince of
               *E. E. Hewitt.*

**395** IN the heart of Jesus
    There is love for you,
Love most pure and tender,
    Love most deep and true;
Why should you be lonely,
    Why for friendship sigh,
When the heart of Jesus
    Has a full supply?

2 In the mind of Jesus
    There is thought for you,
Warm as summer sunshine,
    Sweet as morning dew;

Why should you be fearful,
Why take anxious thought,
Since the mind of Jesus
Cares for those He bought?

3 In the field of Jesus
There is work for you;
Such as even angels
Might rejoice to do:
Why stand idly sighing
For some life-work grand,
While the field of Jesus
Seeks your reaping hand?

4 In the home of Jesus
There's a place for you;
Glorious, bright, and joyous,
Calm and peaceful too:
Why then, like a wanderer,
Roam with weary pace,
If the home of Jesus
Holds for you a place?

*Alice Pugh.*

**396** JESUS keep me near the Cross,
There a precious fountain,
Free to all, a healing stream,
Flows from Calv'ry's mountain.

In the Cross, in the Cross,
Be my glory ever ;
Till my raptured soul shall find
Rest beyond the river.

2 Near the Cross, a trembling soul,
Love and mercy found me;
There the bright and morning Star
Shed its beams around me.

3 Near the Cross! O Lamb of God,
Bring its scenes before me;
Help me walk from day to day,
With its shadow o'er me.

4 Near the Cross I'll watch and wait,
Hoping, trusting ever,
Till I reach the golden strand,
Just beyond the river.

*Fanny J. Crosby.*

**397** HARK, my soul, it is the Lord;
'Tis thy Saviour; hear His word;
Jesus speaks, and speaks to thee,
"Say, poor sinner, lov'st thou Me?"

2 " I delivered thee when bound,
And when bleeding, healed thy wound; [right,
Sought thee wand'ring, set thee
Turned thy darkness into light.

3 " Can a woman's tender care
Cease towards the child she bare?
Yes, she may forgetful be,
Yet will I remember thee.

4 " Mine is an unchanging love,
Higher than the heights above,
Deeper than the depths beneath,
Free and faithful, strong as death.

5 " Thou shalt see My glory soon,
When the work of grace is done;
Partner of My throne shalt be;
Say, poor sinner, lov'st thou Me?"

6 Lord, it is my chief complaint
That my love is weak and faint;
Yet I love Thee, and adore;
Oh for grace to love Thee more.

*W. Cowper.*

**398** NEW ev'ry morning is the love
Our wakening and uprising prove;
Through sleep and darkness safely brought, [thought.
Restored to life, and pow'r and

2 New mercies each returning day
Hover around us while we pray;
New perils past, new sins forgiven,
New thoughts of God, new hopes of heaven.

3 If on our daily course our mind
Be set to hallow all we find,
New treasures still of countless price
God will provide for sacrifice.

4 Old friends, old scenes, will lovelier be,
As more of heaven in each we see:
Some softening gleam of love and prayer
Shall dawn on every cross and care.

5 The trivial round, the common task,
Will furnish all we ought to ask;
Room to deny ourselves; a road
To bring us, daily, nearer God.

6 Only, O Lord, in Thy great love
Fit us for perfect rest above;
And help us this and every day,
To live more nearly as we pray.

*John Keble.*

**399** JESUS, let me ever be
Firmly grounded upon Thee,
Ever in Thy work abide,
Ever in Thy wounds reside.

2 Plant, and root, and fix in me
  All the mind that was in Thee;
Settled peace I then shall find;
  Jesu's is a quiet mind.

3 Anger I no more shall feel,
  Always even, always still,
Meekly on my God reclined;
  Jesu's is a gentle mind.

4 I shall suffer and fulfil
  All my Father's gracious will,
Be in all alike resigned;
  Jesu's is a patient mind.

5 When 'tis deeply rooted here,
  Perfect love shall cast out fear;
Fear doth servile spirits bind,
  Jesu's is a noble mind.

6 I shall nothing know beside
  Jesus, and Him crucified;
Perfectly to Him be joined,
  Jesu's is a loving mind.

7 I shall triumph evermore,
  Gratefully my God adore,
God so good, so true, so kind,
  Jesu's is a thankful mind.

8 Lowly, loving, meek, and pure,
  I shall to the end endure,
Be no more to sin inclined;
  Jesu's is a constant mind.

9 I shall fully be restored
  To the image of my Lord,
Witnessing to all mankind,
  Jesu's is a perfect mind.
*Charles Wesley.*

**400** NEARER, my God to Thee,
  Nearer to Thee;
E'en though it be a cross
  That raiseth me,
Still all my song shall be,
Nearer my God to Thee,
  Nearer to Thee.

2 Though, like the wanderer,
  The sun gone down,
Darkness be over me,
  My rest a stone,
Yet in my dreams I'd be
Nearer, my God, to Thee,
  Nearer to Thee!

3 There let the way appear
  Steps unto heaven;
All that Thou send'st to me
  In mercy given;

Angels to beckon me
Nearer, my God, to Thee,
  Nearer to Thee!

4 Then, with my waking thoughts
  Bright with Thy praise,
Out of my stony griefs
  Bethel I'll raise;
So by my woes to be
Nearer, my God, to Thee,
  Nearer to Thee!

5 Or if on joyful wing
  Cleaving the sky,
Sun, moon, and stars forgot,
  Upwards I fly,
Still all my song shall be,
Nearer, my God, to Thee,
  Nearer to Thee!
*Sarah F. Adams.*

**401** O TELL me more of Christ, my
    Saviour;     [o'er;
  On this glad theme dwell o'er and
His boundless grace, His saving
  favour,     [more!
  His precious name, O tell me

O tell me more ! so much I need
His power to keep, His hand to lead ;
O tell me more of Him I love,
Until I see His face above.

2 O tell me more of love's sweet
    story,     [me;
  If you would cheer and comfort
How Jesus wept, the King of glory,
  Those tender tears of sympathy.

3 O tell me more! and I repeating,
  The happy news shall spread the
    joy;     [completing,
Come, blessèd Lord, Thy work
  Till songs of praise our lips em-
    ploy.     *E. E. Hewitt.*

**402** EARTHLY pleasures vainly call
    me,
  I would be like Jesus;
Nothing worldly shall enthrall me,
  I would be like Jesus.

    Be like Jesus, this my song,
    In the home and in the throng ;
    Be like Jesus, all day long !
    I would be like Jesus.

2 He has broken every fetter,
  I would be like Jesus;
That my soul may serve Him better,
  I would be like Jesus.

3 All the way from earth to glory,
    I would be like Jesus;
Telling o'er and o'er my story,
    I would be like Jesus.

4 That in heaven He may meet me,
    I would be like Jesus; [greet me,
That His words " Well done " may
    I would be like Jesus.
                        *J. Rowe.*

**403** THRICE-BLESSED Spirit! Giver
    of salvation,    [of shame;
Purchased by Jesus on the cross
Dwell in our hearts; transform
    them with Thy beauty—
Fairest adorning of our Saviour's
    name.

2 Thy nine-fold grace bestow upon us
    freely: —
    Love, deep and full, to God and
    all mankind;     [sorrow;
Joy in the Lord, 'mid every earthly
    Peace, calm and sweet, that
    guardeth heart and mind.

3 Make us long-suff'ring, 'mid earth's
    provocations;     [ing wrong;
    Gentleness give us, when endur-
Goodness impart, that we e'en foes
    may succour;
Faithfulness grant, to change our
    toil to song.

4 Meekness bestow, with humble self-
    abasement,    [controlling might;
    And self-control, through Thy
And as we list to every call of duty,
May we do all as in Thy search-
    ing sight.

5 Then with the gift of holiness with-
    in us;     [more Divine;
    We not less human, but made
Our lives replete with heaven's
    supernal beauty,    [is Thine.
Ever declare—That beauty, Lord,
                    *J. Mountain.*

**404** JESU, my Lord, my God, my
    All,
Hear me, blest Saviour, when I call;
Hear me, and from Thy dwelling-
    place
Pour down the riches of Thy grace:

Jesu, my Lord, I Thee adore ;
Oh, make me love Thee more and more.

2 Jesu, too late I Thee have sought;
How can I love Thee as I ought?
And how extol Thy matchless fame,
The glorious beauty of Thy name?

3 Jesu, what didst Thou find in me
That Thou hast dealt so lovingly?
How great the joy that Thou hast
    brought,
So far exceeding hope or thought!

4 Jesu, of Thee shall be my song;
To Thee my heart and soul belong;
All that I have or am is Thine,
And Thou, blest Saviour, Thou art
    mine.     *Henry Collins.*

**405** IF you want pardon, if you
    want peace,     [cease,
If you want sorrow or sighing to
Look up to Jesus who died on the
    tree,
    To purchase a full salvation.

Living beneath the shade of the Cross,
Counting the jewels of earth but dross ;
Cleansed in the blood that flows from His
    side.
Enjoying a full salvation.

2 If you want Jesus to reign in your
    soul,     [shall be whole;
Plunge in the fountain and you
Washed in the blood of the Cruci-
    fied One,
    Enjoying a full salvation.

3 If you want boldness, take part in
    the fight;     [light;
If you want purity, walk in the
If you want liberty, shout and be
    free,
    Enjoying a full salvation.

4 If you want holiness, cling to the
    cross,     [dross;
Counting the riches of earth as
Down at His feet you'll be cleansed
    and made free,
    Enjoying a full salvation.

**406** LOWER and lower, dear Lord,
    at Thy feet,
Seeking Thy Spirit, Thy mercy so
    sweet;     [we fall,
Down in our need, blessèd Master,
Lower and lower; be Thou all in all.

Lower and lower, down at Thy cross,
All the world's treasure counting but dross ;
Down at Thy feet, blessèd Saviour we fall,
Lower, still lower, Christ all in all.

2 Lower and lower, dear Saviour, we
    pray,      [day:
Losing the self-life still more every
Weak and unworthy, we're looking
    above;      [love.
Empty us, Jesus; then fill us with
3 Lower and lower; yet higher we
    rise,      [skies;
Lifted in Jesus, led on to the
Humbly we follow the way of the
    cross,      [for all loss
Then, crowns of glory, and gain
        *E. E. Hewitt.*

**407** WE shall see the desert as the
    rose,
    Walking in the King's highway;
There'll be singing where salvation
    goes,
    Walking in the King's highway.
There's a highway there, and a way, . . .
Where sorrow shall flee away, . . .
And the light shines bright as the day . . .
Walking in the King's highway.

2 We shall see the glory of the Lord,
    Walking in the King's highway;
And behold the beauty of His
    Word,
    Walking in the King's highway.
3 There the rain shall come upon the
    ground,
    Walking in the King's highway;
And the springs of water will be
    found
    Walking in the King's highway.
4 There no rav'nous beast shall make
    afraid,
    Walking in the King's highway;
For the purified the way is made,
    Walking in the King's highway.
5 No unclean thing shall pass o'er
    here,
    Walking in the King's highway;
But the ransomed ones without a
    fear,
    Walking in the King's highway.
        *Florence Horton.*

**408** ARE you trusting Jesus,
    All along the way?
Does He grow more precious
    To your heart each day?
Are you His disciple?
    Test His word and see,
He will give the Spirit
    More abundantly.

More . . . abundantly, more . . . abundantly,
"That they might have life, and more
  abundantly."

2 For His matchless favour
    Magnify the name
Of our gracious Saviour
    Who from glory came;
Let the saints adore Him
    For this wondrous word,
Sealing our redemption
    Through the crimson flood.
3 Come to Him believing,
    Harken to His call;
All from Him receiving,
    Yield to Him your all;
Jesus will accept you
    When to Him you flee;
He will grant His blessing
    More abundantly.   *Thoro Harris.*

**409** ONCE far from God and dead
    in sin,
    No light my heart could see;
But in God's Word the light I
    found,
    Now Christ liveth in me.
    Christ liveth in me, . . .
    Christ liveth in me, . . .
  Oh, what a salvation this,
  That Christ liveth in me.
2 As rays of light from yonder sun
    The flowers of earth set free,
    So life and light and love came
    forth
    From Christ living in me.
3 As lives the flower within the seed,
    As in the cone the tree,
    So, praise the God of truth and
    grace,
    His Spirit dwelleth in me.
4 With longing all my heart is filled,
    That like Him I may be,
    As on the wondrous thought I
    dwell,
    That Christ liveth in me.
        *El Nathan.*

**410** DEEPER, deeper in the love of
    Jesus
    Daily let me go;
Higher, higher in the school of wis-
    More of grace to know.  [dom,
  O deep . . . er yet I pray, . . .
  And high . . . er every day, . . .
  And wis . . . er, blessèd Lord, . . .
  In Thy precious, holy word.

2 Deeper, deeper! blessèd Holy
Take me deeper still, [Spirit,
Till my life is wholly lost in Jesus
And His perfect will.

3 Deeper, deeper! though it cost hard
Deeper let me go! [trials,
Rooted in the holy love of Jesus,
Let me fruitful grow.

4 Deeper, higher every day in Jesus,
Till all conflict past,
Finds me conquror, and in His
Perfected at last. [own image

*Charles Price Jones.*

**411** IN the blood from the Cross
I have been washed from sin;
But to be free from dross,
Still I would enter in.

Deeper yet, deeper yet,
Into the crimson flood ;
Deeper yet, deeper yet,
Under the precious blood.

2 Day by day, hour by hour
Blessings are sent to me;
But for more of His power,
Ever my prayer shall be.

3 Near to Christ I would live,
Following Him each day;
What I ask He will give,
So then with faith I pray.

4 Now I have peace, sweet peace,
While in this world of sin;
But to pray I'll not cease
Till I am pure within.

*Johnson Oatman, Jr.*

**412** O TO be like Thee, blessèd Re-
deemer, [prayer;
This is my constant longing and
Gladly I'll forfeit all of earth's
treasures, [wear.
Jesus, Thy perfect likeness to

O, to be like Thee, O, to be like Thee,
Blessèd Redeemer, pure as Thou art ;
Come in Thy sweetness, come in Thy
fulness ; [heart.
Stamp Thine own image deep on my

2 O to be like Thee, full of com-
passion, [kind
Loving, forgiving, tender and
Helping the helpless, cheering the
fainting, [find.
Seeking the wand'ring sinner to

3 O to be like Thee, lowly in spirit,
Holy and harmless, patient and
brave ;

Meekly enduring cruel reproaches,
Willing to suffer, others to save.

4 O to be like Thee, Lord, I am com-
ing, [divine
Now to receive th'anointing
All that I am and have I am bring-
ing, [be Thine.
Lord, from this moment all shall

5 O to be like Thee, while I am
pleading, [love,
Pour out Thy Spirit, fill with Thy
Make me a temple meet for Thy
dwelling.
Fit me for life and heaven above.

*T. O. Chisholm.*

**413** JESUS, lead me up the moun-
tain,
Where the whitest robes are seen,
Where the saints can see the foun-
tain,
Where the pure are keeping clean.

Bring me high . . . er up the mountain,
Into fel . . . lowship with Thee ; . . .
In Thy light . . . I see the Fountain,
And the blood that cleanseth me. . . .

2 Higher up, where light increases,
Rich above all earthly good,
Where the life of sinning ceases,
Where the Spirit comes in flood.

3 Bring me higher, nothing dreading,
In the race that has no stop,
In Thy footsteps keep me treading,
Give me strength to reach the top.

4 Make me better, make me purer,
Keep me where the fire refines,
Where the breath of God is sweeter,
Where the brightest glory shines.

**414** TAKE time to be holy, speak
oft with thy Lord;
Abide in Him always, and feed on
His Word;
Make friends of God's children,
help those who are weak;
Forgetting in nothing His blessing
to seek.

2 Take time to be holy, the world
rushes on; [Jesus alone—
Spend much time in secret with
By looking to Jesus, like Him thou
shalt be; [ness shall see.
Thy friends in thy conduct His like-

3 Take time to be holy, let Him be
   thy Guide;        [betide;
And run not before Him, whatever
In joy or in sorrow still follow thy
   Lord,           [His word.
And, looking to Jesus, still trust in

4 Take time to be holy, be calm in
   thy soul;    [neath His control:
Each thought and each temper be-
Thus led by His Spirit to fountains
   of love,        [vice above.
Thou soon shalt be fitted for ser-
                *W. D. Longstaff.*

**415** OH, the bitter shame and
   sorrow,
   That a time could ever be,
When I let the Saviour's pity
   Plead in vain, and proudly an-
   swered,
"All of self, and none of Thee!"

2 Yet He found me; I beheld Him
   Bleeding on the accursèd tree,
Heard Him pray, "Forgive them
   Father!"       [faintly—
   And my wistful heart said
"Some of self, and some of Thee."

3 Day by day His tender mercy,
   Healing, helping, full, and free,
Sweet and strong, and, ah! so
   patient.        [pered,
   Brought me lower, while I whis-
"Less of self, and more of Thee."

4 Higher than the highest heavens,
   Deeper than the deepest sea,
Lord, Thy love at last hath con-
   quered;        [tion—
   Grant me now my supplica-
"None of self, and all of Thee."
                *Thomas Monod.*

**416** OUT of my bondage, sorrow
   and night,
   Jesus I come, Jesus, I come;
Into Thy freedom, gladness and
   Jesus I come to Thee;    [light,
Out of my sickness into Thy health,
Out of my want and into Thy
   wealth,
Out of my sin and into Thyself,
   Jesus, I come to Thee.

2 Out of my shameful failure and
   loss,
   Jesus, I come, Jesus, I come;

Into the glorious gain of Thy cross,
   Jesus, I come to Thee;
Out of earth's sorrows into Thy
   balm,          [calm,
Out of life's storms and into Thy
Out of distress to jubilant psalm,
   Jesus, I come to Thee.

3 Out of unrest and arrogant pride,
   Jesus, I come, Jesus, I come;
Into Thy blessèd will to abide,
   Jesus, I come to Thee;
Out of myself to dwell in Thy love,
Out of despair into raptures above,
Upward for aye on wings like a
   dove,
   Jesus, I come to Thee.

4 Out of the fear and dread of the
   tomb,
   Jesus, I come, Jesus, I come;
Into the joy and light of my home,
   Jesus, I come to Thee;
Out of the depths of ruin untold,
Into the peace of Thy sheltering
   fold,
Ever Thy glorious face to behold,
   Jesus, I come to Thee.
               *William T. Sleeper.*

**417** HE walks with God, who
   speaks to God in prayer,
And daily brings to Him his daily
   care;         [knows
Possessing inward peace, he truly
A heart's refreshment and a soul's
   repose.

2 He walks with God, who, as he
   onward moves,    [he loves,
Follows the footsteps of the Lord
And keeping Him for ever in his
   view,          [too.
His Saviour sees and his example

3 He walks with God, who turns his
   face to Heaven, [Jesus given,
And keeps the blest commands by
His life upright, his end untroubled
   peace,     [labours cease.
Whom God will crown when all his

**418** O JESUS Christ, grow Thou in
   me,
   And all things else recede!
My heart be daily nearer Thee,
   From sin be daily freed.

2 Each day let Thy supporting might
    My weakness still embrace;
My darkness vanish in Thy light,
    Thy life my death efface.

3 In Thy bright beams which on me
    Fade every evil thought;  [fall
That I am nothing, Thou art all,
    I would be daily taught.

4 More of Thy glory let me see
    Thou Holy, Wise, and True!
I would Thy living image be,
    In joy and sorrow too.

5 Fill me with gladness from above,
    Hold me by strength Divine:
Lord, let the glow of Thy great love
    Through my whole being shine.

6 Make this poor self grow less and
    Be Thou my life and aim;  [less,
Oh, make me daily through Thy
    grace
    More meet to bear Thy name!
        *J. C. Lavater ; tr. Mrs. E.L. Smith.*

**419** IN the cross of Christ I glory,
    Towering o'er the wrecks of
        time;
All the light of sacred story
    Gathers round its head sublime.

2 When the woes of life o'ertake me,
    Hopes deceive and fears annoy,
Never shall the cross forsake me,
    Lo! it glows with peace and joy.

3 When the sun of bliss is beaming
    Light and love upon my way,
From the cross the radiance stream-
Adds new lustre to the day. [ing

4 Bane and blessing, pain and plea-
By the cross are sanctified : [sure,
    Peace is there that knows no mea-
    sure,
    Joys that through all time abide.
        *John Bowring.*

**420** WALK in the light! so shalt
    thou know
That fellowship of love
His Spirit only can bestow,
    Who reigns in light above.

2 Walk in the light! and sin ab-
Shall ne'er defile again;  [horred
The blood of Jesus Christ thy Lord
    Shall cleanse from every stain.

3 Walk in the light! and thou shalt
    Thy heart made truly His, [find
Who dwells in cloudless light en-
    shrined,
    In Whom no darkness is.

4 Walk in the light! and thou shalt
    Thy darkness passed away, [own
Because that light hath on thee
    In which is perfect day. [shone

5 Walk in the light! and e'en the
    tomb
    No fearful shade shall wear;
Glory shall chase away its gloom,
    For Christ hath conquered there.

6 Walk in the light! and thine shall
    be
    A path, though thorny, bright;
For God by grace shall dwell in
    And God Himself is Light. [thee
        *Bernard Barton.*

**421** ONWARD still, and upward,
    Follow evermore
Where our mighty Leader
    Goes in love before;
" Looking unto Jesus,"
    Reach a helping hand,
To a struggling neighbour,
    Helping him to stand.

    Marching on ... ward, ... up ... ward, ...
    Marching steadily onward, Jesus leads the
      way,
    Marching on ... ward, ... up ... ward, ...
    Onward unto glory, to the perfect day.

2 Onward, ever onward,
    Through the pastures green,
Where the streams flow softly
    Under skies serene;
Or, if need be, upward,
    O'er the rocky steep,
Trusting Him to guide us,
    Strong to save and keep.

3 Upward, ever upward,
    T'ward the radiant glow,
Far above the valley,
    Where the mist hangs low;
On, with songs of gladness,
    Till the march shall end,
Where ten thousand thousand
    Hallelujahs blend.
        *E. E. Hewitt.*

**422** BLEST are the humble souls
    that see
Their emptiness and poverty;

Treasures of grace to them are
given,                              [heaven.
And crowns of joy laid up in

2 Blest are the men of broken heart,
Who mourn for sin and inward
smart;
The blood of Christ divinely flows,
A healing balm for all their woes.

3 Blest are the souls that long for
grace,                              [ness;
Hunger and thirst for righteous-
They shall be well supplied and fed,
With living streams and living
bread.

4 Blest are the pure, whose hearts are
clean
From the defiling power of sin;
With endless pleasure they shall see
The God of spotless purity.

5 Blest are the sufferers, who partake
Of pain and shame for Jesu's sake;
Their souls shall triumph in the
Lord;
Glory and joy are their reward.
                              *Isaac Watts.*

**423** COME, O Thou Traveller un-
known,
Whom still I hold but cannot see;
My company before is gone,
And I am left alone with Thee;
With Thee all night I mean to stay,
And wrestle till the break of day.

2 I need not tell Thee who I am;
My misery or sin declare;
Thyself hast called me by my name,
Look on Thy hands, and read it
there.
But who, I ask Thee, who art Thou?
Tell me Thy name, and tell me now.

3 Yield to me now, for I am weak,
But confident in self-despair;
Speak to my heart, in blessings
speak,                              [prayer:
Be conquered by my instant
Speak, or Thou never hence shalt
move,
And tell me if Thy name is Love.

4 'Tis Love! 'tis Love! Thou diedst
for me!
I hear Thy whisper in my heart;

The morning breaks, the shadows
flee;
Pure, universal Love Thou art:
To me, to all, Thy mercies move;
Thy nature and Thy name is Love.

5 My prayer hath power with God:
the grace
Unspeakable I now receive;
Through faith I see Thee face to
face,
I see Thee face to face, and live;
In vain I have not wept and strove,
Thy nature and Thy name is Love.

6 I know Thee, Saviour, who Thou
art,
Jesus, the feeble sinner's friend;
Nor wilt Thou with the night de-
part,
But stay and love me to the end.
Thy mercies never shall remove;
Thy nature and Thy name is Love.
                              *Charles Wesley.*

**424** THE mercy of God is an ocean
divine,                              [flood;
A boundless and fathomless
Launch out in the deep, cut away
the shore line,                              [God.
And be lost in the fulness of

Launch out . . . into the deep, . . .
Oh, let the shore-line go,
Launch out, launch out in the ocean Divine,
Out where the full tides flow.

2 But many, alas! only stand on the
shore
And gaze on the ocean so wide;
They never have ventured its depths
to explore,                              [tide,
Or to launch on the fathomless

3 And others just venture away from
the land,
And linger so near to the shore;
That the surf and the slime that
beat over the strand,
Dash o'er them in floods evermore.

4 Oh, let us launch out on this ocean
so broad,                              [flow;
Where the floods of salvation e'er
Oh, let us be lost in the mercy of
God,                              [know.
Till the depth of His fulness we
                              *A. B. Simpson.*

## (3) CONFLICT AND VICTORY

**425** MARCHING on in the light of
God,
  Marching on, I'm marching on:
Up the path that the Master trod,
  Marching, marching on.

A robe of white, a crown of gold,
A harp, a home, a mansion fair,
A victor's palm, a joy untold,
Are mine when I get there,
For Jesus is my Saviour, He's washed my
  sins away,
Paid my debt on Calv'ry's mountain,
Happy in His dying love, singing all the day,
I'm living, yes, I'm living in the Fountain.

2 Marching on through the hosts of
sin,
  Marching on, I'm marching on:
Victory's mine while I've Christ
  Marching on, marching on. [within,

3 Marching on while the worldlings
sneer,
  Marching on, I'm marching on:
Perfect love casteth out all fear,
  Marching, marching on.

4 Marching on in the Spirit's might,
  Marching on, I'm marching on;
More than conqueror in every fight,
  Marching, marching on.

5 Marching on to the realms above,
  Marching on, I'm marching on:
There to sing of redeeming love,
  Marching, marching on.
                                    *R. Johnson.*

**426** THROUGH the night of doubt
and sorrow
  Onward goes the pilgrim band,
Singing songs of expectation,
  Marching to the Promised Land.

2 Clear before us through the dark-
ness,                        [light;
  Gleams and burns the guiding
Brother clasps the hand of brother
  Stepping fearless through the
night.

3 One the light of God's own pre-
sence,
  O'er His ransomed people shed,
Chasing far the gloom and terror,
  Brightening all the path we tread.

4 One the object of our journey,
  One the faith that never tires,
One the earnest looking forward,
  One the hope our God inspires.

5 One the strain that lips of thous-
ands
  Lift as from the heart of one;
One the conflict, one the peril,
  One the march in God begun.

6 One the gladness of rejoicing
  On the far, eternal shore,
Where the One Almighty Father
  Reigns in love for evermore.

7 Onward, therefore, pilgrim bro-
thers,
  Onward with the Cross our aid!
Bear its shame, and fight its battle,
  Till we rest beneath its shade.

8 Soon shall come the great awaking,
  Soon the rending of the tomb;
Then the scattering of all shadows,
  And the end of toil and gloom.
                            *tr. S. Baring-Gould.*

**427** WHEN upon life's billows you
are tempest-tossed,
  When you are discouraged, think-
ing all is lost,
Count your many blessings, name
  them one by one,
And it will surprise you what the
  Lord hath done.

Count your blessings, name them one by one,
Count your blessings, see what God hath
  done ;
Count your blessings, name them one by one,
And it will surprise you what the Lord hath
  done.

2 Are you ever burdened with a load
  of care?        [called to bear?
Does the cross seem heavy you are
  Count your many blessings, every
  doubt will fly,          [go by.
And you will be singing as the days

3 When you look at others with their
  lands and gold,
Think that Christ has promised you
  His wealth untold,
Count your many blessings, money
  cannot buy
Your reward in heaven, nor your
  home on high.

4 So amid the conflict, whether great
  or small,            [over all,
Do not be discouraged, God is
  Count your many blessings, angels
  will attend,
Help and comfort give you to your
  journey's end.
                        *Johnson Oatman, Jr.*

**428** QUIT you like men, be strong!
Wax valiant in the fight;
See! yonder Captain leads the throng,
In Whom is your delight.

2 Though battle's thunders roar,
And hosts of darkness press,
He is alive for evermore,
And succours our distress.

3 List to the swelling strains
Of those who fought and won,
They laud the Lamb, the crimson stains
His vesture are upon:

4 'Twas through His precious Confession to His Name, [blood,
And lives laid down, that they once stood
And every foe o'ercame.

5 Shall we, then, faint and fall
When strength seems all but gone?
Nay, rather, on your Captain call
And look to Him alone;

6 " For I am strong when weak,"
O count this saying true, [speak
The Lord doth strength and comfort
As no one else can do.

*Ernest T. Mellor.*

**429** ONWARD, Christian soldiers!
Marching as to war,
Looking unto Jesus,
Who is gone before;
Christ, the Royal Master,
Leads against the foe;
Forward into battle,
See His banners go.
Onward, Christian soldiers !
Marching as to war,
Looking unto Jesus,
Who is gone before.

2 At the name of Jesus
Satan's host doth flee;
On then, Christian soldiers,
On to victory!
Hell's foundations quiver
At the shout of praise:
Brothers, lift your voices,
Loud your anthems raise.

3 Like a mighty army
Moves the church of God:
Brothers, we are treading
Where the saints have trod.

We are not divided,
All one body we—
One in hope and doctrine,
One in charity.

4 Crowns and thrones may perish,
Kingdoms rise and wane;
But the church of Jesus
Constant will remain:
Gates of hell can never
'Gainst that church prevail;
We have Christ's own promise—
And that cannot fail.

5 Onward then, ye people,
Join our happy throng;
Blend with ours your voices
In the triumph song:
" Glory, praise and honour,
Unto Christ the King,"—
This, through countless ages,
Men and angels sing.

*S. Baring-Gould.*

**430** OFT in danger, oft in woe,
Onward, Christians, onward go;
Fight the fight, maintain the strife,
Strengthened with the Bread of Life.

2 Shrink not, Christians: will ye yield?
Will ye quit the painful field?
Will ye flee in danger's hour?
Know ye not your Captain's power?

3 Let your drooping hearts be glad;
March in heavenly armour clad:
Fight, nor think the battle long;
Soon shall victory tune your song.

4 Let not sorrow dim your eye,
Soon shall every tear be dry;
Let not fears your course impede,
Great your strength if great your need.

5 Onward then to glory move
More than conquerors ye shall prove;
Though opposed by many a foe,
Christian soldiers, onward go.

*H. K. White and F. S. Colquhoun.*

**431** WHO is on the Lord's side?
Who will serve the King?
Who will be His helpers,
Other lives to bring?
Who will leave the world's side?
Who will face the foe?

Who is on the Lord's side?
  Who for Him will go?
By Thy call of mercy,
  By Thy grace divine,
We are on the Lord's side,
  Saviour, we are Thine!

2 Not for weight of glory,
    Not for crown and palm,
  Enter we the army,
    Raise the warrior psalm;
  But for love that claimeth
    Lives for whom He died:
  He whom Jesus nameth
    Must be on His side!
  By Thy love constraining,
    By Thy grace divine,
  We are on the Lord's side,
    Saviour, we are Thine!

3 Jesus, Thou hast bought us,
    Not with gold or gem,
  But with Thine own life-blood
    For Thy diadem;
  With Thy blessing filling
    All who come to Thee,
  Thou hast made us willing.
    Thou hast made us free.
  By Thy grand redemption,
    By Thy grace divine,
  We are on the Lord's side,
    Saviour, we are Thine!

4 Fierce may be the conflict,
    Strong may be the foe;
  But the King's own army
    None can overthrow:
  Round His standard ranging,
    Vict'ry is secure,
  For His truth unchanging
    Makes the triumph sure.
  Joyfully enlisting,
    By Thy grace divine,
  We are on the Lord's side,
    Saviour, we are Thine!
                *Frances R. Havergal.*

**432** FIGHT the good fight with all
        thy might,        [thy right;
  Christ is thy strength, and Christ
  Lay hold on life, and it shall be
  Thy joy and crown eternally.

2 Run the straight race through God's
        good grace,        [Face;
  Lift up thine eyes, and seek His
  Life with its way before thee lies,
  Christ is the path, and Christ thy
  prize.

3 Cast care aside, lean on thy Guide;
  His boundless mercy will provide;
  Lean, and the trusting soul shall
        prove,
  Christ is its life, and Christ its love.

4 Faint not, nor fear, His arms are
        near,
  He changeth not, and thou art dear;
  Only believe, and thou shalt see
  That Christ is all in all to thee.
                *J. S. B. Monsell.*

**433** SOLDIERS of Christ, arise—
        And put your armour on,
  Strong in the strength which God
        supplies
    Through His eternal Son!

2 Strong in the Lord of hosts,
    Stand in His mighty power;
  Who in the strength of Jesus trusts
    Is more than conqueror!

3 Stand then in His great might,
    With all His strength endued;
  And take, to arm you for the fight,
    The panoply of God.

4 To keep your armour bright,
    Attend with constant care;
  Still marching in your Captain's
        sight,
    And watching unto prayer.

5 From strength to strength go on,
    Wrestle and fight and pray,
  Tread all the powers of darkness
        down
    And win the well-fought day.

6 Then, having all things done,
    And every conflict past—
  Accepted each through Christ alone,
    You shall be crowned at last.
                *Charles Wesley.*

**434** A SAFE stronghold our God is
        still,
  A trusty shield and weapon;
  He'll help us clear from all the ill
    That hath us now o'ertaken.
      The ancient prince of hell
      Hath risen with purpose fell;
      Strong mail of craft and power
      He weareth in this hour;
    On earth is not his fellow.

2 With force of arms we nothing can,
  Full soon were we down-ridden;
But for us fights the proper Man,
  Whom God Himself hath bidden.
    Ask ye: Who is this same?
    Christ Jesus is His name,
    The Lord Sabaoth's Son;
    He, and no other one,
  Shall conquer in the battle.

3 And were this world all devils o'er,
  And watching to devour us,
We lay it not to heart so sore;
  Not they can overpower us.
    And let the prince of ill
    Look grim as e'er he will,
    He harms us not a whit:
    For why? His doom is writ;
  A word shall quickly slay him.

4 God's word, for all their craft and
    force
  One moment will not linger,
But, spite of hell, shall have its
    course;
  'Tis written by His finger.
    And though they take our life,
    Goods, honour, children, wife.
    Yet is their profit small:
    These things shall vanish all;
  The city of God remaineth.
        *Martin Luther ; tr. Thomas Carlyle.*

**435** HE who would valiant be
    'Gainst all disaster,
  Let him in constancy
    Follow the Master.
  There's no discouragement
  Shall make him once relent
  His first avowed intent
    To be a pilgrim.

2 Who so beset him round
    With dismal stories,
  Do but themselves confound—
    His strength the more is.
  No foes shall stay his might,
  Though he with giants fight:
  He will make good his right
    To be a pilgrim.

3 Since, Lord, thou dost defend
    Us with thy Spirit,
  We know we at the end
    Shall life inherit.

Then fancies flee away!
I'll fear not what men say,
I'll labour night and day,
  To be a pilgrim.
            *John Bunyan and others.*

**436** SOUND the battle cry!
    See! the foe is nigh;
  Raise the standard high
      For the Lord;
  Gird your armour on,
  Stand firm ev'ry one;
  Rest your cause upon
      His holy word.

  Rouse, then, soldiers ! rally round the
      banner !
  Ready, steady, pass the word along ;
  Onward, forward, shout aloud Hosanna !
    Christ is Captain of the mighty throng.

2 Strong to meet the foe,
  Marching on we go,
  While our cause we know
      Must prevail;
  Shield and banner bright
  Gleaming in the light;
  Battling for the right,
      We ne'er can fail.

3 O! Thou God of all,
  Hear us when we call;
  Help us one and all,
      By Thy grace;
  When the battle's done,
  And the vict'ry won,
  May we wear the crown
      Before Thy face.
            *W. F. Sherwin.*

**437** FORWARD! be our watchword,
    Steps and voices joined;
  Seek the things before us,
    Not a look behind;
  Burns the fiery pillar
    At our army's head;
  Who shall dream of shrinking,
    By our Captain led?
  Forward through the desert,
    Through the toil and fight;
  Canaan lies before us,
    Zion beams with light.

2 Forward! flock of Jesus,
    Salt of all the earth,
  Till each yearning purpose
    Spring to glorious birth:
  Sick, they ask for healing,
    Blind, they grope for day;

Pour upon the nations
  Wisdom's loving ray!
Forward, out of error,
  Leave behind the night;
Forward through the darkness,
  Forward into light.

3 Glories upon glories
    Hath our God prepared,
  By the souls that love Him
    One day to be shared:
  Eye hath not beheld them;
    Ear hath never heard;
  Nor of these hath uttered
    Thought or speech a word;
  Forward, ever forward,
    Clad in armour bright;
  Till the veil be lifted,
    Till our faith be sight.

4 Far o'er yon horizon
    Rise the city towers,
  Where our God abideth;
    That fair home is ours!
  Flash the gates with jasper,
    Shine the streets with gold;
  Flows the gladdening river,
    Shedding joys untold;
  Thither, onward, thither,
    In the Spirit's might:
  Pilgrims, to your country,
    Forward into light!   *H. Alford.*

**438**  STAND up! stand up for Jesus,
        Ye soldiers of the Cross;
  Lift high His royal banner;
    It must not suffer loss.
  From vict'ry unto vict'ry
    His army shall He lead,
  Till every foe is vanquished,
    And Christ is Lord indeed.

> Stand up for Jesus,
>   Ye soldiers of the Cross !
> Lift high His royal banner,
>   It must not suffer loss !

2 Stand up! stand up for Jesus!
    The trumpet call obey;
  Forth to the mighty conflict,
    In this His glorious day;
  Ye that are men now serve Him
    Against unnumbered foes;
  Let courage rise with danger,
    And strength to strength oppose.

3 Stand up! stand up for Jesus!
    Stand in His strength alone;
  The arm of flesh will fail you,
    Ye dare not trust your own;

Put on the gospel armour,
  And watching unto prayer;
Where duty calls, or danger,
  Be never wanting there.

4 Stand up! stand up for Jesus!
    The strife will not be long;
  This day the noise of battle,
    The next the victor's song;
  To him that overcometh,
    A crown of life shall be;
  He with the King of glory
    Shall reign eternally.   *G. Duffield.*

**439**  A LIFE of overcoming,
        A life of ceaseless praise,
  Be this thy blessèd portion
    Throughout the coming days.
  The victory was purchased
    On Calv'ry's cross for thee,
  Sin shall not have dominion,
    The Son hath made thee free.

2 And would'st thou know the secret
    Of constant victory?
  Let in the Overcomer,
    And He will conquer thee!
  Thy broken spirit taken
    In sweet captivity
  Shall glory in His triumph
    And share His victory.

3 Though all the path before thee
    The host of darkness fill,
  Look to thy Father's promise,
    And claim the vict'ry still.
  Faith sees the heavenly legions,
    Where doubt sees naught but
      foes,
  And through the very conflict
    Her life the stronger grows.

4 More stern will grow the conflict
    As nears our King's return,
  And they alone can face it
    Who this great lesson learn:—
  That from them God asks nothing
    But to unlatch the door
  Admitting Him who, through them,
    Will conquer evermore.
                *Freda Hanbury Allen.*

**440**  BLESSED Lord, in Thee is
          refuge,
  Safety for my trembling soul,
  Power to lift my head when droop-
      ing,
    'Midst the angry billows' roll.
      I will trust Thee,
  All my life Thou shalt control.

2 In the past too unbelieving
  'Midst the tempest I have been,
And my heart has slowly trusted
  What my eyes have never seen.
    Blessèd Jesus,
  Teach me on Thine arm to lean.

3 Oh, for trust that brings me tri-
    umph,            [near!
  When defeat seems strangely
Oh, for faith that changes fighting
  Into vict'ry's ringing cheer!
    Faith triumphant!
  Knowing not defeat or fear.

4 Faith triumphant—blessèd vict'ry!
  Every barrier swept away!
Heaven descending, joy and fulness,
  Dawn of everlasting day!
    Jesus only—
  Him to love and Him obey.
                    *H. H. Booth.*

**441** THEY who know the Saviour
    shall in Him be strong,
Mighty in the conflict of the right
    'gainst wrong.    [God's word,
This the blessed promise given in
Doing wondrous exploits, they who
    know the Lord.

  Victory! victory! blessed blood-bought
    victory,
  Victory! victory! vict'ry all the time.
  **As Jehovah liveth, strength divine He giveth,**
    Unto those who know Him vict'ry all the
    time.

2 In the midst of battle be not thou
    dismayed,
  Though the powers of darkness
    'gainst thee are arrayed;
  God, thy strength, is with thee,
    causing thee to stand,
  Heaven's allied armies wait at thy
    command.

3 Brave to bear life's testing, strong
    the foe to meet,
  Walking like a hero midst the fur-
    nace heat,        [Spirit's sword
  Doing wondrous exploits with the
  Winning souls for Jesus, praise, O
    praise the Lord.
                    *Mrs. C. H. Morris.*

**442** LORD of our life, and God of
    our salvation,
Star of our night, and hope of every
    nation,            [supplication,
Hear and receive Thy Church's
    Lord God Almighty.

2 See round Thine ark the hungry
    billows curling;    [unfurling;
See how Thy foes their banners are
Lord, while their darts envenomed
    they are hurling,
    Thou canst preserve us.

3 Lord, Thou canst help when earthly
    armour faileth;    [sin assaileth;
Lord, Thou canst save when deadly
Lord, o'er Thy rock nor death nor
    hell prevaileth:
    Grant us Thy peace, Lord.

4 Grant us Thy help till foes are
    backward driven;
  Grant them Thy truth that they
    may be forgiven;
  Grant peace on earth, and, after
    we have striven,
    Peace in Thy heaven.
              *M. A. Lowenstern and P. Pusey.*

**443** WE never need be vanquished,
    We never need give in,
  Though waging war with Satan,
    And compassed round by sin.
  Temptations will beset us,
    Allurements oft assail,
  But in the name of Jesus,
    We shall, we must prevail.

    Victory in Jesus' name,
    Victory our hearts proclaim,
    Victory, glorious victory.

2 He leads us on in triumph,
    An overcoming band,
  While vict'ry crowns His progress,
    "For none can stay his hand."
  Our eyes are on our Leader,
    His presence is our might;
  He arms us for the conflict,
    And trains our hands to fight.

3 God wills not that His people
    By sin enthralled should be,
  But that their lives henceforward
    Be lives of victory;
  And so at our disposal,
    He places all His power,
  That we from its resources
    May draw in danger's hour.

4 Herein is hid the secret
    Of an all-glorious life,
  Whereby we conquer Satan,
    And rise above sin's strife.

Abiding in the Saviour,
  Self prostrate in the dust,
We live to do His bidding,
  In glad perpetual trust.

5 We in ourselves are nothing,
    A small and feeble host,
  Nor have we aught of prowess
    Wherewith to make our boast,
  Our stronghold is Christ Jesus,
    His grace alone we plead,
  His name our shield and banner,
    Himself just all we need.
                    *W. A. Garratt.*


**444**  Ho, my comrades! see the sig-
           nal
         Waving in the sky!
       Reinforcements now appearing,
         Victory is nigh!

    "Hold the fort, for I am coming,"
      Jesus signals still ;
    Wave the answer back to heaven,
      "By Thy grace we will."

2 See the mighty host advancing,
    Satan leading on:
  Mighty men around us falling,
    Courage almost gone!

3 See the glorious banner waving!
    Hear the trumpet blow!
  In our Leader's name we'll triumph
    Over every foe!

4 Fierce and long the battle rages,
    But our help is near:
  Onward comes our great Com-
      mander,
    Cheer, my comrades, cheer!
                        *P. P. Bliss*


**445**  Our souls cry out, hallelujah!
         And our faith enraptured
             sings,        [standard
       While we throw to the breeze the
         Of the mighty King of kings.

    On the vict'ry side, on the vict'ry side,
    In the ranks of the Lord are we ;
    On the vict'ry side we will boldly stand,
    Till the glory-land we see.

2 Our souls cry out, hallelujah!
    For the Lord Himself comes
      near,
  And the shout of a royal army
    On the battle-field we hear.

3 Our souls cry out, hallelujah!
    For the tempter flies apace,
  And the chains he has forged are
      breaking,        [grace.
    Through the power of redeeming

4 Our souls cry out, hallelujah!
    And our hearts beat high with
      praise,          [conquer,
  Unto Him, in whose name we'll
    And our song of triumph raise.
                    *James L. Black.*


(4) GUIDANCE AND SECURITY

**446**  Precious promise God hath
             given
         To the weary passer-by,
       On the way from earth to heaven,
         "I will guide thee with Mine
             eye."

    "I will guide thee, I will guide thee,
    I will guide thee with Mine eye ;
    On the way from earth to heaven,
    I will guide thee with Mine eye."

2 When temptations almost win thee,
    And thy trusted watchers fly,
  Let this promise ring within thee:
    "I will guide thee with Mine
        eye."

3 When thy secret hopes have
        perished
    In the grave of years gone by,
  Let this promise still be cherished,
    "I will guide thee with Mine
        eye."

4 When the shades of life are falling,
    And the hour has come to die,
  Hear thy trusty Leader calling,
    "I will guide thee with Mine
        eye."
                        *N. Niles.*


**447**  O God of Bethel, by whose
             hand
         Thy people still are fed,
       Who through this weary pilgrim-
       Hast all our fathers led.    [age

2 Our vows, our prayers we now pre-
      sent
    Before Thy throne of grace;
  God of our fathers, be the God
    Of their succeeding race.

3 Through each perplexing path of
life
Our wandering footsteps guide:
Give us, each day, our daily bread,
And raiment fit provide.

4 O spread thy covering wings
around,
Till all our wanderings cease,
And at our Father's loved abode
Our souls arrive in peace.

5 Such blessings from Thy gracious
hand
Our humble prayers implore;
And Thou shalt be our chosen God,
And portion evermore.
*Doddridge and Logan.*

**448** THINE for ever! Lord of love,
Hear us from Thy throne
above;
Thine for ever may we be,
Here and in eternity.

2 Thine for ever! Lord of life,
Shield us through our earthly strife;
Thou the Life, the Truth, the Way,
Guide us to the realms of day.

3 Thine for ever! O how blest
They who find in Thee their rest!
Saviour, Guardian, Heavenly
O defend us to the end! [Friend,

4 Thine for ever! Shepherd, keep
These Thy frail and trembling
sheep;
Safe alone beneath Thy care,
Let us all Thy goodness share.

5 Thine for ever! Thou our guide,
All our wants by Thee supplied,
All our sins by Thee forgiven,
Lead us, Lord, from earth to
heaven. *Mary Fowler Maude.*

**449** LEAD us, heavenly Father, lead
us
O'er the world's tempestuous sea:
Guard us, guide us, keep us, feed
us,
For we have no help but Thee,
Yet possessing every blessing
If our God our Father be.

2 Saviour, breathe forgiveness o'er us;
All our weakness Thou dost
know; [us,
Thou didst tread this earth before

Thou didst feel its keenest woe;
Lone and dreary, faint and weary,
Through the desert Thou didst
go.

3 Spirit of our God, descending,
Fill our hearts with heavenly joy,
Love with every passion blending,
Pleasure that can never cloy;
Thus provided, pardoned, guided,
Nothing can our peace destroy.
*James Edmeston.*

**450** I NEED Jesus, my need I now
confess; [distress;
No one like Him in times of deep
I need Jesus, the need I gladly own;
Though some may bear their load
Yet I need Jesus. [alone,

I need Jesus . . . I need Jesus . . .
I need Jesus every day ! . . .
Need Him in the sunshine hour,
Need Him when the storm-clouds low'r;
Ev'ry day along my way,
Yes, I need Jesus.

2 I need Jesus, I need a Friend like
Him, [life are dim;
A Friend to guide when paths of
I need Jesus, when foes my soul
assail;
Alone I know I can but fail,—
So I need Jesus.

3 I need Jesus, I need Him to the
end; [ners' Friend;
No one like Him—He is the sin-
I need Jesus, no other friend will
do; [true,—
So constant, kind, so strong, and
Yes, I need Jesus.
*G. O. Webster.*

**451** JUST lean upon the arms of
Jesus, [along;
He'll help you along, help you
If you will trust His love unfailing,
He'll fill your heart with song.

Lean on . . . His arms, . . . trusting in His
love ;
Lean on . . . His arms, . . . all His mercies
prove :
Lean on . . . His arms . . . looking home
above,
Just lean on the Saviour's arms !

2 Just lean upon the arms of Jesus,
He'll brighten the way, brighten
the way :
Just follow gladly where He lead-
His gentle voice obey. [eth,

3 Just lean upon the arms of Jesus,
   Oh bring every care, bring every
      care!                    [heavy,
   The burden that has seemed so
   Take to the Lord in prayer.

4 Just lean upon the arms of Jesus,
   Then leave all to Him, leave all
      to Him;
   His heart is full of love and mercy,
   His eyes are never dim.

5 Just lean upon the arms of Jesus,
   He meets every need, meets every
      need.
   To all who take Him as a Saviour,
   He is a Friend indeed.
         *Edgar Lewis and William W. Rock.*

**452** WHERE He may lead me I will
         go,                    [so,
   For I have learned to trust Him
   And I remember 'twas for me,
   That He was slain on Calvary.

   Jesus shall lead me night and day.
   Jesus shall lead me all the way ;
   He is the truest Friend to me,
   For I remember Calvary.

2 Oh, I delight in His command,
   Love to be led by His dear hand,
   His divine will is sweet to me,
   Hallowed by blood-stained Calvary.

3 Onward I go, nor doubt nor fear,
   Happy with Christ, my Saviour,
      near,
   Trusting some day that I shall see,
   Jesus, my Friend of Calvary.
                        *W. C. Martin.*

**453** HOLD Thou my hand! so weak
         I am, and helpless;
   I dare not take one step without
      Thy aid!         [loving Saviour,
   Hold Thou my hand! for then, O
   No dread of ill shall make my
   soul afraid.

2 Hold Thou my hand! and closer,
      closer draw me
   To Thy dear self—my hope, my
      joy, my all;      [should wander,
   Hold Thou my hand! lest haply I
   And missing Thee, my trembling
   feet should fall.

3 Hold Thou my hand! the way is
   dark before me
   Without the sunlight of Thy face
   divine;

But when by faith I catch its radiant glory,
   What heights of joy, what rapturous songs are mine!

4 Hold Thou my hand! that, when I
   reach the margin         [cross for me,
   Of that lone river Thou didst
   A heavenly light may flash along
      its waters,        [bright shall be.
   And every wave like crystal
                        *Grace J. Frances.*

**454** OH, safe to the Rock that is
         higher than I,
   My soul in its conflicts and sorrows
      would fly.            [would I be;
   So sinful, so weary, Thine, Thine
   Thou blest " Rock of Ages," I'm
   hiding in Thee.

   Hiding in Thee, hiding in Thee,
   Thou blest " Rock of Ages," I'm hiding in
   Thee.

2 In the calm of the noontide, in
      sorrow's lone hour,
   In times when temptation casts
      o'er me its power;
   In the tempests of life, on its wide,
      heaving sea,        [hiding in Thee.
   Thou blest "Rock of Ages," I'm

3 How oft in the conflict, when
      pressed by the foe,
   I have fled to my Refuge and
      breathed out my woe;
   How often when trials like sea
      billows roll,       [Rock of my soul.
   Have I hidden in Thee, O Thou
                        *W. O. Cushing.*

**455** ALL the way my Saviour
         leads me:
   What have I to ask beside?
   Can I doubt His tender mercy,
   Who through life has been my
      Guide?
   Heavenly peace, divinest comfort,
   Here by faith in Him to dwell!
   For I know whate'er befall me,
   Jesus doeth all things well.

2 All the way my Saviour leads me,
   Cheers each winding path I tread,
   Gives me grace for every trial,
   Feeds me with the Living Bread.
   Though my weary steps may falter,
   And my soul athirst may be,
   Gushing from the Rock before me,
   Lo! a spring of joy I see.

3 All the way my Saviour leads me;
    Oh, the fulness of His love!
Perfect rest to me is promised
    In my Father's house above.
When my spirit, clothed, immortal,
    Wings its flight to realms of day,
This my song through endless ages,
    Jesus led me all the way.
*                 Fanny J. Crosby.*

**456** O PILGRIM, bound for the
        heavenly land,
    Never lose sight of Jesus!
He'll lead you gently with loving
    Never lose sight of Jesus! [hand:
      Never lose sight of Jesus!
      Never lose sight of Jesus!
      **Day and night He will lead you right;**
      Never lose sight of Jesus!

2 When you are tempted to go astray,
    Never lose sight of Jesus!
Press onward, upward, the narrow
    Never lose sight of Jesus! [way;

3 Though dark the pathway may
      seem ahead,
    Never lose sight of Jesus!
"I will be with you," His word hath
    Never lose sight of Jesus! [said:

4 When death is knocking outside the
      door,
    Never lose sight of Jesus! [shore:
Till safe with Him on the golden
    Never lose sight of Jesus!
*                 J. Oatman (arr.)*

**457** I HAVE a Shepherd, One I love
        so well; [never tell;
How He has blessed me tongue can
On the Cross He suffered, shed His
    blood and died, [fide.
That I might ever in His love con-
    Following Jesus, ever day by day,
    Nothing can harm me when He leads the way;
    Darkness or sunshine, what'er befall,
    Jesus, the Shepherd, is my All in All.

2 Pastures abundant doth His hand
      provide, [side,
Still waters flowing ever at my
Goodness and mercy follow on my
    track, [I lack.
With such a Shepherd nothing can

3 When I would wander from the
      path astray, [the way;
**Then He will draw me back into**

In the darkest valley I need fear no
    ill, [me still.
For He, my Shepherd, will be with

4 When labour's ended and the jour-
    ney done, [home;
Then He will lead me safely to my
There I shall dwell in rapture sure
    and sweet, [round His feet.
With all the loved ones gathered
*                 Leonard Weaver.*

**458** BE not dismayed whate'er be-
        tide,
    God will take care of you!
Beneath His wings of love abide,
    God will take care of you!
    **God will take care of you,**
    Through every day, o'er all the way;
    He will take care of you:
    God will take care of you!

2 Through days of toil when heart
      doth fail,
    God will take care of you!
When dangers fierce your path
      assail,
    God will take care of you!

3 All you may need He will provide,
    God will take care of you! [fied,
Trust Him, and you will be satis-
    God will take care of you!

4 Lonely or sad, from friends apart,
    God will take care of you!
He will give peace to your aching
    heart,
    God will take care of you!

5 No matter what may be the test,
    God will take care of you!
Lean, weary one, upon His breast,
    God will take care of you!
*      C. D. Martin and H. C. A. D.*

**459** ALL the way my Lord is lead-
        ing me;
    Praise His name, praise His name!
With His heavenly manna feeding
    me;
    Praise His holy name.
    Halelujah! this is my song,
    Jesus, Jesus, the whole day long;
    Swell the chorus, mighty and strong,
    Praise His holy name.

2 When I faint, His grace upholdeth
    me;
    Praise His name, praise His name!
When I fear, His arm enfoldeth me;
    Praise His holy name.

3 Cares of life have overtaken me;
  Praise His name, praise His name!
Yet He never has forsaken me;
  Praise His holy name.
                    *Chas. H. Gabriel.*

**460** BEGONE, unbelief; my Saviour
       is near,            [appear:
And for my relief will surely
By prayer let me wrestle, and He
  will perform;        [the storm.
With Christ in the vessel, I smile at

2 Though dark be my way, since He
    is my Guide,            [vide:
  'Tis mine to obey, 'tis His to pro-
  Though cisterns be broken and
    creatures all fail,
  The word He hath spoken shall
    surely prevail.

3 His love in time past forbids me to
    think                  [sink;
  He'll leave me at last in trouble to
  While each Ebenezer I have in re-
    view             [me quite through.
  Confirms His good pleasure to help

4 Why should I complain of want or
    distress,           [no less;
  Temptation or pain? He told me
  The heirs of salvation, I know from
    His word,
  Through much tribulation must
    follow their Lord.

5 Since all that I meet shall work for
    my good,             [food;
  The bitter is sweet, the medicine
  Though painful at present, 'twill
    cease before long;
  And then, O how pleasant the con-
    queror's song!    *John Newton.*

**461** ETERNAL Father, strong to
       save,             [wave,
Whose arm hath bound the restless
Who bidd'st the mighty ocean deep
Its own appointed limits keep;
  O hear us when we cry to Thee
  For those in peril on the sea.

2 O Christ, Whose voice the waters
    heard,              [word,
  And hushed their raging at Thy
  Who walkedst on the foaming deep,
  And calm amid the storm didst
    sleep;
  O hear us when we cry to Thee
  For those in peril on the sea.

3 O Holy Spirit, Who did'st brood
  Upon the waters dark and rude,
  And bid their angry tumult cease,
  And give, for wild confusion, peace;
    O hear us when we cry to Thee
    For those in peril on the sea.

4 O Trinity of love and power,
  Our brethren shield in danger's
    hour              [foe,
  From rock and tempest, fire and
  Protect them, wheresoe'er they go:
    Thus evermore shall rise to Thee
    Glad hymns of praise from land
      and sea.    *William Whiting.*

**462** GUIDE me, O Thou Great
       Jehovah!
Pilgrim through this barren land;
I am weak, but Thou art mighty,
Hold me with Thy powerful
  Bread of heaven!       [hand:
Feed me now and evermore.

2 Open Thou the crystal fountain,
  Whence the healing stream doth
  Let the fiery, cloudy pillar  [flow:
  Lead me all my journey through:
    Strong Deliverer!     [shield.
    Be Thou still my strength and

3 If I tread the verge of Jordan,
  Bid my anxious fears subside:
  Bear me through the swelling tor-
    rent,
    Land me safe on Canaan's side:
    Songs of praises
    I will ever give to Thee.

4 Saviour, come! we long to see
    Thee,
  Long to dwell with Thee above;
  And to know in full communion,
  All the sweetness of Thy love.
    Come, Lord Jesus!
    Take Thy waiting people home.
                        *W. Williams.*

**463** ONLY in Thee, O Saviour
       mine,
Dwelleth my soul in peace divine—
Peace that the world, though all
  combine,
  Never can take from me!
Pleasures of earth, so seemingly
  sweet,
Fail at the last my longings to meet;
Only in Thee my bliss is complete,
  Only, dear Lord, in Thee!

2 Only in Thee a radiance bright
Shines like a beacon in the night,
Guiding my pilgrim barque aright
Over life's trackless sea!
Only in Thee, when troubles molest,
When with temptation I am op-
pressed,
There is a sweet pavilion of rest,
Only, dear Lord, in Thee!

3 Only in Thee, when days are drear,
When neither sun nor stars appear—
Still I can trust and feel no fear,
Sing when I cannot see!
Only in Thee, whatever betide,
All of my need is freely supplied:
There is no hope or helper beside,
Only, dear Lord, in Thee!

4 Only in Thee, dear Saviour slain,
Losing Thy life my own to gain,
Trusting, I'm cleansed from every
stain—
Thou art my only plea!
Only in Thee my heart will delight,
Till in that land where cometh no
night,                    [sight—
Faith will be lost in heavenly
Only, dear Lord, in Thee!

*T. O. Chisholm.*

**464** LORD Jesus, Thou dost keep
Thy child     [tempests wild;
Through   sunshine   or   through
Jesus, I trust in Thee!
Thine is such wondrous power to
save,
Thine is the mighty love that gave
It's all on Calvary.

2 O glorious Saviour! Thee I praise;
To Thee my new glad song I raise,
And tell of what Thou art.
Thy grace is boundless in its store;
Thy face of love shines evermore:
Thou givest me Thy heart.

3 Upon Thy promises I stand,
Trusting in Thee: Thine own right
hand
Doth keep and comfort me!
My soul doth triumph in Thy
Word;                    [Lord,
Thine, Thine be all the praise, dear
As Thine the victory.

4 Love perfecteth what it begins;
Thy power doth save me from my
sins—

Thy grace upholdeth me.
This life of trust—how glad, how
sweet!        ,          [meet
My need and Thy great fulness
And I have all in Thee.

*Jean Sophia Pigott.*

**465** IT may be in the valley, where
countless dangers hide;
It may be in the sunshine, that I
in peace abide;
But this one thing I know—if it
be dark or fair,        [where!
If Jesus is with me, I'll go any-
If Jesus goes with me, I'll go . . . anywhere !
'Tis heaven to me, where'er I may be, if He
is there !
I count it a privilege here . . . His cross to
bear ;
If Jesus goes with me, I'll go anywhere.

2 It may be I must carry the blessèd
word of life
Across the burning deserts to those
in sinful strife;
And though it be my lct to bear
my colours there,        [where!
If Jesus goes with me, I'll go any-

3 But if it be my portion to bear
my cross at home,
While others bear their burdens be-
yond the billow's foam,
I'll prove my faith in Him—confess
His judgments fair, [anywhere!
And if He stays with me, I'll stay

4 It is not mine to question the
judgments of my Lord,
It is but mine to follow the lead-
ings of His Word;
But if I go or stay, or whether
here or there,        [anywhere!
I'll be with my Saviour, content

*C. Austin Miles.*

**466** CHRIST shall lead us in the
time of youth,        [truth,
Christ shall lead us in the way of
Christ shall lead us in the love of
Homeward to the light.     [right
Though the way be long and dreary
Though in darkest night we roam,
By His side we never weary,
Christ shall lead us home.

2 Christ shall lead us in the hour of
gloom,                  [tomb;
He hath known it, Victor o'er the
When from grief we vainly seek
He can give us peace.    [release,

3 Christ shall lead us in the hour of strife, [life,
Fill our hearts with everlasting
Give us, even with our latest breath,
Vict'ry over death.

4 Christ shall lead us when the fight shall cease,
To the fields of everlasting peace,
Where the soul that all the way
Resteth calm in God. [hath trod,
*Colin Sterne.*

**467** ALL scenes alike engaging prove
To souls imprest with sacred love;
Where'er they dwell, they dwell in Thee,
In heav'n, in earth, or on the sea.

2 To me remains nor place nor time;
My country is in every clime;
I can be calm, and free from care,
On any shore, since God is there.

3 While place we seek, or place we shun,
The soul finds happiness in none;
But with my God to guide my way,
'Tis equal joy to go or stay.

4 Could I be cast where Thou art not,
That were indeed a dreadful lot:
But regions none remote I call,—
Secure of finding God in all.
*Madam Guyon.*

**468** I COULD not do without Thee,
O Saviour of the lost,
Whose precious blood redeemed me
At such tremendous cost;
Thy righteousness, Thy pardon,
Thy precious blood must be
My only hope and comfort,
My glory and my plea.

2 I could not do without Thee,
I cannot stand alone,
I have no strength or goodness,
No wisdom of my own;
But Thou, belovèd Saviour,
Art all in all to me,
And weakness will be power
If leaning hard on Thee.

3 I could not do without Thee;
No other friend can read
The spirit's strange deep longings,
Interpreting its need:

No human heart can enter
Each dim recess of mine,
And soothe, and hush, and calm it,
O blessèd Lord, but Thine.

4 I could not do without Thee;
For years are fleeting fast,
And soon in solemn loneness
The river must be passed:
But Thou wilt never leave me;
And though the waves roll high,
I know Thou wilt be near me,
And whisper, "It is I!"
*Frances R. Havergal.*

**469** THE Lord's our Rock, in Him we hide:
A shelter in the time of storm!
Secure whatever ill betide:
A shelter in the time of storm!

Oh, Jesus is a Rock in a weary land !
A weary land, a weary land ;
Oh, Jesus is a Rock in a weary land,
A shelter in the time of storm !

2 A shade by day, defence by night:
A shelter in the time of storm!
No fears alarm, no foes affright:
A shelter in the time of storm!

3 The raging storms may round us beat:
A shelter in the time of storm!
We'll never leave our safe retreat,
A shelter in the time of storm!

4 O Rock Divine, O Refuge dear:
A shelter in the time of storm!
Be Thou our helper ever near,
A shelter in the time of storm!
*V. J. C.*

**470** MY times are in Thy hand;
My God, I wish them there;
My life, my friends, my soul I leave
Entirely to Thy care.

2 My times are in Thy hand,
Whatever they may be,
Pleasing or painful, dark or bright,
As best may seem to Thee.

3 My times are in Thy hand;
Why should I doubt or fear?
My Father's hand will never cause
His child a needless tear.

4 My times are in Thy hand,
Jesus, the crucified! [pierced
Those hands my cruel sins had
Are now my guard and guide.

5 My times are in Thy hand;
  I'll always trust in Thee;
And, after death, at Thy right hand
  I shall for ever be.  *W. F. Lloyd.*

**471** ALL they who put their trust
  in God
  Can never be removed;
They stand secure like Zion's
  By many ages proved.  [mount,
  Like the mount . . . of God, . . . like the
    mount . . . of God ; . . .
  They stand secure like Zion's mount,
  By many ages proved.
  They can ne . . . ver be . . . removed, . . .
    removed ; . . .
  They stand secure like Zion's mount,
  They can never be removed.

2 As round about Jerusalem
    The rugged mountains lie,
  So round about His holy saints
    Our God is ever nigh.

3 Though fierce the storm in fury
    beat
  And awful thunders roar,
  The children of the mighty God
    Are safe for evermore.

4 Thus overshadowed by His love,
    Where harm can ne'er betide,
  Within this refuge safe and sure
    I ever would abide.
                       *C. M. Seamans.*

**472** AS I journey through the land,
    singing as I go,
  Pointing souls to Calvary—to the
    crimson flow,
  Many arrows pierce my soul from
    without, within;
  But my Lord leads me on, through
    Him I must win.
    Oh, I want to see Him, look upon His face,
    There to sing for ever of His saving
      grace ; . . .
    On the streets of Glory let me lift my voice ;
    Cares all past, home at last, ever to rejoice.

2 When in service for my Lord, dark
    may be the night,
  But I'll cling more close to Him,
    He will give me light;
  Satan's snares may vex my soul,
    turn my thoughts aside;
  But my Lord goes ahead, leads
    whate'er betide.

3 When in valleys low I look toward
    the mountain height,
  And behold my Saviour there,
    leading in the fight,

With a tender hand outstretched
    toward the valley low,     [go.
Guiding me, I can see, as I onward

4 When before me billows rise from
    the mighty deep,
  Then my Lord directs my barque;
    He doth safely keep,
  And He leads me gently on
    through this world below,
  He's a real Friend to me, oh, I
    love Him so.   *R. H. Cornelius.*

**473** IN heavenly love abiding,
    No change my heart shall
  And safe is such confiding,  [fear;
    For nothing changes here:
  The storm may roar without me,
    My heart may low be laid;
  But God is round about me,
    And can I be dismayed?

2 Wherever He may guide me,
    No want shall turn me back;
  My Shepherd is beside me,
    And nothing can I lack:
  His wisdom ever waketh,
    His sight is never dim;
  He knows the way He taketh,
    And I will walk with Him.

3 Green pastures are before me,
    Which yet I have not seen;
  Bright skies will soon be o'er me,
    Where the dark clouds have
      been:
  My hope I cannot measure,
    My path to life is free;
  My Saviour has my treasure,
    And He will walk with me.
                       *Anna L. Waring.*

**474** TEACH me Thy way, O Lord,
    Teach me Thy way!
  Thy gracious aid afford,
    Teach me Thy way!
  Help me to walk aright,
  More by faith, less by sight;
  Lead me with heavenly light:
    Teach me Thy way!

2 When doubts and fears arise,
    Teach me Thy way!
  When storms o'erspread the skies,
    Teach me Thy way!
  Shine through the cloud and rain,
  Through sorrow, toil, and pain;
  Make Thou my pathway plain:
    Teach me Thy way!

3 Long as my life shall last,
Teach me Thy way!
Where'er my lot be cast,
Teach me Thy way!
Until the race is run,
Until the journey's done,
Until the crown is won,
Teach me Thy way!
*B. M. Ramsay.*

**475** SWEET is the promise " I will
not forget thee";
Nothing can molest or turn my
soul away;                  [in the valley,
E'en though the night be dark with-
Just beyond is shining an eternal
day.

I . . . will not forget thee or leave thee,
In My hands I'll hold thee, in My arms
I'll fold thee ;
I . . . will not forget thee or leave thee—
I am Thy Redeemer, I will care for thee.

2 How can I show my gratitude to
Jesus,                      [tender care?
For His love unfailing and His
I will proclaim to others His salva-
tion,                     [His promise share.
That they may accept Him and

3 Trusting the promise " I will not
forget thee,"           [joy and praise;
Onward will I go with songs of
Though earth despise me, though
my friends forsake me,
Jesus will be near me, gladdening my days.

4 When at the golden portals I am
standing,                  [sorrows past,
All my tribulations, all my
How sweet to hear the blessèd pro-
clamation :            [home at last."
" Enter faithful servant, welcome
*Charles H. Gabriel (arr.)*

### (5) TRUST AND OBEDIENCE

**476** HUSHED was the evening
hymn,
The temple courts were dark,
The lamp was burning dim
Before the sacred ark;
When suddenly a voice divine
Rang through the silence of the
shrine.

2 The old man, meek and mild,
The priest of Israel, slept;
His watch the temple-child,

The little Levite, kept;
And what from Eli's sense was
sealed
The Lord to Hannah's son revealed.

3 Oh, give me Samuel's ear!
The open ear, O Lord,
Alive and quick to hear
Each whisper of Thy word;
Like him to answer at Thy call,
And to obey Thee first of all.

4 Oh give me Samuel's heart!
A lowly heart that waits
Where in Thy house Thou art,
Or watches at Thy gates,
By day and night, a heart that still
Moves at the breathing of Thy will.

5 Oh, give me Samuel's mind!
A sweet unmurmuring faith,
Obedient and resigned
To Thee in life and death;
That I may read with child-like eyes
Truths that are hidden from the
wise.                         *J. D. Burns.*

**477** WHEN we walk with the Lord,
In the light of His word,
What a glory He sheds on our way!
While we do His good will
He abides with us still,
And with all who will trust and
obey.

Trust and obey ! For there's no other way
To be happy in Jesus, but to trust and obey.

2 Not a shadow can rise,
Not a cloud in the skies,
But His smile quickly drives it
Not a doubt nor a fear,       [away;
Not a sigh nor a tear
Can abide while we trust and obey.

3 Not a burden we bear,
Not a sorrow we share,
But our toil He doth richly repay;
Not a grief nor a loss,
Not a frown nor a cross,
But is blest if we trust and obey.

4 But we never can prove
The delights of His love,
Until all on the altar we lay,
For the favour He shows
And the joy He bestows      [obey.
Are for them who will trust and

5 Then in fellowship sweet
   We will sit at His feet,
Or we'll walk by His side in the
What He says we will do, [way;
Where He sends we will go,
Never fear, only trust and obey.
   *J. H. Sammis.*

**478** JESUS, I will trust Thee,
      Trust Thee with my soul,
Guilty, lost, and helpless,
   Thou canst make me whole:
There is none in heaven
   Or on earth like Thee:
Thou hast died for sinners—
   Therefore, Lord, for me.
   Jesus, I will trust Thee,
      Trust Thee with my soul :
   Guilty, lost, and helpless,
      Thou canst make me whole.

2 Jesus, I must trust Thee,
   Pondering Thy ways,
Full of love and mercy
   All Thine earthly days:
Sinners gathered round Thee,
   Lepers sought Thy face:
None too vile or loathsome
   For a Saviour's grace.

3 Jesus, I can trust Thee,
   Trust Thy written Word,
Though Thy voice of pity
   I have never heard:
When Thy Spirit teacheth,
   To my taste how sweet!
Only may I hearken,
   Sitting at Thy feet.

4 Jesus, I do trust Thee,
   Trust without a doubt;
Whosoever cometh,
   Thou wilt not cast out:
Faithful is Thy promise,
   Precious is Thy blood:
These my soul's salvation,
   Thou my Saviour God!
      *Mary J. Walker.*

**479** FATHER of Jesus Christ, my Lord,
   My Saviour, and my Head,
I trust in Thee, whose powerful word
   Hath raised Him from the dead.

2 Eternal life to all mankind
   Thou hast in Jesus given;
And all who seek, in Him shall find
   The happiness of heaven.

3 Faith in Thy power Thou seest I have
   For Thou this faith hast wrought;
Dead souls Thou callest from their grave,
   And seekest worlds from nought.

4 In hope, against all human hope,
   Self-desperate, I believe;
Thy quickening word shall raise me up,
   Thou shalt Thy Spirit give. [up,

5 The thing surpasses all my thought,
   But faithful is my Lord;
Through unbelief I stagger not
   For God hath spoke the word.

6 Faith, mighty faith, the promise sees,
   And looks to that alone; [sees,
Laughs at impossibilities,
   And cries: It shall be done!
      *Charles Wesley.*

**480** SIMPLY trusting every day,
      Trusting through a stormy way;
Even when my faith is small,
   Trusting Jesus, that is all.
   Trusting as the moments fly,
   Trusting as the days go by ;
   Trusting Him what'er befall,
   Trusting Jesus, that is all.

2 Brightly doth His Spirit shine
   Into this poor heart of mine;
While He leads I cannot fall;
   Trusting Jesus, that is all.

3 Singing if my way be clear:
   Praying if the path be drear;
If in danger, for Him call;
   Trusting Jesus, that is all.

4 Trusting Him while life shall last,
   Trusting Him till earth be past;
Till within the jasper wall:
   Trusting Jesus, that is all.
      *E. Page.*

**481** WHY should I charge my soul with care?
   The wealth in every mine
Belongs to Christ, God's Son and Heir,
   And He's a Friend of mine.
   Yes, He's a Friend of mine,
   And He with me doth all things share ;
   Since all is Christ's and Christ is mine,
   Why should I have a care ?
   For Jesus is a Friend of mine.

2 The silver moon, the golden sun,
   And all the stars that shine,
Are His alone, yes, every one,
   And He's a Friend of mine.

3 He daily spreads a glorious feast,
  And at His table dine.
The whole creation, man and beast,
  And He's a Friend of mine.

4 And when He comes in bright
    array,
  And leads the conquering line,
It will be glory then to say,
  That He's a Friend of mine.
                            *J. H. Sammis.*

**482** I LAY my sins on Jesus,
    The spotless Lamb of God;
He bears them all and frees us
  From the accursèd load.
I bring my guilt to Jesus,
  To wash my crimson stains
White in His blood most precious,
  Till not a spot remains.

2 I lay my wants on Jesus;
    All fulness dwells in Him;
He heals all my diseases,
  He doth my soul redeem.
I lay my griefs on Jesus,
  My burdens and my cares:
He from them all releases,
  He all my sorrows shares.

3 I rest my soul on Jesus,
    This weary soul of mine:
His right hand me embraces,
  I on His breast recline.
I love the name of Jesus,
  Immanuel, Christ, the Lord;
Like fragrance on the breezes,
  His name abroad is poured.

4 I long to be like Jesus,
    Meek, loving, lowly, mild;
I long to be like Jesus,
  The Father's holy child;
I long to be with Jesus,
  Amid the heavenly throng,
To sing with saints His praises,
  To learn the angels' song.
                            *H. Bonar.*

**483** SOMETIMES a light surprises
    The Christian while he sings;
It is the Lord who rises
  With healing in His wings;
When comforts are declining,
  He grants the soul again
A season of clear shining,
  To cheer it after rain.

2 In holy contemplation,
    We sweetly then pursue
The theme of God's salvation,
  And find it ever new.
Set free from present sorrow,
  We cheerfully can say,
E'en let th'unknown to-morrow
  Bring with it what it may:

3 It can bring with it nothing
    But He will bear us through;
Who gives the lilies clothing
  Will clothe His people too:
Beneath the spreading heavens
  No creature but is fed;
And He who feeds the ravens
  Will give His children bread.

4 Though vine nor fig-tree neither
    Their wonted fruit should bear,
Though all the field should wither,
  Nor flocks nor herds be there,
Yet, God the same abiding,
  His praise shall tune my voice;
For, while in Him confiding,
  I cannot but rejoice.
                            *W. Cowper.*

**484** WHAT a fellowship, what a joy
    divine,
  Leaning on the everlasting arms;
What a blessedness, what a peace
    is mine,
  Leaning on the everlasting arms.

Lean . . . ing, lean . . . ing,
  Safe and secure from all alarms ;
Lean . . . ing, lean . . . ing,
  Leaning on the everlasting arms.

2 Oh, how sweet to walk in this pil-
    grim way,
  Leaning on the everlasting arms;
Oh, how bright the path grows
    from day to day,
  Leaning on the everlasting arms.

3 What have I to dread, what have
    I to fear,
  Leaning on the everlasting arms;
I have blessèd peace with my Lord
    so near,
  Leaning on the everlasting arms.
                            *E. A. Hoffman.*

**485** ABIDING, oh, so wondrous
    sweet!
I'm resting at the Saviour's feet,
I trust in Him, I'm satisfied,
I'm resting in the Crucified!

Abid . . . ing, abid . . . ing,
  Oh, so wondrous sweet ! . . .
I'm rest . . . ing, rest . . . ing
  At the Saviour's feet. . . .

2 He speaks, and by His word is
    given            [heaven!
  His peace, a rich foretaste of
  Not as the world He peace doth
    give,            [shall live.
  'Tis through this hope my soul

3 I live; not I; through Him alone
  By Whom the mighty work is done,
  Dead to myself, alive to Him,
  I count all loss His rest to gain.

4 Now rest, my heart, the work is
    done,
  I'm saved through the Eternal Son!
  Let all my powers my soul employ,
  To tell the world my peace and joy.
                    *Chas. B. J. Root.*

**486** MY heart is fixed, eternal God,
    Fixed on Thee,
  And my immortal choice is made:
    Christ for me.
  He is my Prophet, Priest and King
  Who did for me salvation bring;
  And while I've breath I mean to
    Christ for me.         [sing:

2 In Him I see the Godhead shine;
    Christ for me.
  He is the Majesty Divine;
    Christ for me.
  The Father's well-belovèd Son,
  Co-partner of His royal throne,
  Who did for human guilt atone;
    Christ for me.

3 In pining sickness or in health,
    Christ for me.
  In deepest poverty or wealth,
    Christ for me.
  And in that all-important day,
  When I the summons must obey,
  And pass from this dark world
    Christ for me.         [away,

4 Let others boast of heaps of gold,
    Christ for me.
  His riches never can be told,
    Christ for me!         [away,
  Your gold will waste and wear
  Your honours perish in a day,
  My portion never can decay:
    Christ for me!
                    *Richard Jukes.*

**487** MASTER, speak! Thy servant
    heareth,
  Waiting for Thy gracious word,
  Longing for Thy voice that cheer-
    Master, let it now be heard. [eth,
  I am listening, Lord, for Thee:
  What hast Thou to say to me?

2 Speak to me by name, O Master,
    Let me know it is to me;
  Speak, that I may follow faster,
    With a step more firm and free,
  Where the Shepherd leads the flock
  In the shadow of the Rock.

3 Master, speak! though least and
    lowest,
    Let me not unheard depart;
  Master, speak! for oh, Thou know-
    All the yearning of my heart, [est
  Knowest all its truest need;
  Speak! and make me blest indeed.

4 Master, speak! and make me ready,
    When Thy voice is truly heard,
  With obedience glad and steady,
    Still to follow every word.
  I am listening, Lord, for Thee:
  Master, speak, oh, speak to me!
                    *Frances R. Havergal.*

**488** AWAY, my needless fears,
    And doubts no longer mine;
  A ray of heavenly light appears,
    A messenger divine.

2 Thrice comfortable hope,
    That calms my troubled breast;
  My Father's hand prepares the cup,
    And what He wills is best.

3 If what I wish is good,
    And suits the will divine;
  By earth and hell in vain withstood,
    I know it shall be mine.

4 Still let them counsel take
    To frustrate His decree,
  They cannot keep a blessing back
    By heaven designed for me.

5 Here then I doubt no more,
    But in His pleasure rest, [power
  Whose wisdom, love, and truth and
    Engage to make me blest.

6 To accomplish His design
    The creatures all agree;
  And all the attributes divine
    Are now at work for me.
                    *Charles Wesley.*

**489** THE Lord hath declared and
the Lord will perform:
" Behold! I am near to deliver,
A refuge and fortress, a covert in
storm;"
He keepeth His promise for ever.
For ever ! for ever ! Oh, not for a day !
He keepeth His promise for ever !
To all who believe, to all who obey,
He keepeth His promise for ever !

2 Who seek Him shall find Him,
shall find Him today,
The word is to all, "whosoever"!
No soul that entreateth He turneth
away;
He keepeth His promise for ever.

3 Though often my toil seems but
labour in vain,        [our!
I leave with the Lord my endeav-
I patiently wait for the sunshine
and rain,
He keepeth His promise for ever.

4 The bonds that unite us in earth's
dearest ties,        [sever;
The rude hand of Time will dis-
But we shall renew them again in
the skies;
He keepeth His promise for ever.
*S. C. Kirk.*

**490** ALL things are possible to him
That can in Jesu's name be-
lieve;        [pheme,
Lord, I no more Thy name blas-
Thy truth I lovingly receive.
I can, I do believe in Thee,
All things are possible to me.

2 'Twas most impossible of all
That here sin's reign in me should
cease;
Yet shall it be, I know it shall;
Jesus, I trust Thy faithfulness!
If nothing is too hard for Thee,
All things are possible to me.

3 Though earth and hell the Word
gainsay,        [fail;
The Word of God shall never
The Lord can break sin's iron sway;
'Tis certain, though impossible.
The thing impossible shall be,
All things are possible to me.

4 All things are possible to God;
To Christ, the power of God in
man;

To me when I am all renewed,
In Christ am fully formed again.
And from the reign of sin set
free,—
All things are possible to me.

5 All things are possible to God;
To Christ, the power of God in
me;
Now shed Thy mighty Self abroad,
Let me no longer live, but Thee;
Give me this hour in Thee to prove
The sweet omnipotence of love.
*Charles Wesley.*

**491** I CLASP the hand of Love
divine,
I claim the gracious promise mine,
And add to His my countersign,
" I take—He undertakes."
I take Thee, blessèd Lord,
I give myself to Thee,
And Thou, according to Thy word,
Dost undertake for me.

2 I take salvation full and free,
Through Him who gave His life for
me,
He undertakes my All to be,
" I take—He undertakes."

3 I take Him as my holiness,
My spirit's spotless heavenly dress,
I take the Lord, my Righteousness,
" I take—He undertakes."

4 I take the promised Holy Ghost,
I take the power of Pentecost,
To fill me to the uttermost,
" I take—He undertakes."

5 I take Him for this mortal frame,
I take my healing through His
name,
And all His risen life I claim,
" I take—He undertakes."
*A. B. Simpson.*

**492** DOWN in the valley with my
Saviour I would go,
Where the flowers are blooming
and the sweet waters flow;
Everywhere He leads me I would
follow, follow on;
Walking in His footsteps till the
crown be won.
Follow ! follow ! I would follow Jesus ;
Anywhere, everywhere, I would follow on !
Follow ! follow ! I would follow Jesus !
Everywhere He leads me I would follow
on !

2 Down in the valley with my
    Saviour I would go,
Where the storms are sweeping and
    the dark waters flow;
With His hand to lead me I will
    never, never fear;
Danger cannot harm me if my
    Lord is near.

3 Down in the valley or upon the
    mountain steep,
Close beside my Saviour would my
    soul ever keep;
He will lead me safely in the path
    that He has trod,
Up to where they gather on the
    hills of God.

*W. O. Cushing.*

**493**  I AM trusting Thee, Lord Jesus,
    Trusting only Thee!
Trusting Thee for full salvation,
    Great and free.

2 I am trusting Thee for pardon,
    At Thy feet I bow;
For Thy grace and tender mercy,
    Trusting now.

3 I am trusting Thee for cleansing,
    In the crimson flood;
Trusting Thee to make me holy,
    By Thy blood.

4 I am trusting Thee to guide me,
    Thou alone shalt lead,
Every day and hour supplying
    All my need.

5 I am trusting Thee for power,
    Thine can never fail;
Words which Thou Thyself shalt
Must prevail.    [give me,

6 I am trusting Thee, Lord Jesus,
    Never let me fall!
I am trusting Thee for ever,
    And for all.

*Frances R. Havergal.*

**494**  FIRM are the promises stand-
    ing,
    Nor can they ever fail,
Sealed with the blood of our Jesus,
    They must, they shall avail!

    Heaven and earth may perish,
    Mountain and hill may vanish ;
    Yet stands the Word we cherish,
    Ever to faith made sure.

2 Follow in Abraham's footsteps,
    Turn to the heavens your eyes;
Counting the stars without number,
    Your faith, your hope will rise.

3 Trust, though the darkness be fall-
    Soon will the sun arise,    [ing—
Shedding bright beams in the morn-
    O'er earth and sea and skies. [ing

4 Trust, though the world may beset
    Faith has no dread or fear : [you;
Lo, in the fiery furnace
    The Son of God draws near!

5 Trust, though your friends dis-
    appoint you,
    Leaving you one by one;
Jesus, true Friend, will stand by you
    Till pilgrim days are done.

6 Trust Him, whatever betide you;
    Soon in the mansions bright
All will be clear as the noonday:
    Faith turned to glorious sight!

*Lewi Pethrus ;*
*English Version by L. F. W. Woodford.*

**495**  GOD holds the key of all un-
    known,
    And I am glad:
If other hands should hold the key,
Or if He trusted it to me,
    I might be sad.

2 What if to-morrow's cares were
    Without its rest?    [here
I'd rather He unlocked the day,
And, as the hours swing open, say,
    " My will is best."

3 The very dimness of my sight
    Makes me secure;
For groping in my misty way,
I feel His hand; I hear Him say,
    " My help is sure."

4 I cannot read His future plans;
    But this I know:
I have the smiling of His face,
And all the refuge of His grace,
    While here below.

5 Enough: this covers all my wants;
    And so I rest!
For what I cannot, He can see,
And in His care I saved shall be,
    For ever blest.

*J. Parker.*

**496** IN the secret of His presence
how my soul delights to hide!
Oh, how precious are the lessons
which I learn at Jesus' side!
Earthly cares can never vex me,
neither trials lay me low;
For when Satan comes to tempt
me, to the secret place I go.

2 When my soul is faint and thirsty,
'neath the shadow of His wing
There is cool and pleasant shelter,
and a fresh and crystal spring;
And my Saviour rests beside me,
as we hold communion sweet;
If I tried, I could not utter what He
says when thus we meet.

3 Only this I know: I tell Him all
my doubts and griefs and fears;
Oh, how patiently He listens! and
my drooping soul He cheers:
Do you think He ne'er reproves
me? what a false friend He
would be,
If He never, never told me of the
sins which He must see!

4 Would you like to know the sweetness of the secret of the Lord?
Go and hide beneath His shadow;
this shall then be your reward;
And whene'er you leave the silence
of that happy meeting place,
You will bear the shining image of
the Master in your face.
*Ellen Lakshmi Goreh.*

**497** I WORSHIP Thee, sweet Will of
God!
And all Thy ways adore;
And every day I live, I long
To love Thee more and more.

2 I have no cares, O blessèd Will!
For all my cares are Thine;
I live in triumph, Lord! for Thou
Hast made Thy triumphs mine.

3 Ride on, ride on triumphantly,
Thou glorious Will, ride on!
Faith's pilgrim-sons behind Thee
take
The road that Thou hast gone.

4 He always wins who sides with
To him no chance is lost; [God,
God's Will is sweetest to him when
It triumphs at his cost.

5 Ill that He blesses is our good;
And unblest good is ill; [wrong,
And all is right that seems most
If it be His sweet Will!
*F. W. Faber.*

**498** GIVE to the winds thy fears;
Hope, and be undismayed:
God hears thy sighs, and counts
thy tears,
God shall lift up thy head.

2 Through waves, and clouds, and
storms
He gently clears thy way:
Wait thou His time; so shall this
Soon end in joyous day. [night

3 Still heavy is thy heart?
Still sink thy spirits down?
Cast off the weight, let fear depart,
Bid every care be gone.

4 What though thou rulest not?
Yet heaven, and earth, and hell
Proclaim: God sitteth on the
throne,
And ruleth all things well!

5 Leave to His sovereign sway
To choose and to command;
So shalt thou, wondering, own His
way
How wise, how strong His hand.

6 Far, far above thy thought
His counsel shall appear,
When fully He the work hath
wrought
That caused thy needless fear.
*Gerhardt ; tr. J. Wesley.*

### (6) LOVE, JOY, AND PEACE

**499** O CHRIST, in Thee my soul
hath found,
And found in Thee alone,
The peace, the joy I sought so long,
The bliss till now unknown.
Now none but Christ can satisfy,
None other name for me,
There's love and life and lasting joy,
Lord Jesus found in Thee.

2 I sighed for rest and happiness,
I yearned for them, not Thee;
But while I passed my Saviour by,
His love laid hold on me.

3 I tried the broken cisterns, Lord,
But, ah! the waters failed!
E'en as I stooped to drink they fled,
And mocked me as I wailed.

4 The pleasures lost I sadly mourned,
  But never wept for Thee;
Till grace my sightless eyes received,
  Thy loveliness to see.

*B. E. (arr.)*

**500** GOD's abiding peace is in my
    soul today,        [now;
  Yes, I feel it now, yes, I feel it
He has taken all my doubts and
    fears away,
  Though I cannot tell you how.

It is mine, . . . mine, . . . blessèd be His name !
  He has given peace, perfect peace to me ;
It is mine, . . . mine, . . . blessèd be His name !
  Mine for all eternity !

2 He has wrought in me a sweet and
    perfect rest,        [it now;
  In my raptured heart I can feel
He each passing moment keeps me
    saved and blest,        [brow.
  Floods with light my heart and

3 He has given me a never failing joy,
  Oh, I have it now! oh, I have it
    now!        [powers employ,
To His praise I will my ransomed
  And renew my grateful vow.

4 Oh, the love of God is comforting
    my soul,        [love is mine!
  For His love is mine, yes, His
Waves of joy and gladness o'er my
    spirit roll,
  Thrilling me with life divine.

*Elisha A. Hoffman.*

**501** IMMORTAL Love, for ever full,
    For ever flowing free,
For ever shared, for ever whole,
  A never-ebbing sea!

2 We may not climb the heavenly
    steeps
  To bring the Lord Christ down:
In vain we search the lowest deeps,
  For Him no depths can drown.

3 But warm, sweet, tender even yet
    A present help is He;
And faith has still its Olivet,
  And love its Galilee.

4 The healing of His seamless dress
    Is by our beds of pain;
We touch Him in life's throng and
  And we are whole again. [press,

5 O Lord and Master of us all,
    Whate'er our name or sign,
We own Thy sway, we hear Thy
  We test our lives by Thine. [call,

*J. G. Whittier.*

**502** I HAVE found His grace is all
    complete,
  He supplieth every need;
While I sit and learn at Jesus' feet,
  I am free, yes, free indeed.

It is joy unspeakable and full of glory,
Full of glory, full of glory ;
It is joy unspeakable and full of glory,
  Oh, the half has never yet been told.

2 I have found the pleasure I once
    craved,
  It is joy and peace within;
What a wondrous blessing! I am
    saved
  From the awful gulf of sin.

3 I have found that hope so bright
    and clear,
  Living in the realm of grace;
Oh, the Saviour's presence is so
  I can see His smiling face. [near,

4 I have found the joy no tongue can
    tell,
  How its waves of glory roll!
It is like a great o'erflowing well,
  Springing up within my soul.

*B. E. Warren.*

**503** OH, how sweet to whisper of
    Jesus,        [died,
  And to tell the lost of One who
That the vilest might be forgiven,
  And to point them to Christ the
    crucified.
Oh, the joy that fills the spirit
  When the tear is sparkling with
    delight,
As the soul goes into the glory,
  And the day passes grandly out
    of night.

Oh, the precious name of Jesus,
  It is beauty, fragrance, and delight,
It is music, sweetness, and rapture.
  'Tis my song in the day and in the night.

2 Oh, how sweet to whisper of Jesus,
    And to tell the wanderers of One
Who can lead them back to the
    Father,        [great have won.
  On the path which His sorrows
Of the bells that ring up yonder,

Of the joy that fills the souls in bliss,
When the lost are home with the [Father,
Oh, there's no joy that will compare with this.

3 By and by this whisper of Jesus
Will be changed to shouts that rend the sky,
As a king He's coming to own us
Where He came once to suffer and to die.
All these wanderers will be with [Him,
And will make His triumph hour complete,
And will swell the loud hallelujah
We shall sing when our glorious Lord we meet.

*J. Wakefield MacGill.*

**504** MASTER, the tempest is raging!
The billows are tossing high!
The sky is o'ershadowed with blackness,
No shelter or help is nigh:
"Carest Thou not that we perish?"
How canst Thou lie asleep,
When each moment so madly is threatening
A grave in the angry deep?

"The winds and the waves shall obey My will,
Peace, . . . be still! . . .
Whether the wrath of the storm-tossed sea,
Or demons, or men, or whatever it be,
No waters can swallow the ship where lies
The Master of ocean, and earth, and skies,
They all shall sweetly obey My will:
Peace, be still! Peace, be still!
They all shall sweetly obey My will:
Peace, peace, be still!"

2 Master, with anguish of spirit
I bow in my grief today;
The depths of my sad heart are troubled;
Oh, waken and save, I pray!
Torrents of sin and of anguish
Sweep o'er my sinking soul;
And I perish! I perish! dear Master:
Oh hasten, and take control.

3 Master, the terror is over,
The elements sweetly rest;
Earth's sun in the calm lake is mirrored,
And heaven's within my breast;

Linger, O blessèd Redeemer,
Leave me alone no more;
And with joy I shall make the blest harbour,
And rest on the blissful shore.

*Mary A. Baker.*

**505** SINCE Christ my soul from sin set free,
This world has been a heav'n to me; [woe,
And 'mid earth's sorrows and its
'Tis heav'n my Jesus here to know.

O hallelujah, yes, 'tis heav'n.
'Tis heav'n to know my sins forgiven;
On land or sea, what matters where,
Where Jesus is, 'tis heaven there.

2 Once heaven seemed a far-off place,
Till Jesus showed His smiling face;
Now it's begun within my soul,
'Twill last while endless ages roll.

3 What matters where on earth we dwell?
On mountain top, or in the dell?
In cottage, or in mansion fair,
Where Jesus is, 'tis heaven there.

*C. F. Butler.*

**506** LIKE a river, glorious,
Is God's perfect peace,
Over all victorious
In its bright increase;
Perfect, yet it floweth
Fuller ev'ry day,—
Perfect, yet it groweth
Deeper all the way.

Stayed upon Jehovah,
Hearts are fully blest;
Finding, as He promised,
Perfect peace and rest.

2 Hidden in the hollow
Of His blessèd hand,
Never foe can follow,
Never traitor stand;
Not a surge of worry,
Not a shade of care,
Not a blast of hurry
Touch the spirit there.

3 Every joy or trial
Falleth from above,
Traced upon our dial
By the Sun of Love.
We may trust Him fully,
All for us to do,
They who trust Him wholly
Find Him wholly true.

*Frances R. Havergal.*

**507** A WONDERFUL Saviour is Jesus
my Lord,
A wonderful Saviour to me,
He hideth my soul in the cleft of
the rock,
Where rivers of pleasure I see.

He hideth my soul in the cleft of the rock,
That shadows a dry thirsty land ;
He hideth my life in the depths of His love,
And covers me there with His hand.

2 A wonderful Saviour is Jesus my
Lord,
He taketh my burden away,
He holdeth me up, and I shall not
be moved,
He giveth me strength as my day

3 With numberless blessings each
moment He crowns, [divine,
And filled with His fulness
I sing in my rapture, oh, glory to
God
For such a Redeemer as mine.

4 When clothed in His brightness
transported I rise, [sky,
To meet Him in clouds of the
His perfect salvation, His wonder-
ful love, [high,
I'll shout with the millions on
*Fanny J. Crosby.*

**508** RICH are the moments of bless-
ing
Jesus my Saviour bestows;
Pure is the well of salvation
Fresh from His mercy that flows.

Ever He walketh beside me,
Brightly His sunshine appears,
Spreading a beautiful rainbow
Over the valley of tears.

2 Rich are the moments of blessing
Lovely and hallowed and sweet,
When from my labour at noontide
Calmly I rest at His feet.

3 Why should I ever grow weary?
Why should I faint by the way?
Has He not promised to give me
Strength for the toils of the day?

4 Though by the mist and the
shadow
Sometimes my sky may be dim,
Rich are the moments of blessing
Spent in communion with Him.
*Fanny J. Crosby.*

**509** I SING the love of God, my
Father,
Whose Spirit abides within;
Who changes all my grief to glad-
And pardons me all my sin. [ness,
Though clouds may lower, dark
and dreary,
Yet He has promised to be near;
He gives me sunshine for my
shadow,
And " beauty for ashes," here.

He gives me joy . . . in place of sor . . . row ;
He gives me love . . . that casts out
fear ; . . .
He gives me sunshine for my shadow,
And " beauty for ashes," here.

2 I sing the love of Christ, my
Saviour,
Who suffered upon the tree;
That, in the secret of His presence,
My bondage might freedom be,
He comes " to bind the broken-
hearted," [cheer;
He comes the fainting soul to
He gives me " oil of joy " for
mourning,
And " beauty for ashes," here.

3 I sing the beauty of the Gospel
That scatters not thorns, but
flowers;
That bids me scatter smiles and
sunbeams
Wherever are lonely hours.
The " garment of His praise " it
offers
For " heaviness of spirit," drear;
It gives me sunshine for my
shadow,
And " beauty for ashes," here.
*J. G. Crabbe.*

**510** IT is glory just to walk with
Him whose blood has ran-
somed me; [day,
It is rapture for my soul each
It is joy divine to feel Him near
where'er my path may be,
Bless the Lord, it's glory all the
way!

It is glory just to walk with Him,
It is glory just to walk with Him,
He will guide my steps aright,
Through the vale and o'er the height ;
It is glory just to walk with Him.

2 It is glory when the shadows fall
  to know that He is near;
  Oh, what joy to simply trust and
  pray!
It is glory to abide in Him when
  skies above are clear;
  Yes, with Him, it's glory all the
  way!

3 'Twill be glory when I walk with
  Him on heaven's golden shore,
  Never from His side again to
  stray.
'Twill be glory, wondrous glory
  with the Saviour evermore,
  Everlasting glory all the way!
  *Avis M. Burgeson.*

**511** Down from His splendour in
  glory He came,
  Into a world of woe; [my shame,
Took on Himself all my guilt and
  Why should He love me so?

  How can I help but love Him,
    When He loved me so?
  How can I help but love Him,
    When He loved me so?

2 I am unworthy to take of His grace,
  Wonderful grace so free; [place,
  Yet Jesus suffered and died in my
  E'en for a soul like me.

3 He is the fairest of thousands to
  His love is sweet and true; [me,
  Wonderful beauty in Him I now see,
  More than I ever knew.
  *Elton M. Roth.*

**512** Jesus the Saviour, dying on
  Calv'ry,
  Purchased my pardon, setting me
  free; [serve Him,
  Love so abundant, should I not
  When He so gladly suffered for
  me?

  Lord, . . . I am Thine, . . . Sa . . .viour
    Divine! . . .
  Oh, . . . what a joy . . . just to know . . .
    Thou art mine! . . .

2 Oh, what a Saviour, tender and
  loving, [should stray;
  Guarding my footsteps, lest I
  Love so abundant, leading me ever
  Out of the darkness into the day.

3 Constant Companion, leaving me
  never, [His side:
  Bidding me follow close by

He is my Refuge, safely I shelter,
  Knowing He loves me, whate'er
  betide.
  *G. C. Tullar.*

**513** Christ will me His aid afford,
  Never to fall, never to fall;
While I find my precious Lord,
  Sweeter than all, sweeter than all.

  Jesus is now and ever will be
    Sweeter than all the world to me,
  Since I heard His loving call,
    Sweeter than all, sweeter than all.

2 I will follow all the way [call,
  Hearing Him call, hearing Him
  Finding Him, from day to day,
  Sweeter than all, sweeter than all.

3 Though a vessel I may be, [small,
  Broken and small, broken and
  Yet His blessings fall on me,
  Sweeter than all, sweeter than all.

4 When I reach the crystal sea,
  Voices will call, voices will call,
  But my Saviour's voice will be
  Sweeter than all, sweeter than all.
  *Johnson Oatman, Jr.*

**514** Love, wonderful love of God,
  So boundless and so free,
To think that Christ His only Son
  Should die on Calvary.
Oh, love so great, so vast, so high,
  That He should for the sinner die.

  Love, wonderful love, the love of God to me,
  Love, wonderful love, so great, so rich, so
    free:
  Wide, as wide as the ocean, deep, as deep
    as the sea,
  High, as high as the heav'ns above, His love
    to me.

2 Love, wonderful love of God,
  To me has been made known,
  To me the Spirit freely gives,
  And claims me for His own.
  Oh, love so wondrous, so divine,
  That I am His and He is mine.

3 Love, wonderful love of God,
  With joy I now proclaim,
  To sinners lost that they may have
  Salvation through His Name.
  That they may now with others
  prove,
  "Christ's dying, and undying love."
  *Seth Sykes.*

**515** WONDERFUL love does Jesus show,
Wonderful grace He does bestow,
Wonderful peace in Him I know,
Bless His holy name!
Wonderful, wonderful Jesus!
Wonderful, wonderful Jesus!
Oh! He's a wonderful Saviour!
Bless His holy name!

2 Wonderful! He is always near,
Wonderful! I have naught to fear,
Wonderful is His voice so dear,
Bless His holy name!

3 Wonderful help does Jesus send,
Wonderful keeping to the end;
Wonderful is this constant Friend,
Bless His holy name!

4 Wonderful day, so pure, so bright,
Wonderful living in His sight;
Wonderful! 'round me all is light,
Bless His holy name!
*W. J. Stuart.*

**516** I FEEL like singing all the time,
My tears are wiped away;
For Jesus is a Friend of mine,
I'll serve Him every day.
I'll praise Him! praise Him! praise Him
all the time!
Praise Him! praise Him! I'll praise Him
all the time!

2 When on the cross my Lord I saw,
Nailed there by sins of mine,
Fast fell the burning tears; but now
I'm singing all the time.

3 When fierce temptations try my heart,
I'll sing, "Jesus is mine!"
And so, though tears at times may start,
I'm singing all the time.

4 The wondrous story of the Lamb
Tell with that voice of thine,
Till others, with the glad new song,
Go singing all the time.
*E. P. Hammond.*

**517** JESUS my King, my wonderful Saviour,
All of my life is given to Thee;
I am rejoicing in Thy salvation,
Thy precious blood now maketh me free.
Wonderful Saviour, wonderful Saviour,
Thou art so near, so precious to me;
Wonderful Saviour, wonderful Saviour,
My heart is filled with praises to Thee.

2 Freedom from sin, oh, wonderful story! [than snow,
All of its stains washed whiter
Jesus has come to live in His temple, [aglow.
And with His love my heart is

3 Jesus my Lord, I'll ever adore Thee,
Lay at Thy feet my treasures of love; [glory,
Lead me in ways to show forth Thy
Ways that will end in heaven above.

4 When in that bright and beautiful city
I shall behold Thy glories untold,
I shall be like Thee, wonderful Saviour,
And I will sing while ages unfold.
*J. M. Harris.*

**518** WHO can cheer the heart like Jesus,
By His presence all divine?
True and tender, pure and precious,
O how blest to call Him mine!
All that thrills my soul is Jesus;
He is more than life to me;
And the fairest of ten thousand,
In my blessèd Lord I see.

2 Love of Christ so freely given,
Grace of God beyond degree,
Mercy higher than the heaven,
Deeper than the deepest sea.

3 What a wonderful redemption!
Never can a mortal know [son,
How my sin, though red like crim-
Can be whiter than the snow.

4 Ev'ry need His hand supplying,
Ev'ry good in Him I see;
On His strength divine relying,
He is all in all to me.

5 By the crystal-flowing river
With the ransomed I will sing,
And for ever and for ever
Praise and glorify the King.
*Thoro Harris.*

**519** I HAVE a song that Jesus gave me,
It was sent from heav'n above;
There never was a sweeter melody,
'Tis a melody of love.
In my heart there rings a melody,
There rings a melody with heaven's harmony;
In my heart there rings a melody;
There rings a melody of love.

2 I love the Christ that died on Calv'ry,
    For He washed my sins away;
    He put within my heart a melody,
    And I know it's there to stay.

3 'Twill be my endless theme in glory,
    With the angels I will sing;
    'Twill be a song with glorious harmony,
    When the courts of heaven ring.
    *Elton M. Roth.*

**520** THERE'S within my heart a melody,
    Jesus whispers sweet and low,
" Fear not, I am with thee, peace be still,"
    In all of life's ebb and flow.

    Jesus, Jesus, Jesus,
      Sweetest name I know,
    Fills my ev'ry longing,
      Keeps me singing as I go.

2 All my life was wrecked by sin and strife,
    Discord filled my heart with pain,
Jesus swept across the broken strings,     [again
    Stirred the slumb'ring chords

3 Feasting on the riches of His grace,
    Resting 'neath His shelt'ring wing,
Always looking on His smiling face,
    That is why I shout and sing.

4 Though sometimes He leads through waters deep,
    Trials fall across the way,
Though sometimes the path seems rough and steep,
    See His footprints all the way.

5 Soon He's coming back to welcome
    Far beyond the starry sky; [me;
I shall wing my flight to worlds unknown,
    I shall reign with Him on high.
    *L. B. Bridgers.*

**521** I HAVE found a wondrous Saviour,
    Jesus Christ, the soul's delight;
Ev'ry blessing of His favour
    Fills my heart with hope so bright.

    Jesus is the Joy of Living,
      He's the King of Life to me ;
    Unto Him my all I'm giving,
      His for evermore to be.

    I will do what He commands me,
      Anywhere He leads I'll go ;
    Jesus is the Joy of Living,
      He's the dearest Friend I know.

2 Life is growing rich with beauty,
    Toil has lost its weary strain,
Now a halo crowns each duty,
    And I sing a glad refrain.

3 Heav'nly wisdom He provides me,
    Grace to keep my spirit free;
In His own sweet way He guides me
    When the path I cannot see.

4 O what splendour, O what glory,
    O what matchless power divine,
Is the Christ of Gospel story,
    Christ the Saviour, who is mine.
    *A. H. Ackley.*

**522** I AM saved! I am saved!
    Jesus bids me go free!
He has bought with a price,
    Even me, even me.

    Hallelujah ! Hallelujah ! Hallelujah to my Saviour !
    Hallelujah ! Hallelujah ! Hallelujah !
      Amen.

2 I am cleansed! I am cleansed!
    I am whiter than snow;
He is mighty to save,
    This I know, this I know.

3 Wondrous love! wondrous love!
    Now the gift I receive;
I have rest in His word—
    I believe, I believe.

4 I was weak, I am strong,
    In the power of His might,
And my darkness He turns
    Into light, into light.

5 Praise the Lord! Praise the Lord!
    Ye His saints everywhere;
I shall join in the throng
    Over there, over there.

**523** A FRIEND of Jesus, oh, what bliss
    That one so weak as I
Should ever have a friend like this
    To lead me to the sky.

    Friendship with Jesus,
      Fellowship divine ;
    Oh, what blessèd sweet communion,
    Jesus is a friend of mine.

2 A friend when other friendships
   cease,
   A friend when others fail;
A friend who gives me joy and
   peace,
   A friend who will prevail.

3 A friend to lead me in the dark,
   A friend who knows the way;
A friend to steer my weak, frail
   bark,
   A friend my debts to pay.

4 A friend when sickness lays me low,
   A friend when death draws near;
A friend as through the vale I go,
   A friend to help and cheer.

5 A friend when life's rough voyage
   is o'er,
   A friend when death is past;
A friend to greet on heaven's shore,
   A friend when home at last.

*J. C. Ludgate.*

**524** MY Jesus, I love Thee, I know
   Thou art mine,
For Thee all the pleasures of sin I
   resign;          [art Thou,
My gracious Redeemer, my Saviour
If ever I loved Thee, my Jesus, 'tis
   now!

2 I love Thee because Thou hast first
   lovèd me,   [nailed to the tree;
And purchased my pardon when
I love Thee for wearing the thorns
   on Thy brow,          [now!
If ever I loved Thee, my Jesus, 'tis

3 I'll love Thee in life, I will love
   Thee in death,
And praise Thee as long as Thou
   lendest me breath,
And say, should the death-dew lie
   cold on my brow,       [now!
If ever I loved Thee, my Jesus, 'tis

4 In mansions of glory and endless
   delight,            [bright;
I'll ever adore Thee in heaven so
I'll sing with the glittering crown
   on my brow,          [now!
If ever I loved Thee, my Jesus, 'tis

*W. R. Featherstone.*

**525** THERE'S a song that's ringing
   in my heart today,
For I've found a loving Friend,
   He'll be with me to the end;

Though the tempter's snares beset
   my path below,
He is ever by my side, I know.

In my heart a song is ringing, . . .
For He's pardoned me I know,
Just because He loved me so,
And I'm singing, singing, singing, . . .
Just because He loved me so.

2 There's a song that's ringing in my
   heart today,
   Jesus' power has set me free,
   And He gives me victory;
All my sin-stains vanished in the
   crimson flow,        [know
And He'll keep me ev'ry hour, I

3 There's a song that's ringing in my
   heart today,
   For I'll see my Saviour's face,
   At the ending of the race;
Wear a spotless robe as white as
   driven snow,         [know.
Hear the welcome from the King I

*Major Sidney Cox.*

**526** ONCE I thought I walked with
   Jesus,
   Yet such changeful moods I had;
Sometimes trusting, sometimes
   doubting,
   Sometimes joyful, sometimes sad.

Oh, the peace my Saviour gives,
Peace I never knew before ;
For my way has brighter grown,
Since I learned to trust Him more.

2 For He called me closer to Him,
   Bade my doubting tremors cease;
And when I had fully trusted—
   Filled my soul with perfect peace.

3 Now I'm trusting ev'ry moment,
   Less than this is not enough;
And my Saviour bears me gently,
   O'er the places once so rough.

4 Blessèd Saviour, Thou dost keep me
   By Thy power from day to day,
And my heart is full of gladness,
   For Thou'lt keep me all the way.

*F. A. Blackmer.*

**527** WHEN peace, like a river
   attendeth my way,      [roll;
   When sorrows, like sea billows
Whatever my lot, Thou hast taught
   me to know,          [soul."
   " It is well, it is well with my

It is well, . . . with my soul, . . .
It is well, it is well with my soul.

2 Though Satan should buffet, if
    trials should come,
  Let this blest assurance control,
That Christ hath regarded my help-
    less estate,          [my soul.
  And hath shed His own blood for

3 My sin—oh, the bliss of this glori-
    ous thought—          [whole
  My sin—not in part, but the
Is nailed to His cross; and I bear
    it no more:
  Praise the Lord, praise the Lord,
    O my soul.

4 For me, be it Christ, be it Christ
    hence to live!
  If Jordan above me shall roll,
No pang shall be mine, for in death
    as in life          [my soul.
  Thou wilt whisper Thy peace to

5 But Lord, 'tis for Thee, for Thy
    coming we wait,          [goal:
  The sky, not the grave, is our
Oh, trump of the angel! oh, voice
    of the Lord!          [soul.
  Blessèd hope! blessèd rest of my
                    *H. G. Spafford.*

**528** PEACE like a river is flooding
    my soul,          [me whole;
  Since Christ, my Saviour, maketh
Sweet peace abiding my portion
    shall be—          [me.
  Jesus, my Saviour, is precious to

  Pre . . . cious to me, . . .
  Pre . . . cious is He : . . .
  Je . . . sus shall ever . . . be pre . . .
    cious to me. . . .

2 Joy is abounding—my heart gaily
    sings,          [wings;
  Cleave I the heavens, mount up on
Christ hath exalted, my soul He set
    free—          [me.
  Jesus, my Saviour, is precious to

3 Oh precious Jesus, how lovely Thou
    art!
  Come and abiding rule in my heart;
Break ev'ry fetter, Thy face let me
    see—          [to me.
  Then thou shalt ever be precious
                    *G. C. Tullar.*

**529** PEACE, perfect peace, in this
    dark world of sin?
  The blood of Jesus whispers peace
    within.

2 Peace, perfect peace, by thronging
    duties pressed?
  To do the will of Jesus, this is rest.

3 Peace, perfect peace, with sorrows
    surging round?
  On Jesus' bosom naught but calm
    is found.

4 Peace, perfect peace, with loved
    ones far away?
  In Jesus' keeping we are safe and
    they.

5 Peace, perfect peace, our future all
    unknown?
  Jesus we know, and He is on the
    throne.

6 Peace, perfect peace, death shadow-
    ing us and ours?
  Jesus has vanquished death and all
    its powers.

7 It is enough; earth's struggles soon
    shall cease,
  And Jesus call us to heaven's per-
    fect peace.
                    *E. H. Bickersteth.*

**530** MY God, I am Thine;
    What a comfort divine,
  What a blessing to know that my
    Jesus is mine!
  In the heavenly Lamb
  Thrice happy I am,
An·l my heart it doth dance at the
    sound of His name.

2 True pleasures abound
    In the rapturous sound;
  And whoever hath found it hath
    paradise found.
  My Jesus to know,
  And feel His blood flow,
'Tis life everlasting, 'tis heaven
    below.

3 Yet onward I haste
    To the heavenly feast:
  That, that is the fulness; but this is
    the taste!
  And this I shall prove,
  Till with joy I remove
To the heaven of heavens in Jesus's
    love.
                    *Charles Wesley.*

## (7) PRAYER

**531** PRAYER is the soul's sincere desire,
Uttered or unexpressed!
The motion of a hidden fire,
That trembles in the breast.

2 Prayer is the burden of a sigh,
The falling of a tear,
The upward glancing of an eye,
When none but God is near.

3 Prayer is the simplest form of speech
That infant lips can try: [speech
Prayer, the sublimest strains that reach
The Majesty on high. [reach

4 Prayer is the Christian's vital breath,
The Christian's native air:
His watchword at the gates of death,
He enters heaven with prayer.

5 The saints in prayer appear as one,
In word, and deed, and mind;
While with the Father and the Son,
Sweet fellowship they find.

6 O Thou by Whom we come to God,
The Life, the Truth, the Way!
The path of prayer Thyself hast trod,
Lord, teach us how to pray!
*Jas. Montgomery.*

**532** WHAT a friend we have in Jesus,
All our sins and griefs to bear;
What a privilege to carry
Ev'rything to God in prayer.
Oh, what peace we often forfeit,
Oh, what needless pain we bear—
All because we do not carry
Ev'rything to God in prayer.

2 Have we trials and temptations?
Is there trouble anywhere?
We should never be discouraged,
Take it to the Lord in prayer.
Can we find a Friend so faithful,
Who will all our sorrows share?
Jesus knows our ev'ry weakness,
Take it to the Lord in prayer.

3 Are we weak and heavy laden,
Cumbered with a load of care?
Precious Saviour, still our refuge,—
Take it to the Lord in prayer.

Do thy friends despise, forsake thee?
Take it to the Lord in prayer;
In His arms He'll take and shield thee,
Thou wilt find a solace there.
*Joseph Scriven.*

**533** Ho, reapers in the whitened harvest!
Oft feeble, faint, and few;
Come, wait upon the blessèd Master,
Our strength He will renew.
For " they that wait upon the Lord shall
renew their strength,
They shall mount up with wings,
They shall mount up with wings as eagles :
They shall run and not be weary ;
They shall walk and not faint."

2 Too oft a-weary and discouraged,
We pour a sad complaint;
Believing in a living Saviour,
Why should we ever faint?

3 Rejoice! for He is with us alway,
Lo, even to the end! [ward—
Look up! take courage and go for-
All needed grace He'll send!
*J. McGranahan.*

**534** SPEAK to my soul Lord Jesus,
Speak now in tend'rest tone;
Whisper in loving-kindness:
" Thou art not left alone."
Open my heart to hear Thee,
Quickly to hear Thy voice,
Fill Thou my soul with praises,
Let me in Thee rejoice.
Speak Thou in softest whispers,
Whispers of love to me :
" Thou shalt be always conq'ror,
Thou shalt be always free."
Speak Thou to me each day, Lord,
Always in tend'rest tone :
Let me now hear Thy whisper :
" Thou art not left alone."

2 Speak to Thy children ever,
Lead in the holy way;
Fill them with joy and gladness,
Teach them to watch and pray,
May they in consecration
Yield their whole lives to Thee,
Hasten Thy coming kingdom,
Till our dear Lord we see.

3 Speak now as in the old time
Thou didst reveal Thy will;
Let me know all my duty,
Let me Thy law fulfil.

Lead me to glorify Thee,
Help me to show Thy praise,
Gladly to do Thy bidding,
Honour Thee all my days.
*L. L. Pickett.*

**535** FROM ev'ry stormy wind that blows,
From ev'ry swelling tide of woes,
There is a calm, a sure retreat;
'Tis found beneath the mercy-seat.

2 There is a place where Jesus sheds
The oil of gladness on our heads—
A place than all beside more sweet;
It is the blood-stained mercy-seat.

3 There is a scene where spirits blend,
And friend holds fellowship with [friend;
Though sundered far, by faith we meet
Around one common mercy-seat.

4 There, there on eagle wing we soar,
And time and sense seem all no more;
And heaven comes down our souls [to greet,
And glory crowns the mercy-seat.
*Hugh Stowell.*

**536** BREATHE on me, Breath of God,
Fill me with life anew,
That I may love what Thou dost [love,
And do what Thou wouldst do.

2 Breathe on me, Breath of God,
Until my heart is pure,
Until with Thee I will one will,
To do and to endure.

3 Breathe on me, Breath of God,
Till I am wholly Thine,
Till all this earthly part of me
Glows with Thy fire divine.

4 Breathe on me, Breath of God,
So shall I never die,
But live with Thee the perfect life
Of Thine eternity. *Edwin Hatch.*

**537** MY God, is any hour so sweet,
From blush of morn to ev'ning star,
As that which calls me to Thy feet,
The hour of prayer?

2 Blest be that tranquil hour of morn,
And blest that hour of solemn eve,
When, on the wings of prayer [upborne,
The world I leave.

3 For then a day-spring shines on me,
Brighter than morn's ethereal glow;
And richer dews descend from [Thee
Than earth can know.

4 Then is my strength by Thee renewed;
Then are my sins by Thee for- [given;
Then dost Thou cheer my solitude
With hope of heaven.

5 No words can tell what blest relief.
There for my every want I find;
What strength for warfare, balm for grief;
What peace of mind.

6 Hushed is each doubt, gone every fear;
My spirit seems in heaven to [stay;
And e'en the penitential tear
Is wiped away.

7 Lord, till I reach yon blissful shore,
No privilege so dear shall be,
As thus my inmost soul to pour
In prayer to Thee.
*Charlotte Elliott.*

**538** COME, my soul, thy suit prepare,
Jesus loves to answer prayer;
He Himself has bid thee pray,
Therefore will not say thee nay.

2 Thou art coming to a King,
Large petitions with thee bring;
For His grace and power are such,
None can ever ask too much.

3 Lord, I come to Thee for rest,
Take possession of my breast;
There Thy blood-bought right maintain,
And without a rival reign.

4 As the image in the glass
Answers the beholder's face,
Thus unto my heart appear,
Print Thine own resemblance there.

5 While I am a pilgrim here,
Let Thy love my spirit cheer;
As my guide, my guard, my friend,
Lead me to my journey's end.
*J. Newton.*

**539** BEHOLD the throne of grace!
The promise calls me near;
There Jesus shows a smiling face,
And waits to answer prayer.

2  That rich atoning blood,
    Which sprinkled round I see,
  Provides for those who come to
    An all-prevailing plea.   [God,

3  My soul, ask what thou wilt,
    Thou canst not be too bold;
  Since His own blood for thee He
    spilt,
    What else can He withhold?

4  Beyond thine utmost wants,
    His love and power can bless:
  To praying souls He always grants
    More than they can express.

5  Thine image, Lord, bestow,
    Thy presence and Thy love:
  I ask to serve Thee here below,
    And reign with Thee above.
*J. Newton.*

**540**  HOLY Father, in Thy mercy,
    Hear our anxious prayer;
  Keep our loved ones, now far dist-
    'Neath Thy care.     [ant

2  Jesus, Saviour, let Thy presence
    Be their light and guide;
  Keep, oh, keep them, in their weak-
    At Thy side.     [ness,

3  When in sorrow, when in danger,
    When in loneliness,
  In Thy love look down and com-
    Their distress.     [fort

4  May the joy of Thy salvation
    Be their strength and stay,
  May they love and may they praise
    Day by day.     [Thee

5  Holy Spirit, let Thy teaching
    Sanctify their life;
  Send Thy grace, that they may con-
    In the strife.     [quer

6  Father, Son, and Holy Spirit,
    God the One in Three,
  Bless them, guide them, save them,
    Near to Thee.    [keep them
*I. S. Stevenson.*

**541**  I NEED Thee ev'ry hour,
    Most gracious Lord;
  No tender voice like Thine
  Can peace afford.

    I need Thee, oh, I need Thee,
     Ev'ry hour I need Thee;
    Oh, bless me now, my Saviour,
     I come to Thee!

2  I need Thee every hour,
    Stay Thou near by;
  Temptations lose their power,
    When Thou art nigh.

3  I need Thee every hour,
    In joy or pain;
  Come quickly and abide,
    Or life is vain.

4  I need Thee every hour,
    Teach me Thy will;
  And Thy rich promises
    In me fulfil.

5  I need Thee every hour,
    Most Holy One;
  Oh, make me Thine indeed,
    Thou blessèd Son!
*Annie Hawkes.*

## (8) SERVICE

**542**  I LOVE, I love my Master,
    I will not go out free!
  For He is my Redeemer;
    He paid the price for me.
  I would not leave His service,
    It is so sweet and blest;
  And in the weariest moments
    He gives the truest rest.

2  My Master shed His life-blood
    My vassal life to win,
  And save me from the bondage
    Of tyrant self and sin.
  He chose me for His service,
    And gave me power to choose
  That blessèd, perfect freedom,
    Which I shall never lose.

3  I would not halve my service,
    His only it must be!
  His *only*—Who so loved me,
    And gave Himself for me.
  Rejoicing and adoring,
    Henceforth my song shall be—
  "I love, I love my Master,
    I will not go out free!"
*F. R. Havergal.*

**543**  LIVING for Jesus a life that is
    true,     [I do,
  Striving to please Him in all that
  Yielding allegiance, gladhearted
    and free,     [for me.
  This is the pathway of blessing

O Jesus, Lord and Saviour,
　I give myself to Thee ;
For Thou, in Thine atonement,
　Didst give Thyself for me ;
I own no other Master,
　My heart shall be Thy throne,
My life I give, henceforth to live,
　O Christ, for Thee alone.

2 Living for Jesus who died in my
　　place,　　　　　　[grace,
Bearing on Calv'ry my sin and dis-
Such love constrains me to answer
　His call,　　　　　　[my all.
Follow His leading and give Him

3 Living for Jesus wherever I am,
Doing each duty in His Holy
　Name,
Willing to suffer affliction or loss,
Deeming each trial a part of my
　cross.

4 Living for Jesus through earth's
　　little while,　　　[His smile,
My dearest treasure, the light of
Seeking the lost ones He died to
　redeem,　　　　　　[Him.
Bringing the weary to find rest in
　　　　　　　　*T. O. Chisholm.*

**544** SEND the gospel of salvation,
　To a world of dying men ;
Tell it out to ev'ry nation,
　Till the Lord shall come again.

　Go and tell them, go and tell them,
　　Jesus died for sinful men.
　Go and tell them, go and tell them,
　　He is coming back again.

2 'Tis the church's great commission,
　'Tis the Master's last command ;
Christ has died for every creature,
　Tell it out in every land.

3 Christ is gathering out a people,
　To His name from every race ;
Haste to give the invitation
　Ere shall end the day of grace.

4 Give the gospel as a witness,
　To a world of sinful men ;
Till the Bride shall be completed,
　And the Lord shall come again.
　　　　　　　　　*A. B. Simpson.*

**545** JESUS, and shall it ever be,
　A mortal man ashamed of
　　Thee ?　　　　　[praise,
Ashamed of Thee, whom angels
Whose glories shine through end-
　less days !

2 Ashamed of Jesus ! sooner far
Let evening blush to own a star ;
He shed the beams of light divine
O'er this benighted soul of mine.

3 Ashamed of Jesus ! just as soon
Let midnight be ashamed of noon :
'Twas midnight with my soul till
　He,　　　　　　　[flee.
Bright morning star, bade darkness

4 Ashamed of Jesus ! that dear
　　Friend　　　　　[pend !
On whom my hopes of heaven de-
No ! when I blush be this my
　shame
That I no more revere His Name.

5 Ashamed of Jesus, yes, I may
When I've no guilt to wash away ;
No tear to wipe, no good to crave,
No fears to quell, no soul to save.

6 Till then—nor is my boasting vain—
Till then I boast a Saviour slain ;
And oh ! may this my glory be,
That Christ is not ashamed of me.
　　　　　　　　　*J. Griggs.*

**546** O THOU who camest from
　　above
The pure celestial fire to impart,
Kindle a flame of sacred love
On the mean altar of my heart !

2 There let it for Thy glory burn
With inextinguishable blaze ;
And trembling to its source return,
In humble prayer and fervent
　praise.

3 Jesus, confirm my heart's desire
To work, and speak, and think
　for Thee ;
Still let me guard the holy fire,
And still stir up Thy gift in me.

4 Ready for all Thy perfect will,
My acts of faith and love repeat,
Till death Thy endless mercies seal,
And make the sacrifice complete.
　　　　　　　　　*Charles Wesley.*

**547** IT may not be on the moun-
　　tain's height,
Or over the stormy sea ;
It may not be at the battle's front
My Lord will have need of me ;

But if by a still, small voice He calls
  To paths that I do not know,
I'll answer, dear Lord, with my hand in Thine,
  I'll go where you want me to go.

I'll go where you want me to go, dear Lord,
  Over mountain, or plain, or sea :
I'll say what you want me to say, dear Lord,
  I'll be what you want me to be.

2 Perhaps today there are loving words         [speak;
  Which Jesus would have me
There may be now in the paths of sin
  Some wand'rer whom I should seek;
O Saviour, if Thou wilt be my guide,
  Though dark and rugged the way,
My voice shall echo the message sweet,        [say.
  I'll say what you want me to

3 There's surely somewhere a lowly place,
  In earth's harvest fields so wide,
Where I may labour through life's short day
  For Jesus the crucified :
So trusting my all to Thy tender care,
  And knowing Thou lovest me,
I'll do Thy will with a heart sincere,
  I'll be what you want me to be.
                          *Mary Brown.*


**548** How I praise Thee, precious Saviour,
  That Thy love laid hold of me;
Thou hast saved and cleansed and filled me,
  That I might Thy channel be.

Channels only, blessèd Master,
  But with all Thy wondrous power,
Flowing through us, Thou canst use us
  Ev'ry day and ev'ry hour.

2 Just a channel, full of blessing,
  To the thirsty hearts around;
To tell out Thy full salvation,
  All Thy loving message sound.

3 Emptied that Thou shouldest fill me,
  A clean vessel in Thy hand;
With no power but as Thou givest,
  Graciously with each command.

4 Witnessing Thy power to save me,
  Setting free from self and sin;
Thou hast bought me to possess me,
  In Thy fulness, Lord, come in.

5 Jesus, fill now with Thy Spirit,
  Hearts that full surrender know;
That the streams of living water
  From our inner man may flow.
                    *Mary E. Maxwell.*


**549** LORD! it is good for us to be
  High on the mountain here with Thee :
Here in an ampler, purer air,
Above the stir of toil and care:
Lord, it is good for us to be
Entranced, enwrapped alone with Thee        [glow,
Watching the glist'ning raiment
Whiter than Hermon's whitest snow.

2 Lord, it is good for us to be
  Here at the mountain foot with Thee,
Where ills afflict and demons vex,
And woes the sons of men perplex.
Our human hands and tears are vain,
But Thou art strong to heal again,
Foul devils vanish at Thy voice,
And loosened hearts and tongues rejoice.

3 Lord, it is good for us to be
  High in the heavenly place with Thee,        [light,
Where drinking beams of holy
And storing rays of heavenly might,
We too with Thee may seek the shade        [made,
Where sons of night are captive
And set them dancing in Thy Name,
And shouting praises to the Lamb!

4 Lord! it is good for us to be
In any place or clime with Thee;
On dazzling peak or darkling plain,
'Mid human joy or gloom or pain.
Be Thou transfigured in our sight,
'Mid shining saints or Satan's blight,
Thy mercy still the people bless,
And save them from their deep distress.
              *A. P. Stanley and Harold Horton.*

**550** WE are marching on, with
    shield and banner bright;
We will work for God, and battle
    for the right;
We will praise His name, rejoicing
    in His might,
    And we'll work till Jesus calls.
From the youthful ranks our army
    we prepare,   [standard here;
As we rally round our blessèd
And the Saviour's cross we early
    learn to bear,
    While we work till Jesus calls.

    Then awake, . . . then awake, . . .
      Happy song, . . . happy song, . . .
    Shout for joy, . . . shout for joy, . . .
      As we gladly march along.
    We are marching onward, singing as we go,
    To the promised land where living waters
      flow ;
    Come and join our ranks as pilgrims here
      below,
    Come and work till Jesus calls.

2 We are marching on: our Captain,
    ever near,   [voice we hear:
Will protect us still, His gentle
Let the foe advance, we'll never,
    never fear,
    For we'll work till Jesus calls.
Then awake, awake, our happy,
    happy song;   [march along;
We will shout for joy, and gladly
In the Lord of hosts let ev'ry heart
    be strong,
    While we work till Jesus calls.

3 We are marching on the strait and
    narrow way,   [ing day,
That will lead to life and everlast-
To the smiling fields, that never
    will decay:
    But we'll work till Jesus calls.
We are marching on, and pressing
    t'wards the prize,
To a glorious crown beyond the
    glowing skies,
To the radiant fields where pleasure
    never dies,
    And we'll work till Jesus calls.
              *Fanny J. Crosby.*

**551** COMING now to Thee, O Christ
    my Lord,   [word.
Trusting only in Thy precious
Let my humble prayer to Thee be
    heard,   [soul.
    And send a great revival in my

    Send a great revival in my soul,
    Send a great revival in my soul ;
    Let the Holy Spirit come and take control,
    And send a great revival in my soul.

2 Send a great revival, Lord, in me,
Help me that I may rejoice in
    Thee;   [tory,
Give me strength to win the vic-
    And send a great revival in my
    soul.

3 Help me go for Thee, dear Lord,
    today,   [astray;
To some lonely soul that's gone
Help me lead them in the home-
    ward way,   [soul.
    Oh, send a great revival in my
              *B. B. McKinney.*

**552** THROW out the Life-line across
    the dark wave,
There is a brother whom someone
    should save :   [will dare
Somebody's brother! oh, who then
To throw out the Life-line his peril
    to share?

    Throw out the Life-line !
    Throw out the Life-line !
    Some one is drifting away ;
    Throw out the Life-line !
    Throw out the Life-line !
    Some one is sinking today.

2 Throw out the Life-line with hand
    quick and strong;
Why do you tarry, why linger so
    long?
See! he is sinking, oh, hasten to-
    day—   [then, away!
    And out with the Life-boat! away,

3 Throw out the Life-line to danger-
    fraught men,   [never been:
Sinking in anguish where you've
Winds of temptation and billows of
    woe   [the dark waters flow.
    Will soon hurl them back where

4 Soon will the season of rescue be
    o'er,   [shore,
Soon will they drift to eternity's
Haste then, my brother, no time
    for delay;
But throw out the Life-line and save
    them today.    *E. S. Ufford.*

**553** GIVE me the faith which can
    remove   [plain;
    And sink the mountain to a
Give me the child-like praying love,

Which longs to build Thy house
   again;
Thy love let it my heart o'er-power,
And all my simple soul devour.

2 I want an even strong desire,
   I want a calmly fervent zeal,
To save poor souls out of the fire,
To snatch them from the verge
   of hell,
And turn them to a pardoning God
And quench the brands in Jesu's
   blood.

3 I would the precious time redeem,
   And longer live for this alone,
To spend, and to be spent, for them
   Who have not yet my Saviour
      known;
Fully on these my mission prove,
And only breathe, to breathe Thy
   love.

4 My talents, gifts, and graces, Lord,
   Into Thy blessèd hands receive;
And let me live to preach Thy
   word,
And let me to Thy glory live;
My every sacred moment spend
In publishing the sinner's Friend.

5 Enlarge, inflame, and fill my heart
   With boundless charity divine!
So shall I all my strength exert,
   And love them with a zeal like
      Thine;
And lead them to Thy open side,
The sheep for whom their Shepherd
   died.

*Charles Wesley.*

**554** SAVIOUR! Thy dying love
   Thou gavest me,
Nor should I aught withhold,
   My Lord, from Thee;
In love my soul would bow,
My heart fulfil its vow,
Some off'ring bring Thee now,
   Something for Thee.

2 At the blest mercy-seat,
   Pleading for me,
My feeble faith looks up,
   Jesus, to Thee:
Help me the cross to bear,
Thy wondrous love declare,
Some song to raise, or prayer,
   Something for Thee.

3 Give me a faithful heart—
   Likeness to Thee—
That each departing day
   Henceforth may see
Some work of love begun,
Some deed of kindness done,
Some wanderer sought and won,
   Something for Thee.

4 All that I am and have—
   Thy gifts so free—
In joy, in grief, through life,
   O Lord, for Thee!
And when Thy face I see,
My ransomed soul shall be,
Through all eternity,
   Something for Thee. *S. D. Phelps.*

**555** SING the wondrous love of
      Jesus,
   Sing His mercy and His grace;
In the mansions, bright and blessèd,
   He'll prepare for us a place.

When we all . . . get to heaven,
   What a day of rejoicing that will be ! . . .
When we all . . . see Jesus,
   We'll sing and shout the victory . . .

2 While we walk the pilgrim path-
      way,
   Clouds will overspread the sky;
But when trav'ling days are over,
   Not a shadow, not a sigh.

3 Let us, then, be true and faithful,
   Trusting, serving every day;
Just one glimpse of Him in glory,
   Will the toils of life repay.

4 Onward to the prize before us!
   Soon His beauty we'll behold;
Soon the pearly gates will open,
   We shall tread the streets of gold.
      *E. E. Hewitt.*

**556** FATHER, I know that all my
      life
   Is portioned out for me,
And the changes that are sure to
      I do not fear to see;      [come
But I ask Thee for a present mind,
   Intent on pleasing Thee.

2 I ask Thee for a thoughtful love,
   Through constant watching wise,
To meet the glad with joyful
      smiles,
   And wipe the weeping eyes;
And a heart at leisure from itself,
   To soothe and sympathize.

3 I would not have the restless will
  That hurries to and fro,
Seeking for some great thing to do
  Or secret thing to know;
I would be treated as a child,
  And guided where I go.

4 Wherever in the world I am,
  In whatsoe'er estate,
I have a fellowship with hearts
  To keep and cultivate;
And a work of lowly love to do
  For the Lord on whom I wait.

5 So I ask Thee for the daily
    strength,
  To none that ask denied,
And a mind to blend with outward
    Still keeping at Thy side;  [life,
  Content to fill a little space
  If Thou be glorified.

6 There are briers besetting every
    path,
  That call for patient care;
There is a cross in every lot,
  And a constant need for prayer:
Yet a lowly heart, that leans on
  Is happy anywhere.    [Thee,

7 In a service which Thy will
    appoints
  There are no bonds for me:
For my inmost soul is taught the
    truth
  That makes Thy children free,
And a life of self-renouncing love
  Is a life of liberty.
                    *Anna L. Waring.*

**557** BLESSED is the service of our
      Lord and King,
Precious are the jewels we may
  help to bring;    [counsel ring,
Down the passing ages words of
He that winneth souls is wise.

    He that winneth souls is wise ; . . .
    In the home beyond the skies, . . .
    There's a crown of glory, oh, the wondrous
      prize !
    He that winneth souls is wise.

2 In the quiet home-life, showing
    love's bright ray,    [ev'ry day,
More and more like Jesus living
We may guide a dear one to the
    heavenward way,
He that winneth souls is wise.

3 Out upon the highway, going forth
    with prayer,    [everywhere,
For the lost and straying, seeking
Close beside the Shepherd, we His
    joy may share,
He that winneth souls is wise.

4 Sow beside all waters, sow the gos-
    pel seed,    [ing deed,
Here a word in season, there a lov-
Sinners to the Saviour, be it ours
    to lead,
He that winneth souls is wise.
                    *E. E. Hewitt.*

**558** THERE is joy in serving Jesus,
      As I journey on my way,
Joy that fills the heart with praises,
  Ev'ry hour and ev'ry day.
    There is joy, joy,
    Joy in serving Jesus,
      Joy that throbs within my heart ;
    Ev'ry moment, ev'ry hour,
    As I draw upon His pow'r,
    There is joy, joy,
      Joy that never shall depart.

2 There is joy in serving Jesus,
    Joy that triumphs over pain;
Fills my soul with heaven's music,
  Till I join the glad refrain.

3 There is joy in serving Jesus,
    As I walk alone with God;
'Tis the joy of Christ, my Saviour,
  Who the path of suffering trod.

4 There is joy in serving Jesus,
    Joy amid the darkest night,
For I've learned the wondrous
    secret,
  And I'm walking in the light.
                    *Oswald J. Smith.*

**559** HEAR the Lord of harvest
      sweetly calling,
  " Who will go and work for Me
    today?    [and dying?
Who will bring to Me the lost
Who will point them to the
    narrow way!"
    Speak, my Lord, . . . speak to me, . . .
    Speak, and I'll be quick to answer Thee ; . . .
    Speak, my Lord, . . . speak to me,
    Speak, and I will answer, "Lord, send
      me" . . .

2 When the coal of fire touched the
    prophet,    [be,
  Making him as pure, as pure can
When the voice of God said,
    "Who'll go for us?"
  Then he answered, "Here I am,
    send me."

3 Millions now in sin and shame are
    dying;
  Listen to their sad and bitter cry:
Hasten, brother, hasten to the res-
  cue;           [am I."
  Quickly answer, " Master, here

4 Soon the time for reaping will be
    over;         [home:
  Soon we'll gather for the harvest-
May the Lord of harvest smile up-
  on us,       [well done!"
  May we hear His blessèd, "Child,
                *Geo. Bennard.*

**560** FORTH in Thy name, O Lord,
    I go,
  My daily labour to pursue,
Thee, only Thee, resolved to know
In all I think, or speak, or do.

2 The task Thy wisdom hath assigned
  O let me cheerfully fulfil,
In all my works Thy presence find,
And prove Thy acceptable will.

3 Thee may I set at my right hand,
  Whose eyes my inmost substance
    see,
And labour on at Thy command,
And offer all my works to Thee.

4 Give me to bear Thy easy yoke,
  And every moment watch and
    pray,
And still to things eternal look,
And hasten to Thy glorious day:

5 For Thee delightfully employ
  Whate'er Thy bounteous grace
    hath given,
And run my course with even joy,
And closely walk with Thee to
  heaven.      *Charles Wesley.*

**561** RESCUE the perishing,
    Care for the dying. [the grave:
Snatch them in pity from sin and
  Weep o'er the erring one,
  Lift up the fallen,
Tell them of Jesus, the Mighty to
    save.

   Rescue the perishing, care for the dying ;
   Jesus is merciful, Jesus will save.

2 Though they are slighting Him,
  Still He is waiting,
Waiting the penitent child to re-
  Plead with them earnestly, [ceive.
  Plead with them gently;
He will forgive if they only believe.

3 Down in the human heart,
  Crushed by the tempter,
Feelings lie buried that grace can
    restore;
  Touched by a loving hand,
  Wakened by kindness,
Chords that were broken will vi-
    brate once more.

4 Rescue the perishing,
  Duty demands it: [will provide;
Strength for thy labour the Lord
  Back to the narrow way
  Patiently win them;
Tell the poor wand'rer a Saviour
  has died.    *Fanny J. Crosby.*

**562** Is your life a channel of bless-
    ing?
  Is the love of God flowing
    through you?    [Saviour?
Are you telling the lost of the
  Are you ready His service to
    do?

   Make me a channel of blessing today,
   Make me a channel of blessing, I pray :
   My life possessing, my service blessing,
   Make me a channel of blessing today.

2 Is your life a channel of blessing?
  Are you burdened for those that
    are lost?    [are straying,
Have you urged upon those who
  The Saviour who died on the
    cross?

3 Is your life a channel of blessing?
  Is it daily telling for Him?
Have you spoken the word of
    salvation
  To those who are dying in sin?

4 We cannot be channels of blessing
  If our lives are not free from all
    sin;
We will barriers be and a hindrance
  To those we are trying to win.
                *H. G. Smyth.*

**563** DISCIPLES of Jesus, why stand
    ye here idle?
  Go work in His vineyard, He
    calls you today;
The night is approaching, when no
    man can labour,
  Our Master commands us, and
    shall we delay?

   The field is the world !
   The field is the world !
  Look up, for the harvest is near ;
   When the reapers from glory
   Will shout as they come,
  And the Lord of the harvest appear.

2 Our field is the world, and our
work is before us,
To each is appointed a message
to bear,                [or palace,
At home or abroad, in the cottage
Wherever directed, our mission is
there.

3 Perhaps we are called from the
highways and hedges,
To gather the lowly, despised,
and oppressed;
If this be our duty, then why
should we falter?
We'll do it, and trust to our
Saviour the rest.

4 O'er islands that sleep in the wave-
crested ocean,
We'll scatter the truth, and its
fruit it shall bear;
O'er ice-covered regions and rock-
girded mountains
The Lord will protect as His
children are there.

5 Instead of the thorn shall the
myrtle be planted,
The desert shall blossom and
bloom as the rose;
The palm-tree rejoicing shall spread
forth her branches
The lamb and the lion together
repose.

**564** Jesus calls us o'er the tumult
Of our life's wild, restless
sea,                    [eth,
Day by day His sweet voice sound-
Saying, "Christian, follow Me!"

2 As, of old, apostles heard it
By the Galilean lake,     [kindred,
Turned from home, and toil, and
Leaving all for His dear sake.

3 Jesus calls us from the worship
Of the vain world's golden store,
From each idol that would keep us,
Saying, "Christian, love Me
more."

4 In our joys and in our sorrows,
Days of toil and hours of ease,
Still He calls, in cares and pleas-
ures,                    [these."
"Christian, love Me more than

5 Jesus calls us; by Thy mercies,
Saviour, may we hear Thy call,

Give our hearts to Thy obedience,
Serve and love Thee best of all.
*C. F. Alexander.*

**565** Oh, where are the reapers that
garner in
The sheaves of the good from the
fields of sin?      [work be done,
With sickles of truth must the
And no one may rest till the "harvest home."

Where are the reapers? Oh, who will come
And share in the glory of the "harvest
home"?
Oh, who will help us to garner in
The sheaves of good from the fields of sin?

2 Go out in the by-ways and search
them all:          [weeds are tall;
The wheat may be there, though the
Then search in the highway, and
pass none by,         [on high.
But gather from all for the home

3 The fields are all rip'ning, and far
and wide,              [tide,
The world is awaiting the harvest
But reapers are few, and the work
is great,          [harvest wait.
And much will be lost should the

4 So come with your sickles, ye sons
of men,               [grain;
And gather together the golden
Toil on till the Lord of the harvest
come,             [vest home."
Then share in the joy of the "har-
*E. E. Rexford.*

**566** Far and near the fields are
teeming,
With the waves of ripened grain;
Far and near their gold is gleaming,
O'er the sunny slope and plain.
Lord of harvest, send forth reapers!
Hear us, Lord, to Thee we cry;
Send them now the sheaves to gather,
Ere the harvest time pass by.

2 Send them forth with morn's first
beaming,
Send them in the noontide's glare;
When the sun's last rays are gleam-
ing,
Bid them gather everywhere.

3 O thou, whom thy Lord is sending,
Gather now the sheaves of gold,
Heav'nward then at evening wend-
ing
Thou shalt come with joy untold.
*J. O. Thompson.*

**567** O MASTER, let me walk with Thee
In lowly paths of service free;
Thy secret tell; help me to bear
The strain of toil, the fret of care.

2 Help me the slow of heart to move
By some clear winning word of love;
Teach me the wayward feet to stay,
And guide them in the homeward way.

3 Teach me Thy patience; still with [Thee
In closer, dearer company,
In work that keeps faith sweet and strong,
In trust that triumphs over wrong.

4 In hope that sends a shining ray
Far down the future's broadening way,
In peace that only Thou canst give,
With Thee, O Master, let me live!

*Washington Gladden.*

**568** To the work! to the work!
we are servants of God,
Let us follow the path that our Master has trod;
With the balm of His counsel our strength to renew,
Let us do with our might what our hands find to do.

Toiling on, . . . toiling on, . . .
Toiling on, . . . toiling on ; . . .
Let us hope, . . . let us watch, . . .
And labour till the Master comes.

2 To the work! to the work! let the hungry be fed,
To the fountain of life let the weary be led!
In the cross and its banner our glory shall be,
While we herald the tidings, " Salvation is free!"

3 To the work! to the work! there is labour for all,
For the kingdom of darkness and error shall fall:
And the name of Jehovah exalted shall be,
In the loud-swelling chorus, " Salvation is free!"

4 To the work! to the work! in the strength of the Lord,
And a robe and a crown shall our labour reward,

When the home of the faithful our dwelling shall be,
And we shout with the ransomed, " Salvation is free!"

*Fanny J. Crosby.*

**569** THE Master hath come, and He calls us to follow
The track of the footprints He leaves on our way;
Far over the mountain, and through the deep hollow,
The path leads us on to the mansions of day.
The Master hath called us, the children who fear Him,
Who march 'neath Christ's banner, His own little band;
We love Him, and seek Him, we long to be near Him,
And rest in the light of His beautiful land.

2 The Master hath called us; the road may be dreary,
And dangers and sorrows are strewn on the track;
But God's Holy Spirit shall comfort the weary—
We follow the Saviour, and cannot turn back.
The Master hath called us: though doubt and temptation
May compass our journey, we cheerfully sing,
" Press onward, look upward," through much tribulation
The children of Zion must follow their King.

3 The Master hath called us: in life's early morning
With spirits as fresh as the dew on the sod:
We turn from the world, with its smiles and its scorning,
To cast in our lot with the people of God.
The Master hath called us, His sons and His daughters,
We plead for His blessing, and trust in His love;
And through the green pastures, beside the still waters,
He'll lead us at last to His kingdom above.

*Sarah Doudney.*

**570** THERE'S a work for Jesus
Ready at your hand,
'Tis a task the Master
Just for you has planned.
Haste to do His bidding,
Yield Him service true;
There's a work for Jesus,
None but you can do.

Work for Jesus, day by day,
Serve Him ever, falter never, Christ obey.
Yield Him service, loyal, true ;
There's a work for Jesus none but you can do.

2 There's a work for Jesus,
Humble though it be,
'Tis the very service

He would ask of thee.
Go where fields are whitened,
And the labourers few;
There's a work for Jesus,
None but you can do.

3 There's a work for Jesus,
Precious souls to bring,
Tell them of His mercies,
Tell them of your King,
Faint not, grow not weary,
He will strength renew;
There's a work for Jesus,
None but you can do.

*Elsie Yale.*

# Section VIII

## CONSECRATION AND HOLINESS

**571** O LOVE that wilt not let me
go,
I rest my weary soul in Thee:
I give Thee back the life I owe,
That in Thine ocean depths its flow
May richer, fuller be.

2 O light that follow'st all my way,
I yield my flick'ring torch to
Thee:
My heart restores its borrowed ray,
That in Thy sunshine's blaze its
May brighter, fairer be. [day

3 O Joy that seekest me through
pain,
I cannot close my heart to Thee:
I trace the rainbow through the
rain,
And feel the promise is not vain,
That morn shall tearless be.

4 O Cross that liftest up my head,
I dare not ask to fly from Thee;
I lay in dust life's glory dead,
And from the ground there blos-
soms red
Life that shall endless be.

*George Matheson.*

**572** BURN, fire of God! my ransomed soul possessing;
Pure fire Thou art, and I would
dwell in Thee.

Light of my life, true source of
ev'ry blessing, [flame to be.
Grant all my days one holy

2 Burn, fire of God! Thy grace and
glory knowing, [within:
My cleansèd heart shall be all fire
Love all-constraining, tenderness
o'erflowing, [to win.
One kindling passion other lives

3 Burn, fire of God! Thy cloven
tongue bestowing, [energy.
Baptizing me with heavenly
Touched with live coals from off
Thine altar glowing, [of Thee.
My purgèd lips shall speak alone

4 Burn, fire of God! with seven-fold
refining. [Thine eyes shall see
Till, mirrored from my deeps
In purest gold Thy perfect image
shining: [irradiancy.
Thy Christ revealed in clear

5 Burn, fire of God! by Thine own
love transcending,
Let all I hold be Thine, and
Thine alone!
Heart, mind and will, a sacrifice
ascending, [fiery Throne.
Consumed by fire from out Thy

*L. F. W. Woodford.*

**573** HAVE Thine own way, Lord!
　　Have Thine own way!
Thou art the Potter;
　　I am the clay.
Mould me and make me
　　After Thy will,
While I am waiting
　　Yielded and still.

2 Have Thine own way, Lord!
　　Have Thine own way!
Search me and try me,
　　Master, today!
Whiter than snow, Lord,
　　Wash me just now,
As in Thy presence
　　Humbly I bow.

3 Have Thine own way, Lord!
　　Have Thine own way!
Wounded and weary
　　Help me, I pray!
Power—all power—
　　Surely is Thine!
Touch me and heal me,
　　Saviour Divine!

4 Have Thine own way, Lord!
　　Have Thine own way!
Hold o'er my being
　　Absolute sway!
Fill with Thy Spirit
　　Till all shall see
Christ only, always,
　　Living in me!

　　　　　　　　*A. A. Pollard.*

**574** O JESUS, I have promised
　　To serve Thee to the end;
Be Thou for ever near me,
　　My Master and my Friend:
I shall not fear the battle
　　If Thou art by my side,
Nor wander from the pathway
　　If Thou wilt be my Guide.

2 O let me feel Thee near me;
　　The world is ever near;
I see the sights that dazzle,
　　The tempting sounds I hear;
My foes are ever near me,
　　Around me and within;
But, Jesus, draw Thou nearer,
　　And shield my soul from sin.

3 O let me hear Thee speaking
　　In accents clear and still,
Above the storms of passion,
　　The murmurs of self-will;

O speak to reassure me,
　　To hasten or control;
O speak and make me listen,
　　Thou Guardian of my soul.

4 O Jesus, Thou hast promised
　　To all who follow Thee,
That where Thou art in glory
　　There shall Thy servant be;
And, Jesus, I have promised
　　To serve Thee to the end;
O give me grace to follow
　　My Master and my Friend.

　　　　　　　　*John Ernest Bode.*

**575** THOU sweet belovèd will of
　　　　God,　　　　　　[hill,
　　My anchor ground, my fortress
My spirit's silent, fair abode,
　　In Thee I hide me, and am still.

2 O Will, that willest good alone,
　　Lead Thou the way, Thou guidest
A little child, I follow on,　　[best:
　　And trusting, lean upon Thy
　　　　breast.

3 Oh, lightest burden, sweetest yoke!
　　It lifts, it bears my happy soul,
It giveth wings to this poor heart;
　　My freedom is Thy grand con-
　　　　trol.

4 Upon God's will I lay me down,
　　As child upon its mother's breast;
No silken couch, nor softest bed,
　　Could ever give me such deep
　　　　rest.

5 Thy wonderful grand will, my God,
　　With triumph now I make it
　　　　mine;
And faith shall cry a joyous, Yes!
　　To every dear command of
　　　　Thine.

　　　　　*Tersteegen and Jean Sophia Pigott.*

**576** JESUS, I my cross have taken,
　　All to leave and follow Thee,
Destitute, despised, forsaken,
　　Thou from hence, my all shalt
Perish ev'ry fond ambition,　　[be.
　　All I've sought, and hoped and
　　　　known:
Yet how rich is my condition!
　　God and heaven are still my own.

2 Let the world despise and leave me:
　　They have left my Saviour too—
Human hearts and looks deceive
　　me:

Thou art not, like them, untrue.
And whilst Thou shalt smile upon
me,
God of wisdom, love, and might,
Foes may hate, and friends disown
me:
Show Thy face and all is bright.

3 Man may trouble and distress me,
'Twill but drive me to Thy
breast;
Life with trials hard may press me,
Heav'n will bring me sweeter
rest.
Oh, 'tis not in grief to harm me,
While Thy love is left to me;
Oh! 'twere not in joy to charm me,
Were that joy unmixed with
Thee.

*H. F. Lyte.*

**577** I MUST needs go home by the
way of the cross,
There's no other way but this;
I shall ne'er get sight of the Gates
of Light,
If the way of the cross I miss.

The way of the cross leads home,
The way of the cross leads home,
It is sweet to know, as I onward go,
The way of the cross leads home.

2 I must needs go on in the blood-
sprinkled way,
The path that the Saviour trod,
If I ever climb to the heights sub-
lime,                [God.
Where the soul is at home with

3 Then I bid farewell to the way of
the world,
To walk in it nevermore;
For my Lord says "Come," and I
seek my home,
Where He waits at the open
door.

*J. B. Pounds.*

**578** I AM thine, O Lord, I have
heard Thy voice
And it told Thy love to me
But I long to rise in the arms of
faith,
And be closer drawn to Thee.

Draw me near ... er, ... nearer blessèd
Lord,
To the cross where Thou hast died;
Draw me nearer, nearer, nearer, blessèd
Lord,
To Thy precious, bleeding side.

2 Consecrate me now to Thy service,
Lord,
By the power of grace divine;
Let my soul look up with a stead-
fast hope,
And my will be lost in Thine.

3 O the pure delight of a single hour,
That before Thy throne I spend,
When I kneel in prayer, and with
Thee my God,
I commune as friend with friend.

4 There are depths of love that I can-
not know
Till I cross the narrow sea.
There are heights of joy that I may
not reach
Till I rest in peace with Thee.

*Fanny J. Crosby.*

**579** IF thou would'st have the dear
Saviour from heaven
Walk by thy side from the morn
till the even,          [must follow,
There is a rule that each day you
Humble thyself to walk with
God.

Humble thyself and the Lord will draw near
thee,
Humble thyself and His presence shall cheer
thee ;
He will not walk with the proud or the
scornful,
Humble thyself to walk with God.

2 Just as the Lord in the world's early
ages                 [prophets and sages,
Walked and communed with the
He will come now if you meet the
conditions,            [God.
Humble thyself to walk with

3 Just as the stream finds a bed that
is lowly,            [the holy;
So Jesus walks with the pure and
Cast out thy pride, and in heartfelt
contrition,          [God.
Humble thyself to walk with

*J. Oatman.*

**580** THY life was giv'n for me!
Thy blood, O Lord, was shed
That I might ransomed be,
And quickened from the dead.
Thy life was giv'n for me:
What have I giv'n for Thee?

2 Long years were spent for me
    In weariness and woe,
That through eternity
    Thy glory I might know.
Long years were spent for me:
Have I spent one for Thee?

3 Thy Father's home of light,
    Thy rainbow-circled throne,
Were left for earthly night
    For wanderings sad and lone.
Yea, all, was left for me:
Have I left aught for Thee?

4 Thou, Lord, hast borne for me
    More than my tongue can tell
Of bitterest agony,
    To rescue me from hell.
Thou suff'redst all for me:
What have I borne for Thee?

5 And Thou hast brought to me,
    Down from Thy home above,
Salvation full and free,
    Thy pardon and Thy love.
Great gifts Thou broughtest me:
What have I brought to Thee?

6 Oh, let my life be given,
    My years for Thee be spent;
World-fetters all be riven,
    And joy with suff'ring blent:
To Thee my all I bring,
My Saviour and my King!
                              *F. R. Havergal.*

**581** ALL, all to Jesus, I consecrate
        anew:
    He is my portion for ever.
Only His glory henceforth will I
        pursue:
    He is my portion for ever.

Take, take the world, with all its gilded toys,
Take, take the world, I covet not its joys,
Mine is a wealth no moth nor rust destroys :
Jesus my portion for ever.

2 All, all to Jesus, my trusting heart
        can say:
    He is my portion for ever.
Led by His mercy, I'm walking
        ev'ry day:
    He is my portion for ever.

3 Though He may try me, this blessèd
        truth I know:
    He is my portion for ever.
He will not leave me, His promise
        tells me so:
    He is my portion for ever.

4 All, all to Jesus, I cheerfully
        resign:
    He is my portion for ever.
I have the witness that He, my
        Lord, is mine:
    He is my portion for ever.
                              *J. Wakefield MacGill.*

**582** TAKE my life, and let it be
        Consecrated, Lord, to Thee;
Take my moments and my days,
Let them flow in ceaseless praise.

2 Take my hands, and let them move
At the impulse of Thy love;
Take my feet, and let them be
Swift and beautiful for Thee.

3 Take my voice and let me sing
Always, only, for my King;
Take my lips and let them be
Filled with messages from Thee.

4 Take my silver and my gold;
Not a mite would I withhold;
Take my intellect, and use
Every power as Thou shalt choose.

5 Take my will and make it Thine,
It shall be no longer mine:
Take my heart, it is Thine own;
It shall be Thy royal throne.

6 Take my love; my Lord, I pour
At Thy feet its treasure-store;
Take myself, and I will be
Ever, only, all for Thee.
                              *F. R. Havergal.*

**583** SEARCH me, O God! my ac-
        tions try,
    And let my life appear,
As seen by Thine all-searching
        eye—
    To mine my ways make clear.

2 Search all my sense, and know my
        heart,
    Who only canst make known,
And let the deep, the hidden part
    To me be fully shown.

3 Throw light into the darkened cells,
    Where passion reigns within;
Quicken my conscience till it feels
    The loathsomeness of sin.

4 Search all my thoughts, the secret
        springs,
    The motives that control;
The chambers where polluted things
    Hold empire o'er the soul.

5 Search, till Thy fiery glance has
cast
Its holy light through all,
And I by grace am brought at last
Before Thy face to fall.

6 Thus prostrate I shall learn of
Thee,
What now I feebly prove,
That God alone in Christ can be
Unutterable love.　　*F. Bottome.*

**584** My stubborn will at last hath
yielded;
I would be Thine and Thine
alone;
And this the prayer my lips are
bringing,　　　　　　　[done.
Lord, let in me Thy will be

Sweet will of God, still fold me closer,
Till I am wholly lost in Thee;
Sweet will of God, still fold me closer,
Till I am wholly lost in Thee.

2 I'm tired of sin, footsore and weary,
The darksome path hath dreary
grown,　　　　　　　　　[me!
But now a light has ris'n to cheer
I find in Thee my Star, my Sun.

3 Thy precious will, O conqu'ring
Saviour　　　　　　　　[me;
Doth now embrace and compass
All discords hushed, my peace a
river,
My soul, a prisoned bird set free.

4 Shut in with Thee, O Lord, for
ever,　　　　　　　　　[roam;
My wayward feet no more to
What power from Thee my soul
can sever?　　　　　　　[home.
The centre of God's will my
　　　　　　　*Mrs. C. H. Morris.*

**585** DRAWN to the Cross which
Thou hast blest,
With healing gifts for souls distrest,
To find in Thee my Life, my Rest,
Christ crucified, I come.

2 Wash me, and take away each
stain,
Let nothing of my sin remain;
For cleansing, though it be through
pain,
Christ crucified, I come.

3 And then for work to do for Thee,
Which shall so sweet a service be,
That angels well might envy me,
Christ crucified, I come.

4 A life of labour, prayers, and love,
Which shall my heart's conversion
prove,
Till to a glorious rest above,
Christ crucified, I come.

5 To share with Thee Thy Life
Divine,　　　　　　　　[mine,
Thy Righteousness, Thy Likeness
Since Thou hast made my nature
Thine
Christ crucified, I come.

6 To be what Thou wouldst have me
Accepted, sanctified in Thee, [be,
Through what Thy grace shall
work in me,
Christ crucified, I come.
　　　　　　　　*G. M. Irons.*

**586** O THOU exalted Son of God,
High seated on Thy Father's
throne!
The gifts, the purchase of Thy
blood,　　　　　　　　[known,
To us Thy waiting saints make

2 Come, Holy Ghost, all-sacred Fire!
Come, fill Thy earthly temples
now;
Emptied of ev'ry base desire,
Reign Thou within, and only
Thou.

3 Thy sovereign right, Thy gracious
claim,　　　　　　　　[power;
To every thought and every
Our lives—to glorify Thy name,
We yield Thee in this sacred
hour.

4 Fill every chamber of the soul;
Fill all our thoughts, our passions
fill;
Till under Thy supreme control
Submissive rests our cheerful
will.

5 The altar sanctifies the gift;
The blood ensures the boon
divine;　　　　　　　　[I lift,
My outstretched hands to heaven
And claim the Father's promise
mine.

6 Now rise, exulting rise, my soul,
Triumphant sing the Saviour's
praise;　　　　　　　　[extol
His name through earth and skies
With all thy power through all
thy days.　　　　　*F. Bottome.*

**587** MAKE me a captive, Lord,
  And then I shall be free;
Force me to render up my sword,
  And I shall conqu'ror be.
I sink in life's alarms
  When by myself I stand;
Imprison me within Thine arms,
  And strong shall be my hand.

2 My heart is weak and poor
    Until it master find;
  It has no spring of action sure—
    It varies with the wind.
  It cannot freely move,
    Till Thou hast wrought its chain;
  Enslave it with Thy matchless love,
    And deathless it shall reign.

3 My power is faint and low
    Till I have learned to serve;
  It wants the needed fire to glow,
    It wants the breeze to nerve;
  It cannot drive the world;
    Until itself be driven;
  Its flag can only be unfurled
    When Thou shalt breathe from
      heaven.

4 My will is not my own
    Till Thou hast made it Thine;
  If it would reach a monarch's
    It must its crown resign; [throne
  It only stands unbent,
    Amid the clashing strife,
  When on Thy bosom it has leant
    And found in Thee its life.
                *George Matheson.*

**588** COME, thou burning Spirit,
    come,                     [Thee,
  Lo! we stretch our hands to
From the Father to the Son,
  Let us now Thy glory see.

    Come, O come, great Spirit, come,
    Let the mighty deed be done,
    Satisfy our soul's desire,
    See us waiting for the fire.
      Waiting, waiting,
    See us waiting for the fire.

2 On the altar now we lay
    Soul and body, mind and will;
  All the evil passions slay,
    Come and ev'ry corner fill.

3 Now the sacrifice we make,
    Though as dear as a right eye,
  For our blessèd Saviour's sake
    Who for us did bleed and die.

4 Now, by faith, the gift I claim,
    Bought for me by blood Divine:
  Through the all-prevailing Name,
    All the promises are mine.
                        *C. Fry.*

**589** "CALLED unto holiness,"
      Church of our God,
  Purchase of Jesus, redeemed by His
    blood;
  Called from the world and its idols
    to flee,                    [be free.
  Called from the bondage of sin to

    "Holiness unto the Lord," is our watchword
      and song,
    "Holiness unto the Lord," as we're march-
      ing along :
    Sing . . . it, shout it, loud . . . and long,
    "Holiness unto the Lord," now and for ever.

2 "Called unto holiness," children
      of light,                 [of white;
  Walking with Jesus in garments
  Raiment unsullied, nor tarnished
      with sin,
  God's Holy Spirit abiding within.

3 "Called unto holiness," praise His
      dear name,              [made plain.
  This blessèd secret to faith now
  Not our own righteousness, but
      Christ within,              [sin.
  Living and reigning, and saving from

4 "Called unto holiness," glorious
      thought!                  [brought
  Up from the wilderness wanderings
  Out from the shadows and darkness
      of night
  Into the Canaan of perfect delight.

5 "Called unto holiness," Bride of
      the Lamb,                 [again;
  Waiting the Bridegroom's returning
  Lift up your heads, for the day
      draweth near               [appear,
  When in His beauty the King shall
                    *Mrs. C. H. Morris.*

**590** I THIRST, Thou wounded Lamb
      of God,
  To wash me in Thy cleansing
      blood,                 [then pain
  To dwell within Thy wounds;
  Is sweet, and life or death is gain.

2 Take my poor heart, and let it be
  For ever closed to all but Thee!
  Seal Thou my breast, and let me
      wear
  That pledge of love for ever there.

3 How can it be, Thou heav'nly King,
  That Thou shouldst us to glory
      bring?       [throne,
  Make slaves the partners of Thy
  Decked with a never-fading crown?

4 Hence our hearts melt, our eyes
    o'erflow,       [know,
  Our words are lost: nor will we
  Nor will we think of aught beside,
  " My Lord, my love is crucified!"
                *tr. J. Wesley.*

**591**  COME, Jesus, Lord, with holy
       fire!       [spire.
  Come, and my quickened heart in-
  Cleansed in Thy precious blood.
  Now to my soul Thyself reveal,
  Thy mighty working let me feel,
  Since I am born of God.

2 Let nothing now my heart divide;
  Since with Thee I am crucified,
    And live to God in Thee.
  Dead to the world and all its toys,
  Its idle pomp, and fading joys,
    Jesus, my glory be!

3 Me with a quenchless thirst inspire,
  A longing, infinite desire,
    And fill my craving heart.
  Less than Thyself, oh, do not give;
  In might Thyself within me live,
  Come, all Thou hast and art!

4 My will be swallowed up in Thee,
  Light in Thy light still may I see,
    In Thine unclouded face;
  Called the full strength of trust to
    prove,
  Let all my quickened heart be love,
  My spotless life be praise.
              *Charles Wesley.*

**592**  JESUS, see me at Thy feet,
    With my sacrifice complete;
  I am bringing all to Thee,
    Thine alone I'll be.
  Have Thy way, Lord, have Thy way,
  This with all my heart I say ;
  I'll obey Thee, come what may ;
    Dear Lord, have Thy way.

2 O how patient Thou hast been,
  With my pride and inbred sin!
  O what mercy Thou hast shown,
    Grace and love unknown!

3 Lord, I loathe myself and sin,
  Enter now and make me clean;
  Make my heart just like Thine own;
    Come, Lord, take Thy throne.

4 Lord, Thy love has won my all,
  Let Thy Spirit on me fall;
  Burn up every trace of sin;
    Make me pure within.

5 Praise the Lord, the work is done!
  Praise the Lord, the vict'ry's won!
  Now the blood is cleansing me,
    From all sin I'm free.
              *George Bennard.*

**593**  O LAMB of God! Thou won-
    derful sin-bearer;
  Hard after Thee my soul doth
    follow on:     [desert dreary,
  As pants the hart for streams in
    So pants my soul for Thee, O
    Thou life-giving One.
  At Thy feet I fall, yield Thee up my all,
  To suffer, live, or die for my Lord crucified.

2 I mourn, I mourn, the sin that
    drove Thee from me,
    And blackest darkness brought
    into my soul;
  Now, I renounce th'accursèd thing
    that hindered,
    And come once more to Thee, to
    be made fully whole.

3 Descend the heavens, Thou whom
    my soul adoreth!
    Exchange Thy Throne for my
    poor longing heart.
  For Thee, for Thee, I watch as for
    the morning;   [Saviour apart.
  No rest or peace is mine from my

4 Come, Holy Ghost, Thy mighty aid
    bestowing,
    Destroy the works of sin, the
    self, the pride;
  Burn, burn in me, my idols over-
    throwing,
    Prepare my heart for Him—for
    my Lord crucified.
              *C. Booth-Clibborn.*

**594**  I WANT, dear Lord, a heart
    that's true and clean;
  A sunlit heart with not a cloud be-
    tween.
    A heart like Thine, a heart
    divine,
      A heart as white as snow;
  On me, dear Lord, a heart like this
    bestow.

2 I want, dear Lord, a love that feels
    for all;     [every call.
A deep strong love that answers
  A love like Thine, a love divine,
    A love for high and low;
On me, dear Lord, a love like this
  bestow.

3 I want, dear Lord, a soul on fire
    for Thee;     [energy.
A soul baptized with heav'nly
  A willing mind, a ready hand
    To do whate'er I know
To spread Thy light wherever I may
  go.       *George Jackson.*

**595** "NOT my own!" but saved by
    Jesus,
  Who redeemed me by His blood:
Gladly I accept the message,
  I belong to Christ the Lord.

   " Not my own !" . . . oh, " not my
    own !" . . .
   Jesus I . . . belong to Thee ! . . .
  All I have, and all I hope for,
   Thine for all eternity.

2 "Not my own!" to Christ, my
    Saviour,
  I, believing, trust my soul;
Ev'rything to Him committed,
  While eternal ages roll.

3 "Not my own!" my time, my
    talent,
  Freely all to Christ I bring,
To be used in joyful service
  For the glory of the King.

4 "Not my own!" The Lord accepts
    me,
  One among the ransomed throng,
Who in heav'n shall see His glory,
  And to Jesus Christ belong.
         *D. W. Whittle.*

**596** THERE'S a Saviour from all sin;
    If you only let Him in
To your heart, He there will reign,
  While you trust Him.
He will put the evil out,
Save from ev'ry fear and doubt,
And you'll soon begin to shout,
  Hallelujah!

  Hallelujah ! Hallelujah !
  Jesus is my Saviour-King,
  He does full salvation bring,
  Hallelujah ! Hallelujah !
  Now with heart and voice I sing
   Hallelujah !

2 Jesus is a wondrous name,
  Now and evermore the same,
He can cleanse from every stain,
  Only trust Him.
He will fill your soul with joy
And your talents will employ,
Satan's kingdom to destroy;
  Hallelujah!

3 If from every sin you part,
And let Christ have all your heart,
You need fear no fiery dart,
  While you trust Him.
For while Jesus reigns within,
You are proof against all sin,
And his perfect peace you'll win,
  Hallelujah!
         *J. G. Govan.*

**597** IN full and glad surrender
    I give myself to Thee;
Thine utterly, and only,
  And evermore to be.

2 O Son of God, who lov'st me,
  I will be Thine alone;
And all I have, and all I am,
  Shall henceforth be Thine own.

3 Reign over me, Lord Jesus;
  O make my heart Thy throne:
It shall be Thine, my Saviour,
  It shall be Thine alone.

4 O come and reign, Lord Jesus,
  Rule over everything;
And keep me always loyal
  And true to Thee, my King.
         *F. R. Havergal.*

**598** WASH me, O Lamb of God,
    Wash me from sin!
By Thine atoning blood,
  Oh, make me clean!
Purge me from ev'ry stain,
Let me Thine image gain,
In love and mercy reign
  O'er all within.

2 Wash me, O Lamb of God,
    Wash me from sin!
I long to be like Thee—
  All pure within.
Now let the crimson tide,
Shed from Thy wounded side,
Be to my heart applied,
  And make me clean.

3 Wash me, O Lamb of God,
　　Wash me from sin!
　I will not, cannot, rest
　　Till pure within.
　All human skill is vain,
　But Thou canst cleanse each stain
　Till not a spot remain—
　　Made wholly clean.

4 Wash me, O Lamb of God,
　　Wash me from sin!
　By faith Thy cleansing blood
　　Now makes me clean.
　So near art Thou to me,
　So sweet my rest in Thee—
　Oh, blessèd purity,
　　Saved, saved from sin!

5 Wash me, O Lamb of God,
　　Wash me from sin!
　Thou, while I trust in Thee,
　　Wilt keep me clean.
　Each day to Thee I bring
　Heart, life—yea, everything;
　Saved, while to Thee I cling,
　　Saved from all sin!

*H. B. Beagle.*

**599** COME, Saviour, Jesus, from
　　above! [grace;
　Assist me with Thy heavenly
　Empty my heart of earthly love,
　　And for Thyself prepare the
　　place.

2 O let Thy sacred presence fill,
　　And set my longing spirit free!
　Which pants to have no other will,
　　But day and night to feast on
　　Thee.

3 While in this region here below,
　　No other good will I pursue;
　I'll bid this world of noise and
　　show, [adieu!
　With all its glittering snares,

4 That path with humble speed I'll
　　seek, [shine;
　In which my Saviour's footsteps
　Nor will I hear, nor will I speak,
　Of any other love but Thine.

5 Henceforth may no profane delight
　　Divide this consecrated soul;
　Possess it Thou, who hast the right,
　　As Lord and Master of the whole.

6 Wealth, honour, pleasure, and what
　　else

This short-enduring world can
　　give,
　Tempt as ye will, my soul repels,
　　To Christ alone resolved to live.

7 Thee I can love, and Thee alone,
　　With pure delight and inward
　　bliss: [own,
　To know Thou tak'st me for Thine
　O what a happiness is this!

8 Nothing on earth do I desire
　　But Thy pure love within my
　　breast:
　This, only this, will I require,
　　And freely give up all the rest.

*tr. J. Wesley.*

**600** ALL to Jesus I surrender,
　　　All to Him I freely give;
　I will ever love and trust Him,
　　In His presence daily live.

　　I surrender all, . . .
　　I surrender all ; . . .
　All to Thee, my blessed Saviour,
　　I surrender all.

2 All to Jesus I surrender,
　　Humbly at His feet I bow;
　Worldly pleasures all forsaken,
　　Take me, Jesus, take me now.

3 All to Jesus I surrender,
　　Lord, I give myself to Thee;
　Fill me with Thy love and power,
　　Let Thy blessing fall on me.

4 All to Jesus I surrender,
　　Now I feel the sacred flame;
　O the joy of full salvation!
　　Glory, glory to His Name!

*J. Van de Venter.*

**601** COME, Thou Fount of ev'ry
　　blessing,
　Tune my heart to sing Thy grace;
　Streams of mercy never ceasing
　　Call for songs of loudest praise.
　Teach me some melodious measure
　　Sung by flaming tongues above;
　O the vast, the boundless treasure
　　Of my Lord's unchanging love!

2 Here I raise my Ebenezer;
　　Hither by Thy help I'm come;
　And I hope, by Thy good pleasure,
　　Safely to arrive at home.
　Jesus sought me when a stranger,
　　Wand'ring from the fold of God;
　He, to rescue me from danger,
　　Interposed His precious blood.

**3** O to grace how great a debtor
    Daily I'm constrained to be!
Let that grace, Lord, like a fetter,
    Bind my wand'ring heart to
        Thee:
Prone to wander, Lord, I feel it,
    Prone to leave the God I love;
Take my heart, O take and seal it,
    Seal it from Thy courts above!

*R. Robinson.*

**602** CALLED to separation
        With the Crucified,
Temples of the Spirit,
    Saved and sanctified,
Set apart for service,
    By God's hand ordained,
We the cross have taken,
    By His love constrained.

Step by step with Jesus,
    All along life's way,
Now the cross and conflict,
    Then the perfect day.

**2** Christ the veil has entered,
    With the blood He shed,
Sin's great debt is cancelled,
    Love's own feast is spread;
Now in Christ we're chosen
    Kings and priests to be,
Living off'rings bringing.
    His own blood our plea.

**3** Like a boundless ocean
        Ever rolling in,
Comes this flood of blessing,
    Seeking lives to win;
Who such love can fathom,
    From God's heart which flows,
Or such grace e'er measure,
    Which His hand bestows?

**4** Pressing onward, upward,
    Life grows pure and strong,
'Tis the vision splendid
    Saves from all that's wrong;
In the steps of Jesus,
    We would plant our own,
Blessèd path of triumph,
    Leading to the throne.

*E. C. W. Boulton.*

**603** THY way, not mine, O Lord,
        However dark it be: [hand,
Oh, lead me by Thine own right
    Choose Thou the path for me.

**2** Smooth let it be or rough,
    It will be still the best;

Winding or straight, it can but lead
    Right onward to Thy rest.

**3** I dare not choose my lot;
    I would not if I might;
But choose Thou for me, O my
    So shall I walk aright. [God,

**4** Take Thou my cup, and it
    With joy or sorrow fill,
As ever best to Thee may seem;
    Choose Thou my good or ill.

**5** Not mine, not mine the choice
    In things or great or small;
Be Thou to me my Guide, my
        Strength,
    My Wisdom and my All.

*H. Bonar.*

**604** JESUS, Thine all victorious
        love
Shed in my heart abroad;
Then shall my feet no longer rove,
    Rooted and fixed in God.

**2** Oh, that in me the sacred fire
    Might now begin to glow,
Burn up the dross of base desire,
    And make the mountains flow.

**3** Refining fire, go through my heart,
    Illuminate my soul;
Scatter Thy life through every part,
    And sanctify the whole.

**4** My steadfast soul from falling free,
    Shall then no longer move;
While Christ is all the world to me,
    And all my heart is love.

*Charles Wesley.*

**605** WHEN shall Thy love con-
        strain,
    And force me to Thy breast?
When shall my soul return again
    To her eternal rest?

**2** Thy condescending grace
    To me did freely move;
It calls me still to seek Thy face,
    And stoops to ask my love.

**3** Lord, at Thy feet I fall!
    I long to be set free;
I fain would now obey the call,
    And give up all for Thee.

**4** To rescue me from woe,
    Thou didst with all things part!
Didst lead a suff'ring life below,
    To gain my worthless heart.

5   My worthless heart to gain,
The God of all that breathe
Was found in fashion as a man,
   And died a cursèd death.

6   And can I yet delay
   My little all to give?
To tear my soul from earth away,
   For Jesus to receive?

7   Nay, but I yield, I yield!
   I can hold out no more,
I sink, by dying love compelled,
   And own Thee conqueror.
*Charles Wesley.*

**606**  LORD, I believe a rest remains
     To all Thy people known;
A rest where pure enjoyment reigns,
   And Thou art loved alone.

2  A rest, where all our soul's desire
   Is fixed on things above;
Where fear and sin and grief expire,
   Cast out by perfect love.

3  Oh, that I now the rest might
   Believe, and enter in!   [know,
Now, Saviour, now the power bestow,
   And let me cease from sin.

4  Remove this hardness from my
   This unbelief remove:   [heart,
To me the rest of faith impart,
   The Sabbath of Thy love.

5  I would be Thine, Thou know'st I
   would,
   And have Thee all my own;
Thee, O my all-sufficient Good,
   I want, and Thee alone.
*Charles Wesley.*

**607**  OH, for a heart to praise my
     God,
   A heart from sin set free,
A heart that always feels the blood
   So freely shed for me.

2  A heart resigned, submissive, meek,
   My great Redeemer's throne,
Where only Christ is heard to
   speak,
   Where Jesus reigns alone.

3  A humble, holy, contrite heart,
   Believing, true, and clean,
Which neither life nor death can
   part
From Him that dwells within.

4  A heart in every thought renewed,
   And full of love divine,
Perfect, and right, and pure, and
   good,
   A copy, Lord, of Thine!

5  Thy nature, gracious Lord, impart;
   Come quickly from above,
Write Thy new name upon my
   heart,
   Thy new, best name of Love.
*Charles Wesley.*

**608**  ALL for Jesus! all for Jesus!
     All my being's ransomed
     pow'rs;     [doings,
All my thoughts and words and
All my days and all my hours.

2  Let my hands perform His bidding;
   Let my feet run in His ways;
Let mine eyes see Jesus only;
   Let my lips speak forth His
   praise.

3  Worldlings prize their gems of
   beauty;
   Cling to gilded toys of dust;
Boast of wealth, and fame, and
   pleasure;
   Only Jesus will I trust.

4  Since mine eyes were fixed on
   Jesus,
   I've lost sight of all beside;
So enchained my spirit's vision,
   Looking at the Crucified.

5  Oh, what wonder! how amazing!
   Jesus, glorious King of kings,
Deigns to call me His belovèd,
   Lets me rest beneath His wings.
*Mary D. James.*

**609**  BLEST are the pure in heart,
     For they shall see our God:
The secret of the Lord is theirs,
   Their soul is Christ's abode.

2    The Lord, who left the heavens
    Our life and peace to bring,
To dwell in lowliness with men,
   Their pattern and their King:

3    He to the lowly soul
    Doth still Himself impart,
And for His dwelling and His
   throne
   Chooseth the pure in heart.

**4** Lord, we Thy presence seek;
  May ours this blessing be;
Give us a pure and lowly heart,
  A temple meet for Thee.

*J. Keble.*

**610** I want my life to be all filled
    with praise to Thee, [for me,
My precious Lord divine Who died
Let all my will be Thine, con-
    trolled by love divine,
Live out in me Thy life, O mighty
    Saviour.

Thy blessed will divine, with joy I make it
    mine,
My heart shall be Thy throne, and Thine
    alone.
Choose Thou the path I tread and whither
    I am led,
Help me to follow on, O mighty Saviour.

**2** A pilgrim born anew, a stranger go-
    ing through, [am Thine.
Not of this world am I, since I

Weaned from its passing show,
    transformed Thy love to know,
Hold Thou my hand in Thine, O
    mighty Saviour.

**3** When evil foes assail and almost
    would prevail,
In that dark hour be Thou my
    strength and shield.
Lend then Thy strong embrace, up-
    hold me by Thy grace,
In weakness be my strength, O
    mighty Saviour.

**4** Yea, choose the path for me, al-
    though I may not see
The reason Thou dost will to lead
    me so.
I know the toilsome way will lead
    to realms of day
Where I shall dwell with Thee, O
    mighty Saviour.

*H. Tee.*

# Section IX

## WITNESS AND TESTIMONY

**611** I will sing of my Redeemer,
    And His wondrous love to
    me;
On the cruel cross He suffered,
  From the curse to set me free.

Sing, oh sing of my Redeemer,
  With His blood He purchased me,
On the cross He sealed my pardon,
  Paid the debt and made me free.

**2** I will tell the wondrous story,
    How my lost estate to save,
In His boundless love and mercy,
  He the ransom freely gave.

**3** I will praise my dear Redeemer,
    His triumphant power I'll tell;
How the victory He giveth,
  Over sin, and death, and hell.

**4** I will sing of my Redeemer,
    And His heavenly love to me;
He from death to life hath brought
    me,
  Son of God, with Him to be.

*Philipp Bliss.*

**612** I will sing the wondrous story
    Of the Christ who died for
    me;
How He left His home in glory,
  For the Cross on Calvary.

Yes, I'll sing the wondrous story
  Of the Christ who died for me ;
Sing it with the saints in glory,
  Gathered by the crystal sea.

**2** I was lost; but Jesus found me—
    Found the sheep that went astray;
Threw His loving arms around me,
  Drew me back into His way.

**3** I was bruised but Jesus healed me—
    Faint was I from many a fall;
Sight was gone and fears possessed
    me
  But He freed me from them all.

**4** He will keep me till the river
    Rolls its waters at my feet;
Then He'll bear me safely over,
  Where the loved ones I shall
    meet.

*F. H. Rawley.*

**613** I've found a Friend; oh, such
a Friend!
He loved me ere I knew Him;
He drew me with the cords of love,
And thus He bound me to Him;
And round my heart still closely
twine [sever;
Those ties which naught can
For I am His, and He is mine,
For ever and for ever.

2 I've found a Friend; oh, such a
Friend!
He bled, He died to save me;
And not alone the gift of life,
But His own self He gave me.
Naught that I have my own I call,
I hold it for the Giver:
My heart, my strength, my life, my
Are His, and His for ever. [all

3 I've found a Friend; oh, such a
Friend!
All power to Him is given,
To guard me on my onward course
And bring me safe to heaven.
Eternal glories gleam afar,
To nerve my faint endeavour;
So now to watch, to work, to war,
And then to rest for ever.

4 I've found a Friend; oh, such a
Friend!
So kind, and true, and tender!
So wise a Counsellor and Guide,
So mighty a Defender!
From Him who loves me now so
well [sever?
What power my soul shall
Shall life, or death, or earth, or
hell?
No! I am His for ever.
*J. G. Small.*

**614** In sorrow I wandered, my
spirit opprest,
But now I am happy, securely I
rest;
From morning till evening glad
carols I sing. [with the King.
And this is the reason—I walk

I walk with the King, hallelujah !
I walk with the King, praise His name !
No longer I roam, my soul faces home,
I walk and I talk with the King.

2 For years in the fetters of sin I
was bound,
The world could not help me—no
comfort I found;
But now like the birds and the sunbeams of Spring, [the King.
I'm free and rejoicing—I walk with

3 O soul near despair in the lowlands
of strife, [your life;
Look up and let Jesus come into
The joy of salvation to you He
would bring— [with the King.
Come into the sunlight and walk
*James Rowe.*

**615** Christ has for sin atonement
made,
What a wonderful Saviour!
We are redeemed! the price is paid!
What a wonderful Saviour!
What a wonderful Saviour is Jesus, my
Jesus !
What a wonderful Saviour is Jesus, my
Lord !

2 He dwells within me day by day,
What a wonderful Saviour!
And keeps me faithful all the way,
What a wonderful Saviour!

3 He gives me overcoming power,
What a wonderful Saviour!
And triumph in each conflict hour,
What a wonderful Saviour!

4 To Him I've given all my heart,
What a wonderful Saviour!
The world shall never share a part,
What a wonderful Saviour!
*E. A. Hoffman.*

**616** Friends all around me are trying to find
What the heart yearns for, by sin
undermined;
I have the secret, I know where
'tis found; [abound!
Only true pleasures in Jesus

All that I need is in Je . . . sus, . . .
He satisfies, . . . joy He supplies ; . . .
Life would be worthless without . . .
Him, . . .
All things in Jesus I find.

2 Some carry burdens whose weight
has for years
Crushed them with sorrow and
blinded with tears,
Yet One stands ready to help them
just now, [bow.
If they will humbly in penitence

3 No other name thrills the joy-
chords within, [of sin;
And through none else is remission
He knows the pain of the heart
sorely tried, [supplied.
All that we need will by Him be

4 Jesus stands ready and waiting to-
day [way:
Sin to forgive and to guide on the
Blindly we strive in the darkness of
night, [be bright.
One glimpse of Jesus and all will
*Harry Dixon Lees.*

**617** IN tenderness He sought me,
Weary and sick with sin,
And on His shoulders brought me
Back to His fold again.
While angels in His presence sang,
Until the courts of heaven rang.

Oh, the love that sought me !
Oh, the blood that bought me !
Oh, the grace that brought me to the fold,
Wondrous grace that brought me to the fold !

2 He washed the bleeding sin wounds,
And poured in oil and wine;
He whispered to assure me
"I've found thee, thou art Mine;"
I never heard a sweeter voice,
It made my aching heart rejoice!

3 He pointed to the nail-prints,
For me His blood was shed,
A mocking crown so thorny,
Was placed upon His head:
I wondered what He saw in me,
To suffer such deep agony.

4 I'm sitting in His presence,
The sunshine of His face,
While with adoring wonder
His blessings I retrace.
It seems as if eternal days
Are far too short to sound His
praise.

5 So while the hours are passing,
All now is perfect rest;
I'm waiting for the morning,
The brightest and the best,
When He will call us to His side,
To be with Him, His spotless bride.
*W. Spencer Walton.*

**618** JESUS has promised my Shep-
herd to be,
That's why I love Him so;
And to the children He said, "Come
to Me,"
That's why I love Him so.

That's why I love Him,
That's why I love Him,
Because He first loved me ; . . .
When I'm tempted and tried,
He is close by my side,
That's why I love Him so.

2 He the weak lambs to His bosom
will take,
That's why I love Him so;
Never will He for a moment for-
That's why I love Him so. [sake,

3 He has in heaven prepared me a
place,
That's why I love Him so:
Where I may dwell, by His won-
derful grace,
That's why I love Him so.
*Scott Lawrence.*

**619** O HAPPY day, that fixed my
choice,
On Thee, my Saviour and my
God! [rejoice,
Well may this glowing heart
And tell its raptures all abroad.

Happy day, happy day,
When Jesus washed my sins away !
He taught me how to watch and pray,
And live rejoicing ev'ry day.
Happy day, happy day,
When Jesus washed my sins away !

2 'Tis done, the great transaction's
done !
I am my Lord's and He is mine:
He drew me and I followed on,
Charmed to confess the voice
divine.

3 Now rest, my long-divided heart,
Fixed on this blissful centre, rest:
Nor ever from thy Lord depart,
With Him of every good
possessed.

4 High heaven, that heard the solemn
vow, [hear,
That vow renewed shall daily
Till in life's latest hour I bow,
And bless in death a bond so
dear.
*P. Doddridge.*

**620** I'VE found a Friend who is
    all to me,
  His love is ever true;
I love to tell how He lifted me,
  And what His grace can do for
    you.
  Saved . . . by His pow'r divine !
  Saved . . . to new life sublime !
  Life now is sweet and my joy is complete,
    For I'm saved, saved, saved !

2 He saves me from ev'ry sin and
    harm,
  Secures my soul each day;
I'm leaning strong on His mighty
    arm;      [way.
I know He'll guide me all the

3 When poor and needy, and all
    alone,
  In love He said to me,
" Come unto Me, I will lead you
    home,
  To live with Me eternally."
                *J. P. Schofield.*

**621** I HEARD the voice of Jesus say,
    " Come unto Me and rest:
Lay down, thou weary one, lay
    down
  Thy head upon My breast."
I came to Jesus as I was—
  Weary, and worn, and sad;
I found in Him a resting-place,
  And He has made me glad.

2 I heard the voice of Jesus say,
    " Behold, I freely give
The living water; thirsty one,
  Stoop down and drink, and live."
I came to Jesus and I drank
  Of that life-giving stream;
My thirst was quenched, my soul
    revived,
  And now I live in Him.

3 I heard the voice of Jesus say,
    " I am this dark world's Light;
Look unto Me, thy morn shall rise,
  And all thy day be bright."
I looked to Jesus and I found
  In Him my Star, my Sun;
And in that light of life I'll walk,
  Till travelling days are done.
                  *H. Bonar.*

**622** THERE'S no one like my Sav-
    iour;
  No friend can be like Him;
My never-failing sunshine

When earthly lights grow dim;
When summer flow'rs are bloom-
  The brightness of my joy, [ing,
O, may His happy service
  My heart and life employ.
  No one, no one like my precious Saviour,
    No one, no one such a friend can be ;
  No one, no one like my precious Saviour,
    Glory, glory, Jesus cares for me.

2 There's no one like my Saviour;
    In seasons of distress.
He draws me closer to Him,
  To comfort and to bless;
He gives me in temptation,
  The strength of His right arm;
His angels camp around me,
  To keep me from all harm.

3 There's no one like my Saviour,
  He pardons all my sin,
And gives His Holy Spirit,
  A springing well within;
He leads me out to service,
  With gentle touch and mild;
O, wonder of all wonders,
  That I should be His child.

4 There's no one like my Saviour,
  Come now, and find it true!
He gave His life a ransom,
  His blood was shed for you;
Then when we reach the City
  Of everlasting light,
We'll sing with saints and angels,
  All honour, power and might.
                  *E. E. Hewitt.*

**623** IT was down at the feet of
    Jesus,
  O the happy, happy day!
That my soul found peace in be-
    lieving,
  And my sins were washed away.
  Let me tell the old, old story
    Of His grace so full and free,
  For I feel like giving Him the glory
    For His wondrous love to me.

2 It was down at the feet of Jesus,
  Where I found such perfect rest,
Where the light first dawned on my
    spirit,
  And my soul was truly blest.

3 It was down at the feet of Jesus,
  Where I brought my guilt and
    sin,       [gressions,
That He cancelled all my trans-
  And salvation entered in.
              *Elisha A. Hoffman*

**624** WHEN in His beauty my Saviour I see,
When I shall look on His face,
Tongue cannot tell of the joy it will be,
Saved by His wonderful grace.

Saved, . . . saved, . . .
Saved by His wonderful grace ! . . .
Saved, . . . saved, . . .
Granted in heaven a place ; . . .
Saved, . . . saved, . . .
Saved by His wonderful grace ! . . .
Glory to Jesus, I know I am saved,
Saved by His wonderful grace ! . . .

2 Long I had wandered in pathways of sin,
Often His grace had I spurned;
Often resisted His striving within,
Ere to the Saviour I turned.

3 How I rejoice that salvation is free,
That I was not turned away!
How I rejoice that my Saviour I'll see,
Where I may praise Him for aye.
*G. O. Webster.*

**625** I HAD heard the gospel call,
Off'ring pardon free for all,
And I hearkened to the blessèd invitation;
Laid my sins at Jesus' feet,
Tasted there redemption sweet,
And He saved me with an uttermost salvation.

Jesus saves . . . fully saves . . .
Jesus saves me with an uttermost salvation ;
Though I cannot tell you how,
Jesus fully saves me now,
With a full and free, an uttermost salvation.

2 Now the load of sin is gone,
And by faith I travel on,
And I rest no longer under condemnation;
For the blood has been applied,
And my soul is satisfied
With this full and free, this uttermost salvation.

3 From the mire and from the clay,
Jesus took my feet away, [clay,
And He placed them on the Rock, the sure Foundation;
Whether now I live or die,
This shall be my constant cry,
Jesus saves me with an uttermost salvation.
*Mrs. C. H. Morris.*

**626** I WAS sinking deep in sin,
Sinking to rise no more,
Overwhelmed by guilt within,
Mercy I did implore.
Then the Master of the sea
Heard my despairing cry,
Christ my Saviour lifted me,
Now safe am I.

Love lifted me ! . . . Love lifted me ! . . .
When no one but Christ could help,
Love lifted me.

2 Souls in danger, look above,
Jesus completely saves;
He will lift you by His love
Out of the angry waves.
He's the Master of the sea,
Billows His will obey;
He your Saviour wants to be,
Be saved to-day!

3 When the waves of sorrow roll,
When I am in distress,
Jesus takes my hand in His,
Ever He loves to bless.
He will every fear dispel,
Satisfy every need;
All who heed His loving call,
Find rest indeed.
*James Rowe (arranged).*

**627** I'VE a Saviour, kind and tender,
I've a Saviour full of grace,
And a smile of winning sweetness
Ever beams upon His face:
In my heart's shrine of affection
He shall hold the highest place.

How I love Him ! . . . how I love Him ! . . .
Since for me . . . He bled and died . . .
How I love . . . Him, yes, I love Him . . .
More than all . . . the world beside.

2 For my sake He came from heaven
To this world of sin and shame;
Bore my guilt, though He was guiltless, [blame:
And though blameless, took my
Can I ever cease to love Him,
And His goodness to proclaim?

3 Though I've often been unworthy,
He has constant been, and true;
Though I wronged Him, He forgave me
When I would my vows renew;
Though I spurned Him, He with kindness
My rebellious heart did woo.

4 I've a Saviour, kind and tender,
   He would be your Saviour too;
Will you not accept the pardon
   Which He freely offers you?
Take Him now as your Redeemer,
   Earth has not a friend so true.
*Chas. M. Fillmore.*

**628**   I HAVE tried to count His bless-
     ings, and I fail to understand
Why the Lord should so richly
   reward;
Could I count the stars of heaven,
   add to them earth's grains of
   sand,
   Still His blessings are more,
   praise the Lord!

And the end is not yet, praise the Lord, . . .
And the end is not yet, praise the Lord; . . .
Blessings new He's still bestowing,
   And my cup is overflowing,
And the end is not yet, praise the Lord ! . . .

2 Like an army I behold them pass
   before me in review,
Oh, what joy doth the sight now
   afford!
Though they may be long in passing, still they come, battalions
   new,
   And the end is not yet, praise
   the Lord!

3 Surely goodness, love and mercy,
   have been mine along life's
   way,
And my weak heart to strength is
   restored;
And my cup of joy and gladness
   keeps o'erflowing, day by day,
   And the end is not yet, praise the
   Lord!      *E. D. Elliott.*

**629**   THERE'S a sweet and blessèd
     story      [glory,
Of the Christ who came from
Just to rescue me from sin and
   misery;
   He in loving-kindness sought me,
   And from sin and shame hath
     brought me,
Hallelujah! Jesus ransomed me.

Hallelujah ! what a Saviour !
   Who can take a poor lost sinner,
Lift him from the miry clay and set him free;
   I will ever tell the story,
     Shouting glory, glory, glory,
Hallelujah ! Jesus ransomed me.

2 From the depth of sin and sad-
   ness      [ness
To the heights of joy and glad-
Jesus lifted me, in mercy full and
   free;      [bought me,
   With His precious blood He
   When I knew Him not, He
     sought me,      [me.
And in love divine He ransomed

3 From the throne of heav'nly
   glory—
   Oh, the sweet and blessèd story!
Jesus came to lift the lost in sin
   and woe
Into liberty all-glorious,
   Trophies of His grace victorious,
Evermore rejoicing here below.

4 By and by with joy increasing,
   And with gratitude unceasing,
Lifted up with Christ for evermore
   to be;
   I will join the host there singing,
   In the anthem ever ringing,
To the King of love who ransomed
   me.
*Julia H. Johnston.*

**630**   OF Jesu's love I'm singing, I
     praise Him ev'ry day:
   He is my all in all, all in all;
He frees my soul from bondage, He
   takes my guilt away,
   Jesus is my all in all.

All . . . in all, . . . all . . . in all, . . .
A strength in time of weariness, a light where
   shadows fall ;
   All . . . in all, . . . all . . . in all, . . .
Jesus is my all in all. . . .

2 He's patient and so tender, so lov-
   ing and so kind,
   He is my all in all, all in all,
Another friend so faithful my soul
   will never find,
   Jesus is my all in all.

3 In time of need no other to me can
   prove so dear,
   He is my all in all, all in all,
He hears me though I whisper, to
   help me He is near.
   Jesus is my all in all.
*Edgar Lewis.*

**631** I SERVE a risen Saviour, He's
in the world today;
I know that He is living, whatever
men may say;
I see His hand of mercy, I hear
His voice of cheer,
And just the time I need Him He's
always near.

He lives, . . . He lives, . . . . Christ Jesus lives
today !
He walks with me and talks with me along
life's narrow way.
He lives, . . . He lives, . . . salvation to
impart !
You ask me how I know He lives ? He lives
within my heart.

2 In all the world around me I see
His loving care,
And though my heart grows weary
I never will despair;
I know that He is leading, through
all the stormy blast,
The day of His appearing will come
at last.

3 Rejoice, rejoice, O Christian, lift
up your voice and sing
Eternal hallelujahs to Jesus Christ
the King!
The Hope of all who seek Him, the
Help of all who find,
None other is so loving, so good
and kind.          *A. H. Ackley.*

**632** JESUS is my loving Saviour,
He is so precious to me;
O, how I love and adore Him for
all His mercies so free;
When I was lost on the mountains
barren and dark and cold
He sought the sheep that was straying, He brought me back to
the fold.

Jesus, Jesus, dearer than all to me,
Jesus, Jesus, Thine, only Thine I'll be ;
Where Thou dost lead I will follow, where'er
the path may be ;
Then when life's journey is ended, Thy face
in glory I'll see.

2 Jesus, the sweet rose of Sharon,
Jesus the lily so fair;
Jesus my rock and salvation, Jesus
the bright morning star;
He is my portion forever, my all
in all is He;
With Him I cannot be lonely, He
fully satisfies me.

3 Jesus was born in a manger, wept
in the garden alone;
Poured out His life's blood on
Calv'ry, died for our sin to
atone;
Rose from the grave more than
conqueror, went to His home
on high;
Soon He is coming in glory, coming in clouds of the sky.
          *Geo. Bennard.*

**633** HE is not a disappointment!
Jesus is far more to me
Than in all my glowing day-dreams
I had fancied He could be;
And the more I get to know Him,
So the more I find Him true,
And the more I long that others
Should be led to know Him too.

2 He is not a disappointment!
He has saved my soul from sin:
All the guilt and all the anguish,
Which oppressed my heart with-
in,
He has banished by His presence,
And His blessèd kiss of peace
Has assured my heart for ever
That His love will never cease.

3 He is not a disappointment!
He has healed my body too:
What a tender, mighty Saviour,
There is naught He cannot do!
When on earth He healed diseases
As they touched Him in the
throng;
Has He lost His heart of pity?
Is the risen Christ less strong?

4 He is not a disappointment!
He is coming by and by,
In my heart I have the witness
That His coming draweth nigh.
All the scoffers may despise me,
And no change around may see,
But He tells me He is coming,
And that's quite enough for me.

5 He is not a disappointment!
He is all in all to me—
Saviour, Sanctifier, Healer;
The unchanging Christ is He!
He has won my heart's affections,
And He meets my every need;
He is not a disappointment,
For He satisfies indeed.
          *Mary Warburton Booth.*

**634** My song shall be of Jesus;
　　His mercy crowns my days,
He fills my cup with blessings,
　And tunes my heart to praise;
My song shall be of Jesus,
　The precious Lamb of God,
Who gave Himself my ransom,
　And bought me with His blood.

2 My song shall be of Jesus;
　　When sitting at His feet,
I call to mind His goodness,
　In meditation sweet:
My song shall be of Jesus,
　Whatever ill betide;
I'll sing the grace that saves me,
　And keeps me at His side.

3 My song shall be of Jesus;
　　While pressing on my way,
To reach the blissful region
　Of pure and perfect day;
And when my soul shall enter
　The gate of Eden fair,
A song of praise to Jesus
　I'll sing for ever there.
*Fanny J Crosby.*

**635** You ask what makes me
　　happy, my heart so free
　　from care,
It is because my Saviour in mercy
　heard my prayer;
He brought me out of darkness and
　now the light I see;
Oh, blessèd, loving Saviour! to
　Him the praise shall be.
　I will shout His praise in glory, . . .
　And we'll all sing hallelujah in heaven by
　　and by,
　I will shout His praise in glory, . . .
　And we'll all sing hallelujah in heaven by
　　and by.

2 I was a friendless wanderer till
　Jesus took me in,
My life was full of sorrow, my
　heart was full of sin,
But when the blood so precious
　spoke pardon to my soul,
Oh, blissful, blissful moment! 'twas
　joy beyond control.

3 I wish that every sinner before His
　throne would bow;
He waits to bid them welcome, He
　longs to bless them now;
If they but knew the rapture that
　in His love I see,

They'd come and shout salvation,
　and sing His praise with me.

4 I mean to live for Jesus while here
　on earth I stay;
And when His voice shall call me
　to realms of endless day,
As one by one we gather, rejoicing
　on the shore,
We'll shout His praise in glory,
　and sing for evermore.
*P. H. Dingman.*

**636** JESUS, my Saviour, to whom
　　I owe all,
Freedom from self and from sins
　that enthral,
Grave, where thy victory? Death,
　where thy sting?　　[bring.
Praises to Jesus each day I must
　Jesus, first thought in the morning !
　Jesus, the last thought at night !
　Jesus my song all the day long,
　Keeping me happy and bright !

2 Jesus, my Healer, oh help me to
　feel　　　　　　[mighty to heal!
Health from the touch that is
Show forth Thy power and make
　me to be　　　　　[for Thee.
Stronger each day in my service

3 Jesus, my Helper, who keeps my
　faith true,　　　[way through,
Guiding, sustaining me all the
Leading me onward and higher al-
　way,　　　　　　[day.
Bringing me closer to God ev'ry

4 Jesus, my King, who is coming
　again,　　　　　　[reign—
With shout triumphant in glory to
Oh, with what gladness I'll join in
　the song,　　　　[fied throng.
Swelling in praise from the glori-
*J. J. Culley.*

**637** COME with me, visit Calv'ry,
　　Where our Redeemer died;
His blood, it fills the fountain,
　'Tis full, 'tis deep, 'tis wide.
He died from sin to sever,
　Our hearts and lives complete;
He saves and keeps for ever
　Those lying at His feet.
　To the uttermost He saves,
　To the uttermost He saves,
　Dare you now believe and His love receive,
　To the uttermost Jesus saves.

2 I will surrender fully,
  And do His blessèd will;
His blood doth make me holy,
  His presence me doth fill.
He's saving. I'm believing,
  This blessing now I claim:
His Spirit I'm receiving,
  My heart is in a flame.

3 I've wondrous peace through trust-
  A well of joy within;     [ing;
This ' rest is everlasting,
  Each day I triumph win.
He gives me heavenly measure
  ' Pressed down' and 'running
    o'er,'
Oh, what a priceless treasure,
  Glory for evermore!
                        *J. Lawley.*

**638** FULL Salvation! Full Salva-
    tion!
  Lo! the fountain opened wide
Streams through ev'ry land and
    nation
  From the Saviour's wounded side.
    Full Salvation!
  Streams an endless crimson tide.

2 Oh! the glorious revelation!
  See the cleansing current flow;
Washing stains of condemnation
  Whiter than the driven snow;
    Full Salvation!
  Oh! the rapturous bliss to know!

3 Love's resistless current sweeping
  All the regions deep within;
Thought and wish and senses keep-
    ing
  Now, and every instant, clean;
    Full Salvation!
  From the guilt and power of sin.

4 Life immortal, heaven descending,
  Lo! my heart the Spirit's shrine!
God and man in oneness blend-
    ing—
  Oh, what fellowship is mine!
    Full Salvation!
  Raised in Christ to life divine!

5 Care and doubting, gloom and
    sorrow,
  Fear and grief are mine no more:
Faith knows nought of dark to-
    morrow

For my Saviour goes before.
  Full Salvation!
Full and free for evermore.
                        *F. Bottome.*

**639** I'VE something in my heart
    that Jesus gave to me,
  It makes me feel like singing
    glory all the day:
He found my captive soul and gave
    me liberty,             [glory!
  And now I feel like singing

He makes the path grow brighter ev'ry
    passing day ;
He makes the burden lighter, all along the
    way ;
His Word is my delight, His will I now obey,
    And all the time I'm singing glory !

2 My Saviour loosed my tongue that
    I might speak His praise;
  Since then I have been singing
    glory all the day;
I love to tell the lost of Jesus and
    His ways,               [glory!
  And oh, it keeps me singing

3 My Saviour took my feet from out
    the miry clay;
  Since then I have been singing
    glory all the day:
He placed them on the Rock that
    shall not pass away—
  I cannot keep from singing glory!

4 O weary heart and sad, O heavy-
    laden soul,
  If you would feel like singing
    glory all the day,
Just let the Saviour in, and let Him
    take control:            [glory!
  Then you will feel like singing
                        *L. R. Minor.*

**640** I HAVE such a wonderful Sav-
    iour,
  Who helps me wherever I go;
That I must be telling His goodness,
  That ev'rybody should know!

Ev'rybody should know, . . .
  Ev'rybody should know, . .
I have such a wonderful Saviour,
  That ev'rybody should know.

2 His mercy and love are unbounded,
  He makes me with gladness o'er-
    flow;                  [and ":
Oh, He is " the Chief of ten thous-
  That ev'rybody should know.

3 He helps me when trials surround
   me,                       [show:
   His grace and His goodness to
Oh, how can I help but adore Him,
   That ev'rybody should know.

4 My life and my love I will give
   Him,
   And faithfully serve Him below,
Who brought me His wondrous sal-
   vation
   That ev'rybody should know.

*Mrs. Frank A. Breck.*

**641** THE trusting heart to Jesus
   clings,
   Nor any ill forebodes,
But at the cross of Calv'ry sings,
   Praise God for lifted loads!

Singing I go along life's road,
Praising the Lord, praising the Lord,
Singing I go along life's road,
For Jesus has lifted my load.

2 The passing days bring many
   cares,
   "Fear not," I hear Him say,
And when my fears are turned to
   prayers,
   The burdens slip away.

3 He tells me of my Father's love,
   And never slumbering eye;
My everlasting King above
   Will all my needs supply.

4 When to the throne of grace I flee,
   I find the promise true,
The mighty arms upholding me
   Will bear my burdens too.

*E. E. Hewitt.*

**642** JESUS Christ is made to me,
   All I need, all I need,
He alone is all my plea,
   He is all I need.

Wisdom, righteousness and power,
Holiness for evermore ;
My redemption full and sure,
   He is all I need.

2 Jesus is my all in all,
   All I need, all I need,
While He keeps, I cannot fall,
   He is all I need.

3 He redeemed me when He died,
   All I need, all I need,
I with Him am crucified,
   He is all I need.

4 To my Saviour will I cleave,
   All I need, all I need,
He will not His servant leave,
   He is all I need.

5 He's the treasure of my soul,
   All I need, all I need,
He has cleansed and made me
   whole,
   He is all I need.

6 Glory, glory to the Lamb,
   All I need, all I need,
By His Spirit sealed I am,
   He is all I need.

7 Oh, the precious Blood of Christ,
   All I need, all I need,
It's the perfect sacrifice,
   He is all I need.   *Chas. P. Jones.*

**643** I'M happy, glad and free,
   Since the Lord has pardoned
   me,                     [sins away;
And by His blood has washed my
   I now can sing and shout,
   My sins are blotted out,
Oh, happy day that fixed my
   choice in Jesus.

God has blotted them out,
God has blotted them out,
My sins like a cloud hung over me,
He blotted them out when He set me free.
God has blotted them out,
God has blotted them out.

2 Well may my heart rejoice,
   Since the Lord became my
   choice,                [miry clay;
For I've been lifted from the
   I sing along the way,
   My night is turned to day,
I'm fully saved and satisfied in
   Jesus.

3 What rapture doth abound,
   Since I heard the joyful sound
Of full salvation wonderful and
   His word I cannot doubt, [free;
   My sins are blotted out,
And all my need is now supplied in
   Jesus.

4 When in the Glory Land,
   I join the blood-washed band,
I'll sing the song of Jesu's precious
   blood,
   That freed my soul from sin—
   Of grace that took me in,
And gave to me the joy of full sal-
   vation.

5  His word I now proclaim,
How through faith in Jesu's name
You too may know this pardon full
and free;
And then with me you'll shout,
Your sins are blotted out,
Oh, come and find your all in all
in Jesus. *Mr. and Mrs. Seth Sykes.*

**644**  WHAT a wonderful change in
my life has been wrought
Since Jesus came into my heart!
I have light in my soul which so
long I had sought,
Since Jesus came into my heart!

Since Jesus came into my heart, . . .
Since Jesus came into my heart, . . .
Floods of joy o'er my soul like the sea
billows roll,
Since Jesus came into my heart.

2  I have ceased from my wand'ring
and going astray,
Since Jesus came into my heart!
And my sins which were many are
all washed away
Since Jesus came into my heart!

3  I'm possessed of a hope that is
steadfast and sure
Since Jesus came into my heart!
And no dark clouds of doubt now
my pathway obscure,
Since Jesus came into my heart!

4  There's a light in the valley of
death now for me,
Since Jesus came into my heart!
And the gates of the City beyond
I can see,
Since Jesus came into my heart!

5  I shall go there to dwell in that
City I know,
Since Jesus came into my heart!
And I'm happy, so happy as on-
ward I go,
Since Jesus came into my heart!
*R. H. McDaniel.*

**645**  WOULD you know why I love
Jesus?
Why He is so dear to me?
'Tis because my blessèd Saviour
From my sins has ransomed me.

This is why . . . I love my Je . . . sus,
This is why . . . I love Him so ; . . .
He has par . . . doned my transgres . . .sions,
He has washed . . . me white as snow.

2  Would you know why I love Jesus?
Why He is so dear to me?
'Tis because the blood of Jesus
Fully saves and cleanses me.

3  Would you know why I love Jesus?
Why He is so dear to me?
'Tis because, amid temptation,
He supports and strengthens me.

4  Would you know why I love Jesus?
Why He is so dear to me?
'Tis because, in ev'ry conflict,
Jesus gives me victory.

5  Would you know why I love Jesus?
Why He is so dear to me?
'Tis because my Friend and Saviour
He will ever, ever be.
*E. A. Hoffmann.*

**646**  I WAS lost in sin, but Jesus
rescued me,
He's a wonderful Saviour to me;
I was bound by fear, but Jesus set
me free,
He's a wonderful Saviour to me.

For He's a wonderful Saviour to me, . . .
He's a wonderful Saviour to me. . . .
I was lost in sin, but Jesus took me in :
He's a wonderful Saviour to me.

2  He's a Friend so true, so patient
and so kind,
He's a wonderful Saviour to me;
Ev'rything I need in Him I always
find,
He's a wonderful Saviour to me.

3  He is always near to comfort and
to cheer,
He's a wonderful Saviour to me;
He forgives my sins, He dries my
ev'ry tear,
He's a wonderful Saviour to me.

4  Dearer grows the love of Jesus day
by day,
He's a wonderful Saviour to me;
Sweeter is His grace while press-
ing on my way,
He's a wonderful Saviour to me.
·  *Virgil P. Brock.*

**647**  THOUGH life's changing values
may vanish away,
And things that were real become dreams;
How blessèd to walk with the Lord
day by day,
And know He is real as He seems.

Jesus is real to me,
Yes, Jesus is real to me ;
I never will doubt Him, nor journey without
Him,
For He is so real to me.

2 I never have seen Him with these
eyes of mine,
But though He be hid from my
sight,                      [divine,
I know He is with me in Spirit
I live in the strength of His
might.

3 My Saviour and Leader each mo-
ment is He,
My Helper in all that I do;
Companionship with Him is blessèd
to me,                      [true.
His friendship is faithful and

4 My reason the unseen can never
discern,
Nor fully explain the unknown;
But precious the truths of the Spirit
I learn,
When His Spirit speaks to my
own.                  *Geo. H. Carr.*

**648** FAR away the noise of strife
upon my ear is falling,
Then I know the sins of earth
beset on ev'ry hand;
Doubt and fear and things of earth
in vain to me are calling,
None of these shall move me
from Beulah Land.

I'm living on the mountain, underneath a
cloudless sky, . . .
I'm drinking at the fountain that never shall
run dry,
Oh, yes ! I'm feasting on the manna from a
bountiful supply,
For I am dwelling in Beulah Land.

2 Far below the storm of doubt upon
the world is beating,
Sons of men in battle long the
enemy withstand;
Safe am I within the castle of God's
word retreating,
Nothing then can reach me, 'tis
Beulah Land.

3 Let the stormy breezes blow, their
cry cannot alarm me,
I am safely sheltered here pro-
tected by God's hand;
Here the sun is always shining, here
there's naught can harm me,
I am safe for ever in Beulah
Land.

4 Viewing here the works of God, I
sink in contemplation,
Hearing now His blessèd voice,
I see the way is planned;
Dwelling in the spirit, here I learn
of full salvation,
Gladly will I tarry in Beulah
Land.          *C. Austin Miles.*

**649** I AM redeemed, oh, praise the
Lord!
My soul from bondage free,
Has found at last a resting-place
In Him who died for me!

I am redeemed ! . . . I am redeemed ! . . .
I'll sing it o'er and o'er ;
I am redeemed ! . . . oh, praise the Lord !
Redeemed for evermore !

2 I looked, and lo, from Calv'ry's
Cross
A healing fountain streamed;
It cleansed my heart, and now I
sing,
Praise God, I am redeemed!

3 The debt is paid, my soul is free;
And by His mighty power,
The blood that washed my sins
away
Still cleanseth ev'ry hour.

4 All glory be to Jesu's name
I know that He is mine!
For on my heart the Spirit seals
His pledge of love Divine.

5 And when I reach that world more
bright
Than mortal ever dreamed,
I'll cast my crown at Jesu's feet
And cry, "Redeemed, redeemed!"
                    *Julia Sterling.*

**650** I HAVE a Friend whose faith-
ful love
Is more than all the world to me,
'Tis higher than the heights above,
And deeper than the soundless
sea :
So old, so new, so strong, so true;
Before the earth received its
frame,                      [name!
He loved me—Blessèd be His

2 He held the highest place above,
Adored by all the sons of flame,
Yet, such His self-denying love,
He laid aside His crown and came

To seek the lost, and, at the cost
Of heav'nly rank and earthly
fame, [name!
He sought me—Blessèd be His
3 It was a lonely path He trod,
From ev'ry human soul apart,
Known only to Himself and God
Was all the grief that filled His
heart:
Yet from the track He turned not
back [shame
Till where I lay in want and
He found me—Blessèd be His
name!
4 Then dawned at last that day of
dread
When, desolate but undismayed,
With wearied frame and thorn-
crowned head
He, now forsaken and betrayed,
Went up for me to Calvary,
And dying there in grief and
shame [name!
He saved me—Blessèd be His
5 Long as I live my song shall tell
The wonders of His matchless
love:
And when at last I rise to dwell
In the bright home prepared
above,
My joy shall be His face to see,
And bowing then with loud
acclaim, [name!
I'll praise Him—Blessèd be His
*C. A. Tydeman.*

**651** I WAS lost in sin when Jesus
found me, [to His name!
But He rescued me, all glory
And the cords of worldly pleasure
bound me, [shame.
Till He saved me from sin and
'Twas a glad day when Jesus found me,
When His strong arms were thrown around
me,
When my sins He buried in the deepest sea,
And my soul He filled with joy and victory,
'Twas a glad day, oh, hallelujah !
'Twas a glad day He claimed His own ;
I will shout a glad hosanna in glory
When I see Him upon His throne.

2 Oh, the bells of heaven now are
ringing [ransomed soul!
For I hear their tones within my
And my heart is filled with joyful
singing [whole.
Since the Saviour hath made me

3 Oh, the joy when we shall meet in
glory, [home above;
In the mansions of my Father's
And through endless ages tell the
story
Of the Saviour's redeeming love.
*A. S. Reitz.*

**652** THERE is never a day so dreary,
There is never a night so long,
But the soul that is trusting Jesus
Will somewhere find a song.
Wonderful, wonderful Jesus,
In the heart He implanteth a song : . . .
A song of deliv'rance, of courage, of strength,
In the heart He implanteth a song. . . .

2 There is never a cross so heavy,
There is never a weight of woe
But that Jesus will help to carry
Because He loveth so.

3 There is never a care or burden,
There is never a grief or loss,
But that Jesus in love will lighten
When carried to the cross.

4 There is never a guilty sinner,
There is never a wandering one,
But that God can in mercy pardon
Through Jesus Christ, His Son.
*Annie B. Russell.*

**653** ALL the darkness of the night
has passed away,
It is morning in my heart;
I am living in the sunlight of the
It is morning in my heart. [day,
It is morning, it is morning in my heart . . .
Jesus made the gloomy shadows all depart ; . .
Songs of gladness now I sing,
For since Jesus is my King
It is morning, it is morning in my heart.

2 I can hear the songbirds singing
their refrain,
It is morning in my heart;
And I know that life for me begins
again,
It is morning in my heart.

3 Christ has made the world a para-
dise to me,
It is morning in my heart;
Every duty in the light of love I
It is morning in my heart. [see,

4 Joy has come to dwell with me for
evermore,
It is morning in my heart ;
I shall sing it when I reach the
other shore,
It is morning in my heart.
*A. H. Ackley.*

**654** I'VE believed the true report,
　　　　Hallelujah to the Lamb!
I have passed the outer court,
　　O glory be to God!
I am all on Jesus' side,
On the altar sanctified,
To the world and sin I've died,
　　Hallelujah to the Lamb!

　Hallelu . . . jah !  Hallelu . . . jah !
　　I have passed the riven vail, where the
　　　glories never fail,
　Hallelu . . . jah !  Hallelu . . . jah !
　　I am living in the presence of the King.

2 I'm a king and priest to God,
　　Hallelujah to the Lamb!
By the cleansing of the blood,
　　O glory be to God!
By the Spirit's power and light,
I am living day and night,
In the holiest place so bright,
　　Hallelujah to the Lamb!

3 I'm within the holiest pale,
　　Hallelujah to the Lamb!
I have passed the inner vail,
　　O glory be to God!
I am sanctified to God
By the power of the blood,
Now the Lord is my abode,
　　Hallelujah to the Lamb!

　　　　　　　　　　　*C. P. Jones.*

**655** WONDERFUL love that rescued
　　　　　Sunk deep in sin,　　[me,
Guilty and vile as I could be—
　　No hope within :
When every ray of light had fled,
　　O glorious day,
Raising my soul from out the dead,
　　Love found a way.

　Love found a way to redeem my soul,
　Love found a way that could make me
　　　whole ;
　Love sent my Lord to the cross of shame,
　Love found a way, O praise His holy name !

2 Love brought my Saviour here to
　　On Calvary,　　　　　　[die
For such a sinful wretch as I,
　　How can it be?
Love bridged the gulf 'twixt me
　　Taught me to pray ; [and heaven,
I am redeemed, set free, forgiven,
　　Love found a way.

3 Love opened wide the gates of light
　　To heaven's domain,

Where in eternal power and might
　　Jesus shall reign;
Love lifted me from depths of woe
　　To endless day,
There was no help in earth below,
　　Love found a way.

　　　　　　　　　　*Constance B. Ried.*

**656** FOR God so loved the sinful
　　　　　world,
　　His Son He freely gave,
That whosoever would believe,
　　Eternal life should have.

　'Tis true, O yes, 'tis true,
　　God's wonderful promise is true ;
　For I've trusted, and tested, and tried it,
　　And I know God's promise is true.

2 I was a wayward wandering child,
　　A slave to sin and fear,
Until this blessèd promise fell,
　　Like music on my ear.

3 The " whosoever " of the Lord,
　　I trusted was for me;
I took Him at His gracious word,
　　From sin to set me free.

4 Eternal life began below
　　Now fills my heart and soul:
I'll sing His praise for evermore,
　　Who has redeemed my soul.

　　　　　　　　　　　*C. H. Morris.*

**657** SINCE the Saviour came to this
　　　　　heart of mine,
My cup's filled and running over,
Filling my poor soul with His joy
　　divine,
My cup's filled and running over.

　Running over, running over,
　My cup's filled and running over,
　　Since the Lord saved me,
　　I'm as happy as can be,
　My cup's filled and running over.

2 With my Lord so dear, I have
　　naught to fear,
My cup's filled and running over,
Though my way be drear He is
　　ever near,
My cup's filled and running over.

3 Even though I walk through death's
　　darksome vale,
My cup's filled and running over,
Christ my Lord shall be my com-
　　fort still,
My cup's filled and running over.

**4** Sinner, seek the Lord, trust His
precious word,
While the angels round you
hover,        [then will sing,
Heaven's bells will ring, and you
My cup's filled and running over.
*Seth Sykes.*

**658** THERE'S a peace in my heart
that the world never gave,
A peace it can not take away;
Though the trials of life may sur-
round like a cloud,  [to stay.
I've a peace that has come there
Con . . . stantly abid . . . ing, . . . Je . . . sus
is mine ; . . .
Con . . . stantly abid . . . ing, . . . rap . . . ture
divine ; . . .
He . . . never leaves me lone . . . ly, . . .
whispers, O so kind : . . .
"I will never leave thee," Jesus is mine.

**2** All the world seemed to sing of a
Saviour and King,       [heart;
When peace sweetly came to my
Troubles all fled away and my
night turned to day,     [art!
Blessèd Jesus, how glorious Thou

**3** This treasure I have in a temple of
clay,                 [roam;
While here on His footstool I
But He's coming to take me some
glorious day,          [home!
Over there to my heavenly
*Mrs. Will L. Murphy.*

**659** ONCE my way was dark and
dreary,
For my heart was full of sin;
But the sky is bright and cheery,
Since the fulness of His love
came in.
I can never tell how much I love Him,
I can never tell His love for me ;
For it passeth human measure,
Like a deep unfathomed sea ; . . .
'Tis redeeming love in Christ my Saviour,
In my soul the heav'nly joys begin ;
And I live for Jesus only
Since the fulness of His love came in.

**2** There is grace for all the lowly,
Grace to keep the trusting soul;
Power to cleanse and make me
holy,                 [trol.
Jesus shall my yielded life con-

**3** Let me spread abroad the story,
Other souls to Jesus win;
For the cross is now my glory,
Since the fulness of His love
came in.    *E. E. Hewitt.*

**660** CLEANSED in our Saviour's
precious Blood,
Filled with the fulness of our God,
Walking by faith the path He trod,
Hallelujah! hallelujah!

**2** Leaning our heads on Jesus' breast,
Knowing the joy of that sweet rest,
Finding in Him the chief, the best,
Hallelujah! hallelujah!

**3** Kept by His power from day to
day,
Held by His hand, we cannot stray,
Glory to glory all the way,
Hallelujah! hallelujah!

**4** Living in us His own pure life,
Giving us rest from inward strife,
From strength to strength, from
death to life,
Hallelujah! hallelujah!

**5** O what a Saviour we have found!
Well may we make the world
resound,
With one continual joyous sound,
Hallelujah! hallelujah!
*W. Spencer Walton.*

**661** IN sin I once had wandered all
weary, sad and lone,
Till Jesus through His mercy adop-
ted me His own;
E'er since I learned to trust Him,
His grace doth make me free,
And now I feel His pardon, He's
ev'rything to me.
He's ev'rything to me, . . .
From sin He sets me free ; . . .
His peace and love my portion through all
eternity ! . . .
He's ev'rything to me, . . .
More than my dreams could be ; . . .
O praise His name for ever, He's ev'rything
to me.

**2** In sin no more I'll wander, He's
Pilot, Friend and Guide,
He brings me joy and singing, His
Spirit doth abide;
A blessèd, loving Saviour, the Lamb
of Calvary;
He purchased my redemption, He's
ev'rything to me.

**3** No longer will I stray from His
tender, loving care,
Like Him to be my purpose, my
aim, my constant prayer;

And when He bids me welcome
  throughout eternity,
I'll praise His name for ever, He's
  ev'rything to me.

*Hamp Sewell.*

**662** Oh, bless the Lord, my soul!
  His grace to thee proclaim,
And all that is within me join
  To bless His Holy Name.

2  Oh bless the Lord, my soul!
  His mercies bear in mind,
Forget not all His benefits;
  The Lord to thee is kind.

3  He will not always chide;
  He will with patience wait;
His wrath is ever slow to rise
  And ready to abate.

4  He pardons all thy sins,
  Prolongs thy feeble breath;
He healeth thine infirmities,
  And ransoms thee from death.

5  He clothes thee with His love,
  Upholds thee with His truth,
And, like the eagle, He renews
  The vigour of thy youth.

6  Then bless His holy Name,
  Whose grace hath made thee
  whole,                [days;
Whose loving-kindness crowns thy
  Oh, bless the Lord, my soul!

*J. Montgomery.*

**663** I REMEMBER when my burdens
  rolled away,
I had carried them for years,
  night and day;
When I sought the blessèd Lord,
  and I took Him at His word.
Then at once all my burdens
  rolled away.

Rolled away, ... rolled away, ...
I am happy since my burdens rolled away.

2  I remember when my burdens
  rolled away,
That I feared would never leave
  night or day;
Jesus showed to me the loss, so I
  left them at the cross;
I was glad when my burdens
  rolled away.

3  I remember when my burdens
  rolled away,
That had hindered me for years,
  night and day;
As I sought the throne of grace,
  just a glimpse of Jesu's face,
And I knew that my burdens
  could not stay.

4  I am singing since my burdens
  rolled away,
There's a song within my heart
  night and day;
I am living for my King, and with
  joy I shout and sing,
Hallelujah! all my burdens
  rolled away.   *Mrs. M. A. Steele.*

# Section X

## YOUNG PEOPLE

**664** IT is a thing most wonderful,
  Almost too wonderful to be,
That God's own Son should come
  from heaven
  And die to save a child like me.

2  And yet I know that it is true:
  He came to this poor world be-
  low,                [and died,
And wept and toiled and mourned
  Only because He loved us so.

3  I cannot tell how He could love
  A child so weak and full of sin;
His love must be most wonderful,
  If He could die my love to win.

4  It is most wonderful to know
  His love for me so free and sure;
But 'tis more wonderful to see
  My love for Him so faint and
  poor.

5 And yet I want to love Thee, Lord:
　　Oh, light the flame within my
　　　heart,　　　　　　　　　[more
　　And I will love Thee more and
　　Until I see Thee as Thou art.
　　　　　　　　　　*W. W. How.*

**665**　ALL things bright and beauti-
　　　　ful,
　　All creatures great and small,
　　All things wise and wonderful,
　　The Lord God made them all.

2 Each little flower that opens,
　　Each little bird that sings,
　　He made their glowing colours,
　　He made their tiny wings.

　　All things bright and beautiful,
　　All creatures great and small,
　　All things wise and wonderful,
　　The Lord God made them all.

3 The purple-headed mountain,
　　The river running by,
　　The sunset, and the morning
　　That brightens up the sky.

4 The cold wind in the winter,
　　The pleasant summer sun,
　　The ripe fruits in the garden,
　　He made them every one.

5 He gave us eyes to see them,
　　And lips that we might tell
　　How great is God Almighty,
　　Who has done all things well.
　　　　　　　　*Mrs. C. F. Alexander.*

**666**　SAVIOUR, while my heart is
　　　　tender,
　　I would yield that heart to Thee,
　　All my powers to Thee surrender,
　　Thine and only Thine to be.

2 Take me now, Lord Jesus, take me;
　　Let my youthful heart be Thine;
　　Thy devoted servant make me;
　　Fill my soul with love Divine.

3 Send me, Lord, where Thou wilt
　　　send me,
　　Only do Thou guide my way;
　　May Thy grace through life attend
　　Gladly then shall I obey.　　[me,

4 Thine I am, O Lord, for ever,
　　To Thy service set apart;
　　Suffer me to leave Thee never;
　　Seal Thine image on my heart.
　　　　　　　　　　*John Burton.*

**667**　CHILDREN of Jerusalem
　　　　Sang the praise of Jesu's name:
　　Children, too, of modern days,
　　Join to sing the Saviour's praise.

　　Hark, hark, hark ! while infant voices sing,
　　Hark, hark, hark ! while infant voices sing,
　　Loud hosannas, loud hosannas,
　　Loud hosannas to our King.

2 We are taught to love the Lord,
　　We are taught to read His Word,
　　We are taught the way to heaven:
　　Praise for all to God be given.

3 Parents, teachers, old and young,
　　All unite to swell the song;
　　Higher and yet higher rise,
　　Till hosannas reach the skies.
　　　　　　　　　　*John Henley.*

**668**　GOD make my life a little light,
　　　　Within the world to glow;
　　A little flame that burneth bright
　　Wherever I may go.

2 God make my life a little flower,
　　That giveth joy to all;
　　Content to bloom in native bower,
　　Although the place be small.

3 God make my life a little song,
　　That comforteth the sad;
　　That helpeth others to be strong,
　　And makes the singer glad.

4 God make my life a little staff,
　　Whereon the weak may rest;
　　That so what health and strength I
　　　have
　　May serve my neighbours best.

5 God make my life a little hymn
　　Of tenderness and praise,
　　Of faith that never waxeth dim,
　　In all His wondrous ways.
　　　　　　　　*M. Betham-Edwards.*

**669**　I THINK, when I read that
　　　　sweet story of old,
　　When Jesus was here among men,
　　How He called little children as
　　　lambs to His fold,
　　I should like to have been with
　　　Him then;
　　I wish that His hands had been
　　　placed on my head,
　　That His arms had been thrown
　　　around me,
　　And that I might have seen His
　　　kind look when He said:
　　Let the little ones come unto Me!

2 Yet still to His footstool in prayer
   I may go,
     And ask for a share in His love;
And if I now earnestly seek Him
   below,        [above.
   I shall see Him and hear Him
In that beautiful place He has gone
   to prepare      [given;
   For all who are washed and for-
And many dear children are gather-
   ing there      [heaven.
   For of such is the kingdom of

3 But thousands and thousands who
   wander and fall
   Never heard of that heavenly
     home;
   I should like them to know there is
     room for them all,
   And that Jesus has bid them to
     come.      [time,
   I long for the joy of that glorious
   The sweetest and brightest and
     best,
When the dear little children of
   every clime    [blessed.
   Shall crowd to His arms and be
                 *Jemima Luke.*

**670** I AM so glad that our Father
     in heaven
   Tells of His love in the Book He
     has given;
   Wonderful things in the Bible I see;
   This is the dearest, that Jesus loves
     me.

   I am so glad that Jesus loves me,
   Jesus loves me, Jesus loves me,
   I am so glad that Jesus loves me,
   Jesus loves me even me.

2 Jesus loves me and I know I love
   Him;    [soul to redeem;
   Love brought Him down my lost
   Yes, it was love made Him die on
     the tree;    [me.
   Oh, I am certain that Jesus loves

3 In this assurance I find sweetest
   rest,      [blest;
   Trusting in Jesus I know I am
   Satan dismayed from my soul doth
     now flee    [loves me.
   When I just tell him that Jesus

4 Oh, if there's only one song I can
   sing,     [King,
   When in His beauty I see the great

This shall my song in eternity be,
  "Oh, what a wonder that Jesus
   loves me!"

5 If one should ask of me, how can
   I tell?
   Glory to Jesus, I know very well!
   God's Holy Spirit with mine doth
     agree,    [me.
   Constantly witnessing—Jesus loves
                 *P. P. Bliss.*

**671** LOVER of children, I come un-
     to Thee;
   Graciously, tenderly look upon me;
   Jesus on me put Thy kind, gentle
     hands;    [derstands.
   Speak in such words as a child un-

2 Teacher of children, so wise and so
   kind,      [mind;
   O may I ever Thy words keep in
   Learning of Thee as I grow day by
     day,      [may.
   Doing Thy will as a little child

3 Friend of the children, who always
   art near,    [fear;
   Holding Thy hand I have nothing to
   Guided and guarded by Thee I
     would be;    [me.
   No other friend is so precious to

4 Saviour of children, Thou camest
   to die,
   Sinners to ransom, and sinful am I;
   Never, O never such love would I
     grieve;    [cleave.
   Closer and closer to Thee would I

5 Lover of children, Redeemer divine,
   I am so happy to know Thou art
     mine;    [my days,
   Loving me, leading me all through
   Thee will I love, and Thy name
     will I praise.
                 *Edith Greeves.*

**672** SAVIOUR, like a shepherd lead
     us;
   Much we need Thy tender care;
In Thy pleasant pastures feed us,
   For our use Thy folds prepare:
     Blessèd Jesus,    [are.
   Thou hast bought us, Thine we

2 We are Thine, do Thou befriend
   us;
   Be the Guardian of our way;

Keep Thy flock, from sin defend
Seek us when we go astray: [us,
    Blessèd Jesus,
Hear us when we praise and pray.

3 Thou hast promised to receive us,
    Poor and sinful though we be;
Thou hast mercy to relieve us,
    Grace to cleanse, and make us
    Blessèd Jesus,        [free:
Early let us turn to Thee.

4 Early let us seek Thy favour;
    Early let us do Thy will;
Gracious Lord, our only Saviour,
    With Thyself our bosoms fill:
    Blessèd Jesus,
Thou hast loved us—love us still.
*Dorothy A. Thrupp.*

**673** JESUS, the children are calling;
        O draw near!
Fold the young lambs in Thy bosom,
    Shepherd dear.

2 Slow are our footsteps and failing,
        Oft we fall;
Jesus the children are calling;
    Hear their call!

3 Cold is our love, Lord, and narrow;
        Large is Thine,
Faithful, and strong and tender:
    So be mine!

4 Gently, Lord, lead Thou our
    Weary they;        [mothers;
Bless all our sisters and brothers
    Night and day.

5 Fathers themselves are God's chil-
    Teach them still:        [dren;
Let the good Spirit show all men
    God's wise will.

6 Now to the Father, Son, Spirit,
    Three in One,
Bountiful God of our fathers,
    Praise be done!
*Annie Matheson.*

**674** JESUS, high in glory,
        Lend a list'ning ear;
When we bow before Thee,
    Children's praises hear.

2 Though Thou art so holy,
    Heav'ns almighty King,
Thou wilt stoop to listen
    While Thy praise we sing.

3 We are little children,
    Weak and apt to stray;
Saviour, guide and keep us
    In the heavenly way.

4 Save us, Lord, from sinning,
    Watch us day by day;
Help us now to love Thee,
    Take our sins away.

5 Then when Thou shalt call us
    To our heavenly home,
We will gladly answer,
    " Saviour, Lord, we come."

6 In the many mansions,
    From all sin set free,
Loud shall be our praises,
    When Thy face we see.
*Harriet B. McKeever.*

**675** JESU, high and holy,
        Make my heart like Thine,
Humble, meek and lowly,
    Full of love divine,
Keep me in Thy dwelling,
    Pure and undefiled,
Ev'ry fear dispelling,
    Let me be Thy child.

2 Thine alone for ever,
    Saviour would I be;
Let not Satan sever
    My young heart from Thee.
In Thine admonition
    Daily may I grow
To Thy full fruition
    While I live below.

3 Saviour, go beside me,
    Never let me stray;
By Thy counsel guide me
    All my pilgrim way.
Be my joy and treasure,
    Grant me, Lord, to see
Truest peace and pleasure
    Are in serving Thee.
*W. Robinson.*

**676** EV'RY morning the red sun
        Rises warm and bright;
But the evening cometh on,
    And the dark cold night:
There's a bright land far away
Where 'tis never-ending day.

2 Every spring the sweet young
    Open fresh and gay;        [flow'rs
Till the chilly autumn hours
    Wither them away:

There's a land we have not seen
Where the trees are always green.

3 Little birds sing songs of praise
   All the summer long;
   But in colder, shorter days
   They forget their song;
   There's a place where angels sing
   Ceaseless praises to their King.

4 Christ our Lord is ever near
   Those who follow Him;
   But we cannot see Him here,
   For our eyes are dim:
   There's a happy, glorious place
   Where His people see His face.

5 Who shall go to that fair land?
   All who love the right;
   Holy children there shall stand
   In their robes of white;
   For that heaven so bright and blest
   Is our everlasting rest.

*Mrs. C. F. Alexander.*

**677** JESUS is our Shepherd,
        Wiping ev'ry tear;
   Folded in His bosom,
      What have we to fear?
   Only let us follow
      Whither He doth lead,

To the thirsty desert
   Or the dewy mead.

2 Jesus is our Shepherd;
   Well we know His voice;
   How its gentle whisper
      Makes our heart rejoice!
   Even when He chideth,
      Tender is His tone;
   None but He shall guide us;
      We are His alone.

3 Jesus is our Shepherd:
   For the sheep He bled;
   Every lamb is sprinkled
      With the blood He shed:
   Then on each He setteth
      His own secret sign;
   "They that have My Spirit,
      These," saith He, "are Mine."

4 Jesus is our Shepherd;
   Guarded by His arm,
   Though the wolves may raven,
      None can do us harm:
   When we tread death's valley,
      Dark with fearful gloom,
   We will fear no evil,
      Victors o'er the tomb.

*Hugh Stowell.*

# Section XI

## THE CHURCH OF GOD

### (1) THE BODY OF CHRIST

**678** O CHURCH of God, thy Lord
        hath chosen thee, [to be.
   His living witness through the years
   To bear the message of His grace
      To all the tribes of earth,
   Till countless souls of Adam's
        race
      In Christ shall seek new birth.

O Church of God ! . . . O temple fair !
Shrine of Christ's beauty, set apart and rare,
His glorious triumph henceforth thou shalt
   share.

2 O Church of God, your Master's
        call obey, [to-day,
   Go seek the lost while it is called
   The fields are white and workers
        few,

To reap the golden grain;
   O then to Him thy Lord be true,
   To live for Christ is gain.

3 O Church of God, the gates of hell
        shall fail [vail,
   Against thy bulwarks ever to pre-
   Clothed in the might of Christ
        thy Lord,
      Abandoned to His will,
   Thy weapon His all-conquering
        Word,
      Thou shalt God's plan fulfil.

4 O Church of God, thy warfare ne'er
        shall cease [of Peace,
   Till Christ appears the mighty Prince
   Whose arm shall break the ty-
        rant's power,

And set creation free; [hour,
Then watch until that advent
When Christ thine eyes shall
see.

*E. C. W. Boulton.*

**679** CHRIST is the foundation
    Of the house we raise;
Be its walls salvation,
    And its gateways praise:
May its threshold lowly
    To the Lord be dear;
May the hearts be holy
    That shall worship here.

2 Here the vow be sealèd
    By Thy Spirit, Lord;
Here the sick be healèd,
    And the lost restored;
Here the broken-hearted
    Thy forgiveness prove;
Here the friends long parted
    Be restored to love.

3 Here may every token
    Of Thy presence be;
Here may chains be broken,
    Prisoners here set free;
Here may light illumine
    Every soul of Thine,
Lifting up the human
    Into the divine.

4 Here may God the Father,
    Christ the Saviour—Son,
With the Holy Spirit,
    Be adored as One;
Till the whole creation
    At Thy footstool fall,
And in adoration
    Own Thee Lord of all.

*J. S. B. Monsall.*

**680** CHURCH of God, beloved and
    chosen,     [died,
Church of Christ for whom He
Claim Thy gifts and praise the
    Giver,—
"Ye are washed and sanctified."
Sanctified by God the Father,
    And by Jesus Christ His Son,
And by God the Holy Spirit,
    Holy, Holy, Three in One.

2 By His will He sanctifieth,
    By the Spirit's pow'r within;
By the loving hand that chasteneth,
    Fruits of righteousness to win;

By His truth and by His promise,
    By the Word, His gift unpriced,
By His blood, and by our union
    With the risen life of Christ.

3 Holiness by faith in Jesus,
    Not by effort of thine own,—
Sin's dominion crushed and broken
    By the power of grace alone,—
God's own holiness within thee,
    His own beauty on thy brow:
This shall be thy pilgrim bright-
    ness,
    This thy blessèd portion now.

4 He will sanctify thee wholly;
    Body, spirit, soul shall be
Blameless till thy Saviour's coming
    In His glorious majesty!
He hath perfected for ever
    Those whom He hath sanctified;
Spotless, glorious, and holy,
    Is the Church, His chosen Bride.

*F. R. Havergal.*

**681** GOD in heaven hath a treasure,
    Riches none may count or
      tell;
Hath a deep eternal pleasure,
    Christ, the Son, He loveth well.
God hath here on earth a treasure,
    None but He its price may
      know,—
Deep, unfathomable pleasure,
    Christ revealed in saints below.

2 God in tongues of fire descending,
    Chosen vessels thus to fill
With the treasure never ending,
    Ever spent, unfailing still.
God's own hand the vessel filling
    From the glory far above,
Longing hearts for ever stilling
    With the riches of His love.

3 Thus though worn, and tried, and
    tempted,
Glorious calling, saint, is thine;
Let the Lord but find thee emptied,
    Living branch in Christ the vine!
Vessels of the world's despising,
    Vessels weak, and poor, and
      base,     [prizing,
Bearing wealth God's heart is
    Glory from Christ's blessèd face.

4 Oh, to be but emptier, lowlier,
  Mean, un-noticed and unknown,
And to God a vessel holier,
  Filled with Christ and Christ
    alone!
Naught of earth to cloud the glory,
  Naught of self the light to dim,
Telling forth His wondrous story
  Emptied—to be filled with Him.
                *tr. Frances Bevan.*

**682** THE Church's one foundation
    Is Jesus Christ her Lord;
She is His new creation
    By water and the word;
From heaven He came and sought
    To be His holy bride;       [her
With His own blood He bought her,
    And for her life He died.

2 Elect from every nation,
    Yet one o'er all the earth,
Her charter of salvation
    One Lord, one faith, one birth,
One holy name she blesses,
    Partakes one holy food,
And to one hope she presses,
    With every grace endued.

3 Though with a scornful wonder
    Men see her sore oppressed,
By schisms rent asunder,
    By heresies distressed,
Yet saints their watch are keeping
    Their cry goes up, "How long?"
And soon the night of weeping
    Shall be the morn of song.

4 'Mid toil and tribulation,
    And tumult of her war,
She waits the consummation
    Of peace for evermore.
Till with the vision glorious
    Her longing eyes are blest,
And the great Church victorious
    Shall be the Church at rest.

5 Yet she on earth hath union
    With God the Three in One,
And mystic sweet communion
    With those whose rest is won.
O happy ones and holy!
    Lord, give us grace that we
Like them, the meek and lowly,
    On high may dwell with Thee.
                *Samuel John Stone.*

**683** HEAD of Thy Church trium-
        phant,
    We joyfully adore Thee,
    Till Thou appear,
    Thy members here
    Shall sing like those in glory.
We lift our hearts and voices
With blest anticipation,
    And cry aloud,
    And give to God
    The praise of our salvation.

2 The name we still acknowledge
    That burst our bonds asunder,
    And loudly sing
    Our conq'ring King,
    In songs of joy and wonder.
In every day's deliverance
Our Jesus we discover;
    'Tis He, 'tis He
    That smote the sea,
    And led us safely over.

3 While in affliction's furnace,
    And passing through the fire,
    Thy love we praise,
    Which knows our days
    And ever brings us nigher.
We clap our hands exulting
In Thine almighty favour;
    The love divine
    Which made us Thine
    Shall keep us Thine for ever.

4 By faith we see the glory
    To which Thou shalt restore **us**;
    The Cross despise
    For that high prize
    Which Thou hast set before **us**.
And if Thou count us worthy,
We each, as dying Stephen,
    Shall see Thee stand
    At God's right hand
    To take us up to heaven.
                *Charles Wesley.*

**684** WE come unto our fathers'
        God;
    Their Rock is our salvation;
Th'eternal arms, their dear abode,
    We make our habitation;
We bring Thee, Lord, the praise
        they brought;      [sought
We seek Thee as Thy saints have
    In every generation.

2 The fire divine their steps that led
  Still goeth bright before us;
The heav'nly shield around them spread
  Is still high holden o'er us;
The grace those sinners that sub-
  dued,                       [renewed,
The strength those weaklings that
  Doth vanquish, doth restore us.

3 The cleaving sins that brought them
  low
  Are still our souls oppressing;
The tears that from their eyes did
  flow
  Fall fast, our shame confessing;
As with Thee, Lord, prevailed their
  cry,                           [high
So our strong prayer ascends on
  And bringeth down Thy blessing.

4 Their joy unto their Lord we bring;
  Their song to us descendeth;
The Spirit who in them did sing
  To us His music lendeth;
His song in them, in us, is one;
  We raise it high, we send it on,
  The song that never endeth.

5 Ye saints to come, take up the
  strain,                        [our:
  The same sweet theme endeav-
Unbroken be the golden chain;
  Keep on the song for ever;
Safe in the same dear dwelling-
  place,
Rich with the same eternal grace,
  Bless the same boundless giver.
                          *T. H. Gill.*

**685** Glorious things of thee are
  spoken,
    Zion, city of our God;
He whose word cannot be broken,
    Formed thee for His own abode.
On the Rock of Ages founded,
    What can shake thy sure repose?
With salvation's walls surrounded,
    Thou may'st smile at all thy foes.

2 See! the streams of living waters,
    Springing from eternal love,
Well supply Thy sons and daugh-
    ters,
    And all fear of want remove.

Who can faint while such a river
    Ever flows their thirst to assuage?
Grace which, like the Lord, the
    Giver,
    Never fails from age to age.

3 Saviour, if of Zion's city
    I through grace, a member am,
Let the world deride or pity,
    I will glory in Thy Name.
Fading is the worldling's pleasure,
    All his boasted pomp and show;
Solid joys and lasting treasure
None but Zion's children know.
                          *John Newton.*

**686** 'Tis the Church triumphant
  singing
    Worthy the Lamb;
Heaven throughout with praises
    Worthy the Lamb.      [ringing,
Thrones and powers before Him
    bending,
Odours sweet with voice ascending,
Swell the chorus never-ending,
    Worthy the Lamb!

2 Every kindred, tongue and nation,
    Worthy the Lamb;
Join to sing the great salvation,
    Worthy the Lamb.
Loud as mighty thunders roaring,
Floods of mighty waters pouring,
Prostrate at His feet adoring,
    Worthy the Lamb!

3 Harps and songs for ever sounding
    Worthy the Lamb;
Mighty Grace o'er sin abounding,
    Worthy the Lamb.
By His blood He dearly bought us;
Wand'ring from the fold He sought
    us,
And to glory safely brought us:
    Worthy the Lamb!

4 Sing with blest anticipation
    Worthy the Lamb;
Through the vale of tribulation,
    Worthy the Lamb.
Sweetest notes, all notes excelling,
On the theme for ever dwelling,
Still untold, though ever telling,
    Worthy the Lamb!
                          *J. Kent.*

## (2) THE MINISTRY

**687** Go, labour on, spend, and be
 spent,
 Thy joy to do the Father's will;
It is the way the Master went,
 Should not the servant tread it
 still?

2 Go, labour on; 'tis not for nought,
 Thy earthly loss is heavenly gain;
Men heed thee, love thee, praise
 thee not.    [men?
 The Master praises, what are

3 Men die in darkness at your side,
 Without a hope to cheer the
 tomb:     [wide,
Take up the torch, and wave it
 The torch that lights time's thick-
 est gloom.

4 Toil on, and in thy toil rejoice,
 For toil comes rest, for exile
 home;    [groom's voice,
Soon shalt thou hear the Bride-
 The midnight peal, " Behold, I
 come!"

      *Horatius Bonar.*

**688** This is a desert place, but we
 have heard
 That Thou, O Christ, art come
 across the sea:
Hungry we come, Thou hast the
 living Word,
 Athirst, we seek the living fount
 in Thee.

2 Weary with anxious following and
 heartsore   [Saviour now
 With often failing, blessèd
Let Thy compassion help us as of
 yore,    [strong art Thou.
 So weak, so helpless we, so

3 And there are sick among us as of
 old,     [ties:
 Burdened with manifold infirmi-
Thou art the Healer still: oh make
 us bold   [health and ease
 To trust Thy mighty hand for

4 This is a desert place; the night
 comes on:   [no bread.
 No gold have we, no merit and
Give us to eat: though hungry
 every one   [fully fed.
 No pilgrim need depart till

5 How little here upon the wilds of
 earth    [the most:
 Can man provide: a handful at
Lay Thy miraculous hands upon
 our dearth   [hungry host.
 And spread a feast for all the

6 For still Thy crucified and risen
 hands     [much,
 Are all-creative, making little
And evil good; transforming chafing
 bands     [touch.
 To liberating pinions at Thy

7 At Thy command we sit around
 Thy feet:
 Oh bless and break the bread for
 every heart.
Till fully satisfied, give us to eat!
 Then blest and healed and glad
 bid us depart!

      *Harold Horton.*

**689** Lord, speak to me, that I may
 speak
 In living echoes of Thy tone;
As Thou hast sought, so let me
 seek
 Thy erring children lost and lone.

2 Oh, lead me, Lord, that I may lead
 The wandering and the wavering
 feet;
O, feed me, Lord, that I may feed
 Thy hungering ones with manna
 sweet.

3 Oh, strengthen me, that while I
 stand     [Thee,
 Firm on the Rock, and strong in
I may stretch out a loving hand
 To wrestlers with the troubled
 sea.

4 Oh, teach me, Lord, that I may
 teach     [impart,
 The precious things Thou dost
And wing my words that they may
 reach
 The hidden depths of many a
 heart.

5 Oh, give Thine own sweet rest to
 me,     [power
 That I may speak with soothing
A word in season, as from Thee,
 To weary ones in needful hour.

6 Oh, fill me with Thy fulness, Lord,
   Until my very heart o'erflow
In kindling thought, and glowing
   word,                    [show.
   Thy love to tell, Thy praise to

7 Oh, use me, Lord, use even me,
   Just as Thou wilt, and how, and
   where;
Until Thy blessèd face I see,
   Thy rest, Thy joy, Thy glory
   share.
                    *F. R. Havergal.*

**690**  YE servants of the Lord
         Each in his office wait,
Observant of His heavenly word
And watchful at His gate.

2  Let all your lamps be bright,
   And trim the golden flame;
Gird up your loins, as in His sight,
For awful is His name.

3  Watch: 'tis your Lord's com-
   mand;
   And, while we speak, He's near;
Mark the first signal of His hand,
And ready all appear.

4  O happy servant he,
   In such employment found!
He shall His Lord with rapture see,
And be with honour crowned.

5  Christ shall the banquet spread
   With His own royal hand,
And raise that faithful servant's
   head
   Amid the angelic band.
                    *Philip Doddridge.*

**691**  MOVE me, dear Lord, and
         others I shall move
   To do Thy will;          [fair
Mould Thou this life into a vessel
   Thyself to fill;
No charm with which to draw do I
   possess,
In Thee I find the secret of success.

2 O  touch these yielded lips and
      through them pour
   Thy living thought;   [the words
I would not give to hungry souls
   That man hath taught;
Shall they who seek for bread a
   stone receive?        [relieve.
It is God's Word alone that can

3 How wonderful a channel thus to
   be,
   To those forlorn,       [hope,
A  messenger of peace and joy and
   To them that mourn;
O grant that I Thy risen life may
   share,                   [bear.
The virtue of Thy name to others

4 Under th'anointing daily let me live,
   A priest and king;
Relying not on fleshly energy
   Thy smile to win
A simple soul in contact with my
   Lord,                  [stored.
In  whom all  fulness  is  forever

5 O teach me, Lord, henceforth with
   Thee to walk
   In union deep;        [neglect
Whilst tending other souls not to
   My own to keep;
A separated soul unto the One
Whose grace and love for me so
   much have done.
                    *E. C. W. Boulton.*

### (3) BELIEVERS' BAPTISM

**692**  " BURIED with Christ," and
         raised with Him too;
What is there left for me to do?
Simply to cease from struggling and
   strife,                 [life."
Simply to " walk in newness of

2 " Risen with Christ," my glorious
   Head,
Holiness now the pathway I tread,
Beautiful thought, while walking
   therein:                [sin."
" He that is dead is freed from

3 " Living with Christ," who " dieth
   no more,"
Following Christ, who goeth be-
   fore;
I am from bondage utterly freed,
Reckoning self as " dead indeed."

4 Living for Christ, my members I
   yield                  [sealed,
Servants to God, for evermore
" Not under law," I'm now " under
   grace,"                [its place.
Sin is dethroned, and Christ takes

5 Growing in Christ; no more shall
  be named      [ashamed,
Things of which now I'm truly
" Fruit unto holiness " will I bear,
Life evermore, the end I shall
  share.        *T. Ryder.*

**693** STAND, soldier of the Cross,
  Thy high allegiance claim,
And vow to hold the world but loss
  For thy Redeemer's name.

2  Arise, and be baptized,
  And wash thy sins away;
Thy league with God be solemn-
  ised,
  Thy faith avouched today.

3  No more thine own, but Christ's
  With all the saints of old,
Apostles, seers, evangelists,
  And martyr throngs enrolled—

4  In God's whole armour strong,
  Front hell's embattled powers:
The warfare may be sharp and
  long,
  The victory must be ours.

5  O bright the conqueror's crown,
  The song of triumph sweet,
When faith casts every trophy
  down
    At our great Captain's feet!
        *E. H. Bickersteth.*

**694** GLORY to God, whose Spirit
  draws      [cause,
Fresh soldiers to the Saviour's
Who thus, baptized into His name,
His goodness and their faith pro-
  claim.

2  For these now added to the host,
  Who in their Lord and Saviour
    boast,
  And consecrate to Him their days,
  Accept, O God, our grateful praise.

3  Thus may Thy mighty Spirit draw
  All here to love and keep His law;
  Themselves His subjects to declare,
  And place themselves beneath His
    care.

4  Lead them at once their Lord to
  To glory in His cross alone; [own,
  And then, baptized, His truth to
    teach,      [reach.
His love to share, His heaven to
      *Baptist W. Noel.*

**695** A MIGHTY mystery we set
  forth,
  A wondrous sign and seal;
Lord, give our hearts to know its
  worth,
  And all its truth to feel.

2  Death to the world we thus avow,
  Death to each sinful lust;
The risen life is our life now,
  The risen Christ our trust.

3  Baptized into the Father's name,
  We're children of our God;
Baptized into the Son we claim
  The ransom of His blood.

4  Baptized into the Holy Ghost
  In this accepted hour,
Give us to own the Pentecost,
  And the descending power.
        *G. Rawson.*

## (4) BREAKING OF BREAD

**696** WOUNDED for me, wounded
  for me,
There on the cross He was
  wounded for me;   [am free,
Gone my transgressions and now I
All because Jesus was wounded
  for me.

2  Risen for me, risen for me,
  Up from the grave He has risen for
    me;       [I am free,
  Now evermore from death's sting
  All because Jesus has risen for me.

3  Living for me, living for me,
  There on the Throne He is living
    for me;      [be,
  Saved to the uttermost now I shall
  All because Jesus is living for me.

4  Coming for me, coming for me,
  One day to earth He is coming for
    me;      [I shall see,
  Then with what joy His dear face
  Oh, how I praise Him—He's com-
    ing for me.     *G.W.R.*

**697** HERE, O my Lord, I see Thee
  face to face;
  Here would I touch and handle
    things unseen;
Here grasp with firmer hand
  th'eternal grace,   [lean.
  And all my weariness upon Thee

2 Here would I feed upon the Bread
    of God;
  Here drink with Thee the royal
    Wine of Heaven;
  Here would I lay aside each earthly
    load,              [forgiven.
  Here taste afresh the calm of sin

3 This is the hour of banquet and of
    song,              [for me;
  This is the heav'nly table spread
  Here let me feast, and, feasting,
    still prolong  [ship with Thee.
  The brief, bright hour of fellow-

4 Too soon we rise; the symbols dis-
    appear;            [past and gone;
  The feast, though not the love, is
  The bread and wine remove; but
    Thou art here,     [and Sun.
  Nearer than ever; still my Shield

5 Mine is the sin, but Thine the
    righteousness;
  Mine is the guilt, but Thine the
    cleansing blood:
  Here is my robe, my refuge, and
    my peace—      [Lord, my God.
  Thy blood, Thy righteousness, O

6 Feast after feast thus comes, and
    passes by;         [Feast above,
  Yet, passing, points to the glad
  Giving sweet foretaste of the festal
    joy,               [bliss and love.
  The Lamb's great Bridal Feast of
                    *Horatius Bonar.*

**698** O CHRIST, what burdens bowed
    Thy head!
  Our load was laid on Thee;
  Thou stoodest in the sinner's stead,
  Didst bear all ill for me.
  A Victim led, Thy blood was shed,
    Now there's no load for me.

2 Death and the curse were in our
    cup,
  O Christ, 'twas full for Thee!
  But Thou hast drained the last
    dark drop,
  'Tis empty now for me.
  That bitter cup, love drank it up,
    Now blessing's draught for me.

3 The tempest's awful voice was
    heard,
  O Christ, it broke on Thee!

Thy open bosom was my ward,
  It braved the storm for me:
Thy form was scarred, Thy visage
    marred;
  Now cloudless peace for me.

4 For me, Lord Jesus, Thou hast
    died,
  And I have died in Thee:
Thou'rt risen—my bands are all
    untied;
  And now Thou liv'st in me;
When purified, made white and
  Thy glory then for me!    [tried,
                    *Anne Ross Cousin.*

**699** FAIREST of all the earth beside,
    Chiefest of all unto Thy bride,
  Fulness divine in Thee I see,
  Wonderful Man of Calvary.

    That Man of Calvary
    Has won my heart from me,
    And died to set me free,
    Blest Man of Calvary !

2 Granting the sinner life and peace,
  Granting the captive sweet release,
  Shedding His blood to make us
    free,
  Merciful Man of Calvary!

3 Giving the gifts obtained for men,
  Pouring out love beyond our ken,
  Giving us spotless purity,
  Bountiful Man of Calvary!

4 Comfort of all my earthly way,
  Jesus, I'll meet Thee some sweet
    day;
  Centre of glory Thee I'll see,
  Wonderful Man of Calvary!
                    *M. P. Ferguson.*

**700** WHEN the Paschal evening fell
    Deep on Kedron's hallowed
    dell,
  When around the festal board
  Sate th'Apostles with their Lord,
  Then His parting word He said,
  Blessed the cup and brake the
    bread—
  " This whene'er ye do and see,
  Evermore remember Me."

2 Years have passed: in every clime,
  Changing with the changing time,
  Varying through a thousand forms,
  Torn by factions, rocked by storms,

Still the sacred table spread,
Flowing cup and broken bread,
With that parting word agree,
" Drink and eat; remember Me."

3 When by treason, doubt, unrest,
Sinks the soul, dismayed, opprest;
When the shadows of the tomb
Close us round with deepening gloom,
Then bethink us at that board
Of the sorrowing, suffering Lord,
Who, when tried and grieved as we,
Dying, said, " Remember Me."

4 When in this thanksgiving feast
We would give to God our best,
From the treasures of His might
Seeking life and love and light;
Then, O Friend of human-kind,
Make us true and firm of mind,
Pure of heart, in spirit free;
Thus may we remember Thee.
*A. P. Stanley.*

**701** SWEET the moments, rich in blessing
Which before the Cross I spend,
Life and health and peace possessing,
From the sinner's dying Friend!

2 Here I rest, for ever viewing
Mercy poured in streams of blood:
Precious drops, my soul bedewing,
Plead, and claim my peace with God.

3 Truly blessèd is this station,
Low before His Cross to lie,
While I see divine compassion
Beaming in His languid eye.

4 Here it is I find my heaven,
While upon the Lamb I gaze;
Love I much?—I've much forgiven,—
I'm a miracle of grace.

5 Love and grief my heart dividing,
With my tears His feet I'll bathe;
Constant still in faith abiding,—
Life deriving from His death.
*W. Shirley.*

**702** JESUS, Thou joy of loving hearts, [men!
Thou fount of life, Thou light of

From the best bliss that earth imparts
We turn unfilled to Thee again.

2 Thy truth unchanged hath ever stood, [call;
Thou savest those that on Thee call!
To them that seek Thee, Thou art good, [all!
To them that find Thee, All in all!

3 We taste Thee, O Thou living bread, [still:
And long to feast upon Thee still:
We drink of Thee, the fountain-head, [to fill.
And thirst our souls from Thee to fill.

4 Our restless spirits yearn for Thee,
Where'er our changeful lot is cast, [see,
Glad when Thy gracious smile we see,
Blest when our faith can hold Thee fast.

5 O Jesus, ever with us stay!
Make all our moments calm and bright;
Chase the dark night of sin away:
Shed o'er the world Thy holy light. *Bernard of Clairvaux.*

**703** WHEN I saw the cleansing fountain
Open wide for all my sin,
I obeyed the Spirit's wooing
When He said " Wilt thou be clean?"

I will praise Him, I will praise Him, praise Him,
Praise the Lamb for sinners slain : . . . .
Give Him glory all ye people,
For His blood has washed away my stain.

2 Though the way seemed straight and narrow,
All I claimed was swept away;
My ambition, plans and wishes,
At my feet in ashes lay.

3 Then God's fire upon the altar
Of my heart was set aflame;
I shall never cease to praise Him,
Glory! glory! to His name.

4 Blessèd be the name of Jesus,
I'm so glad He took me in;
He has pardoned my transgressions,
He has cleansed my heart from sin. *Mrs. M. J. Harris.*

**704** ACCORDING to Thy gracious word,
In meek humility,
This will I do, my dying Lord:
I will remember Thee.

2 Thy body, broken for my sake,
My bread from heaven shall be;
Thy testamental cup I take,
And thus remember Thee.

3 Gethsemane can I forget?
Or there Thy conflict see,
Thine agony and bloody sweat,
And not remember Thee?

4 When to the cross I turn mine eyes,
And rest on Calvary,
O Lamb of God, my sacrifice,
I must remember Thee : —

5 Remember Thee, and all Thy pains,
And all Thy love to me;
Yea, while a breath, a pulse remains,
Will I remember Thee.

6 And when these failing lips grow dumb,
And mind and memory flee,
When Thou shalt in Thy kingdom come,
Then, Lord, remember me.
*J. Montgomery.*

**705** FOR the bread and for the wine,
For the pledge that seals Him [mine,
For the words of love divine,
We give Thee thanks, O Lord.

2 For the feast of love and peace,
Bidding all our sorrows cease,
Earnest of the kingdom's bliss,
We give Thee thanks, O Lord.

3 Only bread and only wine,
Yet to faith the solemn sign
Of the heav'nly and divine!
We give Thee thanks, O Lord.

4 For the words that turn our eye
To the cross of Calvary,
Bidding us in faith draw nigh,
We give Thee thanks, O Lord.

5 For the words that fragrance breathe,
These poor symbols underneath,
Words that His own peace bequeath,
We give Thee thanks, O Lord.

6 For the words that tell of home,
Pointing us beyond the tomb,
"Do ye this until I come,"
We give Thee thanks, O Lord.
*Horatius Bonar.*

**706** ONCE, only once, and once for all,
His precious life He gave;
Before the Cross in faith we fall,
And own Him strong to save.

2 "One off'ring, single and complete,"
With lips and hearts we say;
And what He never can repeat
He shows forth day by day.

3 For as the priest of Aaron's line
Within the holiest stood,
And sprinkled all the mercy-seat
With sacrificial blood :

4 So He, who once atonement wrought,
Our Priest of endless power,
Presents Himself for those He bought
In that dark noontide hour.

5 His manhood pleads where now it lives
On heav'n's eternal throne,
And where in mystic pow'r He gives
His presence to His own.

6 And so we show Thy death, O Lord,
Till Thou again appear,
And feel when we approach Thy board,
We have an altar here.
*W. Bright.*

**707** I HEAR the words of love,
I gaze upon the blood,
I see the mighty Sacrifice,
And I have peace with God.

2 'Tis everlasting peace!
Sure as Jehovah's name;
'Tis stable as His steadfast throne,
For evermore the same.

3 The clouds may go and come,
And storms may sweep my sky—
This blood-sealed friendship changes not;
The cross is ever nigh.

4  My love is ofttimes low,
My joy still ebbs and flows;
But peace with Him remains the same,
No change Jehovah knows.

5  I change, He changes not,
The Christ can never die;
His love, not mine, the resting place,
His truth, not mine, the tie.
*Horatius Bonar.*

**708**  BY Christ redeemed, in Christ restored,
We keep the memory adored,
And show the death of our dear Lord
Until He come.  [Lord

2  His body, broken in our stead,
Is seen in this memorial bread;
And so our feeble love is fed
Until He come.

3  The drops of His dread agony,
His life-blood shed for us, we see;
The wine shall tell the mystery
Until He come.

4  And thus that dark betrayal night
With the last advent we unite,
By one blest chain of loving rite,
Until He come.

5  O blessèd hope! With this elate,
Let not our hearts be desolate,
But, strong in faith, in patience wait
Until He come.
*Geo. Rawson.*

**709**  SAVIOUR, we remember Thee!
Thy deep woe and agony,
All Thy suff'ring on the tree:
Saviour, we adore Thee!

2  Calvary! O Calvary!
Mercy's vast unfathomed sea,
Love, eternal love to me:
Saviour, we adore Thee!

3  Darkness hung around Thy head,
When for sin Thy blood was shed,
Victim in the sinner's stead;
Saviour, we adore Thee!

4  Jesus, Lord, Thou now art risen!
Thou hast all our sins forgiven;
Haste we to our home in heaven:
Saviour, we adore Thee!

5  Soon, with joyful, glad surprise,
We shall hear Thy word—Arise!
Mounting upward to the skies:
Glory, glory, glory!

6  Saviour, we Thy love adore;
We will praise Thee more and more;  [shore;
Spread Thy Name from shore to
Saviour, we adore Thee!

**710**  " TILL He come!" Oh, let the words
Linger on the trembling chords;
Let the " little while " between
In their golden light be seen;
Let us think how heaven and home
Lie beyond that " Till He come!"

2  When the weary ones we love
Enter on their rest above—
Seems the earth so poor and vast?—
All our life-joy overcast?
Hush! be every murmur dumb;
It is only " Till He come!"

3  Clouds and conflicts round us press;
Would we have one sorrow less?
All the sharpness of the cross,
All that tells the world is loss—
Death, and darkness, and the tomb—
Only whisper " Till He come!"

4  See, the feast of love is spread,
Drink the wine and break the bread—
Sweet memorials—till the Lord
Call us round His heavenly board;
Some from earth, from glory some,
Severed only " Till He come!"
*E. H. Bickersteth.*

### (5) FELLOWSHIP OF SAINTS

**711**  BEHOLD, how good a thing
It is to dwell in peace;
How pleasing to our King
This fruit of righteousness;
When brethren all in one agree,
Who know the joys of unity!

2  When all are sweetly joined,
(True followers of the Lamb)
The same in heart and mind,
And think and speak the same;
And all in love together dwell;
The comfort is unspeakable.

3 Where unity takes place,
　The joys of heaven we prove;
This is the gospel grace,
　The unction from above,
The Spirit on all believers shed,
　Descending swift from Christ our
　　Head.

4 Where unity is found,
　The sweet anointing grace
Extends to all around,
　And consecrates the place;
To every waiting soul it comes,
And fills it with divine perfumes.

5 Grace every morning new,
　And every night we feel;
The soft refreshing dew
　That falls on Hermon's hill!
On Zion it doth sweetly fall;
The grace of one descends on all.

6 E'en now our Lord doth pour
　The blessing from above,
A kindly, gracious shower
　Of heart-reviving love,
The former and the latter rain,
The love of God and love of man.
*Charles Wesley.*

**712** AND are we yet alive,
　　And see each other's face?
Glory and praise to Jesus give
　For His redeeming grace!

2　Preserved by power divine
　　To full salvation here,
Again in Jesu's praise we join,
　And in His sight appear.

3　What troubles have we seen,
　　What conflicts have we passed,
Fightings without and fears within,
　Since we assembled last!

4　But out of all the Lord
　　Hath brought us by His love;
And still He doth His help afford,
　And hides our life above.

5　Then let us make our boast
　　Of His redeeming power,
Which saves us to the uttermost,
　Till we can sin no more:

6　Let us take up the cross,
　　Till we the crown obtain;
And gladly reckon all things loss,
　So we may Jesus gain.
*Charles Wesley.*

**713**　BLEST be the tie that binds
　　　Our hearts in Christian love;
The fellowship of kindred minds
　Is like to that above.

2　Before our Father's throne,
　　We pour our ardent prayers;
Our fears, our hopes, our aims are
　　one,
　Our comforts and our cares.

3　We share our mutual woes;
　　Our mutual burdens bear;
And often for each other flows
　The sympathizing tear.

4　When we asunder part,
　　It gives us inward pain:
But we shall still be joined in heart,
　And hope to meet again.

5　This glorious hope revives
　　Our courage by the way,
While each in expectation lives,
　And longs to see the day.

6　From sorrow, toil and pain,
　　And sin we shall be free;
And perfect love and friendship
　　reign
　Through all eternity.
*John Fawcett.*

**714**　COME, ye that love the Lord,
　　　And let your joys be known;
Join in a song with sweet accord,
　And thus surround the throne.

We're marching to Zion,
Beautiful, beautiful, Zion :
We're marching upward to Zion,
The beautiful city of God.

2　Let those refuse to sing
　　Who never knew our God:
But children of the heavenly King
　Shall speak their joys abroad.

3　The hill of Zion yields
　　A thousand sacred sweets;
Before we reach the heavenly fields,
　Or walk the golden streets.

4　Then let our songs abound,
　　And every tear be dry;
We're marching through Imman-
　　uel's ground
　To fairer worlds on high.
*Isaac Watts.*

**715** WE love the place, O God,
    Wherein   Thine   honour
        dwells;
The joy of Thine abode
    All earthly joy excels.

2 It is the house of prayer,
    Wherein Thy servants meet;
And Thou, O Lord, art there,
    Thy chosen flock to greet.

3 We love the word of life,
    The word that tells of peace,
Of comfort in the strife
    And joys that never cease.

4 We love to sing below
    Of mercies freely given;
But O we long to know
    The triumph song of heaven!

5 Lord Jesus, give us grace,
    On earth to love Thee more,
In heaven to see Thy face,
    And with Thy saints adore.
            *William Bullock.*

**716** BRETHREN in Christ, and well
      beloved,
    To Jesus and His servants dear,
Enter and show yourselves ap-
      proved;
    Enter and find that God is here.

2 Welcome from earth: lo, the right
      hand
    Of fellowship to you we give!
With open hearts and hands we
      stand,
    And you in Jesus' name receive.

3 Say, are your hearts resolved as
      ours?        [love;
Then let them burn with sacred
Then let them taste the heavenly
      powers,
    Partakers of the joys above.

4 Thou God that answerest by fire,
    The burning Spirit now impart;
And let the flames of pure desire
    Rise from the altar of our heart.

5 In part we only know Thee here,
    But wait Thy coming from
      above:      [near,
And we shall then behold Thee
And we shall all be lost in love.
            *Charles Wesley.*

**717** COME, brethren dear, that
      know the Lord,
Who taste the sweets of Jesus' word,
    In Jesus' ways go on;
Our poverty and trials here,
    Will only make us richer there,
    When we arrive at home.

2 We feel that heaven is now begun,
    It issues from th'eternal throne,
    From Jesus' throne on high;
It comes in floods we can't contain,
We drink, and drink, and drink
    And yet we still are dry. [again,

3 But when to that bright world we
      come      [throne,
    And all surround the glorious
We'll drink a full supply;
Jesus will lead the ransomed forth
To living streams of richest worth,
    That never will run dry.

4 O then we'll shine, and shout, and
      sing,      [ring,
    And make the heavenly arches
    When all the saints get home;
Come on, come on, my brethren
      dear,
We soon shall meet together there,
    For Jesus bids you come.

5 Amen! Amen! my soul replies,
I'm bound to meet Him in the
      skies.
    And claim a mansion there;
Now here's my heart, and here's
    my hand,
To meet you in the heavenly land,
    Where we shall part no more.

**718** ABBA, Father! we approach
      Thee
    In our Saviour's precious name;
We, Thy children, here assembling,
    Access to Thy presence claim.
From our sin His blood hath
      washed us;      [draw near;
'Tis through Him our souls
And Thy Spirit, too, hath taught us,
    " Abba, Father!" name so dear.

2 Once as prodigals we wandered,
    In our folly far from Thee!
But Thy grace, o'er sin abounding,
    Rescued us from misery.
Thou Thy prodigals hast pardoned,

Loved us with a Father's love;
Welcomed us with joy o'erflowing,
E'en to dwell with Thee above.

3 Clothed in garments of salvation,
At Thy table is our place;
We rejoice, and Thou rejoicest,
In the riches of Thy grace.
"It is meet," we hear Thee saying,
"We should merry be and glad;
I have found My once lost chil-
dren,                    [dead."
Now they live who once were

4 Abba, Father! all adore Thee,
All rejoice in heaven above;
While in us they learn the wonders
Of Thy wisdom, power, and love.
Soon, before Thy throne assembled,
All Thy children shall proclaim,
"Glory, everlasting glory,
Be to God and to the Lamb!"

**719** O DAY of rest and gladness,
O day of joy and light,
O balm of care and sadness,
Most beautiful, most bright!
On thee the high and lowly,
Through ages joined in tune,
Sing, holy, holy, holy,
To the great God Triune.

2 On thee, at the creation,
The light first had its birth;
On thee, for our salvation,
Christ rose from depths of earth;
On thee, our Lord victorious
The Spirit sent from heaven:
And thus on thee most glorious
A triple light was given.

3 Thou art a port protected
From storms that round us rise;
A garden intersected
With streams of paradise;
Thou art a cooling fountain
In life's dry dreary sand;
From thee, like Pisgah's mountain,
We view our promised land.

4 Thou art a holy ladder,
Where angels go and come;
Each Sunday finds us gladder,
Nearer to heaven, our home;
A day of sweet refection,
Thou art a day of love;
A day of resurrection
From earth to things above.

5 To-day on weary nations
The heavenly manna falls;
To holy convocations
The silver trumpet calls,
Where gospel light is glowing
With pure and radiant beams,
And living water flowing
With soul-refreshing streams,

6 New graces ever gaining
From this our day of rest,
We reach the rest remaining
To spirits of the blest.
To Holy Ghost be praises,
To Father, and to Son;
The Church her voice upraises
To Thee, blest Three in One.
*C. Wordsworth.*

**720** BEHOLD, what love, what
boundless love,
The Father hath bestowed
On sinners lost, that we should be
Now called the sons of God!

Behold, what manner of love ! . . .
What manner of love the Father hath
bestowed upon us,
That we, that we should be called, . . .
Should be called the sons of God.

2 No longer far from Him, but now
By " precious blood " made nigh;
Accepted in the " Well-beloved,"
Near to God's heart we lie.

3 What we in glory soon shall be,
It doth not yet appear;
But when our precious Lord we see,
We shall His image bear.

4 With such a blessèd hope in view,
We would more holy be,
More like our risen, glorious Lord,
Whose face we soon shall see.
*M. S. Sullivan.*

**721** THE hallowed morn is dear to
me,                    [the day,
When prayer and praise awake
Or friends with sacred minstrelsy,
Call me from earthly cares away;

2 And dear to me the sacred hour
Employed within Thy courts, O
Lord!
To feel devotion's soothing power,
And taste the manna of Thy
word;

3 And dear to me the loud " Amen,"
 Which echoes through the blest
 abode,
Which swells, and sinks, and swells
 again, [God.
Dies on the walls, but lives with

4 In secret I have often prayed,
 And still the anxious tears would
 fall;
But on Thy secret altar laid,
 The fire descends and dries them
 all.

5 Let men of pleasure strike their
 lyre, [charms,
Of broken Sabbaths sing the
But I, in prayer's swift car of fire,
 Will rise to Jesus' sheltering arms.
 *J. W. Cunningham.*

**722** God be with you till we meet
 again, [you,
By His counsels guide, uphold
With His sheep securely fold you:
God be with you till we meet again!

2 God be with you till we meet again,
 'Neath His wings securely hide
 you,
 Daily manna still provide you:
God be with you till we meet again!

3 God be with you till we meet again,
 When life's perils thick con-
 found you, [you:
 Put His arms unfailing round
God be with you till we meet again!

4 God be with you till we meet again,
 Keep love's banner floating o'er
 you, [before you:
 Smite death's threatening wave
God be with you till we meet again!
 *J. E. Rankin.*

## (6) MARRIAGE

**723** O Perfect Love, all human
 thought transcending,
Lowly we kneel in prayer before
 Thy throne,
That theirs may be the love which
 knows no ending
Whom Thou for evermore dost
 join in one.

2 O perfect Life, be Thou their full
 assurance [faith,
 Of tender charity and steadfast
Of patient hope, and quiet brave
 endurance,
 With childlike trust that fears
 nor pain nor death.

3 Grant them the joy which brightens
 earthly sorrow;
 Grant them the peace which
 calms all earthly strife,
And to life's day the glorious unknown morrow
 That dawns upon eternal love
 and life.
 *Dorothy F. Gurney.*

**724** O Father, all-creating,
 Whose wisdom and Whose
 power
First bound two lives together
 In Eden's primal hour;
Today to these Thy children
 Thine earliest gift renew;—
A home by Thee made blessèd,
 A love by Thee kept true.

2 O Saviour, Guest most bounteous
 Of old in Galilee,
Vouchsafe to-day Thy presence,
 With these who wait on Thee;
Their store of earthly gladness
 Transform to heavenly wine,
And teach them, in the tasting,
 To know the gift is Thine.

3 O Spirit of the Father,
 Breathe on them from above,—
So searching in Thy pureness,
 So tender in Thy love;
That guarded by Thy presence,
 From sin and strife kept free,
Their lives may own Thy guidance
 Their hearts be ruled by Thee.

4 Except Thou build it, Father,
 The house is built in vain;
Except Thou, Lord, sustain it,
 The joy will turn to pain:
But nought can break the union
 Of hearts in Thee made one,
And love which Thou hast hal-
 lowed,
 Is endless love begun.
 *John Ellerton.*

**725** THE voice that breathed o'er Eden,
That earliest wedding day,
The primal marriage blessing,
It hath not passed away.

2 Still in the pure espousal
Of Christian man and maid
The Holy Three are with us,
The threefold grace is said,

3 For dower of blessèd children,
For love and faith's sweet sake,
For high mysterious union
Which nought on earth may break.

4 Be present, heavenly Father,
To give away this bride,
As Eve Thou gav'st to Adam
Out of his own pierced side.

5 Be present, gracious Saviour,
To join their loving hands,
As Thou didst bind two natures
In Thine eternal bands.

6 Be present, Holy Spirit,
To bless them as they kneel,
As Thou for Christ the Bridegroom
The heavenly spouse dost seal.

7 O spread Thy pure wings o'er them!
Let no ill power find place,
When onward through life's journey
The hallowed path they trace,

8 To cast their crowns before Thee,
In perfect sacrifice,
Till to the home of gladness
With Christ's own bride they rise.
*John Keble.*

### (7) INFANT DEDICATION

**726** THY Name, O Lord, we bless,
Our thankful hearts adore;
Thy lavish gifts confess,
Of rich and bounteous store.

2 To us Thou hast made known
Heaven's pure felicity;
A gracious gift we own
Of sweet simplicity.

3 What shall we render Thee,
Or how Thy love repay?
This very gift shall be
Our glad response to-day.

4 O Shepherd heart and kind,
Thy tender lamb now bless;
Safe kept by Thee to find
The path of righteousness.

5 Thy grace we seek, O Lord,
This life to guard and teach
According to Thy Word,
By prayerful act and speech.

6 Our charge we undertake,
Humbly Thine aid implore;
Vow Thee, for Thy dear sake,
Our all for evermore.
*L. F. W. Woodford.*

**727** JESUS loves the little children,
Once He took them on His knee,
Gently put His arms around them,
Saying " Let them come to Me!"

2 Oh! He loves to see them kneeling,
And with hands together pray;
Loves to hear them call Him Jesus,
If they mean the words they say.

3 If they trust Him as their Saviour,
He will wash their sins away;
He will take their hand and lead them
All along the narrow way.

4 He would have them love each other,
And be truthful, meek, and mild,
Doing as their parents bid them,
As He did when once a Child.

**728** SEE Israel's gentle Shepherd stand
With all-engaging charms;
Hark! how He calls the tender lambs,
And folds them in His arms.

2 Permit them to approach, He cries,
Nor scorn their humble name!
For 'twas to bless such souls as these
The Lord of angels came.

3 We bring them, Lord, in thankful hands,
And yield them up to Thee;
Joyful that we ourselves are Thine,
Thine let our children be.
*Philip Doddridge.*

**729** WHEN mothers of Salem
Their children brought to
Jesus,
The stern disciples drove them back
And bade them depart:
But Jesus saw them ere they fled,
And sweetly smiled and kindly said,
" Suffer little children to come unto
Me."

2 " For I will receive them,
And fold them in My bosom;
I'll be a Shepherd to those lambs,
Oh, drive them not away!
For if their hearts to Me they give,
They shall with Me in glory live,
" Suffer little children to come unto
Me."

3 How kind was our Saviour
To bid those children welcome!
But there are many thousands
Who have never heard His name;
The Bible they have never read;
They know not that the Saviour said,
" Suffer little children to come unto
Me."

4 Oh! soon may the heathen
Of every tribe and nation
Fulfil Thy blessèd word,
And cast their idols all away;
Oh! shine upon them from above,
And show Thyself a God of love,
Teach the little children to come unto
Thee.

*W. M. Hutchings.*

# Section XII

## DIVINE HEALING

**730** HE healed them all—the blind,
the lame, the palsied,
The sick in body and the weak in
mind,
Whoever came, no matter how
afflicted, [to find.
Were sure a sovereign remedy

2 His word gave health, His touch
restored the vigour
To every weary pain-exhausted
frame;
And all He asked before He gave
the blessing [those who came.
Was simple faith in Him from

3 And is our Lord, the kind, the
good, the tender,
Less loving now than in those
days of old?
Or is it that our faith is growing
feeble, [cold?
And Christian energy is waxing

4 Why do we not with equal expectation, [Lord in prayer
Now bring our sick ones to the
Right through the throng of unbelieving scruples
Up to His very side and leave
them there?

5 He never health refused in bygone
ages, [ment " away;
Nor feared to take the " chastise-
Then why not ask it now, instead
of praying
For " patience " to endure from
day to day?

**731** SHE only touched the hem of
His garment
As to His side she stole,
Amid the crowd that gathered
around Him,
And straightway she was whole.
Oh, touch the hem of His garment,
And thou, too, shalt be free ;
His saving power this very hour
Shall give new life to thee.

2 She came in fear and trembling be-
fore Him,
She knew her Lord had come;
She felt that from Him virtue had
healed her.
The mighty deed was done.

3 He turned with, " Daughter, be of
good comfort,
Thy faith hath made thee whole;"
And peace that passeth all under-
standing
With gladness filled her soul.
*Geo. F. Root.*

**732** AT even, ere the sun was set,
    The sick, O Lord, around
        Thee lay;
O in what divers pains they met!
O with what joy they went away!

2 Once more 'tis eventide and we,
    Oppressed with various ills, draw
        near;
What if Thy form we cannot see,
    We know and feel that Thou art
        here.

3 O Saviour Christ, our woes dispel:
    For some are sick, and some are
        sad,
And some have never loved Thee
    well,          [had.
And some have lost the love they

4 And some are pressed with worldly
    care,         [doubt,
And some are tried with sinful
And some such grievous passions
    tear,          [out,
That only Thou canst cast them

5 And some have found the world is
    vain,        [not free;
    Yet from the world they break
And some have friends who give
    them pain,      [Thee.
Yet have not sought a friend in

6 O Saviour Christ Thou too art
    Man;      [ted, tried;
Thou hast been troubled, temp-
Thy kind but searching glance can
    scan
The very wounds that shame
    would hide!

7 Thy touch has still its ancient
    power;      [less fall;
No word from Thee can fruit-
Hear in this solemn evening hour,
And in Thy mercy heal us all.

                    *H. Twells.*

**733** THINE arm, O Lord, in days of
      old
    Was strong to heal and save;
It triumphed o'er disease and death,
    O'er darkness and the grave.
To Thee they went, the blind, the
      dumb,
    The palsied and the lame,
The leper with his tainted life,
    The sick with fevered frame;

2 And lo! Thy touch brought life
    and health,
    Gave speech, and strength, and
      sight;
And youth renewed, and frenzy
    calmed,
    Owned Thee the Lord of light.
And now, O Lord, be near to bless,
    Almighty as of yore,
In crowded street, by restless couch,
    As by Gennesaret's shore.

3 Be Thou our great Deliverer still,
    Thou Lord of life and death;
Restore and quicken, soothe and
    bless,
    With Thine Almighty breath.
To hands that work, and eyes that
    see,
Give wisdom's heavenly lore,
That whole and sick and weak and
    strong
    May praise Thee evermore.

                *E. H. Plumptre.*

**734** JESUS is the same for ever,
    As of old, so now today;
All the hosts of hell endeavour
    Vainly to obstruct His sway.
In His people's hearts He reigneth,
    Finishes what He begins;
Jesus still " all power " retaineth,
    Saves His people from their sins.

2 Jesus is the same for ever;
    Yes, He heals the sick to-day.
As of old, so now, He never
    Turns one suffering child away.
He can cure the worst diseases,
    For He understands our frame;
Bore our griefs, and so releases
    All who dare their rights to
      claim.

3 Jesus is the same for ever;
    Still He says " In Me abide."
From His love no power can sever
    Those who in their Lord confide.
Sweetly from all care He frees us,
    Ours the comfort—His the
      shame.
Blessèd Saviour; precious Jesus!
    There's no music like Thy name.

                    *T. Price.*

**735** O Saviour Christ, at Thy behest
We gather in Thy Name
As humble suppliants, to be blest,
That in our need so full confessed
Thy healing power may claim.

2 Behold the sick, the blind, the lame!
To whom else can we go?
Oh, show to us Thou art the same
As when Thy touch healed all who came
Thy freedom full to know.

3 For Thou didst share in days of yore
Our sorrow and our woe; [yore
Oh, who can tell Thine anguish sore,
That from Thy stripes and wounds [may pour
A cleansing, healing flow.

4 Thou didst the perfect work complete:
Our all is found in Thee! [plete:
The scars so deep in hands and feet
Are pledge of our redemption sweet,
Deliverance full and free.

5 Our dear High Priest, on Thee we wait,
Thou sympathising Friend.
Thyself dost feel our weak estate;
Do Thou, in Thy compassion great,
Thy grace to each extend.

6 Thy wondrous virtue now impart:
Thy healing power display!
Bid doubt and anxious fear depart,
Inspiring faith in every heart
Thy gift to claim this day.

7 O touch our eyes: so shall we see
That Thou art by our side.
Restored and quickened shall we be,
And blessed with perfect liberty,
Shall in Thy life abide.

*L. F. W. Woodford.*

**736** Our blessèd Lord, in this Thy presence sweet,
Behold us lowly bending at Thy feet.
Fain would we meet Thee on this hallowed ground
Where ev'ry Blood-bought blessing may be found.

2 Drawn by the strength of Thine own mighty love,
Gladly we come Thy healing touch to prove. [Thy word—
All power is Thine—we echo back
In heaven and earth, Thou never-changing Lord.

3 We grasp Thy promises so sure, so free, [on Thee.
To all who in their weakness call
Th'effectual fervent prayer Thou dost receive, [dare believe.
With strength renewing all who

4*Thy servants bless who now before Thee stand, [command;
Who here fulfil the word of Thy
And as the anointing oil shall gently flow, [bestow.
Thy heavenly unction on each life

5*As holy hands now minister, with prayer, [hands that bear
May we discern Thy wondrous
The marks of Thine affliction for our sake; [ing take.
And thus in humble faith Thy heal-

6 If to Thine eye that pierces deep within [stain of sin
There stands revealed the hidden
Still unconfessed, Oh, grant us grace that we [purer be.
May purge our lives afresh and

7 Thus joined to Thee our living Head above, [triumph move:
Thy life we share, and in Thy
Knit with our fellow-members here below, [Thy fulness know.
From strength to strength we shall

* These verses may be omitted where not applicable.

*L. F. W. Woodford.*

**737** He healeth me, O blessèd truth,
His mighty Word renews my youth,
By His own power from sickness free,
My precious Saviour healeth me.

He healeth me, He healeth me,
By His own word He healeth me;
His faithful witness I would be,
For by His word He healeth me.

2 Sometimes through testing times I
go, [woe;
Dark seems the way, and full of
But in the furnace though I be,
My great Physician healeth me.

3 Lord, I would spread this truth
abroad,
The mighty power of Thy word;

It's just the same, the blind now see,
And demons at Thy presence flee.

4 For sin and sickness doth depart,
When Thou dost reign within the
heart;
And I from all the curse am free,
Since Christ, my Saviour, healeth
me.

# Section XIII

## WORLD MISSIONS

**738** LET the song go round the
earth,
Jesus Christ is Lord,
Sound His praises, tell His worth,
Be His name adored;
Ev'ry clime and ev'ry tongue
Join the grand, the glorious song.

2 Let the song go round the earth!
From the Eastern sea,
Where the daylight has its birth,
Glad and bright and free;
China's millions join the strains,
Waft them on to India's plains.

3 Let the song go round the earth!
Lands where Islam's sway
Darkly broods o'er home and
hearth
Cast their bonds away!
Let His praise from Afric's shore
Rise and swell her wide lands o'er.

4 Let the song go round the earth!
Where the summer smiles:
Let the notes of holy mirth
Break from distant isles!
Inland forests dark and dim,
Snowbound coasts give back the
hymn.

5 Let the song go round the earth!
Jesus Christ is King!
With the story of His worth
Let the whole world ring!
Him creation all adore,
Evermore and evermore!

*Sarah G. Stock.*

**739** THERE'S a call comes ringing
o'er the restless wave,
Send the light! Send the light!
There are souls to rescue, there are
souls to save,
Send the light! Send the light!

Send the light, . . . the blessèd gospel light,
Let it shine . . . from shore to shore ! . . .
Send the light ! . . . and let its radiant beams
Light the world . . . for evermore. . . .

2 We have heard the Macedonian call
to-day,
Send the light! Send the light!
And a golden off'ring at the cross
we lay,
Send the light! Send the light!

3 Let us pray that grace may every-
where abound,
Send the light! Send the light!
And a Christlike spirit everywhere
be found,
Send the light! Send the light!

4 Let us not grow weary in the work
of love,
Send the light! Send the light!
Let us gather jewels for a crown
above,
Send the light! Send the light!

*Chas. H. Gabriel.*

**740** FLING out the banner! Let it
float [wide,
Skyward and seaward high and
The sun that lights its shining folds,
The cross on which the Saviour
died.

2 Fling out the banner! Angels bend
  In anxious silence o'er the sign,
And vainly seek to comprehend
  The wonder of the love divine.

3 Fling out the banner! Heathen lands
  Shall see from far the glorious
      sight,
And nations crowding to be born
  Baptize their spirits in its light.

4 Fling out the banner! Let it float
  Skyward and seaward, high and
      wide,
Our glory only in the cross,
  Our only hope the Crucified.

5 Fling out the banner! Wide and
      high,
  Seaward and skyward let it shine:
Nor skill, nor might, nor merit
      ours;
  We conquer only in that sign.
                        *G. W. Doane.*

**741** FROM out the splendour of His
          throne, the Majesty on high,
The Lord stooped down to live as
  man, to suffer and to die;
To bear the sin of many and to triumph o'er the grave,
To pass victorious through the
  heavens, the Mighty One to
  save.

2 But darkness covereth the earth, the
  people sleep in death!
They know not God nor can they
  live without His quickening
  breath.
How shall the light of holy love
  illume their sightless eyes,
Except a herald at His call, with
  trumpet voice arise?

3 Yet see! how swift, how beauti-
  ful, the feet of them that bring
Good tidings of rejoicing from their
  Saviour and their King!
As royal messengers they speed to
  bear the heavenly light
Of full redemption, gifted free, to
  captive sons of night.

4 They move at His Divine command
  and in His conquering Name;
They preach the wonders of His
  love with Pentecostal flame.

The silver tones of Jubilee peal out
  o'er land and sea:
"Awake, awake, ye souls of men!
  Christ Jesus sets you free!"

5 The Isles re-echo to the theme of
  liberty and peace;
A myriad captives hail the Word
  and claim a full release.
They own one Lord and Master
  and they gather round His feet,
One family of freedmen in one
  fellowship complete.

6 Oh make us, Lord, ambassadors, to
  bear this Word of grace
Across the main, o'er hill and plain,
  to every tribe and race!
So shall Thy glory be revealed, Thy
  saving power be known,
And ransomed nations shall return,
  to worship at Thy throne.
                    *L. F. W. Woodford.*

**742** FROM the brightness of the
          glory,
  "Go ye forth," He said;
"Heal the sick, and cleanse the
  Raise the dead."        [lepers,

2 "Freely give I thee the treasure,
    Freely give the same;
Take no store of gold or silver—
    Take My Name.

3 Thou art fitted for the journey,
    How so long it be;
Thou shalt come, unworn, un-
    Back to Me.        [wearied

4 Thou shalt tell me in the glory
    All that thou hast done,
Setting forth alone; returning
    Not alone.

5 Thou shalt bring the ransomed with
    thee,
  They with songs shall come
As the golden sheaves of harvest,
  Gathered home."
                    *tr. Frances Bevan.*

**743** "FOR My sake and the Gos-
          pel's, go
  And tell Redemption's story;"
His heralds answer, "Be it so,
  And Thine, Lord, all the glory!"
They preach His birth, His life, His
  cross,

The love of His atonement,
For whom they count the world but
loss,
His Easter, His enthronement.

2 Hark, hark, the trump of Jubilee
Proclaims to every nation,
From pole to pole, by land and sea,
Glad tidings of salvation:
As nearer draws the day of doom,
While still the battle rages,
The heavenly Dayspring, through
the gloom
Breaks on the night of ages.

3 Still on and on the anthems spread
Of Hallelujah voices,
In concert with the holy dead
The warrior-Church rejoices;
Their snow-white robes are washed
in blood,
Their golden harps are ringing;
Earth, and the Paradise of God,
One triumph-song are singing.

3 He comes, whose Advent Trumpet
drowns
The last of Time's evangels—
Emmanuel crowned with many
crowns,
The Lord of saints and angels:
O Life, Light, Love, the great I
AM,
Triune, who changest never;
The throne of God and of the
Lamb
Is Thine, and Thine for ever!

*E. H. Bickersteth.*

**744** SEE how great a flame aspires,
Kindled by a spark of grace!
Jesu's love the nations fires,
Sets the kingdoms on a blaze.
To bring fire on earth He came;
Kindled in some hearts it is;
O that all might catch the flame,
All partake the glorious bliss!

2 When He first the work begun,
Small and feeble was His day;
Now the word doth swiftly run,
Now it wins its widening way;
More and more it spreads and
Ever mighty to prevail; [grows
Sin's strongholds it now o'erthrows,
Shakes the trembling gates of hell.

3 Sons of God, your Saviour praise!
He the door hath opened wide;
He hath given the word of grace,
Jesu's word is glorified;
Jesus, mighty to redeem,
He alone the work hath wrought;
Worthy is the work of Him,
Him who spake a world from
nought.

4 Saw ye not the cloud arise,
Little as a human hand?
Now it spreads along the skies,
Hangs o'er all the thirsty land:
Lo! the promise of a shower
Drops already from above;
But the Lord will shortly pour
All the Spirit of His love!

*Charles Wesley.*

**745** THE whole wide world for
Jesus—
This shall our watchword be
Upon the highest mountain,
Down by the widest sea—
The whole wide world for Jesus!
To Him all men shall bow,
In city or in prairie
The world for Jesus now!

The whole wide world, the whole wide
world—
Proclaim the Gospel tidings through the
whole wide world ;
Lift up the Cross for Jesus, His banner be
unfurled—
Till every tongue confess Him through the
whole wide world.

2 The whole wide world for Jesus,
Inspires us with the thought
That every son of Adam
Should by His blood be bought;
The whole wide world for Jesus!
O faint not by the way!
The Cross shall surely conquer
In this our glorious day.

3 The whole wide world for Jesus
The marching order sound—
Go ye and preach the Gospel
Wherever man is found,
The whole wide world for Jesus!
Our banner is unfurled—
We battle now for Jesus,
And faith demands the world!

*Catherine Johnson.*

**746** FAR, far away, in heathen
darkness dwelling,
Millions of souls for ever may be
lost;
Who, who will go, salvation's story
telling, [cost?
Looking to Jesus, minding not the

" All power is given unto Me,
All power is given unto Me.
Go ye into all the world and preach the
gospel,
And lo, I am with you alway."

2 See o'er the world wide open doors
inviting, [in!
Soldiers of Christ, arise and enter
Christians, awake! your forces all
uniting, [chains of sin.
Send forth the gospel, break the

3 " Why will ye die?" the voice of
God is calling,
" Why will ye die?" re-echo in
His name!
Jesus hath died to save from death
appalling, [proclaim.
Life and salvation therefore go

4 God speed the day, when those of
ev'ry nation [shall sing;
" Glory to God!" triumphantly
Ransomed, redeemed, rejoicing in
salvation,
Shout " Hallelujah, for the Lord
is King!"

*J. McGranahan.*

**747** TELL the whole wide world of
Jesus, [shore;
Bear the news from shore to
Telling sinners of the Saviour,
Let the light spread more and
more.

Tell the world, . . . the whole wide world :
Bear the news . . . from shore to shore ;
Tell the whole wide world of Jesus,
Praise His name for evermore !

2 Send abroad the gospel heralds,
Let them take the blessèd light
Into every land of darkness,
Piercing through the shades of
night.

3 Yes, we'll send the joyful message
Over mountain, over wave,
Telling everywhere of Jesus,
And His mighty power to save.

4 While we pray for other nations,
Send them help with willing hand,
Let us not forget the home fields—
Jesus for our native land!

*E. E. Hewitt.*

**748** SPEED Thy servants, Saviour,
speed them;
Thou art Lord of wind and
waves: [freed them,
They were bound, but Thou hast
Now they go to free the slaves.
Be Thou with them,
'Tis Thine arm alone that saves.

2 Friends, and home, and all forsaking,
Lord, they go at Thy command;
As their stay Thy promise taking,
While they traverse sea and land:
O be with them!
Lead them safely by the hand.

3 Where no fruit appears to cheer
them,
And they seem to toil in vain,
Then in mercy, Lord, draw near
them,
Then their sinking hopes sustain;
Thus supported,
Let their zeal revive again.

4 In the midst of opposition,
Let them trust, O Lord, in Thee;
When success attends their mission,
Let Thy servants humbler be;
Never leave them,
Till Thy face in heaven they see:

5 There to reap in joy for ever
Fruit that grows from seed here
sown,
There to be with Him who never
Ceases to preserve His own,
And with gladness
Give the praise to Him alone.

*Thomas Kelly.*

**749** FATHER, let Thy kingdom
come,
Let it come with living power;
Speak at length the final word,
Usher in the triumph hour.

2 As it came in days of old,
In the deepest hearts of men,
When Thy martyrs died for Thee,
Let it come, O God, again.

3 Tyrant thrones and idol shrines,
  Let them from their place be
    hurled:
Enter on Thy better reign,
  Wear the crown of this poor
    world.

4 Oh, what long sad years have gone,
  Since Thy Church was taught this
    prayer;                    [wept
  Oh, what eyes have watched and
  For the dawning everywhere.

5 Break, triumphant day of God!
  Break at last our hearts to cheer;
Throbbing souls and holy songs
  Wait to hail Thy dawning here.

6 Empires, temples, sceptres, thrones,
  May they all for God be won;
And, in every human heart,
  Father, let Thy kingdom come.
                    *John Page Hopps.*

**750**  WE have heard a joyful sound,
        Jesus saves;
  Spread the gladness all around,
  Jesus saves;
Bear the news to ev'ry land,
  Climb the steeps and cross the
    waves,
Onward, 'tis our Lord's command,
  Jesus saves.

2 Waft it on the rolling tide,
  Jesus saves;
Tell to sinners far and wide,
  Jesus saves;
Sing, ye islands of the sea,
  Echo back, ye ocean caves,
Earth shall keep her jubilee,
  Jesus saves.

3 Sing above the battle's strife,
  Jesus saves;
By His death and endless life,
  Jesus saves;
Sing it softly through the gloom,
  When the heart for mercy craves,
Sing in triumph o'er the tomb,
  Jesus saves.

4 Give the winds a mighty voice,
  Jesus saves;
Let the nations now rejoice,
  Jesus saves;
Shout salvation full and free,
  Highest hills and deepest caves,
This our song of victory,
  Jesus saves.      *Priscilla J. Owens.*

**751**  FROM Greenland's icy moun-
        tains,
  From India's coral strand,
Where Afric's sunny fountains
  Roll down their golden sand,
From many an ancient river,
  From many a palmy plain,
They call us to deliver
  Their land from error's chain.

2 What though the spicy breezes
  Blow soft o'er Ceylon's Isle,
Though ev'ry prospect pleases,
  And only man is vile;
In vain with lavish kindness,
  The gifts of God are strown,
The heathen in his blindness
  Bows down to wood and stone.

3 Can we, whose souls are lighted
  With wisdom from on high,
Can we to men benighted
  The lamp of life deny?
Salvation! oh, salvation!
  The joyful sound proclaim,
Till each remotest nation
  Has learnt Messiah's name.

4 Waft, waft, ye winds, His story,
  And you, ye waters, roll,
Till, like a sea of glory,
  It spreads from pole to pole;
Till o'er our ransomed nature
  The Lamb for sinners slain,
Redeemer, King, Creator,
  In bliss returns to reign.
                    *Reginald Heber.*

**752**  I HEAR ten thousand voices
        singing
  Their praises to the Lord on high;
Far distant shores and hills are
    ringing                    [joy—
  With anthems of their nations
" Praise ye the Lord! for He has
    given                     [light;
  To lands in darkness hid His
As morning rays light up the
    heaven,                   [night."
  His word has chased away our

2 On China's shores I hear His
    praises,                  [stones;
  From lips that once kissed idol
Soon as His banner He upraises,
  The Spirit moves the breathless
    bones,—                  [and ocean;
" Speed, speed Thy Word o'er land

The Lord in triumph has gone
forth: [tion,
The nations hear with strange emo-
From East to West, from South
to North."

3 The song has sounded o'er the
waters,
And India's plains re-echo joy:
Beneath the moon sit India's daugh-
ters, [ply,—
Soft singing, as the wheel they
" Thanks to Thee, Lord! for hopes
of glory,
For peace on earth to us revealed;

Our cherished idols fell before
Thee,
Thy Spirit has our pardon sealed."

4 Hark! hark! a louder sound is
booming [and sea,
O'er heav'n and earth, o'er land
The angel's trump proclaims His
coming,
Our day of endless Jubilee.
Hail to Thee, Lord! Thy people
praise Thee,
In ev'ry land Thy name we sing,
On heaven's eternal throne upraise
Thee; [glorious King!
Take Thou Thy power, Thou
*H. W. Fox.*

# Section XIV

## THE SECOND COMING OF CHRIST

**753** OUR Lord is now rejected
And by the world disowned:
By the many still neglected,
And by the few enthroned;
But soon He'll come in glory!
The hour is drawing nigh,
For the crowning day is coming
By and by.

Oh, the crowning day is coming!
Is coming by and by,
When our Lord shall come in " power "
And " glory " from on high!
Oh the glorious sight will gladden
Each waiting, watchful eye,
In the crowning day that's coming
By and by.

2 The heav'ns shall glow with
splendour;
But brighter far than they,
The saints shall shine in glory,
As Christ shall them array:
The beauty of the Saviour
Shall dazzle ev'ry eye,
In the crowning day that's coming
By and by.

3 Our pain shall then be over;
We'll sin and sigh no more;
Behind us all of sorrow,
And naught but joy before—

A joy in our Redeemer,
As we to Him are nigh,
In the crowning day that's coming
By and by.

4 Let all that look for hasten
The coming joyful day
By earnest consecration,
To walk the narrow way;
By gath'ring in the lost ones
For whom our Lord did die,
For the crowning day that's coming
By and by.   *El Nathan.*

**754** HAIL to the Lord's Anointed,
Great David's greater Son;
Hail in the time appointed,
His reign on earth begun!
He comes to break oppression,
To set the captive free;
To take away transgression,
And rule in equity.

2 He shall come down like showers
Upon the fruitful earth:
And love, joy, hope, like flowers,
Spring in His path to birth.
Before Him on the mountains
Shall Peace, the herald go;
And righteousness in fountains
From hill to valley flow.

3 Kings shall fall down before Him,
  And gold and incense bring;
All nations shall adore Him,
  His praise all people sing.
For He shall have dominion
  O'er river, sea, and shore,
Far as the eagle's pinion
  Or dove's light wing can soar.
                    *J. Montgomery.*

**755** JESUS may come today,
    Glad day, glad day!
And I would see my Friend;
Dangers and troubles would end
If Jesus should come today.

    Glad day, glad day!
    Is it the crowning day?
    I'll live for today, nor anxious be
    Jesus my Lord I soon shall see.
    Glad day, glad day!
    Is it the crowning day?

2  I may go home today,
    Glad day, glad day!
Seemeth I hear their song;
Hail to the radiant throng!
If I should go home today.

3  Why should I anxious be?
    Glad day, glad day!
Lights appear on the shore,
Storms will affright nevermore,
For He is " at hand " today.

4  Faithful I'll be today,
    Glad day, glad day!
And I will freely tell
Why I should love Him so well,
For He is my all today.
              *George Walker Whitcomb.*

**756** THERE'S a light upon the
    mountains, and the day is at
    the spring,
When our eyes shall see the beauty
    and the glory of the King:
Weary was our heart with waiting,
    and the night-watch seemed so
    long;
But His triumph-day is breaking,
    and we hail it with a song.

2 In the fading of the starlight we can
    see the coming morn;
And the lights of men are paling in
    the splendours of the dawn:
For the eastern skies are glowing as
    with light of hidden fire,
And the hearts of men are stirring
    with the throbs of deep desire.

3 There's a hush of expectation, and
    a quiet in the air;
And the breath of God is moving
    in the fervent breath of prayer:
For the suff'ring, dying Jesus is the
    Christ upon the throne,
And the travail of our spirit is the
    travail of His own.

4 He is breaking down the barriers,
    He is casting up the way;
He is calling for His angels to build
    up the gates of day:
But His angels here are human, not
    the shining hosts above;
For the drum-beats of His army
    are the heart-beats of our love.

5 Hark! we hear a distant music, and
    it comes with fuller swell;
'Tis the triumph-song of Jesus, of
    our King, Immanuel:
Zion, go ye forth to meet Him;
    and my soul, be swift to bring
All thy sweetest and thy dearest for
    the triumph of our King!
                        *H. Burton.*

**757** REJOICE! rejoice! our King is
    coming!
And the time will not be long,
Until we hail the radiant dawning,
And lift us up the glad new song.

    Oh, wondrous day! oh, glorious morning,
    When the Son of Man shall come!
    May we with lamps all trimmed and burning
    Gladly welcome His return!
    Rejoice! rejoice! our King is coming!
    And the time will not be long,
    Until we hail the radiant dawning,
    And lift up the glad new song.

2 With joy we wait our King's return-
    ing
    From His heav'nly mansions fair;
And with ten thousand saints
    appearing
    We shall meet Him in the air.

3 Oh, may we never weary, watching,
    Never lay our armour down,
Until He come, and with rejoicing
    Give to each the promised crown.
                        *Ira D. Sankey.*

**758** WHEN the trump of the great
    archangel
    Its mighty tones shall sound,
And, the end of the world pro-
    claiming,

Shall pierce the depths profound;
When the Son of Man shall come
    in His glory,
With all the saints on high,
What a shouting in the skies from
    the multitudes that rise,
Changed in the twinkling of an
    eye.
Changed in the twinkling of an eye, . . .
Changed in the twinkling of an eye; . . .
The trumpet shall sound, the dead shall be
    raised,
Changed in the twinkling of an eye . . .

2 When He comes in the clouds des-
    cending,
    And they who loved Him here,
From their graves shall awake and
    praise Him
    With joy and not with fear;
When the body and the soul are
    united,
    And clothed no more to die,
What a shouting there will be when
    each other's face we see,
Changed in the twinkling of an
    eye.

3 Oh the seed that was sown in weak-
    ness
    Shall then be raised in power,
And the songs of the blood-bought
    millions
    Shall hail that blissful hour;
When we gather safely home in the
    morning,
    And night's dark shadows fly,
What a shouting on the shore
    when we meet to part no more,
Changed in the twinkling of an
    eye.                 *Fanny J. Crosby.*

**759** IN the Advent Light, O Saviour,
    I am living day by day;
Waiting, working, watching ever,
    Knowing Thou art on Thy way.

2 " Separated " unto Jesus,
    " Loosed " from all the world be-
    side;
Blinded by the Advent glory,
    Hour by hour would I abide.

3 So " from glory unto glory,"
    Gladdened by the Advent ray;
All the path is growing brighter,
    Shining unto " perfect day "!

4 In the Advent Light to witness
    To a dark and dying world;

This the holy ordination—
    May His banner be unfurled.

5 In the Advent Light rejoicing!
    Songs of praise along the road
Seem to make the journey shorter,
    Mounting upward to our God!

6 He is coming! He is coming!
    Pass the heav'nly watchword on!
Go ye forth to meet the Bride-
    groom,
    Hail! to God's anointed Son!

7 See the Advent glory breaking!
    Faith will soon be lost in sight;
" Face to face " I shall behold
    Him—
    Bathed in His eternal light!
                        *E. May Grimes.*

**760** Lo! He comes with clouds
    descending,
    Once for favoured sinners slain;
Thousand thousand saints attending,
    Swell the triumph of His train!
        Hallelujah!
    Jesus comes, and comes to reign.

2 Ev'ry eye shall now behold Him
    Robed in dreadful majesty;
Those who set at naught and sold
    Him,                    [tree,
    Pierced and nailed Him to the
Deeply wailing,
    Shall the true Messiah see.

3 When the solemn trump has
    sounded,
    Heav'n and earth shall flee away;
All who hate Him must, con-
    founded,
    Hear the summons of that day—
        Come to Judgment!
    Come to Judgment, come away!

4 Now redemption, long expected,
    See in solemn pomp appear!
All His saints, by men rejected,
    Now shall meet Him in the air;
        Hallelujah!
    See the day of God appear!

5 Yea, Amen! let all adore Thee,
    High on Thine eternal throne;
Saviour, take the power and glory,
    Claim the kingdom for Thine
    own!
        Oh, come quickly!
    Hallelujah! come, Lord, come!
                *J. Cennick and C. Wesley.*

**761** On that bright and golden
morning when the Son of
Man shall come,
And the radiance of His glory
we shall see:
When from ev'ry clime and nation
He shall call His people home—
What a gath'ring of the ran-
somed that will be!

What a gath . . . 'ring ! what a gath . . .'ring
What a gath'ring of the ransomed in the
summer land of love !
What a gath . . . 'ring ! what a gath . . . 'ring
Of the ransomed in that happy home
above !

2 When the blest who sleep in Jesus
at His bidding shall arise
From the silence of the grave
and from the sea;
And with bodies all celestial they
shall meet Him in the skies
What a gath'ring and rejoicing
there will be!

3 When our eyes behold the city,
with its " many mansions "
bright,
And its river, calm and restful,
flowing free—
When the friends that death has
parted shall in bliss again
unite—
What a gath'ring and a greeting
there will be!

4 Oh, the King is surely coming, and
the time is drawing nigh,
When the blessèd day of
promise we shall see;
Then the changing " in a moment,"
" in the twinkling of an eye,"
And for ever in His presence we
shall be!

*Fanny J. Crosby.*

**762** Sing we the King Who is coming to reign,
Glory to Jesus, the Lamb that was
slain!
Life and salvation His empire
shall bring. [King.
Joy to the nations when Jesus is

Come let us sing . . . praise to our King : . . .
Jesus our King, . . . Jesus our King ; . . .
This is our song who to Jesus belong,
Glory to Jesus, to Jesus our King.

2 All men shall dwell in His mar-
vellous light, [unite,
Races long severed His love shall
Justice and truth from His sceptre
shall spring, [King.
Wrong shall be ended when Jesus is

3 All shall be glad in His Kingdom
of Peace, [increase,
Freedom shall flourish and wisdom
Foe shall be friend when His tri-
umph we sing, [King.
Sword shall be sickle when Jesus is

4 Souls shall be saved from the bur-
den of sin, [within,
Doubt shall not darken His witness
Hell hath no terrors, and Death
hath no sting, [King.
Love is victorious when Jesus is

5 Kingdom of Christ, for Thy com-
ing we pray, [day,
Hasten, O Father, the dawn of the
When this new song Thy creation
shall sing, [King!
Satan is vanquished, for Jesus is

*Silvester Horne.*

**763** When the trumpet of the Lord
shall sound, and time shall
be no more,
And the morning breaks, eternal,
bright and fair;
When the saved of earth shall
gather over on the other shore,
And the roll is called up yonder
I'll be there.

When the roll . . . is called up yon . . . der,
When the roll . . . is called up yon . . . der,
When the roll . . . is called up yonder,
When the roll is called up yonder I'll be
there.

2 On that bright and cloudless morning, when the dead in Christ
shall rise,
And the glory of His resurrection
share:
When His chosen ones shall gather
to their home beyond the skies,
And the roll is called up yonder,
I'll be there.

3 Let us labour for the Master from
the dawn till setting sun,
Let us talk of all His wondrous
love and care,

Then, when all of life is over, and
    our work on earth is done,
And the roll is called up yonder,
    I'll be there.

               *J. M. Black.*

**764**  SAVIOUR, long Thy saints have
    waited—
Centuries have passed away
Since the promise first was given
Of a glorious Advent day.
Grey and old the world is growing,
    Loud the scoffer's boast is heard;
But our hearts are peaceful, know-
    ing
    We may rest upon Thy word.

    " Surely I come quickly !
      Surely I come quickly !
      Surely I come quickly ! "
    Amen, Lord Jesus, come !

2 Lo! the fig-tree buds and blossoms;
    Lo! the shadows flee away;
Glad we lift our heads expectant,
    Brief will now be Thy delay.
Thou to raise the dead art able,
    O'er the grave Thou didst prevail:
Heav'n and earth may prove un-
    stable,
    But Thy word can never fail.

3 Precious, precious parting promise!
    Sweetly linger in our ears;
Brightly gleam amid our darkness,
    Gently soothe away our fears:
Ever nerve us for the conflict,
    Ever fill our souls with joy;
Christ will come and will not
    tarry—
    Nothing can our hope destroy.

             *Mrs. H. A. Guinness.*

**765**  O SHOUT aloud the tidings,
      Repeat the joyful strain;
Let all the waiting nations
    This message hear again:
The spotless Lamb of glory,
    Who once for man was slain,
    Soon o'er all the earth shall
    reign.

    Looking for that blessèd hope, . . .
    Looking for that blessèd hope ; . .
      We know the hour is nearing,
      The hour of His appearing :
    We're looking for that blessèd hope.

2 Signs in the heav'n above us,
    In sun and moon and sky,
Proclaim to all the faithful

Redemption draweth nigh;
The hearts of men are quaking,
    And failing them for fear:
    Jesus' coming draweth near.

3 We'll watch for His returning
    With lamps well trimmed and
    bright;
He cometh to the careless
    As thieves break through at
    night;        [ful "—
" Well done, thou good and faith-
    O may we hear the word,
    " Share the joy of Christ thy
    Lord."

             *Thoro Harris.*

**766**  THE morning breaks, 'tis bright
      and clear,
The shadows of the night are flying
    swift away;
A stirring cry salutes the ear:
    Jesus is coming soon.

    The song of jubilee,
    It sweeps o'er land and sea ;
    With thousand voices strong
    The chorus speeds along—
    One word of hope and cheer !
    The kingdom now is near,
    Jesus is coming soon.

2 By form and creed are millions
    bound,
But God hath sent the word to
    loose the iron band—
Deliv'rance dawns with this glad
    sound:
    Jesus is coming soon.

3 Salvation nears—the saints arise,
    And from the sleep of death the
    slumbering nations wake;
We too shall mount the starry skies,
    Jesus is coming soon.

4 Our glorious King is coming soon—
    It may be darkest night, it may be
    morn or noon;
In glory then His saints will reign,
    Jesus is coming soon.

        *T. B. Barratt,* tr. *Thoro Harris.*

**767**  SWEET is the hope that is
      thrilling my soul—
I know I'll see Jesus some day!
Then what if the dark clouds of
    sin o'er me roll,
    I know I'll see Jesus some day!

I know I'll see Jesus some day ! ...
I know I'll see Jesus some day ! ...
What a joy it will be
When His face I shall see,
I know I'll see Jesus some day !

2 Though I must travel by faith, not
by sight,
I know I'll see Jesus some day !
No evil can harm me, no foe can
affright—
I know I'll see Jesus some day !

3 Darkness is gath'ring, but hope
shines within,
I know I'll see Jesus some day !
What joy when He comes to wipe
out ev'ry sin;
I know I'll see Jesus some day !
*Avis M. Christiansen.*

**768**  WE are just upon the dawning
Of that bright and glorious
morning,
When the Bridegroom comes to
call away His bride;
We'll be then caught up to meet
Him,
Hallelujah, what a greeting,
When the Bridegroom comes, and
we'll with Him abide.

Then we'll shout Hallelujah and sing
Hallelujah,
Glory, Hallelujah to our Lord,
We will bow down before Him, worship and
adore Him,
King of kings and Lord of lords.

2  Get your lamps all trimmed and
burning,
For the Bridegroom is returning,
And the cry, go forth to meet Him,
soon will come;
Be ye wise, make haste to meet
Him,                 [Him,
With your lamps lit, soon to greet
As He comes in clouds descending
for His own.

3  At the mill, two will be grinding,
In the field, two will be binding,
When the Bridegroom comes to
catch away His own;
Only one then will be taken,
And the other one forsaken,
Watch, ye know not what the hour
your Lord doth come.
*E. A. Hinchcliffe.*

**769**  THOU  art  coming,  O  my
Saviour.
Thou art coming, O my King,
In Thy beauty, all resplendent,
In Thy glory, all transcendent;
Well may we rejoice and sing;
Coming in the opening east
Herald brightness slowly swells;
Coming! O my glorious Priest,
Hear we not Thy golden bells?

2 Thou art coming, Thou art coming;
We shall meet Thee on Thy way,
We shall see Thee, we shall know
Thee,                    [Thee
We shall bless Thee, we shall show
All our hearts could never say;
What an anthem that will be,
Ringing out our love to Thee,
Pouring out our rapture sweet,
At Thine own all-glorious feet.

3 O the joy to see Thee reigning,
Thee our own belovèd Lord!
Ev'ry tongue Thy name confessing,
Worship, honour, glory, blessing
Brought to Thee with one accord;
Thee, our Master and our Friend,
Vindicated and enthroned,
Unto earth's remotest end
Glorified, adored and owned!
*Frances R. Havergal.*

**770**  IN these, the closing days of
time,
What  joy  the  glorious  hope
affords,                 [lime!
That soon—O wondrous truth sub-
He shall reign, King of kings
and Lord of lords.

He's coming soon, He's coming soon ;
With joy we welcome His return . . . ing ;
It may be morn, it may be night or noon—
We know He's coming soon. . . .

2 The signs around—in earth and air,
Or painted on the starlit sky,
God's faithful witnesses—declare
That the coming of the Saviour
draweth nigh.

3 The dead in Christ who 'neath us
lie,                       [rise
In countless numbers, all shall
When through the portals of the
sky                   [Paradise.
He shall come to prepare our

4 And we who, living, yet remain,
    Caught up, shall meet our faithful Lord;
This hope we cherish not in vain,
    But we comfort one another by
    this word.     *Thoro Harris.*

**771** Soon will our Saviour from
         heaven appear,
Sweet is the hope and its power to
    cheer;
All will be changed by a glimpse
    of His face—
This is the goal at the end of our
    race.

> Oh, what a change ! . . . Oh, what a
>    change . . .
> When I shall see His wonderful face !
> Oh, what a change ! . . . Oh, what a
>    change . . .
> When I shall see His face !

2 Loneliness changed to reunion complete,
    Absence exchanged for a place at
    His feet,
Sleeping ones raised in a moment
    of time,
Living ones changed to His image
    sublime.

3 Sunrise will chase all the darkness
    away,
Night will be changed to the brightness of day,
Tempests will change to ineffable
    calm,
Weeping will change to a jubilant
    psalm.

4. Weakness will change to magnificent strength,
Failure will change to perfection
    at length,
Sorrow will change to unending
    delight,
Walking by faith change to walking
    by sight.
            *Ada R. Habershon.*

**772** "Upheld by hope," a glorious
         hope,
    As days and years roll by;
The coming of our Lord and King
    Is surely drawing nigh.

2 "Upheld by hope," all toil is sweet
    With this glad thought in view,
The Master may appear to-night
    To call His servants true.

3 "Upheld by hope," that wondrous
    hope,
    That I shall see His face,
And to His likeness be conformed
    When I have run the race.

4 "Upheld by hope," in darkest days
    Faith can the light descry
The deepening glory in the East
    Proclaims deliverance nigh.

5 "Upheld by hope." "Belovèd one,"
    I hear the Bridegroom say,
" Awake, arise! go forth to meet
    My chariot on its way."

6 "Upheld by hope," how glad the
    heart,
    My soul is on the wing,
E'en now His hand is on the door,
    He comes, my glorious King.
            *E. May Grimes.*

**773** It may be at morn, when the
         day is awaking,
When sunlight through darkness
    and shadow is breaking,
That Jesus will come in the fulness
    of glory,     [own."
To receive from the world " His

> O Lord Jesus, how long ?
> How long ere we shout the glad song ?—
> Christ returneth, Hallelujah !
>    Hallelujah ! Amen !
>    Hallelujah ! Amen !

2 It may be at midday, it may be at
    twilight,
It may be, perchance, that the
    blackness of midnight
Will burst into light in the blaze of
    His glory,
    When Jesus receives " His own."

3 While hosts cry " Hosanna!" from
    heaven descending, [attending,
With glorified saints and the angels
With grace on His brow, like a
    halo of glory,
    Will Jesus receive " His own."

4 Oh, joy! oh, delight! should we go
    without dying;
No sickness, no sadness, no dread
    and no crying;
Caught up through the clouds with
    our Lord into glory
    When Jesus receives " His own."
            *H. L. Turner.*

# Section XV

## THE FUTURE LIFE

**774** FATHER, Thou God of tender love and grace,
Thou art, in sorrow's hour, a hiding place. [ance deep:
Here would we rest, in Thine assur-
All, all is well with those in Christ asleep.

2 Though dark awhile our path and veiled from sight,
With Thee the darkness shineth as the light.
Draw near, O Lord! bid earth's repining cease, [holy peace.
And breathe into our lives Thy

3 Thine was a weight of grief beyond compare: [Thou didst bear?
Who could endure the Cross that
Yet not in vain! O Christ, Thou didst arise
From death to ride in triumph through the skies!

4 Living for us, Thine own shall live by Thee. [soon shall see.
Our loved ones gone before we
O come, Lord Jesus, burst the bars of night— [of light.
Ope wide the portals of the realms

5 Then shall we see Thee on Thy sapphire Throne;
Then, in Thy likeness, know as we are known.
The severed bonds of earth be knit again; [pain.
No more the bitter cry, no more the

6 O radiant hope! our eyes behold afar [Morning Star.
Thy shining splendour, Bright and
All glorious breaks the dawn of perfect day, [tears away.
When Thou shalt gently wipe all
*L. F. W. Woodford.*

**775** SLEEP on, belovèd, sleep and take thy rest;
Lay down thy head upon thy Saviour's breast:

We love thee well; but Jesus loves thee best—
Good-night! Good-night! Good-night!

2 Calm is thy slumber as an infant's sleep; [and weep:
But thou shalt wake no more to toil
Thine is a perfect rest, secure and deep—
Good-night! Good-night! Good-night!

3 Until the shadows from this earth are cast; [last;
Until He gathers in His sheaves at
Until the twilight gloom is over-past—
Good-night! Good-night! Good-night!

4 Until the Easter glory lights the skies;
Until the dead in Jesus shall arise,
And He shall come, but not in lowly guise—
Good-night! Good-night! Good-night!

5 Until made beautiful by Love Divine, [shalt shine,
Thou in the likeness of thy Lord
And He shall bring that golden crown of thine—
Good-night! Good-night! Good-night!

6 Only "good-night," belovèd—not "farewell!" [shall dwell
A little while, and all His saints
In hallowed union, indivisible—
Good-night! Good-night! Good-night!

7 Until we meet again before His throne, [gives His own,
Clothed in the spotless robe He
Until we know even as we are known—
Good-night! Good-night! Good-night!
*Sarah Doudney.*

**776** I KNOW that my Redeemer liveth, [stand!
And on the earth again shall
I know eternal life He giveth,
That grace and power are in His hand.

I know, I know . . . that Jesus liveth,
  And on the earth . . . again shall stand ;
I know, I know . . . that life He giveth,
  That grace and power . . . are in His hand.

2 I know His promise never faileth,
The word He speaks, it cannot die; [eth,
Though cruel death my flesh assail-
Yet I shall see Him by and by.

3 I know my mansion He prepareth,
That where He is there I may be;
O wondrous thought, for me He careth
And He at last will come for me.
*Jessie H. Brown.*

**777** LET us sing of His love once again—
Of the love that can never decay,
Of the blood of the Lamb who was slain, [day.
Till we praise Him again in that

In the sweet by and by,
  We shall meet on that beautiful shore.

2 There are cleansing and healing for all [flood;
Who will wash in the life-giving
There is life everlasting and joy
At the right hand of God through the blood.

3 Even now while we taste of His love [His name;
We are filled with delight at
But what will it be when above
We shall join in the song of the Lamb!
*F. Bottome.*

**778** THERE'S a land that is fairer than day,
And by faith we can see it afar:
For the Father waits over the way,
To prepare us a dwelling-place there.

In the sweet by and by,
  We shall meet on that beautiful shore.

2 We shall sing on that beautiful shore
The melodious songs of the blest,
And our spirits shall sorrow no more, [rest.
Not a sigh for the blessing of

3 To our bountiful Father above,
We will offer our tribute of praise,
For the glorious gift of His love,
And the blessings that hallow our days.
*S. Bennett.*

**779** WE shall gather in the morning when our race on earth is run,
We shall gather with our loved ones by and by;
All the years of waiting over, all the tears for ever gone,
By His grace there'll be no parting up on high.

We shall gather in the morning,
  When the waiting days are o'er ;
We shall gather in the morning
  On the blessèd, cloudless shore ;
And redeemed by grace we'll stand
At the Saviour's own right hand,
  In the likeness of the One whom we adore.

2 We shall gather in the morning—
what a morning that will be!
When by grace we stand trans-figured by the side
Of the One who wrought salvation, by His death on Calv'ry's tree,
And for us the gates of glory opened wide.

3 We shall gather in the morning! and the thought of that glad day
Brightens all life's dreary path-way here below;
We are waiting for the morning, and till then we'll watch and pray,
Ever looking for the One who loves us so.
*Avis B. Christiansen.*

**780** FOR ever with the Lord!
Amen, so let it be!
Life from the dead is in that word;
'Tis immortality.
Here in the body pent,
Absent from Him I roam;
Yet nightly pitch my moving tent
A day's march nearer home.

**2** My Father's house on high,
    Home of my soul, how near
At times to faith's foreseeing eye
    Thy golden gates appear!
My thirsty spirit faints
    To reach the land I love,
The bright inheritance of saints—
    Jerusalem above.

**3** For ever with the Lord!
    Father, if 'tis Thy will,
The promise of that faithful word,
    E'en here to me fulfil.
Be Thou at my right hand,
    Then can I never fail;
Uphold Thou me, so I shall stand,
    Fight, and I must prevail.

**4** So when my latest breath
    Shall rend the veil in twain,
By death I shall escape from death,
    And life eternal gain.
Knowing as I am known,
    How shall I love that word!
And oft repeat before the throne,
    For ever with the Lord!
            *James Montgomery.*

**781** FACE to face with Christ my
    Saviour,
  Face to face—what will it be?
When with rapture I behold Him,
  Jesus Christ who died for me.
    Face to face shall I behold Him,
      Far beyond the starry sky ;
    Face to face in all His glory,
      I shall see Him by and by !

**2** Only faintly now I see Him,
  With the darkling veil between,
But a blessèd day is coming,
  When His glory shall be seen.

**3** What rejoicing in His presence,
  When are banished grief and
    pain;         [ened
When the crooked ways are straight-
  And the dark things shall be
    plain.

**4** Face to face! O blissful moment!
  Face to face—to see and know!
Face to face with my Redeemer,
  Jesus Christ who loves me so.
          *Mrs. Frank A. Breck.*

**782** THERE is a land of pure de-
    light
  Where saints immortal reign,
Infinite day excludes the night,
  And pleasures banish pain.

We're feeding on the living Bread,
We're drinking at the fountain-head :
  And whoso drinketh, Jesus said,
    Shall never, never thirst again.
What ! never thirst again ? No, never thirst
    again !
What ! never thirst again ? No, never thirst
    again !
  And whoso drinketh, Jesus said,
    Shall never, never thirst again !

**2** There everlasting spring abides,
  And never-withering flowers:
Death, like a narrow sea, divides
  This heavenly land from ours.

**3** O could we make our doubts re-
    move         [rise,
  Those gloomy thoughts that
And see the Canaan that we love
  With unbeclouded eyes.

**4** Could we but climb where Moses
    stood
  And view the landscape o'er,
Not Jordan's stream, nor death's
    cold flood,
  Should fright us from the shore.

*The following Chorus may be substituted :*
  We're marching through Immanuel's ground,
  And soon shall hear the trumpet sound,
  And then we shall with Jesus reign,
    And never, never part again.
  What ! never part again ? No, never part
    again !
  What ! never part again ? No, never part
    again !
  And then we shall with Jesus reign,
    And never, never part again !
          *Isaac Watts.*

**783** JERUSALEM, my happy home,
    Name ever dear to me!
  When shall my labours have an
    end,
    In joy, and peace, and thee?
When shall these eyes thy heav'n-
    built walls
  And pearly gates behold,
Thy bulwarks with salvation strong,
  And streets of shining gold?

**2** There happier bowers than Eden's
    bloom,
  Nor sin nor sorrow know:
Blest seats, through rude and
    stormy scenes
  I onward press to you.
Why should I shrink at pain and
    woe,
  Or feel, at death, dismay?
I've Canaan's goodly land in view,
  And realms of endless day.

3 Apostles, prophets, martyrs there
    Around my Saviour stand;
And soon my friends in Christ
    below
Will join the glorious band.
Jerusalem, my happy home,
    My soul still pants for thee!
Then shall my labours have an end,
    When I thy joys shall see.
                    *Joseph Bromehead.*

**784** JERUSALEM the golden,
    With milk and honey blest,
Beneath thy contemplation
    Sink heart and voice oppressed;
I know not, oh! I know not,
    What joys await us there,
What radiancy of glory,
    What bliss beyond compare.

2 They stand, those halls of Zion,
    All jubilant with song;
And bright with many an angel,
    And all the martyr throng:
The Prince is ever in them,
    The daylight is serene,
The pastures of the blessèd
    Are decked in glorious sheen.

3 There is the throne of David,
    And there from care released,
The shout of them that triumph,
    The song of them that feast:
And they who with their Leader,
    Have conquered in the fight,
For ever and for ever
    Are clothed in robes of white.

4 Oh, sweet and blessèd country,
    The home of God's elect!
Oh, sweet and blessèd country
    That eager hearts expect!
Jesus, in mercy bring us
    To that dear land of rest,
Who art, with God the Father,
    And Spirit, ever blest.
            *Bernard of Cluny, tr. J. M. Neale.*

**785** FOR all the saints who from
    their labours rest,
Who Thee by faith before the
    world confessed,

Thy name, O Jesu, be for ever blest,
    Alleluia!

2 Thou wast their Rock, their Fort-
        ress, and their Might;
Thou, Lord, their Captain in the
        well fought fight;
Thou in the darkness drear their
        one true Light.
    Alleluia!

3 Oh, may Thy soldiers, faithful, true
        and bold,
Fight as the saints who nobly
        fought of old,
And win, with them, the victor's
        crown of gold.
    Alleluia!

4 O blest communion! fellowship
        Divine!                [shine;
We feebly struggle, they in glory
Yet all are one in Thee, for all are
        Thine.
    Alleluia!

5 And when the strife is fierce, the
        warfare long,
Steals on the ear the distant tri-
        umph-song.
And hearts are brave again, and
        arms are strong.
    Alleluia!

6 The golden evening brightens in
        the west;
Soon, soon to faithful warriors
        comes their rest;
Sweet is the calm of Paradise the
        blest.
    Alleluia!

7 But lo! there breaks a yet more
        glorious day;
The saints triumphant rise in bright
        array:
The King of glory passes on His
        way.
    Alleluia!

8 From earth's wide bounds, from
        ocean's farthest coast,
Through gates of pearl streams in
        the countless host,
Singing to Father, Son, and Holy
        Ghost.
    Alleluia!          *W. W. How.*

**786** LIGHT after darkness,
  Gain after loss,
Strength after weakness,
  Crown after cross;
Sweet after bitter,
  Hope after fears,
Home after wandering,
  Praise after tears.

2 Sheaves after sowing,
  Sun after rain,
Sight after mystery,
  Peace after pain;
Joy after sorrow,
  Calm after blast,
Rest after weariness,
  Sweet rest at last.

3 Near after distant,
  Gleam after gloom,
Love after loneliness,
  Life after tomb;
After long agony,
  Rapture of bliss,
Right was the pathway
  Leading to this.

*Frances R. Havergal.*

**787** Now the labourer's task is
    o'er,
  Now the battle-day is past;
Now upon the farther shore
  Lands the voyager at last.
  Father, in Thy gracious keeping
  Leave we now Thy servant sleeping.

2 There the tears of earth are dried;
  There its hidden things are clear;
There the work of life is tried
  By a juster Judge than here.

3 There the Shepherd, bringing home
  Many a lamb forlorn and strayed,
Shelters each, no more to roam,
  Where the wolf can ne'er invade.

4 There the penitents who turn
  To the cross their dying eyes,
All the love of Jesus learn
  At His feet in paradise.

5 There no more the powers of hell
  Can prevail to mar their peace;
Christ the Lord shall guard them
    well,
  He who died for their release.

6 Earth to earth, and dust to dust,
  Calmly now the words we say;
Left behind, we wait in trust
  For the resurrection day.

*John Ellerton.*

**788** WHO, who are these beside the
    chilly wave,            [grave,
Just on the borders of the silent
Shouting Jesus' power to save,
  "Washed in the blood of the
    Lamb"?

  "Sweeping through the gates" of the New
    Jerusalem,
  "Washed in the blood of the Lamb,"

2 These, these are they who, in their
    youthful days,        [ways
Found Jesus early, and in wisdom's
Proved the fulness of His grace,
  "Washed in the blood of the
    Lamb."

3 These, these are they who, in afflic-
    tion's woes,          [pose,
Ever have found in Jesus calm re-
Such as from a pure heart flows,
  "Washed in the blood of the
    Lamb."

4 These, these are they who, in the
    conflict dire,         [fire;
Boldly have stood amid the hottest
Jesus now says: "Come up higher,"
  "Washed in the blood of the
    Lamb."

5 Safe, safe upon the ever-shining
    shore,                [all are o'er;
Sin, pain, and death, and sorrow,
Happy now and evermore,
  "Washed in the blood of the
    Lamb."

*T. C. O'Kane.*

**789** I SHALL see the King
  Where the angels sing,
I shall see the King some day,
  In the better land,
  On the golden strand,
And with Him shall ever stay.

  In His glory, I shall see the King,
  And for ever endless praises sing ;
  'Twas on Calvary Jesus died for me ;
    I shall see the King some day.

2   In the land of song,
  In the glory throng,
Where there never comes a night,
  With my Lord once slain
  I shall ever reign
In the glory land of light.

3   I shall see the King,
    All my tributes bring,
And shall look upon His face;
    Then my song shall be
    How He ransomed me,
And has kept me by His grace.
                                *W. C. Poole.*

**790** How bright these glorious
            spirits shine!
    Whence all their white array?
How came they to the blissful seats
    Of everlasting day?

2 Lo! these are they from sufferings
        great
    Who came to realms of light;
And in the blood of Christ have
        washed
    Those robes that shine so bright.

3 Now with triumphal palms they
        stand
    Before the throne so high,

And serve the God they love
            amidst
    The glories of the sky.

4 Hunger and thirst are felt no more,
    Nor suns with scorching ray;
God is their Sun, whose cheering
            beams
    Diffuse eternal day.

5 The Lamb which dwells amidst the
            throne,
    Shall o'er them still preside,
Feed them with nourishment
            Divine,
    And all their footsteps guide.

6 'Midst pastures green He'll lead
            His flock,
    Where living streams appear;
And God the Lord from every eye
    Shall wipe off every tear.

7 To Father, Son, and Holy Ghost,
    The God whom we adore,
Be glory, as it was, is now,
    And shall be evermore.
                        *I. Watts* and *W. Cameron.*

# Section XVI

## CLOSING HYMNS

**791** LORD, dismiss us with Thy
            blessing.        [peace;
    Fill our hearts with joy and
Let us each, Thy love possessing,
    Triumph in redeeming grace:
        Oh, refresh us,
    Travelling through this wilder-
        ness!

2 Thanks we give, and adoration,
    For Thy Gospel's joyful sound;
May the fruits of Thy salvation
    In our hearts and lives abound;
        May Thy presence,
    With us evermore be found!

3 So whene'er the signal's given
    Us from earth to call away,
Borne on angels' wings to heaven,
    Glad the summons to obey,
        We shall surely,
    Reign with Christ in endless day.
                                *J. Fawcett.*

**792** FATHER, in high heaven dwell-
            ing,
    May our evening song be telling
        Of Thy mercy large and free;
    Through the day Thy love hath fed
        us,                        [us,
    Through the day Thy care hath led
        With divinest charity.

2 This day's sins, oh, pardon, Saviour,
    Evil thoughts, perverse behaviour,
        Envy, pride, and vanity;
    From the world, the flesh, deliver,
    Save us now, and save us ever,
        O Thou Lamb of Calvary.

3 From enticements of the devil,
    From the might of spirits evil,
        Be our shield and panoply;
    Let Thy power this night defend us,
    And a heavenly peace attend us,
        And angelic company.

4 Whilst the night-dews are distilling,
　Holy Ghost, each heart be filling
　　With Thine own serenity;
　Softly let our eyes be closing,
　Loving souls on Thee reposing,
　　Ever blessèd Trinity.
　　　　　　　　　*George Rawson.*

**793** LORD, it is eventide: the light
　　　of day is waning;
　　Far o'er the golden land earth's
　　　voices faint and fall;
　　Lowly we pray to Thee for strength
　　　and love sustaining,
　　Lowly we ask of Thee Thy peace
　　　upon us all.
　　　　　Oh, grant unto our souls—

　　　Light that groweth not pale
　　　　With day's decrease,
　　　Love that never can fail
　　　　Till life shall cease ;
　　　Joy no trial shall mar,
　　　Hope that shineth afar,
　　　Faith serene as a star,
　　　　And Christ's own peace.

2 Lord, it is eventide: we turn to
　　Thee for healing,
　　Like those of Galilee who came
　　　at close of day;
　Speak to our waiting souls, their
　　hidden founts unsealing;
　　Touch us with hands divine that
　　　take our sin away.
　　　　Oh, grant unto our souls—

3 Saviour, Thou knowest all, the trial
　　and temptation,
　　Knowest the wilfulness and way-
　　　wardness of youth:
　Help us to cling to Thee, our
　　strength and our salvation,
　　Help us to find in Thee the one
　　　eternal Truth.
　　　　Oh, grant unto our souls—

4 Lord, it is eventide: our hearts
　　await Thy giving,
　　Wait for that peace divine that
　　　none can take away,
　Peace that shall lift our souls to
　　loftier heights of living,
　　Till we abide with Thee in ever-
　　　lasting day.
　　　　Oh, grant unto our souls—
　　　　　　　　　*Colin Sterne.*

**794** DAY is dying in the west,
　　　Heav'n is touching earth with
　　　　rest,
　　Wait and worship while the night
　　Sets her evening lamps alight
　　　Through all the sky.

　　Holy, Holy, Holy, Lord God of Hosts !
　　Heav'n and earth are full of Thee ;
　　Heav'n and earth are praising Thee,
　　　O Lord, most high.

2 Lord of life, beneath the dome
　Of the universe, Thy home,
　Gather us who seek Thy face,
　To the fold of Thy embrace,
　　For Thou art nigh.

3 While the deepening shadows fall,
　Heart of love, enfolding all,
　Through the glory and the grace
　Of the stars that veil Thy face,
　　Our hearts ascend.

4 When for ever from our sight
　Pass the stars, the day, the night,
　Lord of angels, on our eyes
　Let eternal morning rise,
　　And shadows end.
　　　　　　　*Mary A. Lathbury.*

**795** SAVIOUR, again to Thy dear
　　　name we raise
　　With one accord our parting hymn
　　　of praise;
　　We stand to bless Thee ere our
　　　worship cease,
　　Then, lowly kneeling, wait Thy
　　　word of peace.

2 Grant us Thy peace upon our
　　homeward way;
　　With Thee began, with Thee shall
　　　end the day;
　　Guard Thou the lips from sin, the
　　　hearts from shame,
　　That in this house have called upon
　　　Thy name.

3 Grant us Thy peace, Lord, through
　　the coming night,
　　Turn Thou for us its darkness into
　　　light;
　　From harm and danger keep Thy
　　　children free,
　　For dark and light are both alike to
　　　Thee.

4 Grant us Thy peace throughout
   our earthly life,
   Our balm in sorrow and our stay
   in strife;
   Then, when Thy voice shall bid our
   conflict cease,
   Call us, O Lord, to Thine eternal
   peace.          *J. Ellerton.*

**796** Sun of my soul, Thou Saviour
   dear,
   It is not night if Thou be near;
   Oh, may no earth-born cloud arise,
   To hide Thee from Thy servant's
   eyes!

2 When the soft dews of kindly sleep
   My wearied eyelids gently steep,
   Be my last thought, how sweet to
   rest
   For ever on my Saviour's breast.

3 Abide with me from morn till eve,
   For without Thee I cannot live;
   Abide with me when night is nigh,
   For without Thee I dare not die.

4 If some poor wandering child of
   Thine          [divine,
   Have spurned today the voice
   Now, Lord, the gracious work
   begin,
   Let him no more lie down in sin.

5 Watch by the sick, enrich the poor
   With blessings from Thy boundless
   store:
   Be every mourner's sleep tonight,
   Like infants' slumbers, pure and
   light.

6 Come near and bless us when we
   wake,          [take;
   Ere through the world our way we
   Till, in the ocean of Thy love,
   We lose ourselves in heaven above.
                    *John Keble.*

**797** Abide with me; fast falls the
   eventide;
   The darkness deepens; Lord, with
   me abide;          [forts flee,
   When other helpers fail, and com-
   Help of the helpless, O abide with
   me.

2 Swift to its close ebbs out life's
   little day;          [pass away;
   Earth's joys grow dim, its glories
   Change and decay in all around I
   see:          [with me!
   O Thou who changest not abide

3 I need Thy presence every passing
   hour;          [tempter's power?
   What but Thy grace can foil the
   Who like Thyself my guide and
   stay can be?          [abide with me.
   Through cloud and sunshine, O

4 I fear no foe, with Thee at hand to
   bless;          [bitterness;
   Ills have no weight, and tears no
   Where is death's sting? where,
   grave, thy victory?          [me.
   I triumph still, if Thou abide with

5 Keep Thou Thy Cross before my
   closing eyes,
   Shine through the gloom, and point
   me to the skies;
   Heaven's morning breaks, and
   earth's vain shadows flee:
   In life, in death, O Lord, abide
   with me!
                    *H. F. Lyte.*

**798** The day Thou gavest, Lord, is
   ended;
   The darkness falls at Thy behest;
   To Thee our morning hymns
   ascended,
   Thy praise shall sanctify our rest.

2 We thank Thee that Thy church
   unsleeping,          [light,
   While earth rolls onward into
   Through all the world her watch is
   keeping,          [night.
   And rests not now by day or

3 As o'er each continent and island
   The dawn leads on another day,
   The voice of prayer is never silent,
   Nor dies the strain of praise
   away

4 The sun that bids us rest is waking
   Our brethren 'neath the western
   sky,
   And hour by hour fresh lips are
   making          [high.
   Thy wondrous doings heard on

5 So be it, Lord! Thy throne shall
   never,          [away;
   Like earth's proud empires, pass
   Thy kingdom stands and grows for
   ever,          [sway.
   Till all Thy creatures own Thy
                    *John Ellerton.*

**799** GOD be in my head,
    And in my understanding;
God be in mine eyes,
    And in my looking;
God be in my mouth,
    And in my speaking;
God be in my heart,
    And in my thinking;
God be at mine end,
    And at my departing.

*Anon., from a Sarum Primer.*

**800** 'TIS eventide, and from Thy house
    We now depart,     [pray,
O let Thy peace, dear Lord, we
    Possess each heart,
Guard Thou our thoughts and let
    them be,
Kept wholly occupied with Thee,
That thus from sin we may be free,
Until Thy face we see.

*E. C. W. Boulton.*

# INDEX OF CHORUSES

# Index of Choruses

# INDEX

## OF FIRST LINES

# Index of First Lines

# Index of First Lines

# Index of First Lines

# Index of First Lines

*Printed in Great Britain by Richard Clay (The Chaucer Press), Ltd.,*
*Bungay, Suffolk.*